TEN DAYS THAT SHOOK THE WORLD

John Reed was born in Portland, Oregon, in 1887.
After college he entered journalism and soon became
the most highly paid ace reporter in America. He
was a correspondent in the Mexican War of 1916 to
1917 and a reporter in the First World War, a job
which took him to Russia – he was in Petrograd in
1917. He became personally involved in the Labour
movement in the States in 1913 when he helped
organize a silk-workers' strike in Paterson, New
Jersey; and when he returned from Russia he toured
the country speaking on the October Revolution
(of 1917) and reporting for the *Liberator*, a very
left-wing journal. In 1919 he chaired the meeting
which founded the Communist-Labour Party, later
the Communist Party of the U.S.A.

John Reed then returned to Soviet Russia, where he
died of typhus in 1920. He was buried in the Red
Square, in the Heroes' Grave; a plaque in the
Kremlin wall commemorates him.

Ten Days That Shook the World

John Reed

Penguin Books

PENGUIN BOOKS

Published by the Penguin Group
Penguin Books Ltd, 80 Strand, London WC2R 0RL, England
Penguin Putnam Inc., 375 Hudson Street, New York, New York 10014, USA
Penguin Books Australia Ltd, 250 Camberwell Road, Camberwell, Victoria 3124, Australia
Penguin Books Canada Ltd, 10 Alcorn Avenue, Toronto, Ontario, Canada M4V 3B2
Penguin Books India (P) Ltd, 11 Community Centre, Panchsheel Park, New Delhi – 110 017, India
Penguin Books (NZ) Ltd, Cnr Rosedale and Airborne Roads, Albany, Auckland, New Zealand
Penguin Books (South Africa) (Pty) Ltd, 24 Sturdee Avenue, Rosebank 2196, South Africa

Penguin Books Ltd, Registered Offices: 80 Strand, London WC2R 0RL, England

www.penguin.com

First published in the United States of America by Boni and Liveright, Inc, 1919
First published in England by
the Communist Party of Great Britain 1926
Published in Great Britain by Martin Lawrence 1932 and
reprinted by Lawrence & Wishart 1961
Published with a chronology in Penguin Books 1966
Reprinted with an introduction by A. J. P. Taylor 1977

026

Introduction copyright © A. J. P. Taylor, 1977
All rights reserved

Printed and bound in Great Britain by Clays Ltd, Elcograf S.p.A.
Set in Monotype Times

ISBN-13: 978-0-14-144212-9

www.greenpenguin.co.uk

Contents

Introduction by A. J. P. Taylor

In 1964 Penguin Books decided to bring out John Reed's classic account of the Bolshevik revolution, *Ten Days That Shook the World*, and asked me to write an introduction. John Reed's widow had given the copyright of the book to the Communist Party of Great Britain. My introduction was submitted to Lawrence & Wishart, their publishers, and came back covered with objections. These were said to be questions of fact, though most of them seemed to me matters of opinion. However, I duly accepted the objections, either by modifying my statements or, where this would have led to plain error, deleting them. The revised introduction was again submitted. They replied that my introduction still had errors and that only a small part of it was acceptable to them – an attitude which I had expected from the outset. Lawrence & Wishart proposed that someone else should write an acceptable introduction. Penguin Books preferred to publish the book without any introduction. The copyright has now expired and my introduction can at last be published. The reader is thus free to judge whether it is acceptable.

John Reed's book has long been a political classic. Its theme is the Bolshevik revolution of 7 November 1917 and, for once, a great theme found the narrator it deserved. George Kennan, the American diplomat and historian, has written: 'Reed's account of the events of that time rises above every other contemporary record for its literary power, its penetration, its command of detail. It will be remembered when all the others are forgotten'. Reed's book is not only the best account of the Bolshevik revolution, it comes near to being the best account of any revolution. Revolutions are tumultuous affairs, difficult to follow while they are on. The participants are too busy to write down their experiences at the time, and the victors are too busy afterwards. Of the leading Bolsheviks only Trotsky wrote a detailed history of the revolution, and that many years afterwards when he was in exile. The defeated had time on their hands, and many of them wrote memoirs. Such memoirs are usually marked by the bewilderment and resentment that follows defeat.

Sukhanov, the reluctant Menshevik, was one of the few who re-captured the spirit of the time.

Foreign observers stood outside the events even when they tried to be sympathetic, and few of them tried. No one would turn with enthusiasm to the accounts of the Bolshevik revolution as given by the British or French ambassadors. Some journalists did better, notably Philips Price of the *Manchester Guardian*. But even the best of these journalists were palpably writing about strange events in a strange country. John Reed occupied a different position. He was not himself engaged in the revolution and so had time to observe what was going on: time to collect newspapers and handbills; time to listen to street conversations; opportunity even to cross the lines and learn what was happening on the other side. But Reed, though not engaged physically in the Bolshevik revolution, was engaged morally. This was his revolution, not an obscure event in a foreign country. Reed was an American radical, educated at Harvard and now a passionate Socialist. He was in Russia as the representative of *The Masses*, then the principal radical and socialist journal in the United States. In his eyes the Bolshevik revolution was not merely a great upheaval in Russia. It was the beginning of the international revolution to which he, like the Bolsheviks, was pledged. Reed understood the Bolshevik outlook, understood why there should be a further revolution and wanted that revolution to succeed. He was too good a journalist to write propaganda, but he made no secret of where his sympathies lay. He had one further quality which completed the others. He was a great writer. To quote Kennan again, ' Reed was a poet of the first order'. This book is evidence that he was a prose artist of the first order also.

Dazzled by Reed's achievement, we may fail to appreciate exactly what it was. This is not history written in detachment, with a large bibliography and a fuller understanding than men had at the time. The book is a contribution to history, not an analysis composed afterwards. It is first-hand evidence when Reed described what he saw and experienced. But much of it is not first-hand. Often Reed sat in the quiet of his hotel room, cigarette in mouth, tapping out on his typewriter copy for *The Masses*. He would piece together fragments of conversations, add imaginative detail of what was likely to have happened and crown all with a brilliant phrase.

For instance Reed often says that Smolny, which housed the Petrograd Soviet, was 'humming with activity', lights blazing all night, messengers and Red Guards crowding its corridors. Smolny appears as a sort of beehive and with little detail of what the bees were up to. Reed did not in fact know. He was a foreign journalist, though a sympathetic one, and the Bolsheviks revealed to him few of their secrets. Again Reed, like any good reporter, gives the impression of an unflagging excitement. In reality nothing was happening for much of the time, and Reed himself was occupied only in talking with other American journalists. Indeed the Bolsheviks themselves were worried that the revolutionary impulse was dying away. This was a powerful factor in pushing them into action before it was too late.

A further warning is necessary. In 1927 Eisenstein, the famous cinema director, made a film for the tenth anniversary of the Bolshevik revolution. He gave it Reed's title, *Ten Days That Shook the World*, and used Reed's book as his script. It is tempting to see the film as somehow confirming what is recounted in the book. This is not the case. Eisenstein's film was not based on contemporary newsreels or on a study of the historical evidence. It translated Reed's book into cinema terms. Much of the film is fiction, as is indeed much of Reed's book itself.

Reed's book is not reliable in every detail. Its achievement is to recapture the spirit of those stirring days. As with most writers, Reed heightened the drama, and this drama sometimes took over from reality. Bolshevik participants, when they looked back, often based their recollections more on Reed's book than on their own memories. This often happens. Veterans of the First World War saw the trenches through the eyes of Robert Graves, Edmund Blunden and Siegfried Sassoon, and their own memories became blurred. In this sense, Reed's book founded a legend, one which has largely triumphed over the facts. Not that the legend was untrue. Most legends spring from facts. But the mood and emotions of the Bolshevik revolution would not stand out so clearly if Reed had not been there to record them. Reed's book is legendary in another way. Reed believed that the Bolshevik leaders knew precisely what they were doing, and the victory of their revolution confirmed this belief. Such records as are available suggest otherwise. All the political leaders moved in a fog of revolution which was much like the fog of battle. The Bolshevik revolution was not a fully orchestrated piece with the music already composed. It was compounded, like most other events, of confusions and misunderstandings, of human endeavours and human failures, where the outcome surprised the victors as much as it stunned the defeated.

Reed's book, as its title indicates, is centred on the events of early November 1917, when the Bolsheviks seized power in Petrograd and so became in time the rulers of Russia. These events were the last act of one drama and the first act of another. The first drama was the Russian revolution which had been in process since March 1917. The second drama was intended to be the victory of international Communism and turned out to be something quite different. Both dramas are implicit in Reed's book.

In August 1914 Imperial Russia became involved in a great European war. Russia was an autocracy, her course determined by the feeble Tsar Nicholas II. There was a parliament, the Duma, with few powers. There were political parties. There was even a Social Democratic party. Its leftwing, the Bolsheviks, had a few thousand members. This was the only party that opposed the war. Its voice went almost unheard. Its daily paper, *Pravda*, was suppressed. Most of its leaders were in exile – some in Siberia, Lenin, the senior of them, in Switzerland. Russia lurched into chaos. An antiquated system succumbed under the strain of running a modern war. The railways were overstrained, carrying supplies to the vast armies. In the towns food ran short except for the rich. The people of Petrograd went hungry. Many politicians canvassed a change of régime. None took action.

In March 1917 there were food riots in Petrograd. The garrison, middle-aged reservists who did not want to be sent to the front, joined the rioters. The Cossacks, usually the guardians of order, remained inactive. The Tsar was at army headquarters. Politicians from the Duma urged him to abdicate. The generals seconded this advice. Nicholas II acquiesced. Such was the Russian revolution of March 1917. It had been made in the streets of Petrograd without leaders and without a programme.

The Tsar had gone. Otherwise nothing was changed. The armies still fought clumsily at the front. The bureaucratic machine still churned out orders in the void. In Trotsky's words, power fell into the street.

A Soviet or council of workers' and soldiers' deputies had been set up in Petrograd during the riots, on the pattern of Russia's first revolution in 1905. Its leaders were moderate Socialists, anxious to do nothing illegal. They implored the Duma politicians to take power, and these politicians duly set up a provisional government. Though called democratic, this government had no popular mandate and little popular support. It simply carried on the old system, just as a hen continues to run round the yard when its head has been cut off. No one knew how to change direction. When the first Bolsheviks, including Stalin, returned from Siberia, they too accepted the provisional government and gave patriotic support to the war.

Far away in Switzerland, Lenin was in despair. In his belief, a great opportunity was being missed – opportunity not only for a socialist revolution in Russia, but for the striking of a spark that would set off revolution all over Europe. If the Russian people ended the war, the workers in every belligerent country would follow their example; there would be general revolution and international socialism would be established. This was the key note of Lenin's policy: revolution for all European countries, not only for Russia. His Bolshevik followers had not grasped this policy, and in Switzerland he was helpless. Somehow he must get back to Russia. The French government refused him permission to cross France. Reluctantly Lenin struck a bargain with the German General Staff and, accompanied by some thirty other Russian revolutionaries, travelled across Germany in a sealed train. Back in Petrograd, he wasted no time. He went directly to Bolshevik headquarters and said: 'I move that we prepare for a second revolution'. Lenin's proposal was defeated by twelve votes to one, Lenin's being the one. He merely laughed and said: 'The Russian people are a hundred times more revolutionary than we are'.

This was shown by the events of the July days which were the second act of the Russian revolution. The first All-Russian Congress of Soviets met in Petrograd. At exactly the same time

Kerensky, a moderate socialist who had become head of the provisional government, ordered a new offensive against the Germans. The offensive was a catastrophic failure. In Petrograd there were great demonstrations, demanding an end of the war and 'All Power to the Soviets'. The Soviet leaders told the demonstrators to go home. Even Lenin recognized that the demonstrations were premature. The people of Petrograd were in a revolutionary mood, but their spirit had not yet spread to the country. Petrograd hung isolated, in the air. Unorganized and without clear leadership, the demonstrations died away.

Kerensky thought that the time had come to end the revolution. Many of the leading Bolsheviks were arrested. The most prominent of these was Trotsky, who had returned from America in May and had just joined the Bolshevik party. His name was to dominate coming events. Lenin, too, wished to be arrested and to challenge a public trial. But the outcry was great against him as a German agent. His Bolshevik colleagues feared that he might be assassinated in prison and insisted that he should go into hiding. Lenin went first to a nearby village, where he swam in the lake and helped to get the hay in. When the police began to make enquiries, he moved to Helsinki, the capital of Finland, then an autonomous province of the Russian empire. Here he lodged with the local chief of police who happened to be a Bolshevik – a convenient arrangement. Lenin was safe, but Helsinki was five hours from Petrograd by train. Lenin had to follow what was happening in Petrograd by reading the newspapers and could influence the Bolsheviks only by letters and pamphlets. He grew impatient, restless. The revolutionary impulse was slowing down. Few people bothered to attend the meetings of the Soviets. The Petrograd Soviet, which had occupied a splendid hall in the centre of the city, was pushed out to Smolny Institute, formerly a suburban high school for the daughters of the nobility. Kerensky believed that he would soon push the Soviet out of existence.

Kerensky miscalculated. He encouraged Kornilov, a reactionary general, to march on Petrograd and restore order. Belatedly he discovered that Kornilov intended to destroy the provisional government as well as the Soviets. Kerensky appealed to the workers of Petrograd to save the revolution, by which he meant himself. The Bolsheviks were released from prison.

Trotsky became president of the Petrograd Soviet, and a military revolutionary committee under his direction organized the Red Guards – equipped ironically at government expense. Kornilov's march on Petrograd was halted. There was little fighting. Kornilov's soldiers simply went home or joined the Red Guards. Kornilov vanished into obscurity and was killed in March 1918 during the civil war.

This is the moment in mid September when Reed's book begins. On the one side were Kerensky and his provisional government, still issuing orders, still speaking in the name of Russia, but with little authority in the country and no force to back it. On the other side, the Bolsheviks now had a majority on the Petrograd Soviet and on many others, including Moscow. They controlled the Red Guards. But they made no use of their power. With Lenin far away, they were at a loss what to do. They made endless speeches. They warned the masses against the danger of counter-revolution, which they believed to be imminent. Then they waited in the atmosphere of tension that Reed describes so well.

On 28 September the central committee of the Bolshevik party met. Lenin, still in Finland, sent a 'Letter from Afar'. He wrote: 'We should at once begin to plan the practical details of a second revolution'. The Bolshevik leaders, who later boasted of their revolutionary prowess – Trotsky, Stalin, Zinoviev, Buharin – were horrified. They resolved unanimously that every copy of Lenin's letter should be destroyed. One survived by chance. Weeks passed. Lenin resolved to defy the order of the central committee that he should remain in Finland. On 20 October he returned to a Petrograd suburb where he went into hiding. As a further disguise he was now clean shaven and on the decisive day of the Bolshevik revolution confronted the Soviet without his customary red beard.

On 23 October the central committee met in Lenin's suburb, ironically at the house of Sukhanov, a Menshevik. Sukhanov's wife was a Bolshevik. She rang up her husband and told him that, as they were both very tired, he should stay the night in Petrograd. Lenin insisted on an immediate seizure of power; the committee finally agreed by ten votes to two, only to find that they had no paper. Lenin borrowed an exercise book from the child of the house and wrote the resolution in pencil on a bit of squared paper. Dawn was breaking. Someone asked: 'Well, what day?'. Lenin, already leaving to get home before the streets were light, answered over his shoulder: '28 October'.

On 28 October nothing happened. The Soviet met as usual. Speeches were made. The day passed. Lenin was furious. He summoned another meeting of the central committee, augmented by delegates from the local party branches. Once more the Bolsheviks resolved to seize power, this time on 2 November. Once more nothing happened. Reed describes yet another meeting at Smolny on 3 November, with Lenin fixing the rising for 7 November, when the second All-Russian Congress of Soviets was to meet. For once Reed's imagination carried him away. There was no such meeting on 3 November. Lenin never came to Smolny until late on 6 November. Nor could he possibly have named 7 November as the day. He was pressing all the time for an immediate seizure of power in the name of the Bolshevik party, not of the Soviets. The other Bolsheviks were less confident that their party alone would command enough support and wished to shelter behind the name of the Soviets. Maybe Trotsky, being President of the Petrograd Soviet, looked on the Soviets with a favourable eye. Some of the Bolsheviks even hoped that a revolution would be unnecessary. The All-Russian Congress would have a Bolshevik majority. The majority would elect a new executive committee, controlled by Bolsheviks, and this committee would in turn become the government almost imperceptibly.

The Bolsheviks were not in fact preparing to seize power, despite Lenin's persistent goading. Their plans were defensive precautions in case Kerensky attempted a counter-revolution. The plans were made by the military revolutionary committee, three obscure men who did not stand high in the party. None of the three achieved fame. One was killed in a car accident a few days after the rising; one died during the civil war; the third fought in Spain twenty years later and was then killed during Stalin's great purge. The leading Bolsheviks were busy making speeches, not planning a revolution. None of them gave the decisive push. Nor for that matter did Lenin himself.

The signal for the revolution was given, strangely enough, by the man against whom the rising was to be directed, none other than Kerensky, the head of the provisional government. Kerensky imagined that he could consolidate his power by appearing as the guardian of order. The July days were much in his mind. Then the masses had demonstrated. They had been dispersed, and Kerensky's stock had gone up. Now all the respectable forces in Russia would surely rally to him again if he struck against the Bolsheviks.

Kerensky believed that the Bolsheviks were on the point of insurrection. Lenin's promptings had become known. Zinoviev and Kamenev, the two Bolsheviks who had opposed them, did not limit their opposition to private discussions. They published an attack on Lenin in a non-Bolshevik paper. Lenin wished to expel them from the party. Stalin was the one who spoke up for tolerance. The protest by Zinoviev and Kamenev was for Kerensky the alarm signal. He was determined to get his blow in first. On 5 November the provisional government resolved to suppress the Bolshevik papers and arrest the leaders of the Petrograd Soviet. That night a detachment of cadets occupied the offices of *Pravda*, stopped the presses and sealed the doors. The printers went home disconsolate. A young girl-typist ran to Smolny, where she found Trotsky and told him what had happened. Trotsky hesitated, then said: 'Break the seals'. It was the moment of defiance. Kerensky had flung down the challenge. Trotsky, not the absent Lenin, picked it up. By the afternoon copies of *Pravda* were again being sold on the streets.

At eleven o'clock that morning the Bolshevik central committee, still thinking in defensive terms, resolved that armed resistance should begin at 2 a.m. the next day. Lenin of course was still in his distant suburb. He knew that the provisional government had taken action. He did not know that the Bolshevik central committee had determined to strike back. Once more, he believed, the decisive opportunity was being lost. Lenin's suburb lay on the far side of the river Neva. He was afraid that the bridges would be raised or closed, as they usually were on days of disturbance. He would be cut off, helpless. He decided to walk to Smolny despite the risk of being arrested by soldiers loyal to Kerensky.

Lenin reached Smolny safely in the late evening and overwhelmed Trotsky with impatient questions. Trotsky explained that the plans would soon be put into action. At two o'clock in the morning of 7 November Trotsky pulled out his watch and said: 'It's begun'. Lenin said: 'From being on the run to supreme power – that's too much. It makes me dizzy', and he made the sign of the cross. The two men lay down on the hard office floor with a rug over them, while they waited for the news which, they hoped, would change the face of the world. The great revolutionary partnership of Lenin and Trotsky had begun.

7 November is the central point of Reed's narrative. Himself tense and excited, he did not perhaps stress enough the small scale of the dramatic events he recounted. This was not a rising of the masses as the March revolution and the July days had been. It was a conflict between two small groups, neither of which had much taste for fighting. Kerensky had no regular troops, only some two thousand cadets – untrained boys still in their teens – and a battalion of Amazons, women soldiers who were an embarrassment to both sides. The Soviet claimed to control ten thousand Red Guards, middle-aged factory workers, but few of them turned out for the fighting. A thousand sailors came up from the naval base at Kronstadt. One sailor was killed when his rifle went off in his hand. Four Red Guards and one sailor were killed by stray bullets. That was the total death toll on this historic day. Most people in Petrograd did not even know that a revolution was taking place. The trams were running, the fashionable restaurants were crowded, the theatres were crowded and Chaliapin was singing at the Opera. The Red Guards kept away from the smart quarter or walked modestly in the gutter.

The revolutionary military committee had planned a desperate resistance against a fierce attack by the provisional government. There was no such attack. Kerensky fled early in the day, protected by the Stars and Stripes, an anticipation perhaps of the much later Cold War. The other members of the provisional government sat helplessly in the Winter Palace. Red Guards took over the Post Office and the principal government buildings. Adhering strictly to programme, they did not reach the Winter Palace until six in the evening. Even then they did not attack it at all seriously. Red Guards filtered in through the kitchen entrance and took over the Palace without a struggle. At 2.25

a.m. on the morning of 8 November Antonov, a member of the military revolutionary committee, broke into the room where the provisional government was still sitting and shouted: 'In the name of the Military Revolutionary Committee I declare you all under arrest'. Such was the end of old Russia.

The prolonged delay caused embarrassment at Smolny. The All-Russian Congress of Soviets was due to meet in the early afternoon. The meeting was postponed until the conquest of power could be announced. Meanwhile Lenin and Trotsky discussed their future plans. Lenin said they must nominate Soviet ministers. Trotsky suggested that they should be called Commissars. Lenin said: 'Yes, that has a good revolutionary sound'. Lenin then suggested that Trotsky should become Chairman of the Council of People's Commissars, while he himself would remain merely leader of the Bolshevik party. Trotsky objected that, as a Jew, he was unsuitable. He added: 'Besides, you will stay outside and criticize'. Lenin reluctantly agreed to become Chairman. He then drew up a list of Commissars, belatedly adding Stalin as Commissar for Nationalities. This is the only time that Stalin's name appears in Reed's book, so little was 'the grey blur', as Sukhanov calls him, then regarded.

At ten in the evening the All-Russian Congress could be put off no longer. Lenin decided to anticipate events at the Winter Palace. He appeared in public for the first time since the July days and informed the astonished delegates that the Soviets had taken power. No sooner was the power in Soviet hands than it was taken away again. Lenin's list of Commissars was read out and the delegates were informed that this was the Soviet government. They duly applauded. There was nothing else they could do. In this way Lenin seized power for the Bolshevik party after all, but from the Soviet Congress, not from Kerensky.

The revolutionary drama was over. The Bolsheviks had a long struggle ahead of them before they consolidated their power. They had to face civil war and a war of intervention conducted by Great Britain and France, the victors of the First World War. They even had to face a rising by the sailors at Kronstadt, once their most devoted supporters. They lost much of Imperial Russia's outlying western territory. But by 1921 they had won. There has not been a revolution in Russia since 7 November 1917,

and the Bolsheviks, changing their name to Communists, have
ruled Russia to the present day.

Such was the achievement, but not the aim, of Lenin's revolution. In his eyes the Russian revolution was a mere preliminary
to a greater revolution which would establish international
socialism. At his first appearance before the All-Russian Congress
of Soviets he read out the Decree on Peace, the essential point in
his programme. Russia, he announced, would at once propose a
general peace on the basis of 'no annexations and no indemnities'. The workers in all other belligerent countries would
embrace this programme. They would revolt against their
imperialist rulers, and socialist governments would be set up
throughout Europe. The drama of international revolution had,
it seemed, begun.

But this first act was not followed by a second, still less carried
to a victorious conclusion. The workers of the other belligerent
countries did not revolt. The Imperialist German government
imposed on Bolshevik Russia the peace of Brest-Litovsk, with
annexations and indemnities thinly disguised. Later in 1918 the
European war was ended by the old method of victory, not by
international revolution. Only war-weariness ended the war of
intervention which Great Britain and France then attempted.

In later years western writers on Bolshevism have discovered
in it specifically Russian characteristics and have pointed to
7 November 1917 as the moment when Russia turned her back
on Europe. This is the reverse of the truth. Lenin made his
revolution for the sake of Europe, not for the sake of Russia,
and he expected Russia's preliminary revolution to be eclipsed
when the international revolution took place. Lenin did not
invent the iron curtain. On the contrary it was invented against
him by the anti-revolutionary Powers of Europe. Then it was
called the *cordon sanitaire*.

Lenin and his followers were bewildered by this outcome.
Trotsky said on 8 November 1917: 'Either the Russian Revolu-
tion will create a revolutionary movement in Europe, or the
European powers will crush the Russian revolution'. Neither
happened. Lenin, like all other Bolsheviks, including at that time
Stalin, believed that socialism was impossible in a single country.
In 1921 he called a halt. The New Economic Policy marked a

cautious return to capitalism, while the Bolsheviks waited for a second wave of international revolution which must surely come. Lenin himself fell ill and died in 1924, doubtful whether Bolshevik idealism would survive a long period of waiting. Trotsky continued to preach international revolution and was driven into exile. Stalin attained supreme power and, at the price of enormous suffering, carried through the Socialism in a Single Country which he and all other Bolsheviks had deemed impossible. In 1940 Trotsky was assassinated, probably by an agent of Stalin's. The great revolutionary duumvirate of Lenin and Trotsky vanished from the scene.

John Reed vanished also. In 1919 he went to the United States where he published *Ten Days That Shook the World*, endorsed by Lenin as 'a truthful and most vivid exposition'. Reed returned to Russia and worked as a secretary in the newly-founded Third (Communist) International. In 1920 he died of typhus and was buried under the Kremlin wall where he still rests, a hero of the revolution. His book had a period of great popularity in Soviet circles and among Socialists abroad. Then came Stalin's dictatorship. In Reed's book Stalin was barely mentioned and Trotsky was the hero of it. The book was banned along with its hero. In the years since Stalin's death, Reed's book has received a grudging tolerance from the Communists and no more. For while Stalin's other victims have been rehabilitated, Trotsky can still not be mentioned and yet no account of the Bolshevik revolution can be given without him. To the present day a citizen of the Soviet Union can find no book – Reed's or any other – to tell him in detail how his state was born. Reed's book will survive the ban. It stands unrivalled as a monument to the Bolshevik revolution and to its two leaders, Lenin and Trotsky.

Introduction

With the greatest interest and with never-slackening attention I read John Reed's book, *Ten Days That Shook the World*. Unreservedly do I recommend it to the workers of the world. Here is a book which I should like to see published in millions of copies and translated into all languages. It gives a truthful and most vivid exposition of the events so significant to the comprehension of what really is the Proletarian Revolution and the Dictatorship of the Proletariat. These problems are widely discussed, but before one can accept or reject these ideas one must understand the full significance of such a decision. John Reed's book will undoubtedly help to clear this question, which is the fundamental problem of the universal workers' movement.

NIKOLAI LENIN
(Vladimir Ilyich Ulyanov)

Preface

This book is a slice of intensified history – history as I saw it. It does not pretend to be anything but a detailed account of the November Revolution, when the Bolsheviki, at the head of the workers and soldiers, seized the state power of Russia and placed it in the hands of the Soviets.

Naturally, most of it deals with 'Red Petrograd', the capital and heart of the insurrection. But the reader must realize that what took place in Petrograd was almost exactly duplicated, with greater or lesser intensity, at different intervals of time, all over Russia.

In this book, the first of several which I am writing, I must confine myself to a chronicle of those events which I myself observed and experienced, and those supported by reliable evidence; preceded by two chapters briefly outlining the background and causes of the November Revolution. I am aware that these two chapters make difficult reading, but they are essential to an understanding of what follows.

Many questions will suggest themselves to the mind of the reader. What is Bolshevism? What kind of a government structure did the Bolsheviki set up? If the Bolsheviki championed the Constituent Assembly before the November Revolution, why did they disgorge it by force of arms afterwards? And if the bourgeoisie opposed the Constituent Assembly until the danger of Bolshevism became apparent, why did they champion it afterwards?

These and many other questions cannot be answered here. In another volume, *Kornilov to Brest-Litovsk*, I trace the course of the Revolution up to and including the German peace. There I explain the origin and functions of the Revolutionary organizations, the evolution of popular sentiment, the dissolution of the Constituent Assembly, the structure of the Soviet state, and the course and outcome of the Brest-Litovsk negotiations. ...

In considering the rise of the Bolsheviki, it is necessary to understand that Russian economic life and the Russian army were the logical result of a process which began as far back as 1915. The corrupt reactionaries in control of the Tsar's Court deliberately undertook to wreck Russia in order to make a separate peace with Germany. The lack of arms on the front, which had caused the great retreat of the summer of 1915, the lack of food in the army and in the great cities, the breakdown of manufactures and transportation in 1916 – all these we know now were part of a gigantic campaign of sabotage. This was halted in time by the March Revolution.

For the first few months of the new régime, in spite of the confusion incident upon a great Revolution, when one hundred and sixty millions of the world's most oppressed peoples suddenly achieved liberty, both the internal situation and the combative power of the army actually improved.

But the 'honeymoon' was short. The propertied classes wanted merely a political revolution, which would take the power from the Tsar and give it to them. They wanted Russia to be a constitutional republic, like France or the United States; or a constitutional monarchy, like England. On the other hand, the masses of the people wanted real industrial and agrarian democracy.

William English Walling, in his book, *Russia's Message*, an account of the Revolution of 1905, describes very well the state of mind of the Russian workers, who were later to support Bolshevism almost unanimously:

They [the working people] saw it was possible that even under a free Government, if it fell into the hands of other social classes, they might still continue to starve. ...

The Russian workman is revolutionary, but he is neither violent, dogmatic, nor unintelligent. He is ready for barricades, but he has studied them, and alone of the workers of the world he has learned about them from actual experience. He is ready and willing to fight his oppressor, the capitalist class, to a finish. But he does not ignore the existence of other classes. He merely asks that the other classes take one side or the other in the bitter conflict that draws near. ...

They [the workers] were all agreed that our [American] political institutions were preferable to their own, but they were not very anxious to exchange one despot for another (i.e., the capitalist class). ...

The working men of Russia did not have themselves shot down, executed by hundreds in Moscow, Riga, and Odessa, imprisoned by thousands in every Russian jail, and exiled to the deserts and the Arctic regions, in exchange for the doubtful privileges of the working men of Goldfields and Cripple Creek. . . .

And so developed in Russia, in the midst of a foreign war, the social revolution on top of the political revolution, culminating in the triumph of Bolshevism.

Mr A. J. Sack, director in this country of the Russian Information Bureau, which opposes the Soviet Government, has this to say in his book *The Birth of the Russian Democracy*:

The Bolsheviki organized their own cabinet, with Nicholas Lenin as Premier and Leon Trotsky Minister of Foreign Affairs. The inevitability of their coming into power became evident almost immediately after the March Revolution. The history of the Bolsheviki, after the Revolution, is a history of their steady growth. . . .

Foreigners, and Americans especially, frequently emphasize the 'ignorance' of the Russian workers. It is true they lacked the political experience of the peoples of the West, but they were very well trained in voluntary organization. In 1917 there were more than twelve million members of the Russian Consumers' Cooperative Societies; and the Soviets themselves are a wonderful demonstration of their organizing genius. Moreover, there is probably not a people in the world so well educated in Socialist theory and its practical application.

William English Walling thus characterizes them:

The Russian working people are for the most part able to read and write. For many years the country has been in such a disturbed condition that they have had the advantage of leadership not only of intelligent individuals in their midst, but of a large part of the equally revolutionary educated class, who have turned to the working people with their ideas for the political and social regeneration of Russia. . . .

Many writers explain their hostility to the Soviet Government by arguing that the last phase of the Russian Revolution was simply a struggle of the 'respectable' elements against the brutal attacks of Bolshevism. However, it was the propertied classes, who, when they realized the growth in power of the popular revolutionary organizations, undertook to destroy them and to halt the Revolution. To this end the propertied classes finally resorted to desperate measures. In order to wreck the Kerensky Ministry and the Soviets, transportation was disorganized and internal troubles provoked; to crush the Factory-Shop Committees, plants were shut down, and fuel and raw materials diverted; to break the Army Committees at the front, capital punishment was restored and military defeat connived at.

This was all excellent fuel for the Bolshevik fire. The Bolsheviki retorted by preaching the class war, and by asserting the supremacy of the Soviets.

Between these two extremes, with the other factions which whole-heartedly or half-heartedly supported them, were the so-called 'moderate' Socialists, the Mensheviki and Socialist Revolutionaries, and several smaller parties. These groups were also attacked by the propertied classes, but their power of resistance was crippled by their theories.

Roughly, the Mensheviki and Socialist Revolutionaries believed that Russia was not economically ripe for a social revolution – that only a *political* revolution was possible. According to their interpretation, the Russian masses were not educated enough to take over the power; any attempt to do so would inevitably bring on a reaction, by means of which some ruthless opportunist might restore the old régime. And so it followed that when the 'moderate' Socialists were forced to assume the power, they were afraid to use it.

They believed that Russia must pass through the stages of political and economic development known to Western Europe, and emerge at last, with the rest of the world, into full-fledged Socialism. Naturally, therefore, they agreed with the propertied classes that Russia must first be a parliamentary State – though with some improvements on the Western democracies. As a consequence, they insisted upon the collaboration of the propertied classes in the Government.

From this it was an easy step to supporting them. The 'moderate' Socialists needed the bourgeoisie. But the bourgeoisie did not need the 'moderate' Socialists. So it resulted in the Socialist Ministers being obliged to give way, little by little, on their entire programme, while the propertied classes grew more and more insistent.

And at the end, when the Bolsheviki upset the whole hollow compromise, the Mensheviki and Socialist Revolutionaries found themselves fighting on the side of the propertied classes. .... In almost every country in the world today the same phenomenon is visible.

Instead of being a destructive force, it seems to me that the Bolsheviki were the only party in Russia with a constructive programme and the power to impose it on the country. If they had not succeeded to the Government when they did, there is little doubt in my mind that the armies of imperial Germany would have been in Petrograd and Moscow in December, and Russia would again be ridden by a Tsar. ...

It is still fashionable, after a whole year of the Soviet Government, to speak of the Bolshevik insurrection as an 'adventure'. Adventure it was, and one of the most marvellous mankind ever embarked upon, sweeping into history at the head of the toiling masses, and staking everything on their vast and simple desires. Already the machinery had been set up by which the land of the great estates could be distributed among the peasants. The Factory-Shop Committees and the trade unions were there to put into operation workers' control of industry. In every village, town, city, district, and province there were Soviets of Workers', Soldiers', and Peasants' Deputies, prepared to assume the task of local administration.

No matter what one thinks of Bolshevism, it is undeniable that the Russian Revolution is one of the great events of human history, and the rise of the Bolsheviki a phenomenon of world-wide importance. Just as historians search the records for the minutest details of the story of the Paris Commune, so they will want to know what happened in Petrograd in November 1917, the spirit which animated the people, and how the leaders looked, talked, and acted. It is with this in view that I have written this book.

In the struggle my sympathies were not neutral. But in telling the story of those great days I have tried to see events with the eye of a conscientious reporter, interested in setting down the truth.

New York, 1 January 1919   J. R.

The Russian Revolution: A Chronology of Events in 1917

(The dates in the first column are according to the old-style Russian calendar, in the second column according to the new style.)

22–6 Feb.	7–11 March	Strikes and demonstrations in Petrograd.
27 Feb.	12 March	Tsarist régime overthrown in Petrograd; Committee of State Duma formed; Petrograd Soviet of Workers' Deputies formed.
1 March	14 March	Petrograd Soviet issues Order No. 1. First Provisional Government under Prince Lvov. Nicholas II abdicates in favour of his brother Michael.
3 March	16 March	Michael abdicates.
14 March	27 March	Petrograd Soviet issues a manifesto calling on all peoples to end the war.
3 April	16 April	Lenin arrives in Petrograd.
7 April	20 April	Lenin publishes 'April Theses'.
18 April	1 May	Milyukov, Foreign Minister of the Provisional Government, sends a Note reaffirming Russia's loyalty to her allies and her pledge not to make a separate peace.
20–2 April	3–5 May	Demonstrations in protest against Milyukov's Note.
27 April	10 May	Prince Lvov invites representatives of the Petrograd Soviet to join the Provisional Government.
2 May	15 May	Official announcement that Milyukov and Guchkov, Minister of War, have resigned.
4 May	17 May	Trotsky arrives in Russia.
5 May	18 May	Coalition Provisional Government formed under Prince Lvov; some

5 May	18 May	Mensheviks and Socialist Revolutionaries take office; Kerensky Minister of War.
3–24 June	16 June–7 July	First Congress of Soviets.
18 June	1 July	War offensive, ordered by Kerensky, opens. Demonstrations in Petrograd; Bolshevik slogans predominate.
2 July	15 July	Constitutional Democrats (Cadets) leave Coalition Provisional Government.
3–5 July	16–18 July	Demonstrations in Petrograd, endorsed on 4 July (17 July in the new-style calendar) by Bolshevik Central Committee; suppressed by 5 July (18 July) with the aid of troops. Measures taken against Bolsheviks: Lenin, Zinoviev, and others go into hiding.
8 July	21 July	Kerensky Prime Minister.
19 July	1 Aug.	Kerensky appoints General Kornilov Commander-in-Chief.
24 July	6 Aug.	Second Coalition Provisional Government under Kerensky; includes Constitutional Democrats (Cadets). Trotsky and Lunacharsky arrested.
26 July–3 Aug.	8–16 Aug.	Sixth Congress of Bolshevik Party. Trotsky's group joins the Bolshevik Party.
12–14 Aug.	25–7 Aug.	Provisional Government convenes State Conference in Moscow.
25 Aug.	7 Sept.	General Kornilov starts to move troops on Petrograd.
28 Aug.	10 Sept.	Kornilov's movement collapses.
31 Aug.	13 Sept.	Petrograd Soviet passes Bolshevik resolution.

1 Sept.	14 Sept.	Kerensky organizes Directory as temporary substitute for cabinet.
4 Sept.	17 Sept.	Kerensky orders dissolution of committees set up to combat Kornilov. Trotsky released.
6 Sept.	19 Sept.	Moscow Soviet for first time shows Bolshevik majority on a vote.
23 Sept.	6 Oct.	Petrograd Soviet elects Trotsky chairman.
25 Sept.	8 Oct.	New Coalition Provisional Government.
7 Oct.	20 Oct.	Pre-Parliament meets.
10 Oct.	23 Oct.	Bolshevik Central Committee, with Lenin attending, decides to organize armed insurrection. Kameniev and Zinoviev voted against.
12 Oct.	25 Oct.	Petrograd Soviet establishes Military Revolutionary Committee.
24 Oct.	6 Nov.	Bolsheviks complete preparations for insurrection. Provisional Government mobilizes, closes down Bolshevik Press. Lenin arrives at Smolny Institute.
25 Oct.	7 Nov.	Second Congress of Soviets opens, with Bolshevik majority. Kerensky leaves Petrograd to organize resistance. Provisional Government overthrown in Petrograd.
26 Oct.	8 Nov.	Soviet Government organized Decrees on Peace and Land.

Notes and Explanations

To the average reader the multiplicity of Russian organizations – political groups, Committee and Central Committees, Soviets, Dumas, and Unions – will prove extremely confusing. For this reason I am giving here a few brief definitions and explanations.

POLITICAL PARTIES

In the elections to the Constituent Assembly, there were seventeen tickets in Petrograd, and in some of the provincial towns as many as forty; but the following summary of the aims and composition of political parties is limited to the groups and factions mentioned in this book. Only the essence of their programmes and the general character of their constituencies can be noticed. ...

1. *Monarchists* of various shades, *Octobrists*, etc. These once-powerful factions no longer existed openly; they either worked underground, or their members joined the *Cadets*, as the *Cadets* came by degrees to stand for their political programme. Representatives in this book, Rodzianko, Shulgin.

2. *Cadets*. So-called from the initials of its name, Constitutional Democrats. Its official name is 'Party of the People's Freedom'. Under the Tsar composed of Liberals from the propertied classes, the *Cadets* were the great party of *political* reform, roughly corresponding to the Progressive Party in America. When the revolution broke out in March 1917 the *Cadets* formed the first Provisional Government. The *Cadet* Ministry was overthrown in April because it declared itself in favour of Allied imperialistic aims, including the imperialistic aims of the Tsar's Government. As the revolution became more and more a *social economic* revolution, the *Cadets* grew more and more conservative. Its representatives in this book are: Milyukov, Vinaver, Shatsky.

(a) *Group of Public Men*. After the *Cadets* had become unpopular through their relations with the Kornilov counter-revolution, the *Group of Public Men* was formed in Moscow. Delegates from the *Group of Public Men* were given portfolios in the last Kerensky Cabinet. The *Group* declared itself non-partisan, although its intellectual leaders were men like Rodzianko and Shulgin. It was composed of the more 'modern' bankers, merchants, and manufacturers, who were intelligent enough to realize that the Soviets must be fought by their own weapon – economic organization. Typical of the *Group*: Lianozov, Konovalov.

3. *Populist Socialists*, or *Trudoviki* (Labour Group). Numerically a small party, composed of cautious intellectuals, the leaders of the cooperative societies, and conservative peasants. Professing to be socialists, the *Populists* really supported the interests of the petty bourgeoisie – clerks, shopkeepers, etc. By direct descent, inheritors of the compromising tradition of the Labour Group in the Fourth Imperial Duma, which was composed largely of peasant representatives. Kerensky was the leader of the *Trudoviki* in the Imperial Duma when the revolution of March 1917 broke out. The *Populist Socialists* are a nationalistic party. Their representatives in this book are: Peshekhanov, Chaikovsky.

4. *Russian Social Democratic Labour Party*. Originally Marxian Socialists. At a party congress held in 1903 the party split, on the question of tactics, into two factions – the Majority (Bolshinstvo), and the Minority (Menshinstvo). From this sprang the names 'Bolsheviki' and 'Mensheviki' – 'members of the majority' and 'members of the minority'. These two wings became two separate parties, both calling themselves 'Russian Social Democratic Labour Party', and both professing to be Marxians. Since the revolution of 1905 the Bolsheviki were really the minority, becoming again the majority in September 1917.

(a) *Mensheviki*. This party includes all shades of socialists who believe that society must progress by natural evolution towards socialism, and that the working class must conquer political power first. Also a nationalistic party. This was the party of the socialist intellectuals, which means: all the means of education having been in the hands of the propertied classes, the intellectuals instinctively reacted to their training, and took the side of the propertied classes. Among their representatives in this book are: Dan, Lieber, Tseretelly.

(b) *Mensheviki Internationalists.* The radical wing of the *Mensheviki*, internationalists, and opposed to all coalition with the propertied classes yet unwilling to break loose from the conservative Mensheviki, and opposed to the dictatorship of the working class advocated by the Bolsheviki. Trotsky was long a member of this group. Among their leaders: Martov, Martinov.

(c) *Bolsheviki.* Now call themselves the *Communist Party*, in order to emphasize their complete separation from the tradition of 'moderate' or 'parliamentary' socialism, which dominates the Mensheviki and the so-called Majority Socialists in all countries. The *Bolsheviki* proposed immediate proletarian insurrection, and seizure of the reins of Government, in order to hasten the coming of socialism by forcibly taking over industry, land, natural resources, and financial institutions. This party expresses the desires chiefly of the factory workers, but also of a large section of the poor peasants.

The name 'Bolshevik' can *not* be translated by 'Maximalist'. The Maximalists are a separate group. (See paragraph 5b.) Among the leaders: Lenin, Trotsky, Lunacharsky.

(d) *United Social Democrats Internationalists.* Also called the *Novaya Zhizn* (New Life) group, from the name of the very influential newspaper which was its organ. A little group of intellectuals with a very small following among the working class, except the personal following of Maxim Gorky, its leader. Intellectuals, with almost the same programme as the *Mensheviki Internationalists*, except that the *Novaya Zhizn* group refused to be tied to either of the two great factions. Opposed the Bolshevik tactics, but remained in the Soviet Government. Other representatives in this book: Avilov, Kramarov.

(e) *Yedinstvo.* A very small and dwindling group, composed almost entirely of the personal following of Plekhanov, one of the pioneers of the Russian Social Democratic movement in the 80s, and its greatest theoretician; now an old man, Plekhanov was extremely patriotic, too conservative even for the Mensheviki. After the Bolshevik *coup d'état, Yedinstvo* disappeared.

5. *Socialist Revolutionary Party*. Called *Essaires* from the initials of their name. Originally the revolutionary party of the peasants, the party of the Fighting Organizations – the Terrorists. After the March Revolution, it was joined by many who had never been socialists. At that time it stood for the abolition of private property in land only, the owners to be compensated in some fashion. Finally the increasing revolutionary feeling of peasants compelled the *Essaires* to abandon the 'compensation' clause, and led to the younger and more fiery intellectuals breaking off from the main party in the fall of 1917 and forming a new party, the *Left Socialist Revolutionary Party*. The *Essaires*, who were afterwards always called by the radical groups '*Right Social Revolutionaries*', adopted the political attitude of the Mensheviki, and worked together with them. They finally came to represent the wealthier peasants, the intellectuals, and the politically un-educated populations of remote rural districts. Among them there was, however, a wider difference of shades of political and economic opinion than among the Mensheviki. Among their leaders mentioned in these pages: Avksentiev, Gotz, Kerensky, Chernov, 'Babushka' Breshkovskaya.

(a) *Left Socialist Revolutionaries*. Although theoretically sharing the Bolshevik programme of dictatorship of the working class, at first were reluctant to follow the ruthless Bolshevik tactics. However, the *Left Socialist Revolutionaries* remained in the Soviet Government, sharing the Cabinet portfolios, especially that of Agriculture. They withdrew from the Government several times, but always returned. As the peasants left the ranks of the *Essaires* in increasing numbers they joined the *Left Socialist Revolutionary Party*, which became the great peasant party supporting the Soviet Government, standing for confiscation with-out compensation of the great landed estates, and their dispo-sition by the peasants themselves. Among the leaders: Spiridon-ova, Karelin, Kamkov, Kalagayev.

(b) *Maximalists*. An offshoot of the *Socialist Revolutionary Party* in the revolution of 1905, when it was a powerful peasant movement, demanding the immediate application of the maxi-mum socialist programme. Now an insignificant group of peasant anarchists.

PARLIAMENTARY PROCEDURE

Russian meetings and conventions are organized after the Continental model rather than our own. The first action is usually the election of officers and the *presidium*.

The *presidium* is a presiding committee, composed of representatives of the groups and political factions represented in the assembly, in proportion to their numbers. The *presidium* arranges the Order of Business, and its members can be called upon by the president to take the chair *pro tem*.

Each question (*vopros*) is stated in a general way and then debated, and at the close of the debate resolutions are submitted by the different factions, and each one voted on separately. The Order of Business can be, and usually is, smashed to pieces in the first half hour. On the plea of 'emergency', which the crowd almost always grants, anybody from the floor can get up and say anything on any subject. The crowd controls the meeting, practically the only functions of the Speaker being to keep order by ringing a little bell, and to recognize speakers. Almost all the real work of the session is done in caucuses of the different groups and political factions, which almost always cast their votes in a body and are represented by floor-leaders. The result is, however, that at every important new point, or vote, the session takes a recess to enable the different groups and political factions to hold a caucus.

The crowd is extremely noisy, cheering or heckling speakers, overriding the plans of the *presidium*. Among the customary cries are: '*Prosim!* Please! Go on!' '*Pravilno!*' or '*Eto vierno!* That's true! Right!' '*Do volno!* Enough!' '*Doloi!* Down with him!' '*Posor!* Shame!' and '*Teeshe!* Silence! Not so noisy!'

POPULAR ORGANIZATIONS

1. *Soviet*. The word *soviet* means 'council'. Under the Tsar the Imperial Council of State was called *Gosudarstvennyi Soviet*. Since the Revolution, however, the term *Soviet* has come to be associated with a certain type of parliament elected by members of working-class economic organizations – the Soviet of Workers', of Soldiers', or of Peasants' Deputies. I have therefore limited the word to these bodies, and wherever else it occurs I have translated it 'Council'.

Besides the local *Soviets*, elected in every city, town, and village of Russia – and in large cities, also Ward (*Raionny*) *Soviets* – there are also the *oblastny* or *gubiernsky* (district or provincial) *Soviets*, and the Central Executive Committee of the All-Russian *Soviets* in the capital, called from its initials *Tsáy-ee-kah*. (See below, 'Central Committees'.)

Almost everywhere the *Soviets* of Workers' and of Soldiers' Deputies combined very soon after the March Revolution. In special matters concerning their peculiar interests, however, the Workers' and the Soldiers' Sections continued to meet separated. The *Soviets* of Peasants' Deputies did not join the other two until after the Bolshevik *coup d'état*. They, too, were organized like the workers and soldiers, with an Executive Committee of the All-Russian Peasants' *Soviets* in the capital.

2. *Trade Unions.* Although mostly industrial in form, the Russian labour unions were still called Trade Unions, and at the time of the Bolshevik Revolution had from three to four million members. These Unions were also organized in an All-Russian body, a sort of Russian Federation of Labour, which had its Central Executive Committee in the capital.

3. *Factory-Shop Committees.* These were spontaneous organizations created in the factories by the workers in their attempt to control industry, taking advantage of the administrative breakdown incident upon the Revolution. Their function was by revolutionary action to take over and run the factories. The *Factory-Shop Committees* also had their All-Russian organization, with a Central Committee at Petrograd, which cooperated with the trade unions.

4. *Dumas.* The word *duma* means roughly 'deliberative body'. The old Imperial Duma, which persisted six months after the revolution, in a democratized form, died a natural death in September 1917. The *City Duma* referred to in this book was the reorganized Municipal Council, often called 'Municipal Self-Government'. It was elected by direct and secret ballot, and its only reason for failure to hold the masses during the Bolshevik Revolution was the general decline in influence of all purely *political* representation in the face of the growing power of organizations based on *economic* groups.

5. *Zemstvos.* May be roughly translated 'country councils'. Under the Tsar semi-political, semi-social bodies with very little administrative power, developed and controlled largely by intellectual Liberals among the landowning classes. Their most important function was education and social service among the peasants. During the War the *Zemstvos* gradually took over the entire feeding and clothing of the Russian army, as well as the buying from foreign countries, and work among the soldiers generally corresponding to the work of the American Y.M.C.A. at the front. After the March Revolution the *Zemstvos* were democratized, with a view to making them the organs of local government in the rural districts. But like the *City Dumas*, they could not compete with the *Soviets*.

6. *Cooperatives.* These were the workers' and peasants' Consumers' Cooperative Societies, which had several million members all over Russia before the revolution. Founded by Liberals and 'moderate' socialists, the cooperative movement was not supported by the revolutionary socialist groups, because it was a substitute for the complete transference of means of production and distribution into the hands of the workers. After the March Revolution the *Cooperatives* spread rapidly, and were dominated by Populist Socialists, Mensheviki, and Socialist Revolutionaries, and acted as a conservative political force until the Bolshevik Revolution. However, it was the *Cooperatives* which fed Russia when the old structure of commerce and transportation collapsed.

7. *Army Committees.* The *Army Committees* were formed by the soldiers at the front to combat the reactionary influence of the old régime officers. Every company, regiment, brigade, division, and corps had its committee, over all of which was elected the *Army Committee.* The *Central Army Committee* cooperated with the General Staff. The administrative breakdown in the army incident upon the revolution threw upon the shoulders of the *Army Committees* most of the work of the Quartermaster's Department, and in some cases even the command of troops.

8. *Fleet Committees.* The corresponding organizations in the navy.

CENTRAL COMMITTEES

In the spring and summer of 1917, All-Russian conventions of every sort of organization were held at Petrograd. There were national congresses of Workers', Soldiers', and Peasants' Soviets, Trade Unions, Factory-Shop Committees, Army and Fleet Committees – besides every branch of the military and naval service, cooperatives, nationalities, etc. Each of these conventions elected a Central Committee, or a Central Executive Committee, to guard its particular interests at the seat of Government. As the Provisional Government grew weaker, these Central Committees were forced to assume more and more administrative powers.

The most important Central Committees mentioned in this book are:

Union of Unions. During the revolution of 1905, Professor Milyukov and other Liberals established unions of professional men – doctors, lawyers, physicians, etc. These were united under one central organization, the *Union of Unions*. In 1905 the *Union of Unions* acted with the revolutionary democracy; in 1917, however, the *Union of Unions* opposed the Bolshevik uprising, and united the Government employees who went on strike against the authority of the Soviets.

Tsay-ee-kah. All-Russian Central Executive Committee of the Soviets of Workers' and Soldiers' Deputies. So called from the initials of its name.

Tsentroflot. 'Centre-Fleet' – the Central Fleet Committee.

Vikzhel. All-Russian Central Committee of the Railway Workers' Union. So called from the initials of its name.

OTHER ORGANIZATIONS

Red Guards. The armed factory workers of Russia. The *Red Guards* were first formed during the revolution of 1905, and sprang into existence again in the days of March 1917, when a force was needed to keep order in the city. At that time they were armed, and all efforts of the Provisional Government to disarm them were more or less unsuccessful. At every great crisis in the revolution the *Red Guards* appeared on the streets, untrained and undisciplined, but full of revolutionary zeal.

White Guards. Bourgeois volunteers, who emerged in the last stages of the revolution, to defend private property from the

Bolshevik attempt to abolish it. A great many of them were university students.

Tekhintsi. The so-called 'Savage Division' in the army, made up of Mohammedan tribesmen from Central Asia, and personally devoted to General Kornilov. The *Tekhintsi* were noted for their blind obedience and their savage cruelty in warfare.

Death Battalions. Or *Shock Battalions.* The Women's Battalion is known to the world as the *Death Battalion*, but there were many *Death Battalions* composed of men. These were formed in the summer of 1917 by Kerensky, for the purpose of strengthening the discipline and combative fire of the army by heroic example. The *Death Battalions* were composed mostly of intense young patriots. These came for the most part from among the sons of the propertied classes.

Union of Officers. An organization formed among the reactionary officers in the army to combat politically the growing power of the Army Committees.

Knights of St George. The Cross of St George was awarded for distinguished action in battle. Its holder automatically became a *Knight of St George.* The predominant influence in the organization was that of the supporters of the military idea.

Peasants' Union. In 1905 the *Peasants' Union* was a revolutionary peasants' organization. In 1917, however, it had become a political expression of the more prosperous peasants, to fight the growing power and revolutionary aims of the Soviets of Peasants' Deputies.

CHRONOLOGY AND SPELLING

I have adopted in this book our calendar throughout, instead of the former Russian calendar, which was thirteen days earlier.

In the spelling of Russian names and words, I have made no attempt to follow any scientific rules for transliteration, but have tried to give the spelling which would lead the English-speaking reader to the simplest approximation of their pronunciation.*

SOURCES

Much of the material in this book is from my own notes. I have

*Note to the Penguin edition: John Reed's spelling has been slightly revised (to accord with current practice), following the same principle.

also relied, however, upon a heterogeneous file of several hundred assorted Russian newspapers, covering almost every day of the time described, of files of the English paper, the *Russian Daily News*, and of the two French papers, *Journal de Russie* and *Entente*. But far more valuable than these is the *Bulletin de la Presse* issued daily by the French Information Bureau in Petrograd, which reports all important happenings, speeches, and the comment of the Russian press. Of this I have an almost complete file from the spring of 1917 to the end of January 1918.

Besides the foregoing, I have in my possession almost every proclamation, decree and announcement posted on the walls of Petrograd from the middle of September 1917 to the end of January 1918. Also the official publication of all Government decrees and orders, and the official Government publication of the secret treaties and other documents discovered in the Ministry of Foreign Affairs when the Bolsheviki took it over.

1 Background

Towards the end of September 1917, an alien professor of socio-
logy visiting Russia came to see me in Petrograd. He had been
informed by business men and intellectuals that the Revolution
was slowing down. The professor wrote an article about it and
then travelled around the country, visiting factory towns and
peasant communities – where, to his astonishment, the Revolution seemed to be speeding up. Among the wage-earners and the
land-working people it was common to hear talk of 'all land to
the peasants, all factories to the workers'. If the professor had
visited the front, he would have heard the whole Army talking
Peace. . . .

The professor was puzzled, but he need not have been; both
observations were correct. The property-owning classes were becoming more conservative, the masses of the people more radical.

There was a feeling among business men and the *intelligentsia*
generally that the Revolution had gone quite far enough, and
lasted too long; that things should settle down. This sentiment
was shared by the dominant 'moderate' Socialist groups, the
oborontsi[1] Mensheviki and Socialist Revolutionaries, who
supported the Provisional Government of Kerensky.

On 14 October the official organ of the 'moderate' Socialists
said:

> The drama of the Revolution has two acts; the destruction of the old
> régime and the creation of the new one. The first act has lasted long
> enough. Now it is time to go on to the second, and to play it as rapidly
> as possible. As a great revolutionist put it, 'Let us hasten, friends, to
> terminate the Revolution. He who makes it last too long will not gather
> the fruits. . . .'

Among the worker, soldier, and peasant masses, however,
there was a stubborn feeling that the 'first act' was not yet played
out. On the front the Army Committees were always running foul
of officers who could not get used to treating their men like human

1. References numbered in this manner refer to the Appendix, p. 273.

beings; in the rear the Land Committees elected by the peasants were being jailed for trying to carry out Government regulations concerning the land; and the workmen[2] in the factories were fighting blacklists and lock-outs. Nay, furthermore, returning political exiles were being excluded from the country as 'undesirable' citizens; and in some cases men who returned from abroad to their villages were prosecuted and imprisoned for revolutionary acts committed in 1905.

To the multiform discontent of the people the 'moderate' Socialists had one answer: Wait for the Constituent Assembly, which is to meet in December. But the masses were not satisfied with that. The Constituent Assembly was all well and good; but there were certain definite things for which the Russian Revolution had been made and for which the revolutionary martyrs rotted in their stark Brotherhood Grave on Mars Field, that must be achieved, Constituent Assembly or no Constituent Assembly: Peace, Land, and Workers' Control of Industry. The Constituent Assembly had been postponed and postponed – would probably be postponed again, until the people were calm enough – perhaps to modify their demands! At any rate here were eight months of the Revolution gone, and little enough to show for it. ....

Meanwhile the soldiers began to solve the peace question by simply deserting, the peasants burned manor-houses and took over the great estates, the workers sabotaged and struck. ... Of course, as was natural, the manufacturers, landowners, and army officers exerted all their influence against any democratic compromise. ...

The policy of the Provisional Government alternated between ineffective reforms and stern repressive measures. An edict from the Socialist Minister of Labour ordered all the Workers' Committees henceforth to meet only after working hours. Among the troops at the front, 'agitators' of opposition political parties were arrested, radical newspapers closed down, and capital punishment applied – to revolutionary propagandists. Attempts were made to disarm the Red Guard. Cossacks were sent to keep order in the provinces. ...

These measures were supported by the 'moderate' Socialists and their leaders in the Ministry, who considered it necessary to cooperate with the propertied classes. The people rapidly deserted them, and went over to the Bolsheviki, who stood for Peace, Land, and Workers' Control of Industry, and a Government of the working class. In September 1917, matters reached a crisis. Against the overwhelming sentiment of the country, Kerensky and the 'moderate' Socialists succeeded in establishing a Government of Coalition with the propertied classes; and as a result, the Mensheviki and Socialist Revolutionaries lost the confidence of the people for ever.

An article in *Rabochi Put* (Workers' Way) about the middle of October, entitled 'The Socialist Ministers', expressing the feeling of the masses of the people against the 'moderate' Socialists:

Here is a list of their services.[3]

Tseretelly: disarmed the workmen with the assistance of General Polovtsev, checkmated the revolutionary soldiers, and approved of capital punishment in the army.

Skobeliev: commenced by trying to tax the capitalists 100 per cent of their profits, and finished – and finished by an attempt to dissolve the Workers' Committees in the shops and factories.

Avksentiev: put several hundred peasants in prison, members of the Land Committees, and suppressed dozens of workers' and soldiers' newspapers.

Chernov: signed the 'Imperial' manifesto, ordering the dissolution of the Finnish Diet.

Savinkov: concluded an open alliance with General Kornilov. If this saviour of the country was not able to betray Petrograd, it was due to reasons over which he had no control.

Zarudny: with the sanction of Alexinsky and Kerensky, put some of the best workers of the Revolution, soldiers and sailors, in prison.

Nikitin: acted as a vulgar policeman against the railway workers.

Kerensky: it is better not to say anything about him. The list of his services is too long. ...

A Congress of delegates of the Baltic Fleet, at Helsingfors, passed a resolution which began as follows:

We demand the immediate removal from the ranks of the Provisional Government of the 'Socialist', the political adventurer – Kerensky, as one who is scandalizing and ruining the great Revolution, and with it the revolutionary masses, by his shameless political blackmail on behalf of the bourgeoisie. ...

The direct result of all this was the rise of the Bolsheviki. ...

Since March 1917, when the roaring torrents of workmen and soldiers beating upon the Tauride Palace compelled the reluctant Imperial Duma to assume the supreme power in Russia, it was the masses of the people, workers, soldiers, and peasants which forced every change in the course of the Revolution. They hurled the Milyukov Ministry down; it was their Soviet which proclaimed to the world the Russian peace terms – 'No annexations, no indemnities, and the right of self-determination of peoples'; and again, in July, it was the spontaneous rising of the unorganized proletariat which once more stormed the Tauride Palace, to demand that the Soviets take over the Government of Russia.

The Bolsheviki, then a small political sect, put themselves at the head of the movement. As a result of the disastrous failure of the rising, public opinion turned against them, and their leaderless hordes slunk back into the Viborg Quarter, which is Petrograd's St Antoine. Then followed a savage hunt of the Bolsheviki; hundreds were imprisoned, among them Trotsky, Madame Kollontai, and Kameniev; Lenin and Zinoviev went into hiding, fugitives from justice; the Bolshevik papers were suppressed. Provocators and reactionaries raised the cry that the Bolsheviki were German agents, until people all over the world believed it.

But the Provisional Government found itself unable to substantiate its accusations; the documents proving pro-German conspiracy were discovered to be forgeries;* and one by one the Bolsheviki were released from prison without trial, on nominal or no bail – until only six remained. The impotence and indecision of the ever-changing Provisional Government was an argument nobody could refute. The Bolsheviki raised again the slogan so dear to the masses, 'All Power to the Soviets!' – and they were not merely self-seeking, for at that time the majority of the Soviets was 'moderate' Socialist, their bitter enemy.

But more potent still, they took the crude, simple desires of the workers, soldiers, and peasants, and from them built their immediate programme. And so, while the *oborontsi* Mensheviki and Socialist Revolutionaries involved themselves in compromise with the bourgeoisie, the Bolsheviki rapidly captured the Russian masses. In July they were hunted and despised; by September the metropolitan workmen, the sailors of the Baltic Fleet, and the

* Part of the famous 'Sisson Documents'.

soldiers had been won almost entirely to their cause. The September municipal elections in the large cities[4] were significant; only 18 per cent of the returns were Menshevik and Socialist Revolutionary, against more than 70 per cent in June. ...

There remains a phenomenon which puzzled foreign observers; the fact that the Central Executive Committees of the Soviets, the Central Army and Fleet Committees,* and the Central Committees of some of the Unions – notably, the Post and Telegraph Workers and the Railway Workers – opposed the Bolsheviki with the utmost violence. These Central Committees had all been elected in the middle of the summer, or even before, when the Mensheviki and Socialist Revolutionaries had an enormous following; and they delayed or prevented any new elections. Thus, according to the constitution of the Soviets of Workers' and Soldiers' Deputies, the All-Russian Congress *should have been called in September*; but the Tsay-ee-kah* would not call the meeting, on the ground that the Constituent Assembly was only two months away, at which time, they hinted, the Soviets would abdicate. Meanwhile, one by one, the Bolsheviki were winning in the local Soviets all over the country, in the Union branches and the ranks of all the soldiers and sailors. The Peasants' Soviets remained still conservative, because in the sluggish rural districts political consciousness developed slowly, and the Socialist Revolutionary party had been for a generation the party which had agitated among the peasants. ... But even among the peasants a revolutionary wing was forming. It showed itself clearly in October, when the left wing of the Socialist Revolutionaries split off, and formed a new political faction, the Left Socialist Revolutionaries.

At the same time there were signs everywhere that the forces of reaction were gaining confidence.[5] At the Troitsky Farce Theatre in Petrograd, for example, a burlesque called *Sins of the Tsar* was interrupted by a group of monarchists, who threatened to lynch the actors for 'insulting the Emperor'. Certain newspapers began to sigh for a 'Russian Napoleon'. It was the usual thing among bourgeois *intelligentsia* to refer to the Soviets of Workers' Deputies (Rabochikh Deputatov) as *Sabachikh* Deputatove – Dogs' Deputies.

* See Notes and Explanations.

On 15 October I had a conversation with a great Russian Capitalist, Stepan Georgevich Lianozov, known as the 'Russian Rockefeller' – a Cadet by political faith.

'Revolution,' he said 'is a sickness. Sooner or later the foreign powers must intervene here – as one would intervene to cure a sick child, and teach it how to walk. Of course, it would be more or less improper, but the nations must realize the danger of Bolshevism in their own countries – such contagious ideas as "proletarian dictatorship", and "world social revolution".... There is a chance that this intervention may not be necessary. Transportation is demoralized, the factories are closing down, and the Germans are advancing. Starvation and defeat may bring the Russian people to their senses.'

Mr Lianozov was emphatic in his opinion that whatever happened, it would be impossible for merchants and manufacturers to permit the existence of the workers' Shop Committees, or to allow the workers any share in the management of industry.

'As for the Bolsheviki, they will be done away with by one of two methods. The Government can evacuate Petrograd, then a state of siege declared, and the military commander of the district can deal with these gentlemen without legal formalities. ... *Or if, for example, the Constituent Assembly manifests any Utopian tendencies, it can be dispersed by force of arms. ...*'

Winter was coming on – the terrible Russian winter. I heard business men speak of it so: 'Winter was always Russia's best friend. Perhaps now it will rid us of Revolution.' On the freezing front miserable armies continued to starve and die without enthusiasm. The railways were breaking down, food lessening, factories closing. The desperate masses cried out that the bourgeoisie was sabotaging the life of the people, causing defeat on the front. Riga had been surrendered just after General Kornilov said publicly, 'Must we pay with Riga the price of bringing the country to a sense of its duty?'*

To Americans it is incredible that the class war should develop to such a pitch. But I have personally met officers on the Northern Front who frankly preferred military disaster to cooperation with the Soldiers' Committees. The secretary of the Petrograd branch

* See *Kornilov to Brest-Litovsk*, by John Reed, Boni and Liveright, N.Y., 1919.

of the Cadet party told me that the breakdown of the country's economic life was part of a campaign to discredit the Revolution. An Allied diplomat, whose name I promised not to mention, confirmed this from his own knowledge. I know of certain coal mines near Kharkov which were fired and flooded by their owners, of textile factories at Moscow whose engineers put the machinery out of order when they left, of railroad officials caught by the workers in the act of crippling locomotives. ...

A large section of the propertied classes preferred the Germans to the Revolution – even to the Provisional Government – and didn't hesitate to say so. In the Russian household where I lived, the subject of conversation at the dinner-table was almost invariably the coming of the Germans, bringing 'law and order'.... One evening I spent at the house of a Moscow merchant; during tea we asked the eleven people at the table whether they preferred 'Wilhelm or the Bolsheviki'. The vote was ten to one for Wilhelm. ...

The speculators took advantage of the universal disorganization to pile up fortunes, and to spend them in fantastic revelry or the corruption of Government officials. Foodstuffs and fuel were hoarded, or secretly sent out of the country to Sweden. In the first four months of the Revolution, for example, the reserve food supplies were almost openly looted from the great Municipal warehouses of Petrograd, until the two years' provision of grain had fallen to less than enough to feed the city for one month. ... According to the official report of the last Minister of Supplies in the Provisional Government, coffee was bought wholesale in Vladivostok for two roubles a pound, and the consumer in Petrograd paid thirteen. In all the stores of the large cities were tons of food and clothing; but only the rich could buy them.

In a provincial town I knew a merchant family turned speculator – *maradior* (bandit, ghoul) the Russians call it. The three sons had bribed their way out of military service. One gambled in foodstuffs. Another sold illegal gold from the Lena mines to mysterious parties in Finland. The third owned a controlling interest in a chocolate factory, which supplied the local Cooperative societies – on condition that the Cooperatives furnished him everything he needed. And so, while the masses of the people got a quarter pound of black bread on their bread cards, he had an

abundance of white bread, sugar, tea, candy, cake, and butter. . . .
Yet, when the soldiers at the front could no longer fight from
cold, hunger, and exhaustion, how indignantly did this family
scream 'Cowards!' – how 'ashamed' they were 'to be Russians'.
. . . When finally the Bolsheviki found and requisitioned vast
hoarded stores of provisions, what 'Robbers' they were.

Beneath all this external rottenness moved the old-time Dark
Forces, unchanged since the fall of Nicholas the Second, secret
still and very active. The agents of the notorious Okhrana still
functioned, for and against the Tsar, for and against Kerensky –
whoever would pay. . . . In the darkness, underground organizations of all sorts, such as the Black Hundreds, were busy attempting to restore reaction in some form or other.

In this atmosphere of corruption, of monstrous half-truths, one
clear note sounded day after day, the deepening chorus of the
Bolsheviki, 'All Power to the Soviets! All Power to the direct
representatives of millions on millions of common workers,
soldiers, peasants. Land, bread, an end to the senseless war, an
end to secret diplomacy, speculation, treachery. . . . The Revolution is in danger and with it the cause of the people all over the
world!'

The struggle between the proletariat and the middle class,
between the Soviets and the Government, which had begun in the
first March days, was about to culminate. Having at one bound
leaped from the Middle Ages into the twentieth century, Russia
showed the startled world two systems of Revolution – the
political and the social – in mortal combat.

What a revelation of the vitality of the Russian Revolution,
after all these months of starvation and disillusionment! The
bourgeoisie should have better known its Russia. Not for a long
time in Russia will the 'sickness' of Revolution have run its
course. . . .

Looking back, Russia before the November insurrection seems
of another age, almost incredibly conservative. So quickly did we
adapt ourselves to the newer, swifter life; just as Russian politics
swung bodily to the Left – until the Cadets were outlawed as
'enemies of the people', Kerensky became a 'counter-revolutionist', the 'middle' Socialist leaders, Tseretelly, Dan, Lieber,
Gotz, and Avksentiev, were too reactionary for their following,

and men like Victor Chernov, and even Maxim Gorky, belonged to the Right Wing. ...

About the middle of December 1917, a group of Socialist Revolutionary leaders paid a private visit to Sir George Buchanan, the British Ambassador, and implored him not to mention the fact that they had been there because they were 'considered too far Right'.

'And to think,' said Sir George, 'one year ago my Government instructed me not to receive Milyukov, because he was so dangerously Left!'

September and October are the worst months of the Russian year – especially the Petrograd year. Under dull grey skies, in the shortening days, the rain fell drenching, incessant. The mud underfoot was deep, slippery, and clinging, tracked everywhere by heavy boots, and worse than usual because of the complete breakdown of the Municipal administration. Bitter damp winds rushed in from the Gulf of Finland, and the chill fog rolled through the streets. At night, for motives of economy as well as fear of Zeppelins, the street-lights were few and far between; in private dwellings and apartment houses the electricity was turned on from six o'clock until midnight, with candles forty cents apiece and little kerosene to be had. It was dark from three in the afternoon to ten in the morning. Robberies and house-breaking increased. In apartment houses the men took turns at all-night guard duty, armed with loaded rifles. This was under the Provisional Government.

Week by week food became scarcer. The daily allowance of bread fell from a pound and a half to a pound, then three-quarters, half, and a quarter-pound. Towards the end there was a week without any bread at all. Sugar one was entitled to at the rate of two pounds a month – if one could get it at all, which was seldom. A bar of chocolate or a pound of tasteless candy cost anywhere from seven to ten roubles – at least a dollar. There was milk for about half the babies in the city; most hotels and private houses never saw it for months. In the fruit season apples and pears sold for a little less than a rouble apiece on the street corner. ...

For milk and bread and sugar and tobacco one had to stand in queue long hours in the chill rain. Coming home from an all-night meeting I have seen the *kvost* (tail) beginning to form before dawn, mostly women, some with babies in their arms. . . . Carlyle, in his *French Revolution*, has described the French people as distinguished above all others by their faculty of standing in queue. Russia had accustomed herself to the practice, begun in the reign of Nicholas the Blessed as long ago as 1915, and from then continued intermittently until the summer of 1917, when it settled down as the regular order of things. Think of the poorly clad people standing on the iron-white streets of Petrograd whole days in the Russian winter! I have listened in the bread-lines, hearing the bitter, acrid note of discontent which from time to time burst up through the miraculous good nature of the Russian crowd. . . .

Of course all the theatres were going every night, including Sundays. Karsavina appeared in a new Ballet at the Marinsky, all dance-loving Russia coming to see her. Chaliapin was singing. At the Alexandrinsky they were reviving Meyerhold's production of Tolstoy's *Death of Ivan the Terrible*; and at that performance I remember noticing a student of the Imperial School of Pages, in his dress uniform, who stood up correctly between the acts and faced the empty Imperial box, with its eagles all erased. . . . The Krivoye Zerkalo staged a sumptuous version of Schnitzler's *Reigen*.

Although the Hermitage and other picture galleries had been evacuated to Moscow, there were weekly exhibitions of paintings. Hordes of the female *intelligentsia* went to hear lectures on Art, Literature, and the Easy Philosophies. It was a particularly active season for Theosophists. And the Salvation Army, admitted to Russia for the first time in history, plastered the walls with announcements of gospel meetings, which amused and astounded Russian audiences. . . .

As in all such times, the petty conventional life of the city went on, ignoring the Revolution as much as possible. The poets made verses – but not about the Revolution. The realistic painters painted scenes from medieval Russian history – anything but the Revolution. Young ladies from the provinces came up to the capital to learn French and cultivate their voices, and the gay young beautiful officers wore their gold-trimmed crimson *bashliki* and their elaborate Caucasian swords around the hotel lobbies.

The ladies of the minor bureaucratic set took tea with each other in the afternoon, carrying each her little gold or silver or jewelled sugar-box, and half a loaf of bread in her muff, and wished that the Tsar were back, or that the Germans would come, or anything that would solve the servant problem.... The daughter of a friend of mine came home one afternoon in hysterics because the woman street-car conductor had called her 'Comrade!'

All around them great Russia was in travail, bearing a new world. The servants one used to treat like animals and pay next to nothing were getting independent. A pair of shoes cost more than a hundred roubles, and as wages averaged about thirty-five roubles a month the servants refused to stand in queue and wear out their shoes. But more than that. In the new Russia every man and woman could vote; there were working-class newspapers, saying new and startling things; there were the Soviets; and there were the Unions. The *izvozchiki* (cab-drivers) had a Union; they were also represented in the Petrograd Soviet. The waiters and hotel servants were organized, and refused tips. On the walls of restaurants they put up signs which read, 'No tips taken here –' or, 'Just because a man has to make his living waiting on table is no reason to insult him by offering him a tip!'

At the front the soldiers fought their fight with the officers and learned self-government through their committees. In the factories, those unique Russian organizations, the Factory-Shop Committees,* gained experience and strength and a realization of their historical mission by combat with the old order. All Russia was learning to read, and *reading* – politics, economics, history – because the people wanted to *know*.... In every city, in most towns, along the front, each political faction had its newspaper – sometimes several. Hundreds of thousands of pamphlets were distributed by thousands of organizations, and poured into the armies, the villages, the factories, the streets. The thirst for education, so long thwarted, burst with the Revolution into a frenzy of expression. From Smolny Institute alone, the first six months, went out every day tons, car-loads, train-loads of literature, saturating the land. Russia absorbed reading matter like hot sand drinks water, insatiable. And it was not fables, falsified history, diluted religion, and the cheap fiction that corrupts – but social

* See Notes and Explanations.

and economic theories, philosophy, the works of Tolstoy, Gogol, and Gorky. . . .

Then the Talk, beside which Carlyle's 'flood of French speech' was a mere trickle. Lectures, debates, speeches – in theatres, circuses, school-houses, clubs, Soviet meeting-rooms, Union headquarters, barracks. . . . Meetings in the trenches at the front, in village squares, factories. . . . What a marvellous sight to see Putilovsky Zavod (the Putilov factory) pour out its forty thousand to listen to Social Democrats, Socialist Revolutionaries, Anarchists, anybody, whatever they had to say, as long as they would talk! For months in Petrograd, and all over Russia, every street-corner was a public tribune. In railway trains, street-cars, always the spurting up of impromptu debate, everywhere. . . .

And the All-Russian Conferences and Congresses, drawing together the men of two continents – conventions of Soviets, of Cooperatives, Zemstvos,* nationalities, priests, peasants, political parties; the Democratic Conference, the Moscow Conference, the Council of the Russian Republic. There were always three or four conventions going on in Petrograd. At every meeting, attempts to limit the time of speakers voted down, and every man free to express the thought that was in him. . . .

We came down to the front of the Twelfth Army, back of Riga, where gaunt and bootless men sickened in the mud of desperate trenches; and when they saw us they started up, with their pinched faces and the flesh showing blue through their torn clothing, demanding eagerly, 'Did you bring anything to *read*?'

What though the outward and visible signs of change were many, what though the statue of Catherine the Great before the Alexandrinsky Theatre bore a little red flag in its hand, and others – somewhat faded – floated from all public buildings; and the Imperial monograms and eagles were either torn down or covered up; and in place of the fierce *gorodovoye* (city police) a mild-mannered and unarmed citizen militia patrolled the streets – still, there were many quaint anachronisms.

For example, Peter the Great's *Tabel o Rangov* – Table of Ranks – which he riveted upon Russia with an iron hand, still held sway. Almost everybody from the schoolboy up wore his prescribed uniform, with the insignia of the Emperor on button

* See Notes and Explanations.

and shoulder-strap. Along about five o'clock in the afternoon the streets were full of subdued old gentlemen in uniform, with portfolios, going home from work in the huge, barrack-like Ministries or Government institutions, calculating perhaps how great a mortality among their superiors would advance them to the coveted *chin* (rank) of Collegiate Assessor, or Privy Councillor, with the prospect of retirement on a comfortable pension, and possibly the Cross of St Anne. ...

There is the story of Senator Sokolov, who in full tide of Revolution came to a meeting of the Senate one day in civilian clothes, and was not admitted because he did not wear the prescribed livery of the Tsar's service!

It was against this background of a whole nation in ferment and disintegration that the pageant of the Rising of the Russian Masses unrolled. ...

2 The Coming Storm

In September General Kornilov marched on Petrograd to make himself military dictator of Russia. Behind him was suddenly revealed the mailed fist of the bourgeoisie, boldly attempting to crush the Revolution. Some of the Socialist Ministers were implicated; even Kerensky was under suspicion.[6] Savinkov, summoned to explain to the Central Committee of his party, the Socialist Revolutionaries, refused and was expelled. Kornilov was arrested by the Soldiers' Committees. Generals were dismissed, Ministers suspended from their functions, and the Cabinet fell.

Kerensky tried to form a new Government, including the Cadets, party of the bourgeoisie. His party, the Socialist Revolutionaries, ordered him to exclude the Cadets. Kerensky declined to obey, and threatened to resign from the Cabinet if the Socialists insisted. However, popular feeling ran so high that for the moment he did not dare oppose it, and a temporary Directorate of Five of the old Ministers, with Kerensky at the head, assumed the power until the question should be settled.

The Kornilov affair drew together all the Socialist groups – 'moderates' as well as revolutionists – in a passionate impulse of self-defence. There must be no more Kornilovs. A new Government must be created, responsible to the elements supporting the Revolution. So the Tsay-ee-kah invited the popular organizations to send delegates to a Democratic Conference, which should meet at Petrograd in September.

In the Tsay-ee-kah three factions immediately appeared. The Bolsheviki demanded that the All-Russian Congress of Soviets be summoned, and that they take over the power. The 'centre' Socialist Revolutionaries, led by Chernov, joined with the Left Socialist Revolutionaries, led by Kamkov and Spiridonova, the Mensheviki Internationalists under Martov, and the 'centre' Mensheviki,* represented by Bogdanov and Skobeliev, in demanding a purely Socialist Government. Tseretelly, Dan, and

* See Notes and Explanations.

Lieber, at the head of the right-wing Mensheviki, and the Right Socialist Revolutionaries under Avksentiev and Gotz, insisted that the propertied classes must be represented in the new Government.

Almost immediately the Bolsheviki won a majority in the Petrograd Soviet, and the Soviets of Moscow, Kiev, Odessa, and other cities followed suit.

Alarmed, the Mensheviki and Socialist Revolutionaries in control of the Tsay-ee-kah decided that after all they feared the danger of Kornilov less than the danger of Lenin. They revised the plan of representation in the Democratic Conference,[7] admitting more delegates from the Cooperative Societies and other conservative bodies. Even this packed assembly at first voted for a *Coalition Government without the Cadets.* Only Kerensky's open threat of resignation, and the alarming cries of the 'moderate' Socialists that 'the Republic is in danger' persuaded the Conference, by a small majority, to declare in favour of the principle of coalition with the bourgeoisie, and to sanction the establishment of a sort of consultative Parliament, without any legislative power, called the Provisional Council of the Russian Republic. In the new Ministry the propertied class practically controlled, and in the Council of the Russian Republic they occupied, a disproportionate number of seats.

The fact is that the Tsay-ee-kah no longer represented the rank and file of the Soviets, and had illegally refused to call another All-Russian Congress of Soviets, due in September. It had no intention of calling this Congress or of allowing it to be called. Its official organ, *Izvestia* (News), began to hint that the function of the Soviets was nearly at an end,[8] and that they might soon be dissolved. ... At this time, too, the new Government announced as part of its policy the liquidation of 'irresponsible organizations' – i.e., the Soviets.

The Bolsheviki responded by summoning the All-Russian Soviets to meet at Petrograd on 2 November and take over the Government of Russia. At the same time they withdrew from the Council of the Russian Republic, stating that they would not participate in a 'Government of Treason to the People'.[9]

The withdrawal of the Bolsheviki, however, did not bring tranquillity to the ill-fated Council. The propertied classes, now in a position of power, became arrogant. The Cadets declared that the Government had no legal right to declare Russia a republic. They demanded stern measures in the Army and Navy to destroy the Soldiers' and Sailors' Committees, and denounced the Soviets. On the other side of the chamber the Mensheviki Internationalists and the Left Socialist Revolutionaries advocated immediate peace, land to the peasants, and workers' control of industry – practically the Bolshevik programme.

I heard Martov's speech in answer to the Cadets. Stooped over the desk of the tribune like the mortally sick man he was, and speaking in a voice so hoarse it could hardly be heard, he shook his finger towards the right benches:

'You call us defeatists, but the real defeatists are those who wait for a more propitious moment to conclude peace, insist upon postponing peace until later, until nothing is left of the Russian army, until Russia becomes the subject of bargaining between the different imperialist groups. . . . You are trying to impose upon the Russian people a policy dictated by the interests of the bourgeoisie. The question of peace should be raised without delay. . . . You will see then that not in vain has been the work of those whom you call German agents, of those Zimmerwaldists* who in all the lands have prepared the awakening of the conscience of the democratic masses. . . .'

Between these two groups the Mensheviki and Socialist Revolutionaries wavered, irresistibly forced to the left by the pressure of the rising dissatisfaction of the masses. Deep hostility divided the chamber into irreconcilable groups.

This was the situation when the long-awaited announcement of the Allied Conference in Paris brought up the burning question of foreign policy. . . .

Theoretically all Socialist parties in Russia were in favour of the earliest possible peace on democratic terms. As long ago as May 1917 the Petrograd Soviet, then under control of the Mensheviki and Socialist Revolutionaries, had proclaimed the famous Russian peace-conditions. They had demanded that the Allies hold a conference to discuss war aims. This conference had been

* Members of the revolutionary international wing of the Socialists of Europe, so-called because of their participation in the International Conference held at Zimmerwald, Switzerland, in 1915.

promised for August; then postponed until September; then until October; and now it was fixed for 10 November.

The Provisional Government suggested two representatives – General Alexeyev, reactionary military man, and Tereshchenko, Minister of Foreign Affairs. The Soviets chose Skobeliev to speak for them and drew up a manifesto, the famous *nakaz*[10] – instructions. The Provisional Government objected to Skobeliev and his *nakaz*; the Allied ambassadors protested and finally Bonar Law in the British House of Commons, in answer to a question, responded coldly, 'As far as I know the Paris Conference will not discuss the aims of the war at all, but only the methods of conducting it. . . .'

At this the conservative Russian press was jubilant, and the Bolsheviki cried, 'See where the compromising tactics of the Mensheviki and Socialist Revolutionaries have led them!'

Along a thousand miles of front the millions of men in Russia's armies stirred like the sea rising, pouring into the capital their hundreds upon hundreds of delegations, crying, 'Peace! Peace!'

I went across the river to the Cirque Moderne, to one of the great popular meetings which occurred all over the city, more numerous night after night. The bare, gloomy amphitheatre, lit by five tiny lights hanging from a thin wire, was packed from the ring up the steep sweep of grimy benches to the very roof – soldiers, sailors, workmen, women, all listening as if their lives depended upon it. A soldier was speaking – from the Five Hundred and Forty-Eighth Division, wherever and whatever that was:

'Comrades,' he cried, and there was real anguish in his drawn face and despairing gestures. 'The people at the top are always calling upon us to sacrifice more, sacrifice more, while those who have everything are left unmolested.

'We are at war with Germany. Would we invite German generals to serve on our Staff? Well we're at war with the capitalists too, and yet we invite them into our Government. . . .

'The soldier says, "Show me what I am fighting for. Is it Constantinople, or is it free Russia? Is it the democracy, or is it the capitalist plunderers? If you can prove to me that I am defending the Revolution then I'll go out and fight without capital punishment to force me."

'When the land belongs to the peasants, and the factories to the workers, and the power to the Soviets, then we'll know we have something to fight for, and we'll fight for it!'

In the barracks, the factories, on the street corners, endless soldier speakers, all clamouring for an end to the war, declaring that if the Government did not make an energetic effort to get peace, the army would leave the trenches and go home.

The spokesman for the Eighth Army:

'We are weak, we have only a few men left in each company. They must give us food and boots and reinforcements, or soon there will be left only empty trenches. Peace or supplies ... either let the Government end the war or support the Army. ...'

For the Forty-Sixth Siberian Artillery:

'The officers will not work with our Committees, they betray us to the enemy, they apply the death penalty to our agitators, and the counter-revolutionary Government supports them. We thought that the Revolution would bring peace. But now the Government forbids us even to talk of such things, and at the same time doesn't give us enough food to live on, or enough ammunition to fight with. ...'

From Europe came rumours of peace at the expense of Russia. ...[11]

News of the treatment of Russian troops in France added to the discontent. The First Brigade had tried to replace its officers with Soldiers' Committees, like their comrades at home, and had refused an order to go to Salonika, demanding to be sent to Russia. They had been surrounded and starved, and then fired on by artillery, and many killed. ...[12]

On 29 October I went to the white marble and crimson hall of the Marinsky Palace, where the Council of the Republic sat, to hear Tereshchenko's declaration of the Government's foreign policy, awaited with such terrible anxiety by all the peace-thirsty and exhausted land.

A tall, impeccably dressed young man with a smooth face and high cheek-bones, suavely reading his careful non-committal speech.[13] Nothing. ... Only the same platitudes about crushing German militarism with the help of the Allies – about the 'State interests' of Russia, about the 'embarrassment' caused by Skobeliev's *nakaz*. He ended with the keynote:

'Russia is a great power. Russia will remain a great power, whatever happens. We must all defend her, we must show that we are defenders of a great ideal, and children of a great power.'

Nobody was satisfied. The reactionaries wanted a 'strong' imperialist policy; the democratic parties wanted an assurance that the Government would press for peace.... I reproduce an editorial in *Rabochi i Soldat* (Worker and Soldier), organ of the Bolshevik Petrograd Soviet:

THE GOVERNMENT'S ANSWER TO THE TRENCHES

The most taciturn of our Ministers, Mr Tereshchenko, has actually told the trenches the following:

1. We are closely united with our Allies. (Not with the peoples, but with the Governments.)

2. There is no use for the democracy to discuss the possibility or impossibility of a winter campaign. That will be decided by the Governments of our Allies.

3. The 1 July offensive was beneficial and a very happy affair. (He did not mention the consequences.)

4. It is not true that our Allies do not care about us. The Minister had in his possession very important declarations. (Declarations? What about deeds? What about the behaviour of the British fleet?[14] The parleying of the British king with exiled counter-revolutionary General Gurko? The Minister did not mention all this.)

5. The *nakaz* to Skobeliev is bad; the Allies don't like it and the Russian diplomats don't like it. In the Allied Conference we must all 'speak one language'.

And is that all? That is all. What is the way out? The solution is, faith in the Allies and in Tereshchenko. When will peace come? When the Allies permit.

That is how the Government replied to the trenches about peace!

Now in the background of Russian politics began to form the vague outlines of a sinister power – the Cossacks. *Novaya Zhizn* (New Life), Gorky's paper, called attention to their activities:

At the beginning of the Revolution the Cossacks refused to shoot down the people. When Kornilov marched on Petrograd they refused to follow him. From passive loyalty to the Revolution the Cossacks have passed to an active political offensive (against it). From the background of the Revolution they have suddenly advanced to the front of the stage. ...

Kaledin, *ataman* of the Don Cossacks, had been dismissed by the Provisional Government for his complicity in the Kornilov affair. He flatly refused to resign, and surrounded by three immense Cossack armies lay at Novocherkask, plotting and menacing. So great was his power that the Government was forced to ignore his insubordination. More than that, it was compelled formally to recognize the Council of the Union of Cossack Armies, and to declare illegal the newly formed Cossack Section of the Soviets. . . .

In the first part of October a Cossack delegation called upon Kerensky, arrogantly insisting that the charges against Kaledin be dropped, and reproaching the Minister-President for yielding to the Soviets. Kerensky agreed to let Kaledin alone, and then is reported to have said, 'In the eyes of the Soviet leaders I am a despot and a tyrant. . . . As for the Provisional Government, not only does it not depend upon the Soviets, but it considers it regrettable that they exist at all.'

At the same time another Cossack mission called upon the British ambassador, treating with him boldly as representatives of 'the free Cossack people'.

In the Don something very like a Cossack Republic had been established. The Kuban declared itself an independent Cossack State. The Soviets of Rostov on Don and Yekaterinburg were dispersed by armed Cossacks, and the headquarters of the Coal Miners' Union at Kharkov raided. In all its manifestations the Cossack movement was anti-Socialist and militaristic. Its leaders were nobles and great landowners, like Kaledin, Kornilov, Generals Dutov, Karaulov, and Bardizhe, and it was backed by the powerful merchants and bankers of Moscow. . . .

Old Russia was rapidly breaking up. In the Ukraine, in Finland, Poland, White Russia, the nationalist movements gathered strength and became bolder. The local Governments, controlled by the propertied classes, claimed autonomy, refusing to obey orders from Petrograd. At Helsingfors the Finnish Senate declined to loan money to the Provisional Government, declared Finland autonomous, and demanded the withdrawal of Russian troops. The bourgeois Rada at Kiev extended the boundaries of the Ukraine until they included all the richest agricultural lands of South Russia, as far east as the Urals, and began the formation of a national army. Premier Vinnichenko hinted at a separate peace with Germany – and the Provisional Government was helpless. Siberia, the Caucasus, demanded separate constituent Assemblies. And in all these countries there was the beginning of a bitter struggle between the authorities and the local Soviets of Workers' and Soldiers' Deputies. . . .

Conditions were daily more chaotic. Hundreds of thousands of soldiers were deserting the front and beginning to move in vast, aimless tides over the face of the land. The peasants of Tambov and Tver Governments, tired of waiting for the land, exasperated by the repressive measures of the Government, were burning manor-houses and massacring landowners. Immense strikes and lock-outs convulsed Moscow, Odessa, and the coal-mines of the Don. Transport was paralysed; the army was starving, and in the big cities there was no bread.

The Government, torn between the democratic and reactionary factions, could do nothing; when forced to act it always supported the interests of the propertied classes. Cossacks were sent to restore order among the peasants, to break the strikes. In Tashkent Government authorities suppressed the Soviet. In Petrograd the Economic Council, established to rebuild the shattered economic life of the country, came to a deadlock between the opposing forces of capital and labour, and was dissolved by Kerensky. The old régime military men, backed by Cadets, demanded that harsh measures be adopted to restore discipline in the Army and Navy. In vain Admiral Verderevsky, the venerable Minister of Marine, and General Verkhovsky, Minister of War, insisted that only a new, voluntary, democratic discipline, based on cooperation with the soldiers' and sailors' committees, could save the army and navy. Their recommendations were ignored.

The reactionaries seemed determined to provoke popular anger. The trial of Kornilov was coming on. More and more openly the bourgeois press defended him, speaking of him as 'the great Russian patriot'. Burtzev's paper, *Obshchee Dielo* (Common Cause), called for a dictatorship of Kornilov, Kaledin, and Kerensky!

I had a talk with Burtzev one day in the press gallery of the Council of the Republic. A small, stooped figure with a wrinkled face, eyes near-sighted behind thick glasses, untidy hair and beard streaked with grey.

'Mark my words, young man! What Russia needs is a Strong Man. We should get our minds off the Revolution now and concentrate on the Germans. Bunglers, bunglers, to defeat Kornilov; and back of the bunglers are the German agents. Kornilov should have won. ...'

On the extreme right the organs of the scarcely veiled Monarchists, Purishkevich's *Narodny Tribun* (People's Tribune), *Novaya Rus* (New Russia), and *Zhivoye Slovo* (Living Word), openly advocated the extermination of the revolutionary democracy. ...

On 23 October occurred the naval battle with a German squadron in the Gulf of Riga. On the pretext that Petrograd was in danger, the Provisional Government drew up plans for evacuating the capital. First the great munitions works were to go, distributed widely throughout Russia; and then the Government itself was to move to Moscow. Instantly the Bolsheviki began to cry out that the Government was abandoning the Red Capital in order to weaken the Revolution. Riga had been sold to the Germans; now Petrograd was being betrayed!

The bourgeois press was joyful. 'At Moscow,' said the Cadet paper *Ryech* (Speech), 'the Government can pursue its work in a tranquil atmosphere, without being interfered with by anarchists.' Rodzianko, leader of the right wing of the Cadet party, declared in *Utro Rossii* (The Morning of Russia) that the taking of Petrograd by the Germans would be a blessing, because it would destroy the Soviets and get rid of the revolutionary Baltic Fleet:

Petrograd is in danger [he wrote]. I say to myself, 'Let God take care of Petrograd.' They fear that if Petrograd is lost the central revolutionary organizations will be destroyed. To that I answer that I rejoice if all these organizations are destroyed; for they will bring nothing but disaster upon Russia. ...

With the taking of Petrograd the Baltic Fleet will also be destroyed. ... But there will be nothing to regret; most of the battleships are completely demoralized. ...

In the face of a storm of popular disapproval the plan of evacuation was repudiated.

Meanwhile the Congress of Soviets loomed over Russia like a

thundercloud, shot through with lightnings. It was opposed, not only by the Government, but by all the 'moderate' Socialists. The Central Army and Fleet Committees, the Central Committees of some of the Trade Unions, the Peasants' Soviets, but most of all the Tsay-ee-kah itself, spared no pains to prevent the meeting. *Izvestia* and *Golos Soldata* (Voice of the Soldier), newspapers founded by the Petrograd Soviet but now in the hands of the Tsay-ee-kah, fiercely assailed it, as did the entire artillery of the Socialist Revolutionary party press, *Dielo Naroda* (People's Cause) and *Volia Naroda* (People's Will).

Delegates were sent through the country, messages flashed by wire to committees in charge of local Soviets, to Army Committees, instructing them to halt or delay elections to the Congress. Solemn public resolutions against the Congress, declarations that the democracy was opposed to the meeting so near the date of the Constituent Assembly, representatives from the front, from the Union of Zemstvos, the Peasants' Union, Union of Cossack Armies, Union of Officers, Knights of St George, Death Battalions,* protesting. . . . The Council of the Russian Republic was one chorus of disapproval. The entire machinery set up by the Russian Revolution of March functioned to block the Congress of Soviets. . . .

On the other hand was the shapeless will of the proletariat – the workmen, common soldiers, and poor peasants. Many local Soviets were already Bolshevik; then there were the organizations of the industrial workers, the Fabrichno-Zavodskiye Comitieti – Factory-Shop Committees; and the insurgent Army and Fleet organizations. In some places the people, prevented from electing their regular Soviet delegates, held rump meetings, and chose one of their number to go to Petrograd. In others they smashed the old obstructionist committees and formed new ones. A ground-swell of revolt heaved and cracked the crust which had been slowly hardening on the surface of revolutionary fires dormant all those months. Only a spontaneous mass movement could bring about the All-Russian Congress of Soviets. . . .

Day after day the Bolshevik orators toured the barracks and factories, violently denouncing 'this Government of civil war'. One Sunday we went, on a top-heavy steam tram that lumbered

* See Notes and Explanations.

through oceans of mud, between stark factories and immense churches, to Obukhovsky Zavod, a Government munitions plant out on the Schlüsselburg Prospekt.

The meeting took place between the gaunt brick walls of a huge unfinished building, ten thousand black-clothed men and women packed around a scaffolding draped in red, people heaped on piles of lumber and bricks, perched high up on shadowy girders, intent and thunder-voiced. Through the dull, heavy sky now and again burst the sun, flooding reddish light through the skeleton windows upon the mass of simple faces upturned to us.

Lunacharsky, a slight, student-like figure with the sensitive face of an artist, was telling why the power must be taken by the Soviets. Nothing else could guarantee the Revolution against its enemies, who were deliberately ruining the country, ruining the army, creating opportunities for a new Kornilov.

A soldier from the Rumanian front, thin, tragical, and fierce, cried, 'Comrades! We are starving at the front, we are stiff with cold. We are dying for no reason. I ask the American comrades to carry word to America that the Russians will never give up their Revolution until they die. We will hold the fort with all our strength until the peoples of the world rise and help us! Tell the American workers to rise and fight for the Social Revolution!'

Then came Petrovsky, slight, slow-voiced, implacable:

'Now is the time for deeds, not words. The economic situation is bad, but we must get used to it. They are trying to starve us and freeze us. They are trying to provoke us. But let them know that they can go too far – that if they dare to lay their hands upon the organizations of the proletariat we will sweep them away like scum from the face of the earth!'

The Bolshevik press suddenly expanded. Besides the two party papers, *Rabochi Put* and *Soldat* (Soldier), there appeared a new paper for the peasants, *Derevenskaya Byednota* (Village Poorest), poured out in a daily half-million edition; and on 17 October, *Rabochi i Soldat*. Its leading article summed up the Bolshevik point of view:

The fourth year's campaign will mean the annihilation of the army and the country. ... There is a danger for the safety of Petrograd. ... Counter-revolutionists rejoice in the people's misfortunes. ... The peasants brought to desperation come out in open rebellion; the landlords and Government authorities massacre them with punitive expeditions; factories and mines are closing down, workmen are threatened with starvation.... The bourgeoisie and its generals want to restore a blind discipline in the army.... Supported by the bourgeoisie, the Kornilovtsi are openly getting ready to break up the meeting of the Constituent Assembly. ...

The Kerensky Government is against the people. He will destroy the country.... This paper stands for the people and by the people – the poor classes, workers, soldiers, and peasants. The people can only be saved by the completion of the Revolution ... and for this purpose the full power must be in the hands of the Soviets. ...

This paper advocates the following:

All power to the Soviets – both in the capital and in the provinces.
Immediate truce on all fronts. An honest peace between peoples.
Landlord estates – without compensation – to the peasants.
Workers' control over industrial production.
A faithfully and honestly elected Constituent Assembly.

It is interesting to reproduce here a passage from that same paper – the organ of those Bolsheviki so well known to the world as German agents:

The German kaiser, covered with the blood of millions of dead people, wants to push his army against Petrograd. Let us call to the German workmen, soldiers, and peasants, who want peace not less than we do, to ... stand up against this damned war!

This can be done only by a revolutionary Government, which would speak really for the workmen, soldiers, and peasants of Russia, and would appeal over the heads of the diplomats directly to the German troops, fill the German trenches with proclamations in the German language. ... Our airmen would spread these proclamations all over Germany. ...

In the Council of the Republic the gulf between the two sides of the chamber deepened day by day.

'The propertied classes,' cried Karelin, for the Left Socialist Revolutionaries, 'want to exploit the revolutionary machine of the State to bind Russia to the war-chariot of the Allies! The revolutionary parties are absolutely against this policy. ...'

Old Nicholas Chaikovsky, representing the Populist Socialists, spoke against giving the land to the peasants, and took the side of the Cadets:

'We must have immediately strong discipline in the army. . . . Since the beginning of the war I have not ceased to insist that it is a crime to undertake social and economic reforms in war-time. We are committing that crime, and yet I am not the enemy of these reforms, because I am a Socialist.'

Cries from the Left, 'We don't believe you!' Mighty applause from the Right. . . .

Adzhemov, for the Cadets, declared that there was no necessity to tell the army what it was fighting for, since every soldier ought to realize that the first task was to drive the enemy from Russian territory.

Kerensky himself came twice, to plead passionately for national unity, once bursting into tears at the end. The assembly heard him coldly, interrupting with ironical remarks.

Smolny Institute, headquarters of the Tsay-ee-kah and of the Petrograd Soviet, lay miles out on the edge of the city, beside the wide Neva. I went there on a streetcar, moving snail-like with a groaning noise through the cobbled, muddy streets, and jammed with people. At the end of the line rose the graceful smoke-blue cupolas of Smolny Convent outlined in dull gold, beautiful, and beside it the great barracks-like façade of Smolny Institute, two hundred yards long and three lofty storeys high, the Imperial arms carved hugely in stone still insolent over the entrance. . . .

Under the old régime a famous convent school for the daughters of the Russian nobility, patronized by the Tsarina herself, the Institute had been taken over by revolutionary organizations of workers and soldiers. Within were more than a hundred huge rooms, white and bare, on their doors enamelled plaques still informing the passer-by that within was 'Ladies' Class-room Number 4' or 'Teachers' Bureau'; but over these hung crudely-lettered signs, evidence of the vitality of the new order: 'Central Committee of the Petrograd Soviet' and 'Tsay-ee-kah' and 'Bureau of Foreign Affairs'; 'Union of Socialist Soldiers', 'Central Committee of the All-Russian Trade Unions', 'Factory-Shop Committees', 'Central Army Committee'; and the central offices and caucus-rooms of the political parties. . . .

The long, vaulted corridors, lit by rare electric lights, were thronged with hurrying shapes of soldiers and workmen, some

bent under the weight of huge bundles of newspapers, proclamations, printed propaganda of all sorts. The sound of their
heavy boots made a deep and incessant thunder on the wooden
floor. .... Signs were posted up everywhere: 'Comrades: For the
sake of your health, preserve cleanliness!' Long tables stood at
the head of the stairs on every floor, and on the landings, heaped
with pamphlets and the literature of the different political parties
for sale. ...

The spacious, low-ceilinged refectory downstairs was still a
dining-room. For two roubles I bought a ticket entitling me to
dinner, and stood in line with a thousand others, waiting to get
to the long serving-tables, where twenty men and women were
ladling from immense cauldrons cabbage soup, hunks of meat and
piles of *kasha*, slabs of black bread. Five kopeks paid for tea in a
tin cup. From a basket one grabbed a greasy wooden spoon. ...
The benches along the wooden tables were packed with hungry
proletarians, wolfing their food, plotting, shouting rough jokes
across the room. ...

Upstairs was another eating-place, reserved for the Tsay-ee-kah
– though everyone went there. Here could be had bread thickly
buttered and endless glasses of tea. ...

In the south wing on the second floor was the great hall of
meetings, the former ballroom of the Institute. A lofty white room
lighted by glazed white chandeliers holding hundreds of ornate
electric bulbs, and divided by two rows of massive columns; at
one end a dais, flanked with two tall many-branched light
standards, and a gold frame behind, from which the Imperial
portrait had been cut. Here on festal occasions had been banked
brilliant military and ecclesiastical uniforms, a setting for Grand
Duchesses. ...

Just across the hall outside was the office of the Credentials
Committee for the Congress of Soviets. I stood there watching the
new delegates come in – burly, bearded soldiers, workmen in
black blouses, a few long-haired peasants. The girl in charge – a
member of Plekhanov's Yedinstvo* group – smiled contemptuously. 'These are very different people from the delegates to the
first *Siezd* (Congress),' she remarked. 'See how rough and ignorant they look! The Dark People. ...' It was true; the depths of

* See Notes and Explanations.

Russia had been stirred, and it was the bottom which came upper-most now. The Credentials Committee, appointed by the old Tsay-ee-kah, was challenging delegate after delegate, on the ground that they had been illegally elected. Karakhan, member of the Bolshevik Central Committee, simply grinned. 'Never mind,' he said, 'when the time comes we'll see that you get your seats. . . .'

Rabochi i Soldat said:

The attention of delegates to the new All-Russian Congress is called to attempts of certain members of the Organizing Committee to break up the Congress, by asserting that it will not take place, and that delegates had better leave Petrograd. . . . Pay no attention to these lies. . . . Great days are coming. . . .

It was evident that a quorum would not come together by 2 November, so the opening of the Congress was postponed to the seventh. But the whole country was now aroused; and the Mensheviki and Socialist Revolutionaries, realizing that they were defeated, suddenly changed their tactics and began to wire frantically to their provisional organizations to elect as many 'moderate' Socialist delegates as possible. At the same time the Executive Committee of the Peasants' Soviets issued an emergency call for a Peasants' Congress, to meet 13 December and offset whatever action the workers and soldiers might take. . . .

What would the Bolsheviki do? Rumours ran through the city that there would be an armed 'demonstration', a *vystuplenie* – 'coming out' of the workers and soldiers. The bourgeois and reactionary press prophesied insurrection, and urged the Government to arrest the Petrograd Soviet, or at least to prevent the meeting of the Congress. Such sheets as *Novaya Rus* advocated a general Bolshevik massacre.

Gorky's paper, *Novaya Zhizn*, agreed with the Bolsheviki that the reactionaries were attempting to destroy the Revolution, and that if necessary they must be resisted by force of arms; but all the parties of the revolutionary democracy must present a united front.

As long as the democracy has not organized its principal forces, so long as the resistance to its influence is still strong, there is no advantage in passing to the attack. But if the hostile elements appeal to force, then the revolutionary democracy should enter the battle to seize the power, and it will be sustained by the most profound strata of the people. ...

Gorky pointed out that both reactionary and Government newspapers were inciting the Bolsheviki to violence. An insurrection, however, would prepare the way for a new Kornilov. He urged the Bolsheviki to deny the rumours. Potressov, in the Menshevik *Dien* (Day), published a sensational story, accompanied by a map, which professed to reveal the secret Bolshevik plan of campaign.

As if by magic the walls were covered with warnings,[15] proclamations, appeals, from the Central Committees of the 'moderate' and conservative factions and the Tsay-ee-kah, denouncing any 'demonstrations', imploring the workers and soldiers not to listen to agitators. For instance, this from the Military Section of the Socialist Revolutionary party:

Again rumours are spreading around the town of an intended *vystuplenie*. What is the source of these rumours? What organization authorizes these agitators who preach insurrection? The Bolsheviki, to a question addressed to them in the Tsay-ee-kah, denied that they have anything to do with it. ... But these rumours themselves carry with them a great danger. It may easily happen that, not taking into consideration the state of mind of the majority of the workers, soldiers, and peasants, individual hot-heads will call out part of the workers and soldiers on the streets, inciting them to an uprising. ... In this fearful time through which revolutionary Russia is passing, any insurrection can easily turn into civil war, and there can result from it the destruction of all organizations of the proletariat, built up with so much labour.... The counter-revolutionary plotters are planning to take advantage of this insurrection to destroy the Revolution, open the front to Wilhelm, and wreck the Constituent Assembly.... Stick stubbornly to your posts! Do not come out!

On 28 October, in the corridors of Smolny, I spoke with Kameniev, a little man with a reddish pointed beard and Gallic gestures. He was not at all sure that enough delegates would come. 'If there *is* a Congress,' he said, 'it will represent the overwhelming sentiment of the people. If the majority is Bolshevik, as I think it will be, we shall demand that the power be given to the Soviets, and the Provisional Government must resign....'

Volodarsky, a tall, pale youth with glasses and a bad complexion,

was more definite. 'The "Lieber-Dans" and the other compromisers are sabotaging the Congress. If they succeed in preventing its meeting – well, then we are realists enough not to
depend on *that*!'

Under date of 29 October I find entered in my notebook the
following items culled from the newspapers of the day:

Moghilev (General Staff Headquarters). Concentration here of loyal
Guard Regiments, the Savage Division, Cossacks, and Death Battalions.

The *yunkers* of the Officers' Schools of Pavlovsk, Tsarskoye Selo
Peterhof ordered by the Government to be ready to come to Petrograd.
Oranienbaum *yunkers* arrive in the city.

Part of the Armoured Car Division of the Petrograd garrison stationed in the Winter Palace.

Upon orders signed by Trotsky, several thousand rifles delivered by
the Government Arms Factory at Sestroretzk to delegates of the
Petrograd workmen.

At a meeting of the City Militia of the Lower Liteiny Quarter, a
resolution demanding that all power be given to the Soviets.

This is just a sample of the confused events of those feverish
days when everybody knew that something was going to happen,
but nobody knew just what.

At a meeting of the Petrograd Soviet in Smolny, the night of
30 October, Trotsky branded the assertions of the bourgeois
press that the Soviet contemplated armed insurrection as 'an
attempt of the reactionaries to discredit and wreck the Congress
of Soviets.... The Petrograd Soviet,' he declared, 'had not
ordered any *vystuplenie*. If it is necessary we shall do so, and we
will be supported by the Petrograd garrison.... They [the
Government] are preparing a counter-revolution; and we shall
answer with an offensive which will be merciless and decisive.'

It is true that the Petrograd Soviet had not ordered a demonstration, but the Central Committee of the Bolshevik party was
considering the question of insurrection. All night long the
twenty-third they met. There were present all the party intellectuals, the leaders – and delegates of the Petrograd workers and
garrison.* Alone of the intellectuals Lenin and Trotsky stood for

* John Reed's facts are not quite accurate here. The Central Committee
decided in principle on an insurrection by a large majority (10–2), without
any such intervention of outside delegates. – Ed.

insurrection. Even the military men opposed it. A vote was taken. Insurrection was defeated!

Then arose a rough workman, his face convulsed with rage. 'I speak for the Petrograd proletariat,' he said harshly. 'We are in favour of insurrection. Have it your own way, but I tell you now that if you allow the Soviets to be destroyed, *we're through with you!*' Some soldiers joined him.... And after that they voted again – insurrection won. ...

However, the right wing of the Bolsheviki, led by Riazanov, Kameniev, and Zinoviev, continued to campaign against an armed rising. On the morning of 31 October appeared in *Rabochi Put* the first instalment of Lenin's 'Letter to the Comrades',[16] one of the most audacious pieces of political propaganda the world has ever seen. In it Lenin seriously presented the arguments in favour of insurrection, taking as text the objections of Kameniev and Riazanov.

'Either we must abandon our slogan, "All Power to the Soviets",' he wrote, 'or else we must make an insurrection. There is no middle course. ...'

That same afternoon Paul Milyukov, leader of the Cadets, made a brilliant, bitter speech[17] in the Council of the Republic, branding the Skobeliev *nakaz* as pro-German, declaring that the 'revolutionary democracy' was destroying Russia, sneering at Tereshchenko, and openly declaring that he preferred German diplomacy to Russian.... The Left benches were one roaring tumult all through. ...

On its part the Government could not ignore the significance of the success of the Bolshevik propaganda. On the twenty-ninth a joint commission of the Government and the Council of the Republic hastily drew up two laws, one for giving the land temporarily to the peasants, and the other for pushing an energetic foreign policy of peace. The next day Kerensky suspended capital punishment in the army. That same afternoon was opened with great ceremony the first session of the new 'Commission for Strengthening the Republican Régime and Fighting Against Anarchy and Counter-Revolution' – of which history shows not the slightest further trace. ... The following morning with two other correspondents I interviewed Kerensky[18] – the last time he received journalists.

'The Russian people,' he said bitterly, 'are suffering from economic fatigue – and from disillusionment with the Allies! The world thinks that the Russian Revolution is at an end. Do not be mistaken. The Russian Revolution is just beginning. ...' Words more prophetic, perhaps, than he knew.

Stormy was the all-night meeting of the Petrograd Soviet the thirtieth of October, at which I was present. The 'moderate' Socialist intellectuals, officers, members of Army Committees, the Tsay-ee-kah, were there in force. Against them rose up workmen, peasants, and common soldiers, passionate and simple.

A peasant told of the disorders in Tver, which he said were caused by the arrest of the Land Committees. 'This Kerensky is nothing but a shield to the *pomieshchiki* (landowners),' he cried. 'They know that at the Constituent Assembly we will take the land anyway, so they are trying to destroy the Constituent Assembly!'

A machinist from the Putilov works described how the superintendents were closing down the departments one by one on the pretext that there was no fuel or raw materials. The Factory-Shop Committee, he declared, had discovered huge hidden supplies.

'It is a *provocatzia*,' said he. 'They want to starve us – or drive us to violence!'

Among the soldiers one began, 'Comrades! I bring you greetings from the place where men are digging their graves and call them trenches!'

Then arose a tall, gaunt young soldier, with flashing eyes, met with a roar of welcome. It was Chudnovsky, reported killed in the July fighting, and now risen from the dead.

'The soldier masses no longer trust their officers. Even the Army Committees, who refused to call a meeting of our Soviet, betrayed us. ... The masses of the soldiers want the Constituent Assembly to be held exactly when it was called for, and those who dare to postpone it will be cursed – and not only platonic curses either, for the Army has guns too. ...'

He told of the electoral campaign for the Constituent Assembly now raging in the Fifth Army. 'The officers, and especially the Mensheviki and the Socialist Revolutionaries, are trying deliberately to cripple the Bolsheviki. Our papers are not allowed to circulate in the trenches. Our speakers are arrested –'

'Why don't you speak about the lack of bread?' shouted another soldier.

'Man shall not live by bread alone,' answered Chudnovsky, sternly. ...

Followed him an officer, delegate from the Vitebsk Soviet, a Menshevik *oboronets*. 'It isn't the question of who has the power. The trouble is not with the Government, but with the war ... and the war must be won before any change –' At this hoots and ironical cheers. 'These Bolshevik agitators are demagogues!' The hall rocked with laughter. 'Let us for a moment forget the class struggle –' But he got no farther. A voice yelled, 'Don't you wish we would!'

Petrograd presented a curious spectacle in those days. In the factories the committee-rooms were filled with stacks of rifles, couriers came and went, the Red Guard* drilled. ... In all the barracks meetings every night, and all day long interminable hot arguments. On the streets the crowds thickened towards gloomy evening, pouring in slow voluble tides up and down the Nevsky, fighting for the newspapers. ... Hold-ups increased to such an extent that it was dangerous to walk down side streets. ... On the Sadovaya one afternoon I saw a crowd of several hundred people beat and trample to death a soldier caught stealing. ... Mysterious individuals circulated around the shivering women who waited in queue long cold hours for bread and milk, whispering that the Jews had cornered the food supply – and that while the people starved, the Soviet members lived luxuriously. ...

At Smolny there were strict guards at the door and the outer gates, demanding everybody's pass. The committee-rooms buzzed and hummed all day and all night, hundreds of soldiers and work-men slept on the floor, wherever they could find room. Upstairs in the great hall a thousand people crowded to the uproarious sessions of the Petrograd Soviet. ...

Gambling clubs functioned hectically from dusk to dawn, with champagne flowing and stakes of twenty thousand roubles. In the centre of the city at night prostitutes in jewels and expensive furs walked up and down, crowded the cafés. ...

* See Notes and Explanations.

Monarchist plots, German spies, smugglers hatching schemes. ...

And in the rain, the bitter chill, the great throbbing city under grey skies rushing faster and faster towards – what?

3 On the Eve

In the relations of a weak Government and a rebellious people there comes a time when every act of the authorities exasperates the masses, and every refusal to act excites their contempt. ...

The proposal to abandon Petrograd raised a hurricane; Kerensky's public denial that the Government had any such intentions was met with hoots of derision.

Pinned to the wall by the pressure of the Revolution [cried *Rabochi Put*], the Government of 'provisional' bourgeois tried to get free by giving out lying assurances that it never thought of fleeing from Petrograd, and that it didn't wish to surrender the capital. ...

In Kharkov thirty thousand coal miners organized, adopting the preamble of the I.W.W. constitution: 'The working class and the employing class have nothing in common.' Dispersed by Cossacks, some were locked out by the mine-owners, and the rest declared a general strike. Minister of Commerce and Industry Konovalov appointed his assistant, Orlov, with plenary powers, to settle the trouble. Orlov was hated by the miners. But the Tsay-ee-kah not only supported his appointment, but refused to demand that the Cossacks be recalled from the Don Basin. ...

This was followed by the dispersal of the Soviet at Kaluga. The Bolsheviki, having secured a majority in the Soviet, set free some political prisoners. With the sanction of the Government Commissar the Municipal Duma called in troops from Minsk, and bombarded the Soviet headquarters with artillery. The Bolsheviki yielded, but as they left the building Cossacks attacked them, crying, 'This is what we'll do to all the other Bolshevik Soviets, including those of Moscow and Petrograd!' This incident sent a wave of panic rage throughout Russia. ...

In Petrograd was ending a regional Congress of Soviets of the North, presided over by the Bolshevik Krylenko. By an immense majority it resolved that all power should be assumed by the All-Russian Congress; and concluded by greeting the Bolsheviki in prison, bidding them rejoice, for the hour of their liberation was at hand. At the same time the first All-Russian Conference of Factory-Shop Committees[19] declared emphatically for the Soviets, and continued significantly:

> After liberating themselves politically from Tsardom, the working class wants to see the democratic régime triumphant in the sphere of its productive activity. This is best expressed by Workers' Control over industrial production, which naturally arose in the atmosphere of economic decomposition created by the criminal policy of the dominating classes. ...

The Union of Railwaymen was demanding the resignation of Liverovsky, Minister of Ways and Communications. ...

In the name of the Tsay-ee-kah, Skobeliev insisted that the *nakaz* be presented at the Allied Conference, and formally protested against the sending of Tereshchenko to Paris. Tereshchenko offered to resign. ...

General Verkhovsky, unable to accomplish his reorganization of the army, only came to Cabinet meetings at long intervals. ...

On 3 November Burtzev's *Obshchee Dielo* came out with great headlines:

> Citizens! Save the fatherland!
> I have just learned that yesterday, at a meeting of the Commission for National Defence, Minister of War, General Verkhovsky, one of the principal persons responsible for the fall of Kornilov, proposed to sign a separate peace, independently of the Allies.
> That is treason to Russia!
> Tereshchenko declared that the Provisional Government had not even examined Verkhovsky's proposition.
> 'You might think,' said Tereshchenko, 'that we were in a madhouse!'
> The members of the Commission were astounded at the General's words.
> General Alexeyev wept.
> No! It is not madness! It is worse. It is direct treason to Russia!
> Kerensky, Tereshchenko, and Nekrassov must immediately answer us concerning the words of Verkhovsky.
> Citizens, arise!
> Russia is being sold!
> Save her!

What Verkhovsky really said was that the Allies must be pressed to offer peace, because the Russian army could fight no longer. . . .

Both in Russia and abroad the sensation was tremendous. Verkhovsky was given 'indefinite leave of absence for ill-health', and left the Government. *Obshchee Dielo* was suppressed. . . .

Sunday, 4 November, was designated as the day of the Petrograd Soviet, with immense meetings planned all over the city, ostensibly to raise money for the organization and the press; really, to make a demonstration of strength. Suddenly it was announced that on the same day the Cossacks would hold a *Krestni Khod* – Procession of the Cross – in honour of the Ikon of 1612, through whose miraculous intervention Napoleon had been driven from Moscow. The atmosphere was electric; a spark might kindle civil war. The Petrograd Soviet issued a manifesto, headed 'Brothers – Cossacks!'

You, Cossacks, are being incited against us, workers and soldiers. This plan of Cain is being put into operation by our common enemies the oppressors, the privileged classes – generals, bankers, landlords, former officials, former servants of the Tsar. . . . We are hated by all grafters, rich men, princes, nobles, generals, including your Cossack generals. They are ready at any moment to destroy the Petrograd Soviet and crush the Revolution. . . .

On the fourth of November somebody is organizing a Cossack religious procession. It is a question of the free consciousness of every individual whether he will or will not take part in this procession. We do not interfere in this matter, nor do we obstruct anybody. . . . However, we warn you, Cossacks! Look out and see to it that under the pretext of a *Krestni Khod*, your Kaledins do not instigate you against workmen, against soldiers. . . .

The procession was hastily called off. . . .

In the barracks and the working-class quarters of the town the Bolsheviki were preaching, 'All Power to the Soviets!' and agents of the Dark Forces were urging the people to rise and slaughter the Jews, shopkeepers, Socialist leaders. . . .

On one side the Monarchist press, inciting to bloody repression – on the other Lenin's great voice roaring, 'Insurrection! . . . We cannot wait any longer!'

Even the bourgeois press was uneasy.[20] *Birzhevya Viedomosti* (Exchange Gazette) called the Bolshevik propaganda an attack on 'the most elementary principles of society – personal security, and the respect for private property'.

But it was the 'moderate' Socialist journals which were the most hostile.[21] 'The Bolsheviki are the most dangerous enemies of the Revolution,' declared *Dielo Naroda*. Said the Menshevik *Dien*, 'The Government ought to defend itself and defend us.' Plekhanov's paper, *Yedinstvo* (Unity),[22] called the attention of the Government to the fact that the Petrograd workers were being armed, and demanded stern measures against the Bolsheviki.

Daily the Government seemed to become more helpless. Even the Municipal administration broke down. The columns of the morning papers were filled with accounts of the most audacious robberies and murders, and the criminals were unmolested.

On the other hand, armed workers patrolled the streets at night, doing battle with marauders and requisitioning arms wherever they found them.

On the first of November Colonel Polkovnikov, Military Commander of Petrograd, issued a proclamation:

Despite the difficult days through which the country is passing, irresponsible appeals to armed demonstrations and massacres are still being spread around Petrograd, and from day to day robbery and disorder increase.

This state of things is disorganizing the life of the citizens, and hinders the systematic work of the Government and the Municipal Institutions.

In full consciousness of my responsibility and my duty before my country, I command:

1. Every military unit, in accordance with special instructions and within the territory of its garrison, to afford every assistance to the Municipality, to the Commissars, and to the militia, in the guarding of Government institutions.

2. The organization of patrols, in cooperation with the District Commander and the representatives of the city militia, and the taking of measures for the arrest of criminals and deserters.

3. The arrest of all persons entering barracks and inciting to armed demonstrations and massacres, and their delivery to the headquarters of the Second Commander of the city.

4. To suppress any armed demonstration or riot at its start, with all armed forces at hand.

5. To afford assistance to the Commissars in preventing unwarranted searches in houses and unwarranted arrests.

6. To report immediately all that happens in the district under charge of the Staff of the Petrograd Military District.

I call upon all Army Committees and organizations to afford their help to the commanders in fulfilment of the duties with which they are charged.

In the Council of the Republic Kerensky declared that the Government was fully aware of the Bolshevik preparations, and had sufficient force to cope with any demonstration.[23] He accused *Novaya Rus* and *Rabochi Put* of both doing the same kind of subversive work. 'But owing to the absolute freedom of the press,' he added, 'the Government is not in a position to combat printed lies....'* Declaring that these were two aspects of the same propaganda, which had for its objects the counter-revolution, so ardently desired by the Dark Forces, he went on:

'I am a doomed man, it doesn't matter what happens to me, and I have the audacity to say that the other enigmatic part is that of the unbelievable provocation created in the city by the Bolsheviki!'

On 2 November, only fifteen delegates to the Congress of Soviets had arrived. Next day there were a hundred, and the morning after that a hundred and seventy-five, of whom one hundred and three were Bolsheviki.... Four hundred constituted a quorum, and the Congress was only three days off. ...

I spent a great deal of time at Smolny. It was no longer easy to get in. Double rows of sentries guarded the outer gates, and once inside the front door there was a long line of people waiting to be let in, four at a time, to be questioned as to their identity and their business. Passes were given out, and the pass system was changed every few hours; for spies continually sneaked through. ...

One day as I came up to the outer gate I saw Trotsky and his wife just ahead of me. They were halted by a soldier. Trotsky searched through his pockets, but could find no pass.

'Never mind,' he said finally. 'You know me. My name is Trotsky.'

'You haven't got a pass,' answered the soldier stubbornly.

* This was not quite candid. The Provisional Government had suppressed Bolshevik papers before, in July, and was planning to do so again.

'You cannot go in. Names don't mean anything to me.'

'But I am the president of the Petrograd Soviet.'

'Well,' replied the soldier, 'if you're as important a fellow as that you must at least have one little paper.'

Trotsky was very patient. 'Let me see the Commandant,' he said. The soldier hesitated, grumbling something about not wanting to disturb the Commandant for every devil that came along. He beckoned finally to the soldier in command of the guard. Trotsky explained matters to him. 'My name is Trotsky,' he repeated.

'Trotsky?' The other soldier scratched his head. 'I've heard the name somewhere,' he said at length. 'I guess it's all right. You can go on in, comrade. ...'

In the corridor I met Karakhan, member of the Bolshevik Central Committee, who explained to me what the new Government would be like.

'A loose organization, sensitive to the popular will as expressed through the Soviets, allowing local forces full play. At present the Provisional Government obstructs the action of the local democratic will, just as the Tsar's Government did. The initiative of the new society shall come from below. ... The form of the Government will be modelled on the Constitution of the Russian Social Democratic Labour Party. The new Tsay-ee-kah, responsible to frequent meetings of the All-Russian Congress of Soviets, will be the parliament; the various Ministries will be headed by *collegia* – committees – instead of by Ministers, and will be directly responsible to the Soviets. ...'

On 30 October, by appointment, I went up to a small bare room in the attic of Smolny, to talk with Trotsky. In the middle of the room he sat on a rough chair at a bare table. Few questions from me were necessary; he talked rapidly for more than an hour. The substance of his talk, in his own words, I give here:

'The Provisional Government is absolutely powerless. The bourgeoisie is in control, but this control is masked by a fictitious coalition with the *oborontsi* parties. Now, during the Revolution, one sees revolts of peasants who are tired of waiting for their promised land; and all over the country, in all the toiling classes, the same disgust is evident. This domination by the bourgeoisie is only possible by means of civil war. The Kornilov method is the only way by which the bourgeoisie can control. But it is force which the bourgeoisie lacks. ... The Army is with us. The conciliators and pacifists, Socialist Revolutionaries, and Mensheviki, have lost all authority – because the struggle between the peasants and the landlords, between the workers and the employers, between the soldiers and the officers, has become more bitter, more irreconcilable than ever. Only by the concerted action of the popular mass, only by the victory of proletarian dictatorship, can the Revolution be achieved and the people saved. ...

'The Soviets are the most perfect representatives of the people – perfect in their revolutionary experience, in their ideas and objects. Based directly upon the army in the trenches, the workers in the factories, and the peasants in the fields, they are the backbone of the Revolution.

'There has been an attempt to create a power without the Soviets – and only powerlessness has been created. Counter-revolutionary schemes of all sorts are now being hatched in the corridors of the Council of the Russian Republic. The Cadet party represents the counter-revolution militant. On the other side, the Soviets represent the cause of the people. Between the two camps there are no groups of serious importance. ... It is the *lutte finale*. The bourgeois counter-revolution organizes all its forces and waits for the moment to attack us. Our answer will be decisive. We will complete the work scarcely begun in March, and advanced during the Kornilov affair. ...'

He went on to speak of the new Government's foreign policy:

'Our first act will be to call for an immediate armistice on all fronts, and a conference of peoples to discuss democratic peace terms. The quantity of democracy we get in the peace settlement depends on the quantity of revolutionary response there is in Europe. If we create here a Government of the Soviets, that will be a powerful factor for immediate peace in Europe; for this Government will address itself directly and immediately to all peoples, over the heads of their Governments, proposing an armistice. At the moment of the conclusion of peace the pressure of the Russian Revolution will be in the direction of "no annexations, no indemnities, the right of self-determination of peoples", and a *Federated Republic of Europe*. ...

'At the end of this war I see Europe re-created, not by the

diplomats, but by the proletariat. The Federated Republic of Europe – the United States of Europe – that is what must be. National autonomy no longer suffices. Economic evolution demands the abolition of national frontiers. If Europe is to remain split into national groups, then Imperialism will recommence its work. Only a Federated Republic of Europe can give peace to the world.' He smiled – that fine, faintly ironical smile of his. 'But without the action of the European masses, these ends cannot be realized – now. ....'

Now while everybody was waiting for the Bolsheviki to appear suddenly on the streets one morning and begin to shoot down people with white collars on, the real insurrection took its way quite naturally and openly.

The Provisional Government planned to send the Petrograd garrison to the front.

The Petrograd garrison numbered about sixty thousand men, who had taken a prominent part in the Revolution. It was they who had turned the tide in the great days of March, created the Soviets of Soldiers' Deputies, and hurled back Kornilov from the gates of Petrograd.

Now a large part of them were Bolsheviki. When the Provisional Government talked of evacuating the city, it was the Petrograd garrison which answered, 'If you are not capable of defending the capital, conclude peace; if you cannot conclude peace, go away and make room for a People's Government which can do both. ....'

It was evident that any attempt at insurrection depended upon the attitude of the Petrograd garrison. The Government's plan was to replace the garrison regiments with 'dependable' troops – Cossacks, Death Battalions. The Army Committee, the 'moderate' Socialists and the Tsay-ee-kah supported the Government. A widespread agitation was carried on at the front and in Petrograd, emphasizing the fact that for eight months the Petrograd garrison had been leading an easy life in the barracks of the capital, while their exhausted comrades in the trenches starved and died.

Naturally there was some truth in the accusation that the garrison regiments were reluctant to exchange their comparative comfort for the hardships of a winter campaign. But there were other reasons why they refused to go. The Petrograd Soviet feared the Government's intentions, and from the front came hundreds of delegates, chosen by the common soldiers, crying, 'It is true we need reinforcements, but more important, we must know that Petrograd and the Revolution are well guarded. ... Do you hold the rear, comardes, and we will hold the front!'

On 25 October, behind closed doors, the Central Committee of the Petrograd Soviet discussed the formation of a special Military Committee to decide the whole question. The next day a meeting of the Soldiers' Section of the Petrograd Soviet elected a Committee, which immediately proclaimed a boycott of the bourgeois newspapers, and condemned the Tsay-ee-kah for opposing the Congress of Soviets. On the twenty-ninth, in open session of the Petrograd Soviet, Trotsky proposed that the Soviet formally sanction the Military Revolutionary Committee. 'We ought,' he said, 'to create our special organization to march to battle, and if necessary to die. ...' It was decided to send to the front two delegations, one from the Soviet and one from the garrison, to confer with the Soldiers' Committees and the General Staff.

At Pskov, the Soviet delegates were met by General Cheremissov, commander of the Northern Front, with the curt declaration that he had ordered the Petrograd garrison to the trenches, and that was all. The garrison committee was not allowed to leave Petrograd. ...

A delegation of the Soldiers' Section of the Petrograd Soviet asked that a representative be admitted to the Staff of the Petrograd District. Refused. The Petrograd Soviet demanded that no orders be issued without the approval of the Soldiers' Section. Refused. The delegates were roughly told, 'We only recognize the Tsay-ee-kah. We do not recognize you; if you break any laws we shall arrest you.'

On the thirtieth a meeting of representatives of all the Petrograd regiments passed a resolution: '*The Petrograd garrison no longer recognizes the Provisional Government. The Petrograd Soviet is our Government. We will obey only the orders of the Petrograd Soviet, through the Military Revolutionary Committee.*' The local military units were ordered to wait for instructions from the Soldiers' Section of the Petrograd Soviet.

Next day the Tsay-ee-kah summoned its own meeting,

composed largely of officers, formed a Committee to cooperate with the Staff, and detailed Commissars in all quarters of the city.

A great soldier meeting at Smolny on the third resolved:

Saluting the creation of the Military Revolutionary Committee, the Petrograd garrison promises it complete support in all its actions, to unite more closely the front and the rear in the interests of the Revolution.

The garrison, moreover, declares that with the revolutionary proletariat it assures the maintenance of revolutionary order in Petrograd. Every attempt at provocation on the part of the Kornilovtsi or the bourgeoisie will be met with merciless resistance.

Now conscious of its power, the Military Revolutionary Committee peremptorily summoned the Petrograd Staff to submit to its control. To all printing plants it gave orders not to publish any appeals or proclamations without the Committee's authorization. Armed Commissars visited the Kronversk arsenal and seized great quantities of arms and ammunition, halting a shipment of ten thousand bayonets which was being sent to Novocherkask, headquarters of Kaledin. . . .

Suddenly awake to the danger, the Government offered immunity if the Committee would disband. Too late. At midnight, 5 November, Kerensky himself sent Malevsky to offer the Petrograd Soviet representation on the Staff. The Military Revolutionary Committee accepted. An hour later General Manikovsky, acting Minister of War, countermanded the offer. . . .

Tuesday morning, 6 November, the city was thrown into excitement by the appearance of a placard signed, 'Military Revolutionary Committee attached to the Petrograd Soviet of Workers' and Soldiers' Deputies'.

To the Population of Petrograd. Citizens!

Counter-revolution has raised its criminal head. The Kornilovtsi are mobilizing their forces in order to crush the All-Russian Congress of Soviets and break the Constituent Assembly. At the same time the *pogromists* may attempt to call upon the people of Petrograd for trouble and bloodshed. The Petrograd Soviet of Workers' and Soldiers' Deputies takes upon itself the guarding of revolutionary order in the city against counter-revolutionary and *pogrom* attempts.

The Petrograd garrison will not allow any violence or disorders. The population is invited to arrest hooligans and Black Hundred agitators and take them to the Soviet Commissars at the nearest barracks. At the first attempt of the Dark Forces to make trouble on the streets of Petrograd, whether robbery or fighting, the criminals will be wiped off the face of the earth!

Citizens! We call upon you to maintain complete quiet and self-possession. The cause of order and Revolution is in strong hands.

Lists of regiments where there are Commissars of the Military Revolutionary Committee. . . .

On the third the leaders of the Bolsheviki had another historic meeting behind closed doors. Notified by Zalkind, I waited in the corridor outside the door; and Volodarsky as he came out told me what was going on.

Lenin spoke: 'November sixth will be too early. We must have an all-Russian basis for the rising; and on the sixth all the delegates to the Congress will not have arrived. . . . On the other hand, November eighth will be too late. By that time the Congress will be organized, and it is difficult for a large organized body of people to take swift, decisive action. We must act on the seventh, the day the Congress meets, so that we may say to it, "Here is the power! What are you going to do with it?"'

In a certain upstairs room sat a thin-faced, long-haired individual, once an officer in the armies of the Tsar, then revolutionist and exile, a certain Avseenko, called Antonov, mathematician and chess-player; he was drawing careful plans for the seizure of the capital.

On its side the Government was preparing. Inconspicuously, certain of the most loyal regiments, from widely separated divisions, were ordered to Petrograd. The *yunker* artillery was drawn into the Winter Palace. Patrols of Cossacks made their appearance in the streets for the first time since the July days. Polkovnikov issued order after order, threatening to repress all insubordination with the 'utmost energy'. Kishkin, Minister of Public Instruction, the worst-hated member of the Cabinet, was appointed Special Commissar to keep order in Petrograd; he named as assistants two men no less unpopular, Rutenburg and Palchinsky. Petrograd, Kronstadt, and Finland were declared in a state of siege – upon which the bourgeois *Novoye Vremya* (New Times) remarked ironically:

Why the state of siege? The Government is no longer a power. It has no moral authority and it does not possess the necessary apparatus to use force. ... In the most favourable circumstances it can only negotiate with anyone who consents to parley. Its authority goes no farther. ...

Monday morning, the fifth, I dropped in at the Marinsky Palace, to see what was happening in the Council of the Russian Republic. Bitter debate on Tereshchenko's foreign policy. Echoes of the Burtzev-Verkhovsky affair. All the diplomats present except the Italian ambassador, who everybody said was prostrated by the Carso disaster. ...

As I came in the Left Socialist Revolutionary Karelin was reading aloud an editorial from the London *Times*, which said, 'The remedy for Bolshevism is bullets!' Turning to the Cadets he cried, 'That's what *you* think, too!'

Voices from the Right, 'Yes! Yes!'

'Yes, I know you think so,' answered Karelin, hotly. 'But you haven't the courage to try it!'

Then Skobeliev, looking like a matinée idol with his soft blond beard and wavy yellow hair, rather apologetically defended the Soviet *nakaz*. Tereshchenko followed, assailed from the Left by cries of 'Resignation! Resignation!' He insisted that the delegates of the Government and of the Tsay-ee-kah to Paris should have a common point of view – his own. A few words about the restoration of discipline in the army, about war to victory. ... Tumult, and over the stubborn opposition of the truculent Left, the Council of the Republic passed to the simple order of the day.

There stretched the rows of Bolshevik seats – empty since that first day when they left the Council, carrying with them so much life. As I went down the stairs it seemed to me that in spite of the bitter wrangling, no real voice from the rough world outside could penetrate this high, cold hall, and that the Provisional Government was wrecked – on the same rock of War and Peace that had wrecked the Miliukov Ministry.... The doorman grumbled as he put on my coat, 'I don't know what is becoming of poor Russia. All these Mensheviki and Bolsheviki and Trudoviki. ... This Ukraine and this Finland and the German imperialists and the English imperialists. I am forty-five years old, and in all my life I never heard so many words as in this place....'

In the corridor I met Professor Shatsky, a rat-faced individual in a dapper frock-coat, very influential in the councils of the Cadet party. I asked him what he thought of the much-talked-of Bolshevik *vystuplenie*. He shrugged, sneering.

'They are cattle – *canaille*,' he answered. 'They will not dare, or if they dare they will soon be sent flying. From our point of view it will not be bad, for then they will ruin themselves and have no power in the Constituent Assembly. ...

'But, my dear sir, allow me to outline to you my plan for a form of Government to be submitted to the Constituent Assembly. You see, I am chairman of a commission appointed from this body, in conjunction with the Provisional Government, to work out a constitutional project. ... We will have a legislative assembly of two chambers, such as you have in the United States. In the lower chamber will be territorial representatives; in the upper, representatives of the liberal professions, zemstvos, Cooperatives – and Trade Unions. ...'

Outside a chill, damp wind came from the west, and the cold mud underfoot soaked through my shoes. Two companies of *yunkers* passed swinging up the Morskaya, tramping stiffly in their long coats and singing an old-time crashing chorus, such as soldiers used to sing under the Tsar. ... At the first cross-street I noticed that the City Militiamen were mounted, and armed with revolvers in bright new holsters; a little group of people stood silently staring at them. At the corner of the Nevsky I bought a pamphlet by Lenin, *Will the Bolsheviki be Able to Hold the Power?* paying for it with one of the stamps which did duty for small change. The usual streetcars crawled past, citizens and soldiers clinging to the outside in a way to make Theodore P. Shonts green with envy. ... Along the sidewalk a row of deserters in uniform sold cigarettes and sunflower seeds. ...

Up the Nevsky in the sour twilight crowds were battling for the latest papers, and knots of people were trying to make out the multitudes of appeal[24] and proclamations pasted in every flat place; from the Tsay-ee-kah, the Peasants' Soviets, the 'moderate' Socialist parties, the Army Committees – threatening, cursing, beseeching the workers and soldiers to stay home, to support the Government. ...

An armoured automobile went slowly up and down, siren screaming. On every corner, in every open space, thick groups were clustered; arguing soldiers and students. Night came swiftly down, the wide-spaced street-lights flickered on, the tides of people flowed endlessly. . . . It is always like that in Petrograd just before trouble. . . .

The city was nervous, starting at every sharp sound. But still no sign from the Bolsheviki; the soldiers stayed in the barracks, the workmen in the factories. . . . We went to a moving picture show near the Kazan Cathedral – a bloody Italian film of passion and intrigue. Down front were some soldiers and sailors, staring at the screen in child-like wonder, totally unable to comprehend why there should be so much violent running about, and so much homicide. . . .

From there I hurried to Smolny. In room 10 on the top floor, the Military Revolutionary Committee sat in continuous session, under the chairmanship of a tow-headed, eighteen-year-old boy named Lazimir. He stopped, as he passed, to shake hands rather bashfully.

'Peter-Paul Fortress has just come over to us,' said he, with a pleased grin. 'A minute ago we got word from a regiment that was ordered by the Government to come to Petrograd. The men were suspicious, so they stopped the train at Gatchina and sent a delegation to us. "What's the matter?" they asked. "What have you got to say? We have just passed a resolution, 'All Power to the Soviets'." . . . The Military Revolutionary Committee sent back word. "Brothers! We greet you in the name of the Revolution. Stay where you are until further instructions!"'

All telephones, he said, were cut off: but communication with the factories and barracks was established by means of military telephonograph apparatus. . . .

A steady stream of couriers and Commissars came and went. Outside the door waited a dozen volunteers, ready to carry word to the farthest quarters of the city. One of them, a gipsy-faced man in the uniform of a lieutenant, said in French, 'Everything is ready to move at the push of a button. . . .'

There passed Podvoisky, the thin, bearded civilian whose brain conceived the strategy of insurrection; Antonov, unshaven, his collar filthy, drunk with loss of sleep; Krylenko, the squat, wide-faced soldier, always smiling, with his violent gestures and tumbling speech; and Dybenko, the giant bearded sailor with the placid face. These were the men of the hour – and of other hours to come.

Downstairs in the office of the Factory-Shop Committees sat Seratov, signing orders on the Government Arsenal for arms – one hundred and fifty rifles for each factory. . . . Delegates waited in line, forty of them. . . .

In the hall I ran into some of the minor Bolshevik leaders. One showed me a revolver. 'The game is on,' he said, and his face was pale. 'Whether we move or not, the other side knows it must finish us or be finished. . . .'

The Petrograd Soviet was meeting day and night. As I came into the great hall Trotsky was just finishing.

'We are asked,' he said, 'if we intend to have a *vystuplenie*. I can give a clear answer to that question. The Petrograd Soviet feels that at last the moment has arrived when the power must fall into the hands of the Soviets. This transfer of government will be accomplished by the All-Russian Congress. Whether an armed demonstration is necessary will depend on . . . those who wish to interfere with the All-Russian Congress. . . .

'We feel that our Government, entrusted to the personnel of the Provisional Cabinet, is a pitiful and helpless Government, which only awaits the sweep of the broom of History to give way to a really popular Government. But we are trying to avoid a conflict, even now, today. We hope that the All-Russian Congress will take . . . into its hands that power and authority which rests upon the organized freedom of the people. If, however, the Government wants to utilize the short period it is expected to live – twenty-four, forty-eight, or seventy-two hours – to attack us, then we shall answer with counter-attacks, blow for blow, steel for iron!'

Amid cheers he announced that the Left Socialist Revolutionaries had agreed to send representatives into the Military Revolutionary Committee. . . .

As I left Smolny, at three o'clock in the morning, I noticed that two rapid-firing guns had been mounted, one on each side of the door, and that strong patrols of soldiers guarded the gates and the near-by street corners. Bill Shatov* came bounding up

* Well known in the American labour movement.

the steps. 'Well,' he cried, 'we're off. Kerensky sent the *yunkers* to close down our papers, *Soldat* and *Rabochi Put*. But our troops went down and smashed the Government seals, and now we're sending detachments to seize the bourgeois newspaper offices!' Exultantly he slapped me on the shoulder, and ran in. ...

On the morning of the sixth I had business with the censor, whose office was in the Ministry of Foreign Affairs. Everywhere, on all the walls, hysterical appeals to the people to remain 'calm'. Polkovnikov emitted *prikaz* after *prikaz*:

I order all military units and detachments to remain in their barracks until further orders from the Staff of the Military District. ... All officers who act without orders from their superiors will be court-martialled for mutiny. I forbid absolutely any execution by soldiers of instructions from other organizations. ...

The morning paper announced that the Government had suppressed the papers *Novaya Rus*, *Zhivoye Slovo*, *Rabochi Put*, and *Soldat*, and decreed the arrest of the leaders of the Petrograd Soviet and the members of the Military Revolutionary Committee. ...

As I crossed the Palace Square several batteries of *yunker* artillery came through the Red Arch at a jingling trot, and drew up before the Palace. The great red building of the General Staff was unusually animated, several armoured automobiles ranked before the door, and motors full of officers were coming and going. ... The censor was very much excited, like a small boy at a circus. Kerensky, he said, had just gone to the Council of the Republic to offer his resignation. I hurried down to the Marinsky Palace, arriving at the end of that passionate and almost incoherent speech of Kerensky's, full of self-justification and bitter denunciation of his enemies.

'I will cite here the most characteristic passage from a whole series of articles published in *Rabochi Put* by Ulyanov-Lenin, a state criminal who is in hiding and whom we are trying to find. ... This state criminal has invited the proletariat and the Petrograd garrison to repeat the experience of 16–18 July, and insists upon the immediate necessity for an armed rising. ... Moreover, other Bolshevik leaders have taken the floor in a series of meetings, and also made an appeal to immediate insurrection. Particularly should be noticed the activity of the present president of the Petrograd Soviet, Bronstein-Trotsky. ...

'I ought to bring to your notice ... that the expressions and the style of a whole series of articles in *Rabochi Put* and *Soldat* resemble absolutely those of *Novaya Rus*. ... We have to do not so much with the movement of such and such political party, as with the exploitation of the political ignorance and criminal instincts of a part of the population, a sort of organization whose object it is to provoke in Russia, cost what it may, an inconscient movement of destruction and pillage; for, given the state of mind of the masses, any movement at Petrograd will be followed by the most terrible massacres, which will cover with eternal shame the name of free Russia. ...

'... By the admission of Ulyanov-Lenin himself, the situation of the extreme left wing of the Social-Democrats in Russia is very favourable.'

Here Kerensky read the following quotation from Lenin's article:

Think of it! ... The German comrades have only one Liebknecht, without newspapers, without freedom of meeting, without a Soviet. ..., They are opposed by the incredible hostility of all classes of society – and yet the German comrades try to act; while we, having dozens of newspapers, freedom of meeting, the majority of the Soviets, we, the best-placed international proletarians of the entire world, can we refuse to support the German revolutionists and insurrectionary organizations? ...

Kerensky then continued:

'The organizers of rebellion recognize thus implicitly that the most perfect conditions for the free action of a political party obtain now in Russia, administered by a Provisional Government, at the head of which is, in the eyes of this party, "a usurper and a man who has sold himself to the bourgeoisie, the Minister-President Kerensky ...".

'... The organizers of the insurrection do not come to the aid of the German proletariat, but of the German governing classes, and they open the Russian front to the iron fists of Wilhelm and his friends. ... Little matter to the Provisional Government the motives of these people, little matter if they act consciously or unconsciously; but in any case, from this tribune, in full consciousness of my responsibility I qualify such acts of a Russian political party as acts of treason to Russia!

'... I place myself at the point of view of the Right, and I propose immediately to proceed to an investigation and make the necessary arrests.' (Uproar from the Left.) 'Listen to me!' he cried in a powerful voice. 'At the moment when the state is in danger, because of conscious or unconscious treason, the Provisional Government, and myself among others, prefer to be killed rather than betray the life, the honour, and the independence of Russia. ...'

At this moment a paper was handed to Kerensky.

'I have just received the proclamation which they are distributing to the regiments. Here is the contents.' Reading:

'"The Petrograd Soviet of Workers' and Soldiers' Deputies is menaced. We order immediately the regiments to mobilize on a war footing and to await new orders. All delay or non-execution of this order will be considered as an act of treason to the Revolution. The Military Revolutionary Committee. For the President, Podvoisky. The Secretary, Antonov."

'In reality this is an attempt to raise the populace against the existing order of things, to break the Constituent and to open the front to the regiments of the iron fist of Wilhelm. ...

'I say "populace" intentionally, because the conscious democracy and its Tsay-ee-kah, all the Army organizations, all that free Russia glorifies, the good sense, the honour and the conscience of the great Russian democracy, protests against these things. ...

'I have not come here with a prayer, but to state my firm conviction that the Provisional Government, which defends at this moment our new liberty – that the new Russian state, destined to a brilliant future, will find unanimous support except among those who have never dared to face the truth. ...

'... The Provisional Government has never violated the liberty of all citizens of the State to use their political rights. ... But now the Provisional Government ... declares: in this moment those elements of the Russian nation, those groups and parties who have dared to lift their hands against the free will of the Russian people, at the same time threatening to open the front to Germany, must be liquidated with decision! ...

'Let the population of Petrograd understand that it will encounter a firm power, and perhaps at the last moment good sense, conscience, and honour will triumph in the hearts of those who still possess them. ....'

All through this speech the hall rang with deafening clamour. When the Minister-President had stepped down, pale-faced and wet with perspiration, and strode out with his suite of officers, speaker after speaker from the Left and Centre attacked the Right, all one angry roaring. Even the Socialist Revolutionaries, through Gotz:

'The policy of the Bolsheviki is demagogic and criminal, in their exploitation of the popular discontent. But there is a whole series of popular demands which have received no satisfaction up to now.... The questions of peace, land, and the democratization of the army ought to be stated in such a fashion that no soldier, peasant, or worker would have the least doubt that our Government is attempting, firmly and infallibly, to solve them....

'We Mensheviki do not wish to provoke a Cabinet crisis, and we are ready to defend the Provisional Government with all our energy, to the last drop of our blood – if only the Provisional Government, on all these burning questions, will speak the clear and precise words awaited by the people with such impatience....'

Then Martov, furious:

'The words of the Minister-President, who allowed himself to speak of "populace" when it is question of the moment of important sections of the proletariat and the army – although led in the wrong direction – are nothing but an incitement to civil war.'

The order of the day proposed by the Left was voted. It amounted practically to a vote of lack of confidence:

1. The armed demonstration which has been preparing for some days past has for its object a *coup d'état*, threatens to provoke civil war, creates conditions favourable to *pogroms* and counter-revolution, the mobilization of counter-revolutionary forces, such as the Black Hundreds, which will inevitably bring about the impossibility of convoking the Constituent, will cause a military catastrophe, the death of the Revolution, paralyse the economic life of the country and destroy Russia;

2. The conditions favourable to this agitation have been created by delay in passing urgent measures, as well as objective conditions caused

by the war and the general disorder. It is necessary before everything to promulgate at once a decree transmitting the land to the peasants' Land Committees, and to adopt an energetic course of action abroad in proposing to the Allies to proclaim their peace terms and to begin peace parleys;

3. To cope with Monarchist manifestations and *pogromist* movements it is indispensable to take immediate measures to suppress these movements, and for this purpose to create at Petrograd a Committee of Public Safety, composed of representatives of the Municipality and the organs of the revolutionary democracy, acting in contact with the Provisional Government. ...

It is interesting to note that the Mensheviki and Socialist Revolutionaries all rallied to this resolution. ... When Kerensky saw it, however, he summoned Avksentiev to the Winter Palace to explain. If it expressed a lack of confidence in the Provisional Government, he begged Avksentiev to form a new Cabinet. Dan, Gotz, and Avksentiev, the leaders of the 'compromisers', performed their last compromise. ... They explained to Kerensky that it was not meant as a criticism of the Government!

At the corner of the Morskaya and the Nevsky, squads of soldiers with fixed bayonets were stopping all private automobiles, turning out the occupants, and ordering them towards the Winter Palace. A large crowd had gathered to watch them. Nobody knew whether the soldiers belonged to the Government or the Military Revolutionary Committee. Up in front of the Kazan Cathedral the same thing was happening, machines being directed back up the Nevsky. Five or six sailors with rifles came along, laughing excitedly, and fell into conversation with two of the soldiers. On the sailors' hat bands were *Avrora* and *Zaria Svobody* – the names of the leading Bolshevik cruisers of the Baltic Fleet. One of them said, 'Kronstadt is coming!' ... It was as if, in 1792, on the streets of Paris, someone had said 'The Marseillais are coming!' For at Kronstadt were twenty-five thousand sailors, convinced Bolsheviki and not afraid to die. .

Rabochi i Soldat was just out, all its front page one huge proclamation:

SOLDIERS! WORKERS! CITIZENS!

The enemies of the people passed last night to the offensive. The Kornilovists of the Staff are trying to draw in from the suburbs *yunkers* and volunteer battalions. The Oranienbaum *yunkers* and the Tsarskoye Selo volunteers refused to come out. A stroke of high treason is being contemplated against the Petrograd Soviet. ... The campaign of the counter-revolutionists is being directed against the All-Russian Congress of Soviets on the eve of its opening, against the Constituent Assembly, against the people. The Petrograd Soviet is guarding the Revolution. The Military Revolutionary Committee is directing the repulse of the conspirators' attack. The entire garrison and proletariat of Petrograd are ready to deal the enemy of the people a crushing blow.

The Military Revolutionary Committee decrees:

1. All regimental, division, and battleship Committees, together with the Soviet Commissars, and all revolutionary organizations, shall meet in continuous session, concentrating in their hands all information about the plans of the conspirators.

2. Not one soldier shall leave his division without permission of the Committee.

3. To send to Smolny at once two delegates from each military unit and five from each Ward Soviet.

4. All members of the Petrograd Soviet and all delegates to the All-Russian Congress are invited immediately to Smolny for an extraordinary meeting.

Counter-revolution has raised its criminal head.

A great danger threatens all the conquests and hopes of the soldiers and workers.

But the forces of the Revolution by far exceed those of its enemies.

The cause of the People is in strong hands. The conspirators will be crushed.

No hesitation or doubts! Firmness, steadfastness, discipline, determination!

Long live the Revolution!

The Military Revolutionary Committee

The Petrograd Soviet was meeting continuously at Smolny, a centre of storm, delegates falling down asleep on the floor and rising again to take part in the debate, Trotsky, Kameniev, Volodarsky speaking six, eight, twelve hours a day. ...

I went down to room 18 on the first floor where the Bolshevik delegates were holding caucus, a harsh voice steadily booming, the speaker hidden by the crowd: 'The compromisers say that we are isolated. Pay no attention to them. Once it begins they must be dragged along with us, or else lose their following. ...'

Here he held up a piece of paper. 'We are dragging them! A

message has just come from the Mensheviki and Socialist Revolutionaries! They say that they condemn our action, but that if the Government attacks us they will not oppose the cause of the proletariat!' Exultant shouting. . . .

As night fell the great hall filled with soldiers and workmen, a monstrous dun mass, deep-humming in a blue haze of smoke. The old Tsay-ee-kah had finally decided to welcome the delegates to that new Congress which would mean its own ruin – and perhaps the ruin of the revolutionary order it had built. At this meeting, however, only members of the Tsay-ee-kah could vote. . . .

It was after midnight when Gotz took the chair and Dan rose to speak, in a tense silence, which seemed to me almost menacing.

'The hours in which we live appear in the most tragic colours,' he said. 'The enemy is at the gates of Petrograd, the forces of the democracy are trying to organize to resist him, and yet we await bloodshed in the streets of the capital, and famine threatens to destroy, not only our homogeneous Government but the Revolution itself. . . .

'The masses are sick and exhausted. They have no interest in the Revolution. If the Bolsheviki start anything, that will be the end of the Revolution. . . .' (Cries, 'That's a lie!') 'The counter-revolutionists are waiting with the Bolsheviki to begin riots and massacres. . . . If there is any *vystuplenie*, there will be no Constituent Assembly. . . .' (Cries, 'Lie! Shame!')

'It is inadmissible that in the zone of military operations the Petrograd garrison shall not submit to the orders of the Staff. . . . You must obey the orders of the Staff and of the Tsay-ee-kah elected by you. All Power to the Soviets – that means death! Robbers and thieves are waiting for the moment to loot and burn. . . . When you have such slogans put before you, "Enter the houses, take away the shoes and clothes from the bourgeoisie –"' (Tumult. Cries, 'No such slogan! A lie! A lie!') 'Well, it may start differently, but it will end that way!

'The Tsay-ee-kah has full power to act, and must be obeyed. . . . We are not afraid of bayonets. . . . The Tsay-ee-kah will defend the Revolution with its body. . . .' (Cries, 'It was a dead body long ago!')

Immense continued uproar, in which his voice could be heard

screaming, as he pounded the desk, 'Those who are urging this are committing a crime!'

Voice: 'You committed a crime long ago, when you captured the power and turned it over to the bourgeoisie!'

Gotz, ringing the chairman's bell: 'Silence, or I'll have you put out!'

Voice: 'Try it!' (Cheers and whistling.)

'Now concerning our policy about peace.' (Laughter.) 'Unfortunately Russia can no longer support the continuation of the war. There is going to be peace, but not permanent peace – not a democratic peace. ... Today, at the Council of the Republic, in order to avoid bloodshed, we passed an order of the day demanding the surrender of the land to the Land Committees and immediate peace negotiations. ...' (Laughter, and cries, 'Too late!')

Then for the Bolsheviki, Trotsky mounted the tribune, borne on a wave of roaring applause that burst into cheers and a rising house, thunderous. His thin, pointed face was positively Mephistophelian in its expression of malicious irony.

'Dan's tactics prove that the masses – the great, dull, indifferent masses – are absolutely with him!' (Titanic mirth.) He turned towards the chairman, dramatically. 'When we spoke of giving the land to the peasants you were against it. We told the peasants, "If they don't give it to you, take it yourselves!" and the peasants followed our advice. And now you advocate what we did six months ago. ...

'I don't think Kerensky's order to suspend the death penalty in the army was dictated by his ideals. I think Kerensky was persuaded by the Petrograd garrison, which refused to obey him. ...

'Today Dan is accused of having made a speech in the Council of the Republic which proves him to be a secret Bolshevik. ... The time may come when Dan will say that the flower of the Revolution participated in the rising of 16 and 18 July. ... In Dan's resolution today at the Council of the Republic there was no mention of enforcing discipline in the army, although that is urged into the propaganda of his party. ...

'No. The history of the last seven months shows that the masses have left the Mensheviki. The Mensheviki and the

Socialist Revolutionaries conquered the Cadets, and then when they got the power they gave it to the Cadets. ...

'Dan tells you that you have no right to make an insurrection. Insurrection is the right of all revolutionists! When the downtrodden masses revolt it is their right. ...

Then the long-faced, cruel-tongued Lieber, greeted with groans and laughter.

'Engels and Marx said that the proletariat had no right to take power until it was ready for it. In a bourgeois revolution like this ... the seizure of power by the masses means the tragic end of the Revolution. ... Trotsky, as a Social-Democratic theorist, is himself opposed to what he is now advocating. ...' (Cries, 'Enough! Down with him!')

Martov constantly interrupted: 'The Internationalists are not opposed to the transmission of power to the democracy, but they disapprove of the methods of the Bolsheviki. This is not the moment to seize the power. ...'

Again Dan took the floor, violently protesting against the action of the Military Revolutionary Committee, which had sent a Commissar to seize the office of *Izvestia* and censor the paper. The wildest uproar followed. Martov tried to speak, but could not be heard. Delegates of the Army and the Baltic Fleet stood up all over the hall, shouting that the Soviet was *their* Government. ...

Amid the wildest confusion Ehrlich offered a resolution, appealing to the workers and soldiers to remain calm and not to respond to provocations to demonstrate, recognizing the necessity of immediately creating a Committee at once to pass decrees transferring the land to the peasants and beginning peace negotiations. ...

Then up leaped Volodarsky, shouting harshly that the Tsay-ee-kah, on the eve of the Congress, had no right to assume the functions of the Congress. The Tsay-ee-kah was practically dead, he said, and the resolution was simply a trick to bolster up its waning power. ...

'As for us, Bolsheviki, we will not vote on this resolution!' Whereupon all the Bolsheviki left the hall and the resolution was passed. ...

Towards four in the morning I met Zorin in the outer hall, a rifle slung from his shoulder.

'We're moving!'[25] said he, calmly, but with satisfaction. 'We pinched the Assistant Minister of Justice and the Minister of Religions. They're down cellar now. One regiment is on the march to capture the Telephone Exchange, another the Telegraph Agency, another the State Bank. The Red Guard is out. ...'

On the steps of Smolny, in the chill dark, we first saw the Red Guard – a huddled group of boys in workmen's clothes, carrying guns with bayonets, talking nervously together.

Far over the still roofs westward came the sound of scattered rifle fire, where the *yunkers* were trying to open the bridges over the Neva, to prevent the factory workers and soldiers of the Viborg quarter from joining the Soviet forces in the centre of the city; and the Kronstadt sailors were closing them again. ...

Behind us great Smolny, bright with lights, hummed like a gigantic hive. ...

4 The Fall of the Provisional Government

Wednesday, 7 November, I rose very late. The noon cannon boomed from Peter-Paul as I went down the Nevsky. It was a raw, chill day. In front of the State Bank some soldiers with fixed bayonets were standing at the closed gates.

'What side do you belong to?' I asked. 'The Government?'

'No more Government,' one answered with a grin. '*Slava Bogu!* Glory to God!' That was all I could get out of him....

The street-cars were running on the Nevsky, men, women, and small boys hanging on every projection. Shops were open, and there seemed even less uneasiness among the street crowds than there had been the day before. A whole crop of new appeals against insurrection had blossomed out on the walls during the night – to the peasants, to the soldiers at the front, to the workmen of Petrograd. One read:

FROM THE PETROGRAD MUNICIPAL DUMA

The Municipal Duma informs the citizens that in the extraordinary meeting of 6 November the Duma formed a Committee of Public Safety, composed of members of the Central and Ward Dumas, and representatives of the following revolutionary democratic organizations: The Tsay-ee-kah, the All-Russian Executive Committee of Peasant Deputies, the Army organizations, the Tsentroflot, the Petrograd Soviet Workers' and Soldiers' Deputies (!), the Council of Trade Unions, and others.

Members of the Committee of Public Safety will be on duty in the building of the Municipal Duma. Telephones No. 15–40, 223–7, 138–36.

7 November 1917

Though I didn't realize it then, this was the Duma's declaration of war against the Bolsheviki.

I bought a copy of *Rabochi Put*, the only newspaper which seemed on sale, and a little later paid a soldier fifty kopeks for a second-hand copy of *Dien*. The Bolshevik paper, printed on large-sized sheets in the conquered office of the *Russkaya Volia*,

had huge headlines: 'ALL POWER – TO THE SOVIETS OF WOR-
KERS, SOLDIERS, AND PEASANTS! PEACE! BREAD! LAND!'
The leading article was signed 'Zinoviev' – Lenin's companion in
hiding. It began:

> Every soldier, every worker, every real Socialist, every honest demo-
> crat, realizes that there are only two alternatives to the present situa-
> tion.
> Either – the power will remain in the hands of the bourgeois-landlord
> crew, and this will mean every kind of repression for the workers,
> soldiers, and peasants, continuation of the war, inevitable hunger and
> death. ...
> Or – the power will be transferred to the hands of the revolutionary
> workers, soldiers, and peasants; in that case it will mean a complete
> abolition of landlord tyranny, immediate check of the capitalists,
> immediate proposal of a just peace. Then the land is assured to the
> peasants, then control of industry is assured to the workers, then bread
> is assured to the hungry, then the end of this nonsensical war! ...

Dien contained fragmentary news of the agitated night. Bolsheviki capture of the Telephone Exchange, the Baltic station,
the Telegraph Agency; the Peterhof *yunkers* unable to reach
Petrograd; the Cossacks undecided; arrest of some of the
Ministers; shooting of Chief of the City Militia Meyer; arrests,
counter-arrests, skirmishes between clashing patrols of soldiers,
yunkers, and Red Guards.[26]
On the corner of the Morskaya I ran into Captain Comberg,
Menshevik *oboronets*, secretary of the Military Section of his
party. When I asked him if the insurrection had really happened
he shrugged his shoulders in a tired manner and replied, '*Chort
znayet!* The devil knows! Well, perhaps the Bolsheviki can seize
the power, but they won't be able to hold it more than three days.
They haven't the men to run a government. Perhaps it's a good
thing to let them try – that will finish them. ...'
The Military Hotel at the corner of St Isaac's Square was
picketed by armed sailors. In the lobby were many of the smart
young officers, walking up and down or muttering together; the
sailors wouldn't let them leave. ...
Suddenly came the sharp crack of a rifle outside, followed by a
scattered burst of firing. I ran out. Something unusual was going
on around the Marinsky Palace, where the Council of the Russian

Republic met. Diagonally across the wide square was drawn a line of sailors, rifles ready, staring at the hotel roof.

'*Provocatzia!* Shot at us!' snapped one, while another went running towards the door.

At the western corner of the Palace lay a big armoured car with a red flag flying from it, newly lettered in red paint: 'S.R.S.D.' (*Soviet Rabochikh Soldatskikh Deputatov*); all the guns trained towards St Isaac's. A barricade had been heaped up across the mouth of Novaya Ulitsa – boxes, barrels, an old bedspring, a wagon. A pile of lumber barred the end of the Moika quay. Short logs from a neighbouring wood-pile were being built up along the front of the building to form breastworks. ...

'Is there going to be any fighting?' I asked.

'Soon, soon,' answered a soldier, nervously. 'Go away, comrade, you'll get hurt. They will come from that direction,' pointing towards the Admiralty.

'Who will?'

'That I couldn't tell you, brother,' he answered, and spat.

Before the door of the Palace was a crowd of soldiers and sailors. A sailor was telling of the end of the Council of the Russian Republic. 'We walked in there,' he said, 'and filled all the doors with comrades. I went up to the counter-revolutionist Kornilovits who sat in the president's chair. "No more Council," I says. "Run along home now!"'

There was laughter. By waving assorted papers I managed to get around to the door of the press gallery. There an enormous smiling sailor stopped me, and when I showed my pass, just said, 'If you were Saint Michael himself, comrade, you couldn't pass here!' Through the glass of the door I made out the distorted face and gesticulating arms of a French correspondent, locked in. ...

Around in front stood a little, grey-moustached man in the uniform of a general, the centre of a knot of soldiers. He was very red in the face.

'I am General Alexeyev,' he cried. 'As your superior officer and as a member of the Council of the Republic I demand to be allowed to pass!' The guard scratched his head, looking uneasily out of the corner of his eye, he beckoned to an approaching officer, who grew very agitated when he saw who it was and saluted before he realized what he was doing.

'*Vashe Vuisokoprevoskhoditelstvo* – your High Excellency – '
he stammered in the manner of the old régime. 'Access to the
Palace is strictly forbidden – I have no right –'

An automobile came by, and I saw Gotz sitting inside, laughing
apparently with great amusement. A few minutes later another,
with armed soldiers on the front seat, full of arrested members of
the Provisional Government. Peters, Lettish member of the
Military Revolutionary Committee, came hurrying across the
Square.

'I thought you bagged all those gentlemen last night,' said I,
pointing to them.

'Oh,' he answered, with the expression of a disappointed
schoolboy. 'The damn fools let most of them go again before we
made up our minds. ....'

Down the Voskressensky Prospect a great mass of sailors were
drawn up, and behind them came marching soldiers, as far as the
eye could reach.

We went towards the Winter Palace by way of the Admiral-
teisky. All the entrances to the Palace Square were closed by
sentries, and a cordon of troops stretched clear across the western
end, besieged by an uneasy throng of citizens. Except for far-away
soldiers who seemed to be carrying wood out of the Palace courtyard and piling it in front of the main gateway, everything was
quiet.

We couldn't make out whether the sentries were pro-Govern-
ment or pro-Soviet. Our papers from Smolny had no effect,
however, so we approached another part of the line with an
important air and showed our American passports, saying,
'Official business!' and shouldered through. At the door of the
Palace the same old *shveitzari*, in their brass-buttoned blue uniforms with the red-and-gold collars, politely took our coats and
hats, and we went upstairs. In the dark, gloomy corridor, stripped
of its tapestries, a few old attendants were lounging about, and in
front of Kerensky's door a young officer paced up and down,
gnawing his moustache. We asked if we could interview the
Minister-President. He bowed and clicked his heels.

'No, I am sorry,' he replied in French. 'Alexander Feodorovich is extremely occupied just now. ....' He looked at us for a
moment. 'In fact, he is not here. ....'

'Where is he?'

'He has gone to the front.[27] And do you know, there wasn't enough gasoline for his automobile. We had to send to the English Hospital and borrow some.'

'Are the Ministers here?'

'They are meeting in some room – I don't know where.'

'Are the Bolsheviki coming?'

'Of course. Certainly they are coming. I expect a telephone call every minute to say that they are coming. But we are ready. We have *yunkers* in the front of the Palace. Through that door there.'

'Can we go in there?'

'No. Certainly not. It is not permitted.' Abruptly he shook hands all round and walked away. We turned to the forbidden door, set in a temporary partition dividing the hall and locked on the outside. On the other side were voices, and somebody laughing. Except for that the vast spaces of the old Palace were as silent as the grave. An old *shveitzar* ran up. 'No, *barin*, you must not go in there.'

'Why is the door locked?'

'To keep the soldiers in,' he answered. After a few minutes he said something about having a glass of tea and went back up the hall. We unlocked the door.

Just inside a couple of soldiers stood on guard, but they said nothing. At the end of the corridor was a large, ornate room with gilded cornices and enormous crystal lustres, and beyond it several smaller ones, wainscoted with dark wood. On both sides of the parqueted floor lay rows of dirty mattresses and blankets, upon which occasional soldiers were stretched out; everywhere was a litter of cigarette butts, bits of bread, cloth, and empty bottles with expensive French labels. More and more soldiers with the red shoulder-straps of the *yunker* schools, moved about in a stale atmosphere of tobacco-smoke and unwashed humanity. One had a bottle of white Burgundy, evidently filched from the cellars of the Palace. They looked at us with astonishment as we marched past, through room after room, until at last we came out into a series of great state-salons, fronting their long and dirty windows on the Square. The walls were covered with huge canvases in massive gilt frames – historical battle scenes....
'12 October 1812' and '6 November 1812' and '16/28 August

1813'. . . . One had a gash across the upper right-hand corner. The place was all a huge barrack, and evidently had been for weeks, from the look of the floor and walls. Machine-guns were mounted on window-sills, rifles stacked between the mattresses.

As we were looking at the pictures an alcoholic breath assailed me from the region of my left ear, and a voice said in thick but fluent French, 'I see, by the way you admire the paintings, that you are foreigners.' He was a short, puffy man with a baldish head as he removed his cap.

'Americans? Enchanted. I am Stabs-Captain Vladimir Artzibashev, absolutely at your service.' It did not seem to occur to him that there was anything unusual in four strangers, one a woman, wandering through the defences of an army awaiting attack. He began to complain of the state of Russia.

'Not only these Bolsheviki,' he said, 'but the fine traditions of the Russian army are broken down. Look around you. These are all students in the officers' training schools. But are they gentlemen? Kerensky opened the officers' schools to the ranks, to any soldier who could pass an examination. Naturally there are many, many who are contaminated by the Revolution. . . .'

Without consequence he changed the subject. 'I am very anxious to get away from Russia. I have made up my mind to join the American army. Will you please go to your Consul and make arrangements? I will give you my address.' In spite of our protestations he wrote it on a piece of paper, and seemed to feel better at once. I have it still – 'Oranienbaumskaya Shkola Praporshchikov 2nd, Staraya Peterhof.'

'We had a review this morning early,' he went on, as he guided us through the rooms and explained everything. 'The Women's Battalion decided to remain loyal to the Government.'

'Are the women soldiers in the Palace?'

'Yes, they are in the back rooms, where they won't be hurt if any trouble comes.' He sighed. 'It is a great responsibility,' said he.

For a while we stood at the window, looking down on the Square before the Palace, where three companies of long-coated *yunkers* were drawn up under arms, being harangued by a tall, energetic-looking officer I recognized as Stankievich, chief Military Commissar of the Provisional Government. After a few minutes two of the companies shouldered arms with a clash, barked three sharp shouts, and went swinging off across the Square, disappearing through the Red Arch into the quiet city.

'They are going to capture the Telephone Exchange,' said someone. Three cadets stood by us, and we fell into conversation. They said they had entered the schools from the ranks, and gave their names – Robert Olev, Alexei Vasilienko, and Erni Sachs, an Estonian. But now they didn't want to be officers any more, because officers were very unpopular. They didn't seem to know what to do, as a matter of fact, and it was plain that they were not happy.

But soon they began to boast. 'If the Bolsheviki come we shall show them how to fight. They do not dare to fight, they are cowards. But if we should be overpowered, well, every man keeps one bullet for himself. ....'

At this point there was a burst of rifle-fire not far off. Out on the Square all the people began to run, falling flat on their faces, and the *izvozchiki* standing on the corners galloped in every direction. Inside all was uproar, soldiers running here and there, grabbing up guns, rifle-belts and shouting, 'Here they come! Here they come!'... But in a few minutes it quieted down again. The *izvozchiki* came back, the people lying down stood up. Through the Red Arch appeared the *yunkers*, marching a little out of step, one of them supported by two comrades.

It was getting late when we left the Palace. The sentries in the Square had all disappeared. The great semi-circle of Government buildings seemed deserted. We went into the Hotel France for dinner, and right in the middle of soup the waiter, very pale in the face, came up and insisted that we move to the main dining-room at the back of the house, because they were going to put out the lights in the café. 'There will be much shooting,' he said.

When we came out on the Morskaya again it was quite dark, except for one flickering street-light on the corner of the Nevsky. Under this stood a big armoured automobile, with racing engine and oil-smoke pouring out of it. A small boy had climbed up the side of the thing and was looking down the barrel of a machine-gun. Soldiers and sailors stood around, evidently waiting for something. We walked back up to the Red Arch, where a knot of soldiers was gathered staring at the brightly lighted Winter Palace and talking in loud tones.

'No, comrades,' one was saying. 'How can we shoot at them? The Women's Battalion is in there – they will say we have fired on Russian women.'

As we reached the Nevsky again another armoured car came around the corner, and a man poked his head out of the turret-top.

'Come on!' he yelled. 'Let's go on through and attack!'

The driver of the other car came over, and shouted so as to be heard above the roaring engine. 'The Committee says to wait. They have got artillery behind the wood-piles in there. . . .'

Here the streetcars had stopped running, few people passed, and there were no lights; but a few blocks away we could see the trams, the crowds, the lighted shop-windows and the electric signs of the moving-picture shows – life going on as usual. We had tickets to the Ballet at the Marinsky Theatre – all the theatres were open – but it was too exciting out of doors. . . .

In the darkness we stumbled over lumber-piles barricading the Police Bridge, and before the Stroganov Palace made out some soldiers wheeling into position a three-inch field-gun. Men in various uniforms were coming and going in an aimless way, and doing a great deal of talking. . . .

Up the Nevsky the whole city seemed to be out promenading. On every corner immense crowds were massed around a core of hot discussion. Pickets of a dozen soldiers with fixed bayonets lounged at the street crossings, red-faced old men in rich fur coats shook their fists at them, smartly-dressed women screamed epithets; the soldiers argued feebly, with embarrassed grins. . . . Armoured cars went up and down the street, named after the first Tsars – Oleg, Rurik, Svietoslav – and daubed with huge red letters, 'R.S.D.R.P.' (*Rossiskaya Sotsial-Demokrateecheskaya Rabochaya Partia*).* At the Mikhailovsky a man appeared with an armful of newspapers, and was immediately stormed by frantic people, offering a rouble, five roubles, ten roubles, tearing at each other like animals. It was *Rabochi i Soldat*, announcing the victory of the Proletarian Revolution, the liberation of the Bolsheviki still in prison, calling upon the Army front and rear

* Russian Social-Democratic Labour Party.

for support ... a feverish little sheet of four pages, running to enormous type, containing no news. ...

On the corner of the Sadovaya about two thousand citizens had gathered, staring up at the roof of a tall building, where a tiny red spark glowed and waned.

'See!' said a tall peasant, pointing to it. 'It is a provocator. Presently he will fire on the people....' Apparently no one thought of going to investigate.

The massive façade of Smolny blazed with lights as we drove up, and from every street converged upon it streams of hurrying shapes dim in the gloom. Automobiles and motor-cycles came and went; an enormous elephant-coloured armoured automobile, with two red flags flying from the turret, lumbered out with screaming siren. It was cold, and at the outer gate the Red Guards had built themselves a bonfire. At the inner gate, too, there was a blaze, by the light of which sentries slowly spelled out our passes and looked us up and down. The canvas covers had been taken off the four rapid-fire guns on each side of the doorway, and the ammunition-belts hung snake-like from their breeches. A dun herd of armoured cars stood under the trees in the courtyard, engines going. The long, bare, dimly illuminated halls roared with the thunder of feet, calling, shouting.... There was an atmosphere of recklessness. A crowd came pouring down the staircase, workers in black blouses and round black fur hats, many of them with guns slung over their shoulders, soldiers in rough dirt-coloured coats and grey fur *shapki* pinched flat, a leader or so – Lunacharsky, Kameniev – hurrying along in the centre of a group all talking at once, with harassed anxious faces, and bulging portfolios under their arms. The extraordinary meeting of the Petrograd Soviet was over. I stopped Kameniev – a quick-moving little man, with a wide, vivacious face set close to his shoulders. Without preface he read in rapid French a copy of the resolution just passed:

The Petrograd Soviet of Workers' and Soldiers' Deputies, saluting the victorious Revolution of the Petrograd proletariat and garrison, particularly emphasizes the unity, organization, discipline, and complete cooperation shown by the masses in this rising; rarely has less blood been spilled, and rarely has an insurrection succeeded so well.

The Soviet expresses its firm conviction that the Workers' and Peasants' Government which, as the government of the Soviets, will be created by the Revolution, and which will assure the industrial proletariat of the support of the entire mass of poor peasants, will march firmly towards Socialism, the only means by which the country can be spared the miseries and unheard-of horrors of war.

The new Workers' and Peasants' Government will propose immediately a just and democratic peace to all the belligerent countries.

It will suppress immediately the great landed property, and transfer the land to the peasants. It will establish workmen's control over production and distribution of manufactured products, and will set up a general control over the banks, which it will transform into a state monopoly.

The Petrograd Soviet of Workers' and Soldiers' Deputies calls upon the workers and peasants of Russia to support with all their energy and all their devotion the Proletarian Revolution. The Soviet expresses its conviction that the city workers, allies of the poor peasants, will assure complete revolutionary order, indispensable to the victory of Socialism. The Soviet is convinced that the proletariat of the countries of Western Europe will aid us in conducting the cause of Socialism to a real and lasting victory.

'You consider it won then?'

He lifted his shoulders. 'There is much to do. Horribly much. It is just beginning. ....'

On the landing I met Riazanov, vice-president of the Trade Unions, looking black and biting his grey beard. 'It's insane! Insane!' he shouted. 'The European working class won't move! All Russia –' He waved his hand distractedly and ran off. Riazanov and Kameniev had both opposed the insurrection,* and felt the lash of Lenin's terrible tongue. ...

It had been a momentous session. In the name of the Military Revolutionary Committee Trotsky had declared that the Provisional Government no longer existed.

'The characteristic of bourgeois governments,' he said, 'is to deceive the people. We, the Soviets of Workers', Soldiers', and Peasants' Deputies, are going to try an experiment unique in history; we are going to found a power which will have no other aim but to satisfy the needs of the soldiers, workers, and peasants.'

* John Reed's statement is not entirely correct. Kameniev was not against an insurrection, but had opposed its commencement at this particular time. For further details see *The Errors of Trotskyism* (C.P.G.B.).

Lenin had appeared, welcomed with a mighty ovation, prophesying world-wide Social Revolution.... And Zinoviev, crying, 'This day we have paid our debt to the international proletariat, and struck a terrible blow at the war, a terrible body-blow at all the imperialists, and particularly at Wilhelm the Executioner....'

Then Trotsky, that telegrams had been sent to the front announcing the victorious insurrection, but no reply had come. Troops were said to be marching against Petrograd – a delegation must be sent to tell them the truth.

Cries, 'You are anticipating the will of the All-Russian Congress of Soviets!'

Trotsky, coldly, 'The will of the All-Russian Congress of Soviets has been anticipated by the rising of the Petrograd workers and soldiers!'

So we came into the great meeting-hall, pushing through the clamorous mob at the door. In the rows of seats, under the white chandeliers, packed immovably in the aisles and on the sides, perched on every window-sill, and even the edge of the platform, the representatives of the workers and soldiers of all Russia waited in anxious silence or wild exultation the ringing of the chairman's bell. There was no heat in the hall but the stifling heat of unwashed human bodies. A foul blue cloud of cigarette smoke rose from the mass and hung in the thick air. Occasionally someone in authority mounted the tribune and asked the comrades not to smoke; then everybody, smokers and all, took up the cry, 'Don't smoke, comrades!' and went on smoking. Petrovsky, Anarchist delegate from the Obukhov factory, made a seat for me beside him. Unshaven and filthy, he was reeling from three nights' sleepless work on the Military Revolutionary Committee.

On the platform sat the leaders of the old Tsay-ee-kah – for the last time dominating the turbulent Soviets, which they had ruled from the first days, and which were now risen against them. It was the end of the first period of the Russian revolution, which these men had attempted to guide in careful ways.... The three greatest of them were not there: Kerensky, flying to the front through country towns all doubtfully heaving up; Chkheidze, the old eagle, who had contemptuously retired to his own Georgian mountains, there to sicken with consumption; and the high-souled Tseretelly, also mortally stricken, who, nevertheless, would return and pour out his beautiful eloquence for the lost cause. Gotz sat there, Dan, Lieber, Bogdanov, Broido, Fillipovsky – white-faced, hollow-eyed and indignant. Below them the second *siezd* of the All-Russian Soviets boiled and swirled, and over their heads the Military Revolutionary Committee functioned white-hot, holding in its hands the threads of insurrection and striking with a long arm. ... It was 10.40 p.m.

Dan, a mild-faced, baldish figure in a shapeless military surgeon's uniform, was ringing the bell. Silence fell sharply, intense, broken by the scuffling and disputing of the people at the door. ...

'We have the power in our hands,' he began sadly, stopped for a moment, and then went on in a low voice. 'Comrades! The Congress of Soviets is meeting in such unusual circumstances and in such an extraordinary moment that you will understand why the Tsay-ee-kah considers it unnecessary to address you with a political speech. This will become much clearer to you if you will recollect that I am a member of the Tsay-ee-kah, and that at this moment our Party comrades are in the Winter Palace under bombardment, sacrificing themselves to execute the duty put on them by the Tsay-ee-kah.' (Confused uproar.)

'I declare the first session of the Second Congress of Soviets of Workers' and Soldiers' Deputies open!'

The election of the presidium took place amid stir and moving about. Avanessov announced that by agreement of the Bolsheviki, Left Socialist Revolutionaries, and Mensheviki Internationalists, it was decided to base the presidium upon proportionality. Several Mensheviki leaped to their feet protesting. A bearded soldier shouted at them, 'Remember what you did to us Bolsheviki when *we* were in the minority!' Result – 14 Bolsheviki, 7 Socialist Revolutionaries, 3 Mensheviki, and 1 Internationalist (Gorky's group). Hendelmann, for the right and centre Socialist Revolutionaries, said that they refused to take part in the presidium, the same from Khinchuk, for the Mensheviki; and from the Mensheviki Internationalists, that until the verification of certain circumstances, they too could not enter the presidium. Scattering applause and hoots. One voice, 'Renegades, you call yourselves Socialists!' A representative of the Ukrainian delegates demanded, and received, a place. Then the old Tsay-ee-kah stepped

down, and in their places appeared Trotsky, Kameniev, Lunacharsky, Madame Kollontai, Nogin.... The hall rose, thundering.
How far they had soared, these Bolsheviki, from a despised and
hunted sect less than four months ago, to this supreme place, the
helm of great Russia in full tide of insurrection!

The order of the day, said Kameniev, was first Organization of
Power; second, War and Peace; and third, the Constitutional
Assembly. Lozovsky, rising, announced that upon agreement of
the bureaux of all factions, it was proposed to hear and discuss
the report of the Petrograd Soviet, then to give the floor to members of the Tsay-ee-kah and the different parties, and finally to
pass to the order of the day.

But suddenly a new sound made itself heard, deeper than the
tumult of the crowd, persistent, disquieting – the dull shock of
guns. People looked anxiously towards the clouded windows, and
a sort of fever came over them. Martov, demanding the floor,
croaked hoarsely, 'The civil war is beginning, comrades! The
first question must be a peaceful settlement of the crisis. On
principle and from a political standpoint we must urgently discuss
a means of averting civil war. Our brothers are being shot down
in the streets! At this moment, when before the opening of the
Congress of Soviets the question of Power is being settled by
means of a military plot organized by one of the revolutionary
parties –' for a moment he could not make himself heard above
the noise, 'All of the revolutionary parties must face the fact!

The first *vopros* (question) before the Congress is the question of
power, and this question is already being settled by force of arms
in the streets!... We must create a power which will be recognized
by the whole democracy. If the Congress wishes to be the voice of
the revolutionary democracy it must not sit with folded hands
before the developing civil war, the result of which may be a
dangerous outburst of counter-revolution.... The possibility of a
peaceful outcome lies in the formation of a united democratic
authority. ... We must elect a delegation to negotiate with the
other Socialist parties and organizations. ...'

Always the methodical muffled boom of cannon through the
windows, and the delegates, screaming at each other.... So,
with the crash of artillery, in the dark, with hatred, and fear, and
reckless daring, new Russia was being born.

The Left Socialist Revolutionaries and the United Social Democrats supported Martov's proposition. It was accepted. A soldier announced that the All-Russian Peasants' Soviets had refused to send delegates to the Congress; he proposed that a committee be sent with a formal invitation. 'Some delegates are present,' he said. 'I move that they be given votes.' Accepted.

Kharash, wearing the epaulettes of a captain, passionately demanded the floor. 'The political hypocrites who control this Congress,' he shouted, 'told us we were to settle the question of Power – and it is being settled behind our backs, before the Congress opens! Blows are being struck against the Winter Palace, and it is by such blows that the nails are being driven into the coffin of the political party which has risked such an adventure!' Uproar. Followed him Gharra: 'While we are here discussing propositions of peace, there is a battle on in the streets. ... The Socialist Revolutionaries and Mensheviki refuse to be involved in what is happening, and call upon all public forces to resist the attempt to capture the power. ...' Kuchin, delegate of the 12th Army and representative of the Trudoviki: 'I was sent here only for information, and I am returning at once to the front, where all the Army Committees consider that the taking of power by the Soviets, only three weeks before the Constituent Assembly, is a stab in the back of the Army and a crime against the people –!' Shouts of 'Lie! You lie!' ... When he could be heard again, 'Let's make an end of this adventure in Petrograd! I call upon all the delegates to leave this hall in order to save the country and the revolution!' As he went down the aisle in the midst of a deafening noise, people surged upon him, threatening. ... Then an officer with a long brown goatee, speaking suavely and persuasively: 'I speak for the delegates from the front. The Army is imperfectly represented in this Congress, and furthermore, the Army does not consider the Congress of Soviets necessary at this time, only three weeks before the opening of the Constituent –' shouts and stamping, always growing more violent. 'The Army does not consider that the Congress of the Soviets has the necessary authority –' Soldiers began to stand up all over the hall.

'Who are you speaking for? What do you represent?' they cried.

'The Central Executive Committee of the Soviet of the Fifth

Army, the Second F— Regiment, the First N— Regiment, the Third S— Rifles. ...'

'When were you elected? You represent the officers, not the soldiers! What do the soldiers say about it?' Jeers and hoots.

'We, the front group, disclaim all responsibility for what has happened and is happening, and we consider it necessary to mobilize all self-conscious revolutionary forces for the salvation of the Revolution! The front group will leave the Congress. ... The place to fight is out on the streets!'

Immense bawling outcry. 'You speak for the Staff – not for the Army!'

'I appeal to all reasonable soldiers to leave this Congress!'

'Kornilovist! Counter-revolutionist! Provocator!' were hurled at him.

On behalf of the Mensheviki, Khinchuk then announced that the only possibility of a peaceful solution was to begin negotiations with the Provisional Government for the formation of a new Cabinet, which would find support in all strata of society. He could not proceed for several minutes. Raising his voice to a shout he read the Menshevik declaration:

'Because the Bolsheviki have made a military conspiracy with the aid of the Petrograd Soviet, without consulting the other factions and parties, we find it impossible to remain in the Congress, and therefore withdraw, inviting the other groups to follow us and to meet for discussion of the situation!'

'Deserter!' At intervals in the almost continuous disturbance Hendelmann, for the Socialist Revolutionaries, could be heard protesting against the bombardment of the Winter Palace. ... 'We are opposed to this kind of anarchy. ...'

Scarcely had he stepped down when a young, lean-faced soldier, with flashing eyes, leaped to the platform, and dramatically lifted his hand:

'Comrades!' he cried, and there was a hush. 'My *familia* (name) is Peterson – I speak for the Second Lettish Rifles. You have heard the statements of two representatives of the Army committees; these statements would have some value *if their authors had been representatives of the Army* –' Wild applause. '*But they do not represent the soldiers!*' Shaking his fist. 'The Twelfth Army has been insisting for a long time upon the re-election of the Great Soviet and the Army Committee, but just as your own Tsay-ee-kah, our Committee refused to call a meeting of the representatives of the masses until the end of September, so that the reactionaries could elect their own false delegates to this Congress. I tell you now, the Lettish soldiers have many times said, "No more resolutions! No more talk! We want deeds – the Power must be in our hands!" Let these impostor delegates leave the Congress! The Army is not with them!'

The hall rocked with cheering. In the first moments of the session, stunned by the rapidity of events, startled by the sound of cannon, the delegates had hesitated. For an hour hammer-blow after hammer-blow had fallen from that tribune, welding them together but beating them down. Did they stand then alone? Was Russia rising against them? Was it true that the Army was marching on Petrograd? Then this clear-eyed young soldier had spoken, and in a flash they knew it for the truth. . . . *This* was the voice of the soldiers – the stirring millions of uniformed workers and peasants were men like them, and their thoughts and feelings were the same. . . .

More soldiers. . . . Gzhelshakh; for the Front delegates, announcing that they had only decided to leave the Congress by a small majority, and that *the Bolshevik members had not even taken part in the vote*, as they stood for division according to political parties, and not groups. 'Hundreds of delegates from the front,' he said, 'are being elected without the participation of the soldiers because the Army Committees are no longer the real representatives of the rank and file. . . .' Lukianov, crying that officers like Kharash and Khinchuk could not represent the Army in this Congress – but only the high command. 'The real inhabitants of the trenches want with all their hearts the transfer of Power into the hands of the Soviets, and they expect very much from it!' . . . The tide was turning.

Then came Abramovich, for the *Bund*, the organ of the Jewish Social-Democrats – his eyes snapping behind thick glasses, trembling with rage.

'What is taking place now in Petrograd is a monstrous calamity! The *Bund* group joins with the declaration of the Mensheviki and Socialist Revolutionaries and will leave the Congress!' He raised his voice and hand. 'Our duty to the Russian proletariat doesn't permit us to remain here and be responsible for these crimes. Because the firing on the Winter Palace doesn't cease, the Municipal Duma together with the Mensheviki and Socialist Revolutionaries, and the Executive Committee of the Peasants' Soviet, has decided to perish with the Provisional Government, and we are going with them! Unarmed we will expose our breasts to the machine-guns of the Terrorists. .... We invite all delegates to this Congress –' The rest was lost in a storm of hoots, menaces, and curses which rose to a hellish pitch as fifty delegates got up and pushed their way out. ....

Kameniev jangled the bell, shouting, 'Keep your seats and we'll go on with our business!' And Trotsky, standing up with a pale, cruel face, letting out his rich voice in cool contempt, 'All these so-called Socialist compromisers, these frightened Mensheviki, Socialist Revolutionaries; *Bund* – let them go! They are just so much refuse which will be swept away into the garbage-heap of history!'

Riazanov, for the Bolsheviki, stated that at the request of the City Duma the Military Revolutionary Committee had sent a delegation to offer negotiations to the Winter Palace. 'In this way we have done everything possible to avoid bloodshed. ...'

We hurried from the place, stopping for a moment at the room where the Military Revolutionary Committee worked at furious speed, engulfing and spitting out panting couriers, dispatching Commissars armed with power of life and death to all corners of the city, amid the buzz of the telephonographs. The door opened, a blast of stale air and cigarette-smoke rushed out, we caught a glimpse of dishevelled men bending over a map under the glare of a shaded electric-light.... Comrade Josephov-Dukhvinski, a smiling youth with a mop of pale yellow hair, made out passes for us.

When we came into the chill night, all the front of Smolny was one huge park of arriving and departing automobiles, above the sound of which could be heard the far-off slow beat of the cannon. A great motor-truck stood there, shaking to the roar of its engine. Men were tossing bundles into it, and others receiving them, with guns beside them.

'Where are you going?' I shouted.

'Down-town – all over – everywhere!' answered a little work-man, grinning, with a large exultant gesture.

We showed our passes. 'Come along!' they invited. 'But there'll probably be shooting –' We climbed in: the clutch slid home with a raking jar, the great car jerked forward, we all toppled backward on top of those who were climbing in; past the huge fire by the gate, and then the fire by the outer gate, glowing red on the faces of the workmen with rifles who squatted around it, and went bumping at top speed down the Suvorovsky Prospect, swaying from side to side. . . . One man tore the wrapping from a bundle and began to hurl handfuls of papers into the air. We imitated him, plunging down through the dark street with a tail of white papers floating and eddying out behind. The late passer-by stooped to pick them up; the patrols around bonfires on the corners ran out with uplifted arms to catch them. Sometimes armed men loomed up ahead, crying '*Stoi!*' and raising their guns, but our chauffeur only yelled something unintelligible and we hurtled on. . . .

I picked up a copy of the paper, and under a fleeting street-light read:

TO THE CITIZENS OF RUSSIA!

The Provisional Government is deposed. The State Power has passed into the hands of the organ of the Petrograd Soviet of Workers' and Soldiers' Deputies, the Military Revolutionary Committee, which stands at the head of the Petrograd proletariat and garrison.

The cause for which the people were fighting: immediate proposal of a democratic peace, abolition of landlord property-rights over the land, labour control over production, creation of a Soviet Government – that cause is securely achieved.

LONG LIVE THE REVOLUTION OF WORKMEN, SOLDIERS, AND PEASANTS!

> *Military Revolutionary Committee*
> *Petrograd Soviet of Workers' and Soldiers' Deputies*

A slant-eyed, Mongolian-faced man who sat beside me, dressed in a goatskin of Caucasian cape, snapped, 'Look out! Here the provocators always shoot from the windows!' We turned into Znamensky Square, dark and almost deserted, careened around Trubetskoy's brutal statue and swung down the wide Nevsky, three men standing up with rifles ready, peering at the windows. Behind us the street was alive with people running and stooping. We could no longer hear the cannon, and the nearer we drew to the Winter Palace end of the city the quieter and more deserted were the streets. The City Duma was all brightly lighted. Beyond that we made out a dark mass of people, and a line of sailors, who yelled furiously at us to stop. The machine slowed down, and we climbed out.

It was an astonishing scene. Just at the corner of the Ekaterina Canal, under an arc-light, a cordon of armed sailors was drawn across the Nevsky, blocking the way to a crowd of people in column of fours. There were about three or four hundred of them, men in frock coats, well-dressed women, officers – all sorts and conditions of people. Among them we recognized many of the delegates from the Congress, leaders of the Mensheviki and Socialist Revolutionaries; Avksentiev, the lean, red-bearded president of the Peasants' Soviets, Sarokin, Kerensky's spokesman, Khinchuk, Abramovich; and at the head white-bearded old Schreider, Mayor of Petrograd, and Prokopovich, Minister of Supplies in the Provisional Government, arrested that morning and released. I caught sight of Malkin, reporter for the *Russian Daily News*. 'Going to die in the Winter Palace,' he shouted cheerfully. The procession stood still, but from the front of it came loud argument. Schreider and Prokopovich were bellowing at the big sailor who seemed in command.

'We demand to pass!' they cried. 'See, these comrades come from the Congress of Soviets! Look at their tickets! We are going to the Winter Palace!'

The sailor was plainly puzzled. He scratched his head with an enormous hand, frowning. 'I have orders from the Committee not to let anybody go to the Winter Palace,' he grumbled. 'But I will send a comrade to telephone to Smolny. . . .'

'We insist upon passing! We are unarmed! We will march on whether you permit us or not!' cried old Schreider, very much excited.

'I have orders –' repeated the sailor sullenly.

'Shoot us if you want to! We will pass! Forward!' came from all sides. 'We are ready to die, if you have the heart to fire on Russians and comrades! We bare our breasts to your guns!'

'No,' said the sailor, looking stubborn, 'I can't allow you to pass.'

'What will you do if we go forward? Will you shoot?'

'No, I'm not going to shoot people who haven't any guns. We won't shoot unarmed Russian people. . . . '

'We will go forward! What can you do?'

'We will do something!' replied the sailor, evidently at a loss. 'We can't let you pass. We will do something.'

'What will you do? What will you do?'

Another sailor came up, very much irritated. 'We will spank you!' he cried energetically. 'And if necessary we will shoot you too. Go home how, and leave us in peace!'

At this there was a great clamour of anger and resentment. Prokopovich had mounted some sort of box, and waving his umbrella, he made a speech:

'Comrades and citizens!' he said. 'Force is being used against us! We cannot have our innocent blood upon the hands of these ignorant men! It is beneath our dignity to be shot down here in the streets by switchmen –' (What he meant by 'switchmen' I never discovered.) 'Let us return to the Duma and discuss the best means of saving the country and the Revolution!'

Whereupon, in dignified silence, the procession marched around and back up the Nevsky, always in column of fours. And taking advantage of the diversion we slipped past the guards and set off in the direction of the Winter Palace.

Here it was absolutely dark, and nothing moved but pickets of soldiers and Red Guards grimly intent. In front of the Kazan Cathedral a three-inch field-gun lay in the middle of the street, slewed sideways from the recoil of its last shot over the roofs. Soldiers were standing in every doorway talking in loud tones and peering down towards the Police Bridge. I heard one voice saying: 'It is possible that we have done wrong. . . .' At the corners patrols stopped all passers-by – and the composition of these patrols was interesting, for in command of the regular troops was invariably a Red Guard. . . . The shooting had ceased.

Just as we came to the Morskaya somebody was shouting: 'The *yunkers* have sent word that they want us to go and get them out!' Voices began to give commands, and in the thick gloom we made out a dark mass moving forward, silent but for the shuffle of feet and the clinking of arms. We fell in with the first ranks.

Like a black river, filling all the street, without song or cheer we poured through the Red Arch, where the man just ahead of me said in a low voice: 'Look out, comrades! Don't trust them. They will fire, surely!' In the open we began to run, stooping low and bunching together, and jammed up suddenly behind the pedestal of the Alexander Column.

'How many of you did they kill?' I asked.

'I don't know. About ten. ...'

After a few minutes huddling there, some hundreds of men, the Army seemed reassured and without any orders suddenly began again to flow forward. By this time, in the light that streamed out of all the Winter Palace windows, I could see that the first two or three hundred men were Red Guards, with only a few scattered soldiers. Over the barricade of fire-wood we clambered, and leaping down inside gave a triumphant shout as we stumbled on a heap of rifles thrown down by the *yunkers* who had stood there. On both sides of the main gateway the doors stood wide open, light streamed out, and from the huge pile came not the slightest sound.

Carried along by the eager wave of men we were swept into the right-hand entrance, opening into a great bare vaulted room, the cellar of the east wing, from which issued a maze of corridors and staircases. A number of huge packing cases stood about, and upon these the Red Guards and soldiers fell furiously, battering them open with the butts of their rifles, and pulling out carpets, curtains, linen, porcelain, plates, glass-ware. ... One man went strutting around with a bronze clock perched on his shoulder; another found a plume of ostrich feathers, which he stuck in his hat. The looting was just beginning when somebody cried, 'Comrades! Don't take anything. This is the property of the People!' Immediately twenty voices were crying, 'Stop! Put everything back! Don't take anything! Property of the People!' Many hands dragged the spoilers down. Damask and tapestry were snatched from the arms of those who had them; two men took away the bronze clock. Roughly and hastily the things were crammed back in their cases, and self-appointed sentinels stood guard. It was all utterly spontaneous. Through corridors and up staircases the cry could be heard growing fainter and fainter in the distance, 'Revolutionary discipline! Property of the People. . . .'

We crossed back over to the left entrance, in the west wing. There order was also being established. 'Clear the Palace!' bawled a Red Guard, sticking his head through an inner door. 'Come, comrades, let's show that we're not thieves and bandits. Everybody out of the Palace except the Commissars, until we get sentries posted.'

Two Red Guards, a soldier and an officer, stood with revolvers in their hands. Another soldier sat at a table behind them, with pen and paper. Shouts of 'All out! All out!' were heard far and near within, and the Army began to pour through the door, jostling, expostulating, arguing. As each man appeared he was seized by the self-appointed committee, who went through his pockets and looked under his coat. Everything that was plainly not his property was taken away, the man at the table noted it on his paper, and it was carried into a little room. The most amazing assortment of objects were thus confiscated; statuettes, bottles of ink, bed-spreads worked with the Imperial monogram, candles, a small oil-painting, desk blotters, gold-handled swords, cakes of soap, clothes of every description, blankets. One Red Guard carried three rifles, two of which he had taken away from *yunkers*; another had four portfolios bulging with written documents. The culprits either sullenly surrendered or pleaded like children. All talking at once the committee explained that stealing was not worthy of the people's champions; often those who had been caught turned around and began to help go through the rest of the comrades.[28]

Yunkers came out in bunches of three or four. The committee seized upon them with an excess of zeal, accompanying the search with remarks like, 'Ah, Provocators! Kornilovists! Counterrevolutionists! Murderers of the People!' But there was no violence done, although the *yunkers* were terrified. They too had their pockets full of small plunder. It was carefully noted down by the scribe, and piled in the little room. . . . The *yunkers* were disarmed. 'Now, will you take up arms against the People any more?' demanded clamouring voices.

'No,' answered the *yunkers*, one by one. Whereupon they were allowed to go free.

We asked if we might go inside. The committee was doubtful, but the big Red Guard answered firmly that it was forbidden. 'Who are you anyway?' he asked. 'How do I know that you are not all Kerenskys?' (There were five of us, two women.)

'*Pazhal'st*', *tovarishchi!* Way, Comrades!' A soldier and a Red Guard appeared in the door, waving the crowd aside, and other guards with fixed bayonets. After them followed single file half a dozen men in civilian dress - the members of the Provisional Government. First came Kishkin, his face drawn and pale, then Rutenberg, looking sullenly at the floor; Tereshchenko was next, glancing sharply around; he stared at us with cold fixity.... They passed in silence; the victorious insurrectionists crowded to see, but there were only a few angry mutterings. It was only later that we learned how the people in the street wanted to lynch them, and shots were fired – but the sailors brought them safely to Peter-Paul....

In the meanwhile unrebuked we walked into the Palace. There was still a great deal of coming and going, of exploring new-found apartments in the vast edifice, of searching for hidden garrisons of *yunkers* which did not exist. We went upstairs and wandered through room after room. This part of the Palace had been entered also by other detachments from the side of the Neva. The paintings, statues, tapestries, and rugs of the great state apartments were unharmed; in the offices, however, every desk and cabinet had been ransacked, the papers scattered over the floor, and in the living-rooms beds had been stripped of their coverings and wardrobes wrenched open. The most highly prized loot was clothing, which the working people needed. In a room where furniture was stored we came upon two soldiers ripping the elaborate Spanish leather upholstery from chairs. They explained it was to make boots with. ...

The old Palace servants in their blue and red and gold uniforms stood nervously about, from force of habit repeating, 'You can't go in there, *barin!* It is forbidden –' We penetrated at length to the gold and malachite chamber with crimson brocade hangings where the Ministers had been in session all that day and night, and where the *shveitzari* had betrayed them to the Red Guards. The long table covered with green baize was just as they had left it, under arrest. Before each empty seat was pen, ink, and paper; the papers were scribbled over with beginnings of plans of action, rough drafts of proclamations and manifestoes. Most of these were scratched out, as their futility became evident, and the rest of the sheet covered with absent-minded geometrical designs, as the writers sat despondently listening while Minister after Minister proposed chimerical schemes. I took one of these scribbled pages, in the handwriting of Konovalov, which read, 'The Provisional Government appeals to all classes to support the Provisional Government –'

All this time, it must be remembered, although the Winter Palace was surrounded, the Government was in constant communication with the front and with provincial Russia. The Bolsheviki had captured the Ministry of War early in the morning, but they did not know of the military telegraph office in the attic, nor of the private telephone line connecting it with the Winter Palace. In that attic a young officer sat all day, pouring out over the country a flood of appeals and proclamations; and when he heard the Palace had fallen, put on his hat and walked calmly out of the building. ...

Interested as we were, for a considerable time we didn't notice a change in the attitude of the soldiers and Red Guards around us. As we strolled from room to room a small group followed us, until by the time we reached the great picture-gallery where we had spent the afternoon with the *yunkers*, about a hundred men surged in upon us. One giant of a soldier stood in our path, his face dark with sullen suspicion.

'Who are you?' he growled. 'What are you doing here?' The others massed slowly around, staring and beginning to mutter. '*Provocatori!*' I heard somebody say, 'Looters!' I produced our passes from the Military Revolutionary Committee. The soldier took them gingerly, turned them upside down and looked at them without comprehension. Evidently he could not read. He handed them back and spat on the floor. '*Bumagi!* Papers!' said he with contempt. The mass slowly began to close in, like wild cattle around a cow-puncher on foot. Over their heads I caught sight of an officer, looking helpless, and shouted to him. He made for us, shouldering his way through.

'I'm the Commissar,' he said to me. 'Who are you? What is it?' The others held back, waiting. I produced the papers.

'You are foreigners?' he rapidly asked in French. 'It is very dangerous. . . .' Then he turned to the mob, holding up our documents. 'Comrades!' he cried, 'These people are foreign comrades – from America. They have come here to be able to tell their countrymen about the bravery and the revolutionary discipline of the proletarian army!'

'How do you know that?' replied the big soldier. 'I tell you they are provocators! They say they came here to observe the revolutionary discipline of the proletarian army, but they have been wandering freely through the Palace, and how do we know they haven't their pockets full of loot?'

'*Pravilno!*' snarled the others, pressing forward.

'Comrades! Comrades!' appealed the officer, sweat standing out on his forehead. 'I am Commissar of the Military Revolutionary Committee. Do you trust me? Well, I tell you that these passes are signed with the same names that are signed to my pass!'

He led us down through the Palace and out through a door opening on to the Neva quay, before which stood the usual committee going through pockets. . . . 'You have narrowly escaped,' he kept muttering, wiping his face.

'What happened to the Women's Battalion?' we asked.

'Oh – the women!' He laughed. 'They were all huddled up in a back room. We had a terrible time deciding what to do with them – many were in hysterics, and so on. So finally we marched them up to the Finland Station and put them on a train to Leva-shovo, where they have a camp. . . .'[29]

We came out into the cold, nervous night, murmurous with obscure armies on the move, electric with patrols. From across the river, where loomed the darker mass of Peter-Paul came a hoarse shout. . . . Underfoot the sidewalk was littered with broken stucco, from the cornice of the Palace where two shells from the battleship *Avrora* had struck; that was the only damage done by the bombardment.

It was now after three in the morning. On the Nevsky all the street-lights were again shining, the cannon gone, and the only signs of war were Red Guards and soldiers squatting around fires. The city was quiet – probably never so quiet in its history; on that night not a single hold-up occurred, not a single robbery.

But the City Duma Building was all illuminated. We mounted

to the galleried Alexander Hall, hung with its great gold-framed, red-shrouded Imperial portraits. About a hundred people were grouped around the platform, where Skobeliev was speaking. He urged that the Committee of Public Safety be expanded, so as to unite all the anti-Bolshevik elements in one huge organization, to be called the Committee for Salvation of Country and Revolution. And as we looked on, the Committee for Salvation was formed – that Committee which was to develop into the most powerful enemy of the Bolsheviki, appearing, in the next week, sometimes under its own partisan name, and sometimes as the strictly non-partisan Committee of Public Safety. ...

Dan, Gotz, Avksentiev were there, some of the insurgent Soviet delegates, members of the Executive Committee of the Peasants' Soviets, old Prokopovich, and even members of the Council of the Republic – among whom Vinaver and other Cadets. Lieber cried that the convention of the Soviets was not a legal convention, that the old Tsay-ee-kah was still in office. ... An appeal to the country was drafted.

We hailed a cab. 'Where to?' But when we said 'Smolny', the *izvozchik* shook his head. '*Niet!*' said he, 'there are devils. ...' It was only after weary wandering that we found a driver willing to take us – and he wanted thirty roubles, and stopped two blocks away.

The windows of Smolny were still ablaze, motors came and went, and around the still-leaping fires the sentries huddled close, eagerly asking everybody the latest news. The corridors were full of hurrying men, hollow-eyed and dirty. In some of the committee-rooms people lay sleeping on the floor, their guns beside them. In spite of the seceding delegates, the hall of meetings was crowded with people roaring like the sea. As we came in, Kameniev was reading the list of arrested Ministers. The name of Tereshchenko was greeted with thunderous applause, shouts of satisfaction, laughter; Rutenberg came in for less; and at the mention of Palchinsky, a storm of hoots, angry cries, cheers burst forth. ... It was announced that Chudnovsky had been appointed Commissar of the Winter Palace.

Now occurred a dramatic interruption. A big peasant, his bearded face convulsed with rage, mounted the platform and pounded with his fist on the presidium table.

'We, Socialist Revolutionaries, insist on the immediate release of the Socialist Ministers arrested in the Winter Palace! Comrades! Do you know that four comrades who risked their lives and their freedom fighting against tyranny of the Tsar, have been flung into Peter-Paul prison -- the historical tomb of Liberty?' In the uproar he pounded and yelled. Another delegate climbed up beside him and pointed at the presidium.

'Are the representatives of the revolutionary masses going to sit here quietly while the Okhrana of the Bolsheviki tortures their leaders?'

Trotsky was gesturing for silence. 'These "comrades" who are now caught plotting the crushing of the Soviets with the adventurer Kerensky -- is there any reason to handle them with gloves? After 16 and 18 July they didn't use much ceremony with us!' With a triumphant ring in his voice he cried, 'Now that the *oborontsi* and the faint-hearted have gone, and the whole task of defending and saving the Revolution rests on our shoulders, it is particularly necessary to work -- work -- work! We have decided to die rather than give up!'

Followed him a Commissar from Tsarskoye Selo, panting and covered with the mud of his ride. 'The garrison of Tsarskoye Selo is on guard at the gates of Petrograd, ready to defend the Soviets and the Military Revolutionary Committee!' Wild cheers. 'The Cycle Corps sent from the front has arrived at Tsarskoye, and the soldiers are now with us; they recognize the power of the Soviets, the necessity of immediate transfer of land to the peasants and industrial control to the workers. The Fifth Battalion of Cyclists, stationed at Tsarskoye, is ours. ....'

Then the delegate of the Third Cycle Battalion. In the midst of delirious enthusiasm he told how the cycle corps had been ordered *three days before* from the South-west front to the 'defence of Petrograd'. They suspected, however, the meaning of the order; and at the station of Peredolsk were met by representatives of the Fifth Battalion from Tsarskoye. A joint meeting was held, and it was discovered that 'among the cyclists not a single man was found willing to shed the blood of his fathers, or to support a Government of bourgeois and landowners!'

Kapelinsky, for the Mensheviki Internationalists, proposed to elect a special committee to find a peaceful solution to the civil war. 'There isn't any peaceful solution!' bellowed the crowd. 'Victory is the only solution!' The vote was overwhelmingly against, and the Mensheviki Internationalists left the Congress in a whirlwind of jocular insults. There was no longer any panic fear. ... Kameniev from the platform shouted after them, 'The Mensheviki Internationalists claimed "emergency" for the question of "peaceful solution", but they always voted for suspension of the order of the day in favour of declarations of factions which wanted to leave the Congress. It is evident,' finished Kameniev, 'that the withdrawal of all these renegades was decided upon beforehand!'

The assembly decided to ignore the withdrawal of the factions, and proceed to the appeal to the workers, soldiers, and peasants of all Russia.

TO WORKERS, SOLDIERS, AND PEASANTS

The Second All-Russian Congress of Soviets of Workers' and Soldiers' Deputies has opened. It represents the great majority of the Soviets. There are also a number of Peasant deputies. Based upon the will of the great majority of the workers, soldiers, and peasants, based upon the triumphant uprising of the Petrograd workmen and soldiers, the Congress assumes power.

The Provisional Government is deposed. Most of the members of the Provisional Government are already arrested.

The Soviet authority will at once propose an immediate democratic peace to all nations, and an immediate truce on all fronts. It will assure the free transfer of landlord, crown, and monastery lands to the Land Committees, defend the soldiers' rights, enforcing a complete democratization of the Army, establish workers' control over production, ensure the convocation of the Constituent Assembly at the proper date, take means to supply bread to the cities and articles of first necessity to the villages, and secure to all nationalities living in Russia a real right to independent existence.

The Congress resolves: that all local power shall be transferred to the Soviets of Workers', Soldiers', and Peasants' Deputies, which must enforce revolutionary order.

The Congress calls upon the soldiers in the trenches to be watchful and steadfast. The Congress of Soviets is sure that the revolutionary Army will know how to defend the Revolution against all attacks of Imperialism, until the new Government shall have brought about the conclusion of the democratic peace which it will directly propose to all nations. The new Government will take all necessary steps to secure

everything needful to the revolutionary Army, by means of a determined policy of requisition and taxation of the propertied classes, and
also to improve the situation of the soldiers' families.

The Kornilovtsi – Kerensky, Kaledin, and others, are endeavouring to
lead troops against Petrograd. Several regiments, deceived by Kerensky,
have sided with the insurgent People.

Soldiers! Make active resistance to the Kornilovets – Kerensky! Be
on guard!

Railway men! Stop all troop-trains being sent by Kerensky against
Petrograd!

Soldiers, Workers, Clerical employees! The destiny of the Revolution
and democratic peace is in your hands!

Long live the Revolution!

> *The All-Russian Congress of Soviets of Workers' and*
> *Soldiers' Deputies Delegates from the Peasants' Soviets*

It was exactly 5.17 a.m. when Krylenko, staggering with fatigue,
climbed to the tribune with a telegram in his hand.

'Comrades! From the Northern Front. The Twelfth Army
sends greetings to the Congress of Soviets, announcing the formation of a Military Revolutionary Committee which has taken
over the command of the Northern Front!' Pandemonium, men
weeping, embracing each other. 'General Chermissov has recognized the Committee – Commissar of the Provisional Government Voitinsky has resigned!'

So. Lenin and the Petrograd workers had decided on insurrec-
tion, the Petrograd Soviet had overthrown the Provisional
Government, and thrust the *coup d'état* upon the Congress of
Soviets. Now there was all great Russia to win – and then the
world! Would Russia follow and rise? And the world – what of it?
Would the peoples answer and rise, a red world-tide?

Although it was six in the morning, night was yet heavy and
chill. There was only a faint unearthly pallor stealing over the
silent streets, dimming the watch-fires, the shadow of a terrible
dawn grey-rising over Russia. . . .

5 Plunging Ahead

Thursday, 8 November. Day broke on a city in the wildest excitement and confusion, a whole nation heaving up in long hissing swells of storm. Superficially all was quiet; hundreds of thousands of people retired at a prudent hour, got up early and went to work. In Petrograd the streetcars were running, the stores and restaurants open, theatres going, an exhibition of paintings advertised. .... All the complex routine of common life – humdrum even in war-time – proceeded as usual. Nothing is so astounding as the vitality of the social organism – how it persists, feeding itself, clothing itself, amusing itself, in the face of the worst calamities. ...

The air was full of rumours about Kerensky, who was said to have raised the front, and to be leading a great army against the capital. *Volia Naroda* published a *prikaz* launched by him at Pskov:

> The disorders caused by the insane attempt of the Bolsheviki place the country on the verge of a precipice, and demand the effort of our entire will, our courage and the devotion of every one of us, to win through the terrible trial which the fatherland is undergoing. ...
>
> Until the declaration of the composition of the new Government – if one is formed – everyone ought to remain at his post and fulfil his duty towards bleeding Russia. It must be remembered that the least interference with existing Army organizations can bring on irreparable misfortunes by opening the front to the enemy. Therefore it is indispensable to preserve at any price the morale of the troops, by assuring complete order and the preservation of the Army from new shocks, and by maintaining absolute confidence between officers and their subordinates. I order all the chiefs and Commissars, in the name of the safety of the country, to stay at their posts as I myself retain the post of Supreme Commander, until the Provisional Government of the Republic declare its will. ...

In answer, this placard on all the walls:

FROM THE ALL-RUSSIAN CONGRESS OF SOVIETS

The ex-Ministers Konovalov, Kishkin, Tereshchenko, Maliantovich, Nikitin, and others have been arrested by the Military Revolutionary Committee. Kerensky has fled. All Army organizations are ordered to take every measure for the immediate arrest of Kerensky and his conveyance to Petrograd.

All assistance given to Kerensky will be punished as a serious crime against the State.

With brakes released the Military Revolutionary Committee whirled, throwing off orders, appeals, decrees, like sparks. . . .[30] Kornilov was ordered to be brought into Petrograd. Members of the Peasant Land Committees imprisoned by the Provisional Government were declared free. Capital punishment in the army was abolished. Government employees were ordered to continue their work, and threatened with severe penalties if they refused. All pillage, plunder, and speculation were forbidden under pain of death. Temporary Commissars were appointed in the various Ministries: Foreign Affairs, Uritsky and Trotsky; Interior and Justice, Rykov; Labour, Shliapnikov; Finance, Menzhinsky; Public Welfare, Madame Kollontai; Commerce, Ways, and Communications, Riazanov; Navy, the sailor Korbir; Posts and Telegraphs, Spiro; Theatres, Muraviov; State Printing Office, Gherbychev; for the City of Petrograd, Lieutenant Nesterov; for the Northern Front, Pozern. . . .

To the Army, appeal to set up Military Revolutionary Committees. To the railway workers, to maintain order, especially not to delay the transport of food to the cities and the front. . . . In return, they were promised representation in the Ministry of Ways and Communications.

Cossack brothers! [said one proclamation]. You are being led against Petrograd. They want to force you into battle with the revolutionary workers and soldiers of the capital. Do not believe a word that is said by our common enemies, the landowners and the capitalists.

At our Congress are represented all the conscious organizations of workers, soldiers, and peasants of Russia. The Congress also wishes to welcome into its midst the worker-Cossacks. The Generals of the Black Band, henchmen of the landowners, of Nikolai the Cruel, are our enemies.

They tell you the Soviets wish to confiscate the land of the Cossacks.

This is a lie. It is only from the great Cossack landlords that the Revolution will confiscate the land to give it to the people.

Organize Soviets of Cossacks' Deputies! Join with the Soviets of Workers' and Soldiers' Deputies!

Show the Black Band that you are not traitors to the People, and that you do not wish to be cursed by the whole of revolutionary Russia. . . .

Cossack brothers, execute no orders of the enemies of the people. Send your delegates to Petrograd to talk it over with us. . . . The Cossacks of the Petrograd garrison, to their honour, have not justified the hope of the People's enemies. . . .

Cossack brothers! The All-Russian Congress of Soviets extends to you a fraternal hand. Long live the brotherhood of the Cossacks with the soldiers, workers, and peasants of all Russia!

On the other side, what a storm of proclamations posted up, handbills scattered everywhere, newspapers – screaming and cursing and prophesying evil. Now raged the battle of the printing-press – all other weapons being in the hands of the Soviets.

First, the appeal of the Committee for Salvation of Country and Revolution, flung broadcast over Russia and Europe;

TO THE CITIZENS OF THE RUSSIAN REPUBLIC

Contrary to the will of the revolutionary masses, on 7 November the Bolsheviki of Petrograd criminally arrested part of the Provisional Government, dispersed the Council of the Republic, and proclaimed an illegal power. Such violence committed against the Government of revolutionary Russia at the moment of its greatest external danger is an indescribable crime against the fatherland.

The insurrection of the Bolsheviki deals a mortal blow to the cause of national defence, and postpones immeasurably the moment of peace so greatly desired.

Civil war, begun by the Bolsheviki, threatens to deliver the country to the horrors of anarchy and counter-revolution, and cause the failure of the Constituent Assembly, which must affirm the republican régime and transmit to the People for ever their right to the land.

Preserving the continuity of the only legal Governmental power, the Committee for Salvation of Country and Revolution, established on the night of 7 November, takes the initiative in forming a new Provisional Government; which, basing itself on the forces of democracy, will conduct the country to the Constituent Assembly and save it from anarchy and counter-revolution. The Committee for Salvation summons you, citizens, to refuse to recognize the power of violence. Do not obey its orders!

Rise for the defence of the country and the Revolution!

Support the Committee for Salvation!

Signed by the Council of the Russian Republic, the Municipal Duma of Petrograd, the Tsay-ee-kah (*First Congress*), the Executive Committee of the Peasants' Soviets, and from the Congress itself the Front group, the factions of Socialist Revolutionaries, Mensheviki, Populist Socialists, Unified Social Democrats, and the group 'Yedinstvo'.

Then posters from the Socialist Revolutionary party, the Mensheviki *oborontsi*, Peasants' Soviets again; from the Central Army Committee, the Tsentroflot. ...

... Famine will crush Petrograd! (they cried). The German armies will trample on our liberty. Black Hundred *pogroms* will spread over Russia, if we all – conscious workers, soldiers, citizens – do not unite. ...

Do not trust the promises of the Bolsheviki! The promise of immediate peace – is a lie! The promise of bread – a hoax! The promise of land – a fairy tale. ...

They were all in this manner.

Comrades! You have been basely and cruelly deceived! The seizure of power has been accomplished by the Bolsheviki alone. ... They concealed their plots from the other Socialist parties composing the Soviet. ...

You have been promised land and freedom, but the counter-revolution will profit by the anarchy called forth by the Bolsheviki, and will deprive you of land and freedom. ...

The newspapers were as violent.

Our duty (said the *Dielo Naroda*) is to unmask these traitors to the working-class. Our duty is to mobilize all our forces and mount guard over the cause of the Revolution! ...

Izvestia, for the last time, speaking in the name of the old Tsay-ee-kah, threatened awful retribution:

'As for the Congress of Soviets, we affirm that there has been no Congress of Soviets! We affirm that it was merely a private conference of the Bolshevik faction! And in that case, they have no right to cancel the powers of the Tsay-ee-kah. ...'

Novaya Zhizn, while pleading for a new Government that should unite all the Socialist parties, criticized severely the action of the Socialist Revolutionaries and the Mensheviki in quitting the Congress, and pointed out that the Bolshevik insurrection meant one thing very clearly: that all illusions about coalition with the bourgeoisie were henceforth demonstrated vain. ...

Rabochi Put blossomed out as *Pravda*, Lenin's newspaper which had been suppressed in July. It crowed, bristling:

Workers, soldiers, peasants! In March you struck down the tyranny of the clique of nobles. Yesterday you struck down the tyranny of the bourgeois gang. ...
The first task is to guard the approaches to Petrograd.
The second is definitely to disarm the counter-revolutionary elements of Petrograd.
The third is definitely to organize the revolutionary power and assure the realization of the popular programme. ...

What few Cadet organs appeared, and the bourgeoisie, generally, adopted a detached, ironical attitude towards the whole business, a sort of contemptuous 'I told you so' to the other parties. Influential Cadets were to be seen hovering around the Municipal Duma, and on the outskirts of the Committee for Salvation. Other than that, the bourgeoisie lay low, abiding its hour – which could not be far off. That the Bolsheviki would remain in power longer than three days never occurred to anybody – except perhaps to Lenin, Trotsky, the Petrograd workers, and the simpler soldiers. ...

In the high, amphitheatrical Nikolai Hall that afternoon I saw the Duma sitting in *permanence*, tempestuous, grouping around it all the forces of opposition. The old Mayor, Schreider, majestic with his white hair and beard, was describing his visit to Smolny the night before, to protest in the name of the Municipal Self-Government. 'The Duma, being the only existing legal Government in the city, elected by equal, direct and secret suffrage, would not recognize the new power,' he had told Trotsky. And Trotsky had answered, 'There is a constitutional remedy for that. The Duma can be dissolved and re-elected. ...' At this report there was a furious outcry.

'If one recognizes a Government by bayonet,' continued the old man, addressing the Duma, 'well, we have one; but I consider legitimate only a Government recognized by the people, by a

majority, and not one created by the usurpation of a minority!'
Wild applause on all benches except those of the Bolsheviki.
Amid renewed tumult the Mayor announced that the Bolsheviki
were violating Municipal autonomy by appointing Commissars
in many departments.

The Bolshevik speaker shouted, trying to make himself heard,
that the decision of the Congress of Soviets meant that all Russia
backed up the action of the Bolsheviki.

'You!' he cried. 'You are not the real representative of the
people of Petrograd!' Shrieks of 'Insult! Insult!' The old Mayor,
with dignity, reminded him that the Duma was elected by
the freest possible popular vote. 'Yes,' he answered, 'but that
was a long time ago – like the Tsay-ee-kah – like the Army
Committee.'

'There has been no new Congress of Soviets!' they yelled at
him.

'The Bolshevik faction refuses to remain any longer in this nest
of counter-revolution –' Uproar. '– and we demand a re-election
of the Duma. ...' Whereupon the Bolsheviki left the chamber,
followed by cries of 'German agents! Down with the traitors!'

Shingariov, Cadet, then demanded that all Municipal functionaries who had consented to be Commissars of the Military
Revolutionary Committee be discharged from their position and
indicted. Schreider was on his feet, putting a motion to the effect
that the Duma protested against the menace of the Bolsheviki to
dissolve it, and as the legal representative of the population, it
would refuse to leave its post.

Outside, the Alexander Hall was crowded for the meeting of
the Committee for Salvation, and Skobeliev was again speaking.
'Never yet,' he said, 'was the fate of the Revolution so acute,
never yet did the question of the existence of the Russian State
excite so much anxiety, never yet did history put so harshly and
categorically the question – is Russia to be or not to be! The great
hour for the salvation of the Revolution has arrived, and in
consciousness thereof we observe the close union of the live
forces of the revolutionary democracy, by whose organized will a
centre for the salvation of the country and the Revolution has
already been created. ...' And much of the same sort. 'We shall
die sooner than surrender our post!'

Amid violent applause it was announced that the Union of Railway Workers had joined the Committee for Salvation. A few moments later the Post and Telegraph Employees came in; then some Mensheviki Internationalists entered the hall, to cheers. The Railway men said they did not recognize the Bolsheviki and had taken the entire railroad apparatus into their own hands, refusing to entrust it to any usurpatory power. The Telegraphers' delegate declared that the operators had flatly refused to work their instruments as long as the Bolshevik Commissar was in the office. The Postmen would not deliver or accept mail at Smolny. ... All the Smolny telephones were cut off. With great glee it was reported how Uritsky had gone to the Ministry of Foreign Affairs to demand the secret treaties and how Neratov had put him out. The Government employees were all stopping work. ...

It was war – war deliberately planned, Russian fashion: war by strike and sabotage. As we sat there the chairman read a list of names and assignments; so-and-so was to make the round of the Ministries; and another was to visit the banks; some ten or twelve were to work the barracks and persuade the soldiers to remain neutral – 'Russian soldiers, do not shed the blood of your brothers!'; a committee was to go and confer with Kerensky; still others were dispatched to provincial cities, to form branches of the Committee for Salvation, and link together the anti-Bolshevik elements.

The crowd was in high spirits. 'These Bolsheviki *will* try to dictate to the *intelligentsia*? We'll show them!' ... Nothing could be more striking than the contrast between this assemblage and the Congress of Soviets. There, great masses of shabby soldiers, grimy workmen, peasants – poor men, bent and scarred in the brute struggle for existence; here the Menshevik and Socialist Revolutionary leaders – Avksentievs, Dans, Liebers – the former Socialist Ministers – Skobelievs, Chernovs – rubbed shoulders with Cadets like oily Shatsky, sleek Vinaver; with journalists, students, intellectuals of almost all camps. This Duma crowd was well fed, well dressed; I did not see more than three proletarians among them all. ...

News came. Kornilov's faithful Tekhintsi* had slaughtered his guards at Bykhov, and he had escaped. Kaledin was marching

* See Notes and Explanations.

north. . . . The Soviet of Moscow had set up a Military Revolutionary Committee, and was negotiating with the commandant of the city for possession of the arsenal, so that the workers might be armed.

With these facts was mixed an astounding jumble of rumours, distortions, and plain lies. For instance, an intelligent young Cadet, formerly private secretary to Milyukov and then to Tereshchenko, drew us aside and told us all about the taking of the Winter Palace.

'The Bolsheviki were led by German and Austrian officers,' he affirmed.

'Is that so?' we replied, politely. 'How do you know?'

'A friend of mine was there and saw them.'

'How could he tell they were German officers?'

'Oh, because they wore German uniforms!'

There were hundreds of such absurd tales, and they were not only solemnly published by the anti-Bolshevik press, but believed by the most unlikely persons – Socialist Revolutionaries and Mensheviki who had always been distinguished by their sober devotion to facts. . . .

But more serious were the stories of Bolshevik violence and terrorism. For example, it was said and printed that the Red Guards had not only thoroughly looted the Winter Palace, but that they had massacred the *yunkers* after disarming them, had killed some of the Ministers in cold blood; and as for the women soldiers, most of them had been violated, and many had committed suicide because of the tortures they had gone through. . . . All these stories were swallowed whole by the crowd in the Duma. But worse still, the mothers and fathers of the students and the women read these frightful details (often accompanied by lists of names), and towards nightfall the Duma began to be besieged by frantic citizens. . . .

A typical case is that of Prince Tumanov, whose body it was announced in many newspapers had been found floating in the Moika Canal. A few hours later this was denied by the Prince's family, who added that the Prince was under arrest, so the press identified the dead man as General Denissov. The General having also come to life, we investigated, and could find no trace of any body having been found whatever. . . .

As we left the Duma building two boy scouts were distributing handbills[31] to the enormous crowd which blocked the Nevsky in front of the door – a crowd composed almost entirely of business men, shopkeepers, *chinovniki*, clerks. One read:

FROM THE MUNICIPAL DUMA

The Municipal Duma in its meeting of 26 October, in view of the events of the day, decrees: To announce the inviolability of private dwellings. Through the House of Committees it calls upon the population of the town of Petrograd to meet with decisive repulse all attempts to enter by force private apartments, not stopping at the use of arms, in the interests of the self-defence of citizens.

Up on the corner of the Liteiny, five or six Red Guards and a couple of sailors had surrounded a newsdealer and were demanding that he hand over his copies of the Menshevik *Rabochaya Gazeta* (Workers' Gazette). Angrily he shouted at them, shaking his fist, as one of the sailors tore the papers from his stand. An ugly crowd had gathered around, abusing the patrol. One little workman kept explaining doggedly to the people and the newsdealer, over and over again, 'It has Kerensky's proclamation in it. It says we killed Russian people. It will make bloodshed. . . .'

Smolny was tenser than ever, if that were possible. The same running men in the dark corridors, squads of workers with rifles, leaders with bulging portfolios arguing, explaining, giving orders as they hurried anxiously along, surrounded by friends and lieutenants. Men literally out of themselves, living prodigies of sleeplessness and work – men unshaven, filthy, with burning eyes who drove upon their fixed purpose full speed on engines of exaltation. So much they had to do, so much! Take over the Government, organize the City, keep the garrison loyal, fight the Duma and the Committee for Salvation, keep out the Germans, prepare to do battle with Kerensky, inform the provinces what had happened, propagandize from Archangel to Vladivostok. . . . Government and Municipal Employees refusing to obey their Commissars, post and telegraph refusing them communication, railroads stonily ignoring their appeals for trains, Kerensky coming, the garrison not altogether to be trusted, the Cossacks waiting to come out. . . . Against them not only the organized

bourgeoisie, but all the other Socialist parties except the Left
Socialist Revolutionaries, a few Mensheviki Internationalists, and
the Social Democrat Internationalists, and even they undecided
whether to stand by or not. With them, it is true, the workers and
the soldier-masses – the peasants an unknown quantity – but
after all the Bolsheviki were a political faction not rich in trained
and educated men. ...

Riazanov was coming up the front steps, explaining in a sort of
humorous panic that he, Commissar of Commerce, knew nothing
whatever of business. In the upstairs café sat a man all by himself
in the corner, in a goatskin cape and clothes which had been – I
was going to say 'slept in', but of course he hadn't slept – and a
three days' growth of beard. He was anxiously figuring on a dirty
envelope, and biting his pencil meanwhile. This was Menzhinsky,
Commissar of Finance, whose qualifications were that he had
once been a clerk in a French bank.... And these four half-
running down the hall from the office of the Military Revolutionary Committee, and scribbling on bits of paper as they run –
these were Commissars dispatched to the four corners of Russia
to carry the news, argue, or fight – with whatever arguments or
weapons came to hand. ...

The Congress was to meet at one o'clock, and long since
the great meeting-hall had filled, but by seven there was yet
no sign of the presidium.... The Bolshevik and Left Social
Revolutionary factions were in session in their own rooms. All the
live-long afternoon Lenin and Trotsky had fought against compromise. A considerable part of the Bolsheviki were in favour of
giving way so far as to create a joint all-Socialist government.
'We can't hold on!' they cried. 'Too much is against us. We
haven't got the men. We will be isolated, and the whole thing will
fall.' So Kameniev, Riazanov, and others.

But Lenin, with Trotsky beside him, stood firm as a rock.*
'Let the compromisers accept our programme and they can come
in! We won't give way an inch. If there are comrades here who
haven't the courage and the will to dare what we dare, let them

* Lenin was not against an All-Socialist Government, provided it was
responsible to the Soviets and accepted the Bolshevik minimum programme. See *The Errors of Trotskyism*.

leave with the rest of the cowards and conciliators! Backed by the
workers and the soldiers we shall go on.'

At five minutes past seven came word from the left Socialist
Revolutionaries to say that they would remain in the Military
Revolutionary Committee.

'See!' said Lenin. 'They are following!'

A little later, as we sat at the press table in the big hall, an
Anarchist who was writing for the bourgeois papers proposed to
me that we go and find out what had become of the presidium.
There was nobody in the Tsay-ee-kah office, nor in the bureau of
the Petrograd Soviet. From room to room we wandered, through
vast Smolny. Nobody seemed to have the slightest idea where to
find the governing body of the Congress. As we went my companion described the ancient revolutionary activities, his long and
pleasant exile in France. . . . As for the Bolsheviki, he confided to
me that they were common, rude, ignorant persons, without
aesthetic sensibilities. He was a real specimen of the Russian
intelligentsia. . . . So we came at last to room 17, office of the
Military Revolutionary Committee, and stood there in the midst
of all the furious coming and going. The door opened and out
shot a squat, flat-faced man in a uniform without insignia, who
seemed to be smiling – which smile, after a minute, one saw to be
the fixed grin of extreme fatigue. It was Krylenko.

My friend, who was a dapper, civilized-looking young man
gave a cry of pleasure and stepped forward.

'Nikolai Vasilievich!' he said, holding out his hand. 'Don't
you remember me, comrade? We were in prison together.'

Krylenko made an effort and concentrated his mind and sight.
'Why, yes,' he answered finally, looking the other up and down
with an expression of great friendliness. 'You are S—. *Zdra'*-
stvuitye!' They kissed. 'What are you doing in all this?' He waved
his arm around.

'Oh, I'm just looking on. . . . You seem very successful.'

'Yes,' replied Krylenko, with a sort of doggedness, 'the proletarian Revolution is a great success.' He laughed. 'Perhaps –
perhaps, however, we'll meet in prison again!'

When we got out into the corridor again my friend went on
with his explanations. 'You see, I'm a follower of Kropotkin. To

us the Revolution is a great failure; it has not aroused the patriotism of the masses. Of course that only proves that the people are not ready for Revolution. ...'

It was just 8.40 when a thundering wave of cheers announced the entrance of the presidium, with Lenin – great Lenin – among them. A short, stocky figure, with a big head set down on his shoulders, bald and bulging. Little eyes, a snubbish nose, wide generous mouth, and heavy chin; clean-shaven now but already beginning to bristle with the well-known beard of his past and future. Dressed in shabby clothes, his trousers much too long for him. Unimpressive, to be the idol of a mob, loved and revered as perhaps few leaders in history have been. A strange popular leader – a leader purely by virtue of intellect; colourless, humourless, uncompromising and detached, without picturesque idiosyncrasies – but with the power of explaining profound ideas in simple terms, of analysing a concrete situation. And combined with shrewdness, the greatest intellectual audacity.

Kameniev was reading the report of the actions of the Military Revolutionary Committee; abolition of capital punishment in the Army, restoration of the free right of propaganda, release of officers and soldiers arrested for political crimes, orders to arrest Kerensky and confiscation of food supplies in private storehouses. .... Tremendous applause.

Again the representative of the *Bund.* The uncompromising attitude of the Bolsheviki would mean the crushing of the Revolution; therefore, the *Bund* delegates must refuse any longer to sit in the Congress. Cries from the audience, 'We thought you walked out last night! How many more times are you going to walk out?'

Then the representative of the Mensheviki Internationalists. Shouts 'What! You here still?' The speaker explained that only part of the Mensheviki Internationalists left the Congress; the rest were going to stay –

'We consider it dangerous and perhaps even mortal for the Revolution to transfer the power to the Soviets' – interruptions – 'but we feel it our duty to remain in the Congress and vote against the transfer here!'

Other speakers followed, apparently without any order. A delegate of the coal-miners of the Don Basin called upon the

Congress to take measures against Kaledin, who might cut off coal and food from the capital. Several soldiers just arrived from the front brought the enthusiastic greetings of their regiments. .... Now Lenin, gripping the edge of the reading stand, letting his little winking eyes travel over the crowd as he stood there waiting, apparently oblivious to the long-rolling ovation, which lasted several minutes. When it finished, he said simply, 'We shall now proceed to construct the Socialist order!' Again that overwhelming human roar.

'The first thing is the adoption of practical measures to realize peace. .... We shall offer peace to the peoples of all the belligerent countries upon the basis of the Soviet terms – no annexations, no indemnities, and the right of self-determination of peoples. At the same time, according to our promise, we shall publish and repudiate the secret treaties. .... The question of War and Peace is so clear that I think that I may, without preamble, read the project of a Proclamation to the Peoples of All the Belligerent Countries. ....'

His great mouth, seeming to smile, opened wide as he spoke; his voice was hoarse – not unpleasantly so, but as if it had hardened that way after years and years of speaking – and went on monotonously, with the effect of being able to go on for ever. .... For emphasis he bent forward slightly. No gestures. And before him, a thousand simple faces looking up in intent adoration.

PROCLAMATION TO THE PEOPLES AND GOVERNMENTS OF ALL THE BELLIGERENT NATIONS

The Workers' and Peasants' Government, created by the revolution of 6 and 7 November and based on the Soviet of Workers', Soldiers', and Peasants' Deputies, proposes to all the belligerent peoples and to their Governments to begin immediately negotiations for a just and democratic peace.

The Government means by a just and democratic peace, which is desired by the majority of the workers and the labouring classes, exhausted and depleted by the war – that peace which the Russian workers and peasants, after having struck down the Tsarist monarchy, have not ceased to demand categorically – immediate peace without annexations (that is to say without conquest of foreign territory, without forcible annexation of other nationalities), and without indemnities.

The Government of Russia proposes to all the belligerent peoples immediately to conclude such a peace, by showing themselves willing to enter upon decisive steps of negotiations aiming at such a peace, at once, without the slightest delay, before the definitive ratification of all the conditions of such a peace by the authorized assemblies of the people of all countries and of all nationalities.

By annexation or conquest of foreign territory the Government means – conformably to the conception of democratic rights in general, and the rights of the working class in particular – all union to a great and strong State of a small or weak nationality, without the voluntary, clear, and precise expression of its consent and desire; whatever be the moment when such an annexation by force was accomplished, whatever be the degree of civilization of the nation annexed by force or maintained outside the frontiers of another State, no matter if that nation be in Europe or in the far countries across the sea.

If any nation is retained by force within the limits of another State; if, in spite of the desire expressed by it (it matters little if that desire be expressed by the press, by popular meetings, decisions of political parties, or by disorders and riots against national oppression), that nation is not given the right of deciding by free vote – without the slightest constraint, after the complete departure of the armed forces of the nation which has annexed it or wishes to annex it or is stronger in general – the form of its national and political organization, such a union constitutes an annexation – that is to say, conquest and an act of violence.

To continue their war in order to permit the strong and rich nations to divide among themselves the weak and conquered nationalities is considered by the Government the greatest possible crime against humanity, and the Government solemnly proclaims its decision to sign a treaty of peace which will put an end to this war upon the above conditions, equally fair for all nationalities without exception.

The Government abolishes secret diplomacy, expressing before the whole country its firm decision to conduct all the negotiations in the light of day before the people, and will proceed immediately to the full publication of all secret treaties confirmed or concluded by the Government of the landowners and capitalists from March until 7 November 1917. All the clauses of the secret treaties which, as occur in the majority of cases, have for their object to procure advantages and privileges for Russian imperialists, are denounced by the Government immediately and without discussion.

In proposing to all Governments and all peoples to engage in public negotiations for peace, the Government declares itself ready to carry on these negotiations by telegraph, by post, or by pourparlers between the different countries, or at a conference of these representatives. To facilitate these pourparlers, the Government appoints its authorized representatives in the neutral countries.

The Government proposes to all the governments and to all the peoples of all the belligerent countries to conclude an immediate armistice, at the same time suggesting that the armistice ought to last three months, during which time it is perfectly possible, not only to hold the necessary pourparlers between the representatives of all the nations and nationalities without exception drawn into the war or forced to take part in it, but also to convoke authorized assemblies of representatives of the people of all countries, for the purpose of the definite acceptance of the conditions of peace.

In addressing this offer of peace to the Governments and to the peoples of all the belligerent countries, the Provisional Workers' and Peasants' Government of Russia addresses equally and in particular the conscious workers of the three nations most devoted to humanity and the three most important nations among those taking part in the present war – England, France, and Germany. The workers of these countries have rendered the greatest services to the cause of progress and Socialism. The splendid examples of the Chartist movement in England, the series of revolutions, of world-wide historical significance, accomplished by the French proletariat – and finally, in Germany, the historic struggle against the Laws of Exception, an example for the workers of the whole world of prolonged and stubborn action, and the creation of formidable organizations of German proletarians – all these models of proletarian heroism, these monuments of history, are for us a sure guarantee that the workers of these countries will understand the duty imposed upon them to liberate humanity from the horrors and consequences of war; and that these workers, by decisive, energetic, and continued action, will help us to bring to a successful conclusion the cause of peace – and at the same time, the cause of the liberation of the exploited working masses from all slavery and all exploitation.

When the grave thunder of applause had died away, Lenin spoke again:

'We propose to the Congress to ratify this declaration. We address ourselves to the Governments as well as to the peoples, for a declaration which would be addressed only to the peoples of the belligerent countries might delay the conclusion of peace. The conditions of peace, drawn up during the armistice, will be ratified by the Constituent Assembly. In fixing the duration of the armistice at three months, we desire to give to the peoples as long a rest as possible after this bloody extermination, and ample time for them to elect their representatives. This proposal of peace will meet with resistance on the part of the imperialist governments – we don't fool ourselves on that score. But we hope that revolution will soon break out in all the belligerent countries; that is why we address ourselves to the workers of France, England, and Germany. ...

'The revolution of 6 and 7 November,' he ended, 'has opened the era of the Social Revolution. ... The labour movement, in the name of peace and Socialism, shall win, and fulfil its destiny. ...'

There was something quiet and powerful in all this, which stirred the souls of men. It was understandable why people believed when Lenin spoke. ...

By crowd vote it was quickly decided that only representatives of political factions should be allowed to speak on the motion and that speakers should be limited to fifteen minutes.

First Karelin for the Left Socialist Revolutionaries. 'Our faction had no opportunity to propose amendments to the text of the proclamation; it is a private document of the Bolsheviki. But we will vote for it because we agree with its spirit. ...'

For the Social Democrat Internationalists Kramarov, long, stoop-shouldered, and near-sighted – destined to achieve some notoriety as the Clown of the Opposition. Only a Government composed of all the Socialist parties, he said, could possess the authority to take such important action. If a Socialist coalition was formed, his faction would support the entire programme; if not, only part of it. As for the proclamation, the Internationalists were in thorough accord with its main points. ...

Then one after another, amid rising enthusiasm; Ukrainian Social Democracy, support; Lithuanian Social Democracy, support; Populist Socialists, support; Polish Social Democracy, support; Polish Socialists, support – but would prefer a Socialist coalition; Lettish Social Democracy, support. ... Something was kindled in these men. One spoke of the 'coming World-Revolution, of which we are the advance-guard'; another of 'the new age of brotherhood, when all the peoples will become one great family...'. An individual member claimed the floor. 'There is contradiction here,' he said. 'First you offer peace without annexations and indemnities, and then you say you will consider all peace offers. To consider means to accept. ...'

Lenin was on his feet. 'We want a just peace, but we are not afraid of a revolutionary war.... Probably the imperialist Governments will not answer our appeal – but we shall not issue an ultimatum to which it will be easy to say no.... If the German proletariat realizes that we are ready to consider all offers of peace, that will perhaps be the last drop which overflows the bowl – revolution will break out in Germany. ...

'We consent to examine all conditions of peace, but that doesn't mean that we shall accept them. ... For some of our terms we shall fight to the end – but possibly for others will find it impossible to continue the war.... Above all, we want to finish the war. ...'

It was exactly 10.35 when Kameniev asked all in favour of the proclamation to hold up their cards. One delegate dared to raise his hand against, but the sudden outburst around him brought it swiftly down. ... Unanimous.

Suddenly, by common impulse, we found ourselves on our feet, mumbling together into the smooth lifting unison of the *Internationale*. A grizzled old soldier was sobbing like a child. Alexandra Kollontai rapidly winked the tears back. The immense sound rolled through the hall, burst windows and doors and soared into the quiet sky. 'The war is ended! The war is ended!' said a young workman near me, his face shining. And when it was over, as we stood there in a kind of awkward hush, someone in the back of the room shouted, 'Comrades! Let us remember those who have died for liberty!' So we began to sing the Funeral March, that slow, melancholy, and yet triumphant chant, so Russian and so moving. The *Internationale* is an alien air, after all. The Funeral March seemed the very soul of those dark masses whose delegates sat in this hall, building from their obscure visions a new Russia – and perhaps more.

You fell in the fatal fight
For the liberty of the people, for the honour of the people.
You gave up your lives and everything dear to you,
You suffered in horrible prisons,
You went to exile in chains. ...

Without a word you carried your chains because you could not
  ignore your suffering brothers,
Because you believed that justice is stronger than the sword. . . .
The time will come when your surrendered life will count.
That time is near; when tyranny falls the people will rise, great and
  free!
Farewell, brothers, you chose a noble path,
At your grave we swear to fight, to work for freedom and the people's
  happiness. . . .

For this did they lie there, the martyrs of March, in their cold
Brotherhood Grave on Mars Field; for this thousands and tens
of thousands had died in the prisons, in exile, in Siberian mines.
It had not come as they expected it would come, nor as the
intelligentsia desired it; but it had come – rough, strong, impatient of formulas, contemptuous of sentimentalism; *real*. . . .

Lenin was reading the Decree on Land:

(1) All private ownership of land is abolished immediately without
compensation.

(2) All landowners' estates and all lands belonging to the Crown, to
monasteries, church lands with all their live stock and inventoried
property, buildings and all appurtenances, are transferred to the disposition of the township Land Committees and the district Soviets of
Peasants' Deputies until the Constituent Assembly meets.

(3) Any damage whatever done to the confiscated property which
from now on belongs to the whole People, is regarded as a serious
crime, punishable by the revolutionary tribunals. The district Soviets
of Peasants' Deputies shall take all necessary measures for the observ-
ance of the strictest order during the taking over of the landowners'
estates, for the determination of the dimensions of the plots of land and
which of them are subject to confiscation, for the drawing up of an
inventory of the entire confiscated property, and for the strictest revolutionary protection of all the farming property on the land, with all
buildings, implements, cattle, supplies of products, etc., passing into the
hands of the people.

(4) For guidance during the realization of the great land reforms until
their final resolution by the Constituent Assembly, shall serve the
following peasant *nakaz* (instructions),[32] drawn up on the basis of 242
local peasant *nakazi* by the editorial board of the '*Izvestia* of the All-
Russian Soviet of Peasants' Deputies', and published in No. 88 of said
'*Izvestia*' (Petrograd, No. 88, 29 August 1917).

The lands of peasants and of Cossacks serving in the Army shall not be confiscated.

'This is not,' explained Lenin, 'the project of former Minister Chernov, who spoke of "erecting a framework" and tried to realize reforms from above. From below, on the spot will be decided the questions of division of the land. The amount of land received by each peasant will vary according to the locality. ...

'Under the Provisional Government, the *pomieshchiki* flatly refused to obey the orders of the Land Committees – those Land Committees projected by Lvov, brought into existence by Shingariov, and administered by Kerensky!'

Before the debates could begin a man forced his way violently through the crowd in the aisle and climbed upon the platform. It was Pianikh, member of the Executive Committee of the Peasants' Soviets, and he was mad clean through.

'The Executive Committee of the All-Russian Soviets of Peasants' Deputies protests against the arrest of our comrades, the Ministers Salazkin and Mazlov!' he flung harshly in the faces of the crowd. 'We demand their instant release! They are now in Peter-Paul fortress. We must have immediate action! There is not a moment to lose!'

Another followed him, a soldier with a disordered beard and flaming eyes. 'You sit here and talk about giving the land to the peasants, and you commit an act of tyrants and usurpers against the peasants' chosen representatives! I tell you' – he raised his fist – 'if one hair of their heads is harmed you'll have a revolt on your hands!' The crowd stirred confusedly.

Then up rose Trotsky, calm and venomous, conscious of power, greeted with a roar. 'Yesterday the Military Revolutionary Committee decided to release the Socialist Revolutionary and Menshevik Ministers, Mazlov, Salazkin, Gvozdov, and Maliantovich – on principle. That they are still in Peter-Paul is only because we have had so much to do. ... They will, however, be detained at their homes under arrest until we have investigated their complicity in the treacherous acts of Kerensky during the Kornilov affair!'

'Never,' shouted Pianikh, 'in any revolution have such things been seen as go on here!'

'You are mistaken,' responded Trotsky. 'Such things have been seen even in this revolution. Hundreds of our comrades were arrested in the July days. .... When Comrade Kollontai was released from prison by the doctor's orders, Avksentiev placed at her door two former agents of the Tsar's secret police!' The peasants withdrew, muttering, followed by ironical hoots.

The representative of the Left Socialist Revolutionaries spoke on the Land Decree. While agreeing in principle, his faction could not vote on the question until after discussion. The Peasants' Soviets should be consulted. ...

The Mensheviki Internationalists, too, insisted on a party caucus.

Then the leader of the Maximalists, the Anarchist wing of the peasants: 'We must do honour to a political party which puts such an act into effect the first day, without jawing about it!'

A typical peasant was in the tribune, long hair, boots and sheepskin coat, bowing to all corners of the hall. 'I wish you well, comrades and citizens,' he said. 'There are some Cadets walking around outside. You arrested our Socialist peasants – why not arrest them?'

This was the signal for a debate of excited peasants. It was precisely like the debate of soldiers of the night before. Here were the real proletarians of the land. ...

'Those members of our Executive Committee, Avksentiev and the rest, whom we thought were the peasants' protectors – they are only Cadets too! Arrest them! Arrest them!'

Another, 'Who are these Pianikhs, these Avksentievs? They are not peasants at all! They only wag their tails!'

How the crowd rose to them, recognizing brothers!

The Left Socialist Revolutionaries proposed a half-hour intermission. As delegates streamed out, Lenin stood up in his place.

'We must not lose time, comrades! News all-important to Russia must be on the press tomorrow morning. No delay!'

And above the hot discussion, argument, shuffling of feet could be heard the voice of an emissary of the Military Revolutionary Committee, crying, 'Fifteen agitators wanted in room 17 at once! To go to the front!' ...

It was almost two hours and a half later that the delegates came straggling back, the presidium mounted the platform, and the session commenced by the reading of telegrams from regiment after regiment, announcing their adhesion to the Military Revolutionary Committee.

In leisurely manner the meeting gathered momentum. A delegate from the Russian troops on the Macedonian front spoke bitterly of their situation. 'We suffer there more from the friendship of our "Allies" than from the enemy,' he said. Representatives of the Tenth and Twelfth Armies, just arrived in hot haste, reported, 'We support you with all our strength!' A peasant soldier protested against the release of 'the traitor Socialists Mazlov and Salazkin'; as for the Executive Committee of the Peasants' Soviets, it should be arrested *en masse*! Here was real revolutionary talk.... A deputy from the Russian Army in Persia declared he was instructed to demand all power to the Soviets. ... A Ukrainian officer, speaking in his native tongue: 'There is no nationalism in this crisis. ... *Da zdravstvuyet* the proletarian dictatorship of all lands!' Such a deluge of high and hot thoughts that surely Russia would never again be dumb!

Kameniev remarked that the anti-Bolshevik forces were trying to stir up disorders everywhere, and read an appeal of the Congress to all the Soviets of Russia:

The All-Russian Congress of Soviets of Workers' and Soldiers' Deputies, including some Peasants' Deputies, calls upon the local Soviets to take immediate energetic measures to oppose all counter-revolutionary anti-Jewish action and all *pogroms* whatever they may be. The honour of the Workers', Peasants', and Soldiers' Revolution demands that no *pogrom* be tolerated.

The Red Guard of Petrograd, the revolutionary garrison and the sailors have maintained complete order in the capital.

Workers, soldiers, and peasants, you should follow everywhere the example of the workers and soldiers of Petrograd.

Comrade soldiers and Cossacks, on us falls the duty of assuring real revolutionary order.

All revolutionary Russia and the entire world have their eyes on us. ...

At two o'clock the Land Decree was put to the vote, with only one against and the peasant delegates wild with joy. ... So plunged the Bolsheviki ahead, irresistible, overriding hesitation and opposition – the only people in Russia who had a definite programme of action while the others talked for eight long months.

Now arose a soldier, gaunt, ragged and eloquent, to protest against the clause of the *nakaz* tending to deprive military deserters from a share in village land allotments. Bawled at and hissed at first, his simple, moving speech finally made silence. 'Forced against his will into the butchery of the trenches,' he cried, 'which you yourselves, in the Peace decree, have voted senseless as well as horrible, he greeted the Revolution with hope of peace and freedom. Peace? The Government of Kerensky forced him again to go forward into Galicia to slaughter and be slaughtered; to his pleas for peace, Tereshchenko simply laughed.... Freedom? Under Kerensky he found his Committees suppressed, his newspapers cut off, his party speakers put in prison.... At home in his village, the landlords were defying his Land Committees, jailing his comrades. ... In Petrograd the bourgeoisie, in alliance with the Germans, were sabotaging the food and ammunition for the Army. ... He was without boots or clothes. ... Who forced him to desert? The Government of Kerensky, which you have overthrown!' At the end there was applause.

But another soldier hotly denounced it: 'The Government of Kerensky is not a screen behind which can be hidden dirty work like desertion! Deserters are scoundrels, who run away home and leave their comrades to die in the trenches alone! Every deserter is a traitor and should be punished....' Uproar, shouts of '*Do volno! Teeshe!*' Kameniev hastily proposed to leave the matter to the Government for decision.[33]

At 2.30 a.m. fell a tense hush. Kameniev was reading the decree of the Constitution of Power:

Until the meeting of the Constituent Assembly, a provisional Workers' and Peasants' Government is formed, which shall be named the Council of People's Commissars.[34]

The administration of the different branches of state activity shall be entrusted to commissions, whose composition shall be regulated to ensure the carrying out of the programme of the Congress, in close union with the mass organizations of working-men, working-women, sailors, soldiers, peasants, and clerical employees. The governmental power is vested in a *collegium* made up of the chairmen of these commissions, that is to say, the Council of the People's Commissars.

Control over the activities of the People's Commissars, and the right to replace them, shall belong to the All-Russian Congress of Soviets of Workers', Peasants', and Soldiers' Deputies, and its Central Committee.

Still silence; as he read the list of Commissars, bursts of applause after each name, Lenin's and Trotsky's especially.

President of the Council: Vladimir Ulyanov (Lenin).
Interior: A. I. Rykov.
Agriculture: V. P. Milyutin.
Labour: A. G. Shliapnikov.
Military and Naval Affairs: A committee composed of V. A. Avseenko (Antonov), N. V. Krylenko, and F. M. Dybenko.
Commerce and Industry: V. P. Nogin.
Popular Education: A. V. Lunacharsky.
Finance: I. I. Skvortsov (*Stepanov*).
Foreign Affairs: L. D. Bronstein (*Trotsky*).
Justice: G. E. Oppokov (*Lomov*).
Supplies: E. A. Teodorovich.
Post and Telegraph: N. P. Avilov (*Gliebov*).
Chairman for Nationalities: I. V. Djugashvili (*Stalin*).
Railroads: To be filled later.

There were bayonets at the edges of the room, bayonets prick-ing up among the delegates; the Military Revolutionary Com-mittee was arming everybody, Bolshevism was arming for the decisive battle with Kerensky, the sound of whose trumpets came up the south-west wind. . . . In the meanwhile nobody went home; on the contrary, hundreds of newcomers filtered in, filling the great room solid with stern-faced soldiers and workmen who stood for hours and hours, indefatigably intent. The air was thick with cigarette smoke, and human breathing, and the smell of coarse clothes and sweat.

Avilov of the staff of *Novaya Zhizn* was speaking in the name of the Social Democratic Internationalists and the remnant of the Mensheviki Internationalists; Avilov, with his young, intelligent face, looking out of place in his smart frock-coat.

'We must ask ourselves where we are going. . . . The ease with which the Coalition Government was upset cannot be explained by the strength of the left wing of the democracy, but only by the incapacity of the Government to give the people peace and bread. And the left wing cannot maintain itself in power unless it can solve these questions. . . .

'Can it give bread to the people? Grain is scarce. The majority of the peasants will not be with you, for you cannot give them the machinery they need. Fuel and other primary necessities are almost impossible to procure. ...

'As for peace, that will be even more difficult. The Allies refused to talk with Skobeliev. They will never accept the proposition of a peace conference from *you*. You will not be recognized either in London and Paris or in Berlin. ...

' You cannot count on the effective help of the proletariat of the Allied countries because in most countries it is very far from the revolutionary struggle; remember, the Allied democracy was unable to convoke the Stockholm Conference. Concerning the German Social Democrats, I have just talked with Comrade Goldenberg, one of our delegates to Stockholm; he was told by the representatives of the Extreme Left that revolution in Germany was impossible during the war....' Here interruptions began to come thick and fast, but Avilov kept on.

'The isolation of Russia will fatally result either in the defeat of the Russian Army by the Germans, and the patching up of a peace between the Austro-German coalition and the Franco-British coalition *at the expense of Russia* – or in a separate peace with Germany.

'I have just learned that the Allied ambassadors are preparing to leave, and that Committees for Salvation of Country and Revolution are forming in all the cities of Russia. ...

'No one party can conquer these enormous difficulties. The majority of the people, supporting a government of Socialist coalition, can alone accomplish the Revolution. ...'

He then read the resolution of the two factions:

Recognizing that for the salvation of the conquests of the Revolution it is indispensable immediately to constitute a government based on the Soviet of Workers', Soldiers', and Peasants' Deputies, recognizing, moreover, that the task of this government is the quickest possible attainment of peace, the transfer of the land into the hands of the agrarian committees, the organization of control over industrial production, and the convocation of the Constituent Assembly on the date decided, the Congress appoints an executive committee to constitute such a government after an agreement with the groups of the democracy which are taking part in the Congress.

In spite of the revolutionary exaltation of the triumphant crowd, Avilov's cool, tolerant reasoning had shaken them.

Towards the end the cries and hisses died away, and when he finished there was even some clapping.

Karelin followed him – also young, fearless, whose sincerity no one doubted – for the Left Socialist Revolutionaries, the party of Marie Spiridonova, the party which almost alone followed the Bolsheviki, and which represented the revolutionary peasants.

'Our party has refused to enter the Council of People's Commissars because we do not wish for ever to separate ourselves from the part of the revolutionary army which left the Congress, a separation which would make it impossible for us to serve as intermediaries between the Bolsheviki and the other groups of the democracy.... And that is our principal duty at this moment. We cannot sustain any government except a government of Socialist coalition. ...

'We protest, moreover, against the tyrannical conduct of the Bolsheviki. Our Commissars have been driven from their posts. Our only organ, *Znamia Truda* (Banner of Labour), was forbidden to appear yesterday. ...

'The Central Duma is forming a powerful Committee for Salvation of Country and Revolution to fight you. Already you are isolated, and your Government is without the support of a single other democratic group. ...'

And now Trotsky stood upon the raised tribune, confident and dominating, with that sarcastic expression about his mouth which was almost a sneer. He spoke in a ringing voice, and the great crowd rose to him.

'These considerations on the danger of isolation of our party are not new. On the eve of insurrection our fatal defeat was also predicted. Everybody was against us; only a faction of the Socialist Revolutionaries of the Left was with us in the Military Revolutionary Committee. How is it that we were able to overturn the Government almost without bloodshed? ... That fact is the most striking proof that we *were not isolated*. In reality the Provisional Government was isolated; the democratic parties which march against us were isolated, are isolated, and for ever cut off from the proletariat!

'They speak of the necessity for a coalition. There is only one coalition possible – the coalition of the workers, soldiers, and poorest peasants; and it is our party's honour to have realized that coalition. .... What sort of coalition did Avilov mean? A coalition with those who supported the Government of Treason to the People? Coalition doesn't always add to strength. For example, could we have organized the insurrection with Dan and Avksentiev in our ranks?' Roars of laughter.

'Avksentiev gave little bread. Will a coalition with the *oborontsi* furnish more? Between the peasants and Avksentiev, who ordered the arrest of the Land Committees, we choose the peasants! Our Revolution will remain the classic revolution of history. ...

'They accuse us of repelling an agreement with the other democratic parties. But is it we who are to blame? Or must we, as Karelin put it, blame it on a "misunderstanding"? No, comrades. When a party in full tide of revolution, still wreathed in powder-smoke, comes to say, "Here is the Power – take it!" – and when those to whom it is offered go over to the enemy, that is not a misunderstanding ... that is a declaration of pitiless war. And it isn't we who have declared war. ...

'Avilov menaces us with failure of our peace efforts – if we remain "isolated". I repeat, I don't see how a coalition with Skobeliev, or even Tereshchenko, can help us to get peace! Avilov tries to frighten us by the threat of a peace at our expense. And I answer that in any case, if Europe continues to be ruled by the imperialist bourgeoisie, revolutionary Russia will inevitably be lost. ...

'There are only two alternatives; either the Russian Revolution will create a revolutionary moment in Europe, or the European powers will destroy the Russian Revolution!'

They greeted him with an immense crusading acclaim, kindling to the daring of it, with the thought of championing mankind. And from that moment there was something conscious and decided about the insurrectionary masses in all their actions, which never left them.

But on the other side, too, battle was taking form. Kameniev recognized a delegate from the Union of Railway Workers, a hard-faced, stocky man with an attitude of implacable hostility. He threw a bombshell.

'In the name of the strongest organization in Russia I demand the right to speak, and I say to you: the Vikzhel charges me to make known the decision of the Union concerning the constitution of Power. The Central Committee refuses absolutely to support the Bolsheviki if they persist in isolating themselves from the whole democracy of Russia!' Immense tumult all over the hall.

'In 1905, and in the Kornilov days, the Railway Workers were the best defenders of the Revolution. But you did not invite us to your Congress –' Cries, 'It was the old Tsay-ee-kah which did not invite you!' The orator paid no attention. 'We do not recognize the legality of this Congress; since the departure of the Mensheviki and Socialist Revolutionaries there is not a legal quorum. ... The Union supports the old Tsay-ee-kah, and declares that the Congress has no right to elect a new Committee. ...

'The Power should be a Socialist and revolutionary Power, responsible before the authorized organs of the entire revolutionary democracy. Until the constitution of such a power, the Union of Railway Workers, which refuses to transport counter-revolutionary troops to Petrograd, at the same time forbids the execution of any order whatever without the consent of the Vikzhel. The Vikzhel also takes into its hands the entire administration of the railroads of Russia.'

At the end he could hardly be heard for the furious storm of abuse which beat upon him. But it was a heavy blow – that could be seen in the concern on the faces of the presidium. Kameniev, however, merely answered that there could be no doubt of the legality of the Congress, as even the quorum established by the old Tsay-ee-kah was exceeded – in spite of the secession of the Mensheviki and Socialist Revolutionaries. ...

Then came the vote on the Constitution of Power, which carried the Council of People's Commissars into office by an enormous majority. ...

The election of the new Tsay-ee-kah, the new parliament of the Russian Republic, took barely fifteen minutes. Trotsky announced its composition: 100 members, of which 70 Bolsheviki. ... As for the peasants, and the seceding factions, places were to be reserved for them. 'We welcome into the Government all parties and groups which will adopt our programme,' ended Trotsky.

And thereupon the Second All-Russian Congress of Soviets

was dissolved, so that the members might hurry to their homes in the four corners of Russia and tell of the great happenings. . . .

It was almost seven when we woke the sleeping conductors and motor-men of the streetcars which the Street-Railway Workers' Union always kept waiting at Smolny to take the Soviet delegates to their homes. In the crowded car there was less happy hilarity than the night before, I thought. Many looked anxious; perhaps they were saying to themselves, 'Now we are masters, how can we do our will?'

At our apartment-house we were held up in the dark by an armed patrol of citizens and carefully examined. The Duma's proclamation was doing its work. . . .

The landlady heard us come in, and stumbled out in a pink silk wrapper.

'The House Committee has again asked that you take your turn on guard duty with the rest of the men,' she said.

'What's the reason for this guard duty?'

'To protect the house and the women and children.'

'Who from?'

'Robbers and murderers.'

'But suppose there came a Commissar from the Military Revolutionary Committee to search for arms?'

'Oh, that's what they'll say they are. . . . And besides, what's the difference?'

I solemnly affirmed that the Consul had forbidden all American citizens to carry arms – especially in the neighbourhood of the Russian *intelligentsia*. . . .

6 The Committee for Salvation

Friday, 9 November. ...

Novocherkask, 8 November.

In view of the revolt of the Bolsheviki, and their attempt to depose the Provisional Government and to seize the power in Petrograd. ... The Cossack Government declares that it considers these acts criminal and absolutely inadmissible. In consequence, the Cossacks will lend all their support to the Provisional Government, which is a government of coalition. Because of these circumstances, and until the return of the Provisional Government to power, and the restoration of order in Russia, I take upon myself, beginning 7 November, all power in that which concerns the region of the Don.

Signed: ATAMAN KALEDIN
President of the Government of
Cossack Troops

Prikaz of the Minister-President Kerensky, dated at Gatchina:

I, Minister-President of the Provisional Government, and Supreme Commander of all the armed forces of the Russian Republic, declare that I am at the head of regiments from the Front who have remained faithful to the fatherland.

I order all the troops of the military District of Petrograd, who through mistake or folly have answered the appeal of the traitors to the country and the Revolution, to return to their duty without delay.

This order will be read in all regiments, battalions, and squadrons.

Signed: *Minister-President of the Provisional*
Government and Supreme Commander
A. F. KERENSKY

Telegram from Kerensky to the General in Command of the Northern Front:

The town of Gatchina has been taken by the loyal regiments without bloodshed. Detachments of Kronstadt sailors, and of the Semionovsky and Ismailovsky regiments gave up their arms without resistance and joined the Government troops.

I order all the designated units to advance as quickly as possible. The Military Revolutionary Committee has ordered its troops to retreat. ...

Gatchina, about thirty kilometres south-west, had fallen during the night. Detachments of the two regiments mentioned – not the sailors – while wandering captainless in the neighbourhood, had indeed been surrounded by Cossacks and given up their arms; but it was not true that they had joined the Government troops. At this very moment crowds of them, bewildered and ashamed, were up at Smolny trying to explain. They did not think the Cossacks were so near. .... They had tried to argue with the Cossacks. ...

Apparently the greatest confusion prevailed along the revolutionary front. The garrisons of all the little towns southward had split hopelessly, bitterly into two factions – or three: the high command being on the side of Kerensky, in default of anything stronger, the majority of the rank and file with the Soviets, and the rest unhappily wavering.

Hastily the Military Revolutionary Committee appointed to command the defence of Petrograd an ambitious regular Army captain, Muraviov; the same Muraviov who had organized the Death Battalions during the summer, and had once been heard to advise the Government that 'it was too lenient with the Bolsheviki; they must be wiped out'. A man of military mind, who admired power and audacity, perhaps sincerely. ...

Beside my door when I came down in the morning were posted two new orders of the Military Revolutionary Committee, directing that all shops and stores should open as usual, and that all empty rooms and apartments should be put at the disposal of the Committee. ...

For thirty-six hours now the Bolsheviki had been cut off from provincial Russia and the outside world. The railwaymen and telegraphers had refused to transmit their dispatches, the postmen would not handle their mail. Only the Government wireless at Tsarskoye Selo launched half-hourly bulletins and manifestoes to the four corners of heaven; the Commissars of Smolny raced the Commissars of the City Duma on speeding trains half across the earth; and two aeroplanes, laden with propaganda, fled high up towards the front. ...

But the eddies of insurrection were spreading through Russia with a swiftness surpassing any human agency. Helsingfors Soviet passed resolutions of support; Kiev Bolsheviki captured the arsenal and the telegraph station, only to be driven out by delegates of the Congress of Cossacks, which happened to be meeting there; in Kazan, a Military Revolutionary Committee arrested the local garrison staff and the Commissar of the Provisional Government; from far Krasnoyarsk, in Siberia, came news that the Soviets were in control of the Municipal institutions; at Moscow, where the situation was aggravated by a great strike of leather workers on one side and a threat of a general lock-out on the other, the Soviets had voted overwhelmingly to support the action of the Bolsheviki in Petrograd. ... Already a Military Revolutionary Committee was functioning.

Everywhere the same thing happened. The common soldiers and the industrial workers supported the Soviets by a vast majority; the officers, *yunkers*, and middle class generally were on the side of the Government – as were the bourgeois Cadets and the 'moderate' Socialist parties. In all these towns sprang up Committees for Salvation of Country and Revolution, arming for civil war. ...

Vast Russia was in a state of solution. As long ago as 1905 the process had begun; the March Revolution had merely hastened it, and giving birth to a sort of forecast of the new order, had ended by merely perpetuating the hollow structure of the old régime. Now, however, the Bolsheviki, in one night, had dissipated it, as one blows away smoke. Old Russia was no more; human society flowed molten in primal heat, and from the tossing sea of flame was emerging the class struggle, stark and pitiless – and the fragile, slowly cooling crust of new planets. ...

In Petrograd sixteen Ministries were on strike, led by the Ministries of Labour and of Supplies – the only two created by the All-Socialist Government of August.

If ever men stood alone, the 'handful of Bolsheviki' apparently stood alone that grey, chill morning, with all storms towering over them.[35] Back against the wall, the Military Revolutionary Committee struck – for its life. ' *De l'audace, encore de l'audace, et toujours de l'audace....*' At five in the morning the Red Guards entered the printing office of the City Government, confiscated thousands of copies of the Appeal-Protest of the Duma, and suppressed the official Municipal organ – the *Viestnik Gorodskovo Samoupravleniya* (Bulletin of the Municipal Self-Government).

All the bourgeois newspapers were torn from the presses, even the *Golos Soldata*, journal of the old Tsay-ee-kah – which, however, changing its name to *Soldatski Golos*, appeared in an edition of a hundred thousand copies, bellowing rage and defiance:

> The men who began their stroke of treachery in the night, who have suppressed the newspapers, will not keep the country in ignorance long. The country will know the truth! It will appreciate you, Messrs the Bolsheviki! We shall see! ...

As we came down the Nevsky a little after midday the whole street before the Duma building was crowded with people. Here and there stood Red Guards and sailors, with bayoneted rifles, each one surrounded by about a hundred men and women – clerks, students, shopkeepers, *chinovniki* – shaking their fists and bawling insults and menaces. On the steps stood Boy Scouts and officers distributing copies of the *Soldatski Golos*. A workman with a red band around his arm and a revolver in hand was trembling with rage and nervousness in the middle of a hostile throng at the foot of the stairs, demanding the surrender of the papers. ... Nothing like this, I imagine, ever occurred in history. On one side a handful of workmen and common soldiers, with arms in their hands, representing a victorious insurrection – and perfectly miserable; on the other side a frantic mob made up of the kind of people that crowd the sidewalks of Fifth Avenue at noontime, sneering, abusing, shouting, 'Traitors! Provocators! *Oprichniki!*'*

The doors were guarded by students and officers with white arm-bands lettered in red, 'Militia of the Committee of Public Safety', and a half-dozen Boy Scouts came and went. Upstairs the place was all commotion. Captain Gomberg was coming down the stairs. 'They're going to dissolve the Duma,' he said. 'The Bolshevik Commissar is with the Mayor now.' As we reached the top Riazanov came hurrying out. He had been to demand that the Duma recognize the Council of People's Commissars, and the Mayor had given him a flat refusal.

In the offices a great babbling crowd, hurrying, shouting, gesticulating – Government officials, intellectuals, journalists, foreign correspondents, French and British officers. ... The City

* Savage bodyguards of Ivan the Terrible, seventeenth century.

Engineer pointed to them triumphantly. 'The Embassies recognize the Duma as the only power now,' he explained. 'For these Bolshevik murderers and robbers it is only a question of hours. All Russia is rallying to us. . . .'

In the Alexander Hall a monster meeting of the Committee for Salvation. Fillipovsky in the chair and Skobeliev again in the tribune, reporting, to immense applause, new adhesions to the Committee; Executive Committee of Peasants' Soviets, old Tsay-ee-kah, Central Army Committee, Tsentroflot, Menshevik, Socialist Revolutionary and Front group delegates from the Congress of Soviets, Central Committees of the Mensheviki, Socialist Revolutionary, Populist Socialist parties, Yedinstvo group, Peasants' Union, Cooperatives, Zemstvos, Municipalities, Post and Telegraph Unions, Vikzhel, Council of the Russian Republic, Union of Unions,* Merchants' and Manufacturers' Association. . . .

'. . . The power of the Soviets is not a democratic power, but a dictatorship – and not the dictatorship of the proletariat, but *against* the proletariat. All those who have felt or know how to feel revolutionary enthusiasm must join now for the defence of the Revolution. . . .

'The problem of the day is not only to render harmless irresponsible demagogues, but to fight against the counter-revolution. . . . If rumours are true that certain generals in the provinces are attempting to profit by events in order to march on Petrograd with other designs, it is only the more proof that we must establish a solid base of democratic government. Otherwise troubles with the Right will follow troubles from the Left. . . .

'The garrison of Petrograd cannot remain indifferent when citizens buying the *Golos Soldata* and newsboys selling the *Rabochaya Gazeta* are arrested in the streets. . . .

'The hour of resolutions has passed. . . . Let those who have no longer faith in the Revolution retire. . . . To establish a united power we must again restore the prestige of the Revolution. . . .

'Let us swear that either the Revolution shall be saved – or we shall perish!'

The hall rose, cheering, with kindling eyes. There was not a single proletarian anywhere in sight. . . .

* See Notes and Explanations.

Then Weinstein:

'We must remain calm, and not act until public opinion is firmly grouped in support of the Committee for Salvation – then we can pass from the defensive to action!'

The Vikzhel representative announced that his organization was taking the initiative in forming the new Government, and its delegates were now discussing the matter with Smolny.... Followed a hot discussion, were the Bolsheviki to be admitted to the new Government? Martov pleaded for their admission; after all, he said, they represented an important political party. Opinions were very much divided upon this, the right wing Mensheviki and Socialist Revolutionaries, as well as the Populist Socialists, the Cooperatives, and the bourgeois elements being bitterly against. ...

'They have betrayed Russia,' one speaker said. 'They have started civil war and opened the front to the Germans. The Bolsheviki must be mercilessly crushed. ...'

Skobeliev was in favour of excluding both the Bolsheviki and the Cadets.

We got into conversation with a young Socialist Revolutionary, who had walked out of the Democratic Conference together with the Bolsheviki that night when Tseretelly and the 'compromisers' forced Coalition upon the democracy of Russia.

'You here?' I asked him.

His eyes flashed fire. 'Yes!' he cried. 'I left the Congress with my party Wednesday night. I have not risked my life for twenty years and more to submit now to the tyranny of the Dark People. Their methods are intolerable. But they have not counted on the peasants. ... When the peasants begin to act then it is a question of minutes before they are done for.'

'But the peasants – will they act? Doesn't the Land decree settle the peasants? What more do they want?'

'Ah, the Land decree! It is our decree – it is the Socialist Revolutionary programme intact! My party framed that policy, after the most careful compilation of the wishes of the peasants themselves. It is an outrage. ...'

'But if it is your own policy, why do you object? If it is the peasants' wishes, why will the people oppose it?'

'You don't understand! Don't you see that the peasants will

immediately realize that it is all a trick – that these usurpers have stolen the Socialist Revolutionary programme?'

I asked if it were true that Kaledin was marching north.

He nodded and rubbed his hands with a sort of bitter satisfaction. 'Yes. Now you see what these Bolsheviki have done. They have raised the counter-revolution against us. The Revolution is lost. The Revolution is lost.'

'But won't you defend the Revolution?'

'Of course we will defend it – to the last drop of our blood. But we won't cooperate with the Bolsheviki in any way. . . .'

'But if Kaledin comes to Petrograd, and the Bolsheviki defend the city. Won't you join with them?'

'Of course not. We will defend the city also, but we won't support the Bolsheviki. Kaledin is the enemy of the Revolution, but the Bolsheviki are equally enemies of the Revolution.'

'Which do you prefer – Kaledin or the Bolsheviki?'

'It is not a question to be discussed!' he burst out impatiently. 'I tell you the Revolution is lost. And it is the Bolsheviki who are to blame. But listen – why should we talk of such things? Kerensky is coming. . . . Day after tomorrow we shall pass to the offensive. . . . Already Smolny has sent delegates inviting us to form a new Government. But we have them now – they are absolutely impotent. . . . We shall not cooperate. . . .'

Outside there was a shot. We ran to the windows. A Red Guard, finally exasperated by the taunts of the crowd, had shot into it, wounding a young girl in the arm. We could see her being lifted into a cab, surrounded by an excited throng, the clamour of whose voices floated up to us. As we looked, suddenly an armoured automobile appeared around the corner of the Mikhailovsky, its guns slung this way and that. Immediately the crowd began to run, as Petrograd crowds do, falling down and lying still in the street, piled in the gutters, heaped up behind telephone-poles. The car lumbered up to the steps of the Duma and a man stuck his head out of the turret, demanding the surrender of the *Soldatski Golos*. The Boy Scouts jeered and scuttled into the building. After a moment the automobile wheeled undecidedly around and went off up the Nevsky, while some hundreds of men and women picked themselves up and began to dust their clothes. . . .

Inside was a prodigious running about of people with armfuls of *Soldatski Golos*, looking for places to hide them. ...

A journalist came running into the room, waving a paper.

'Here's a proclamation from Krasnov!' he cried. Everybody crowded around. 'Get it printed – get it printed quick, and around to the barracks!'

By order of the Supreme Commander I am appointed commandant of the troops concentrated under Petrograd.

Citizens, soldiers, valorous Cossacks of the Don, of the Kuban, and of the Transbaikal, of the Amur, of the Yenissei, to all you who have remained faithful to your oath I appeal; to you who have sworn to guard inviolate your oath of Cossack – I call upon you to save Petrograd from anarchy, from famine, from tyranny, and to save Russia from the indelible shame to which a handful of ignorant men, bought by the gold of Wilhelm, are trying to submit her.

The Provisional Government, to which you swore fidelity in the great days of March, is not overthrown, but by violence expelled from the edifice in which it held its meetings. However, the Government, with the help of the Front armies, faithful to their duty, with the help of the Council of Cossacks, which has united under its command all the Cossacks, and which, strong with the morale which reigns in its ranks, and acting in accordance with the will of the Russian people, has sworn to serve the country as its ancestors served it in the Troublous Times of 1612, when the Cossacks of the Don delivered Moscow, menaced by the Swedes, the Poles, and the Lithuanians. Your Government still exists. ...

The active army considers these criminals with horror and contempt. Their acts of vandalism and pillage, their crimes, the German mentality with which they regard Russia – stricken down but not yet surrendered – have alienated them from the entire people.

Citizens, soldiers, valorous Cossacks of the Garrison of Petrograd; send me your delegates so that I may know who are the traitors to their country and who are not, that there may be avoided an effusion of innocent blood.

Almost the same moment word ran from group to group that the building was surrounded by Red Guards. An officer strode in, a red band around his arm, demanding the Mayor. A few minutes later he left and old Schreider came out of his office, red and pale by turns.

'A special meeting of the Duma!' he cried. 'Immediately!'

In the big hall proceedings were halted. 'All members of the Duma for a special meeting!'

'What's the matter?'

'I don't know – going to arrest us – going to dissolve the Duma – arresting the members at the door –' so ran the excited comments.

In the Nikolai Hall there was barely room to stand. The Mayor announced that troops were stationed at all the doors, prohibiting all exit and entrance, and that a Commissar had threatened arrest and the dispersal of the Municipal Duma. A flood of impassioned speeches from members, and even from the galleries, responded. The freely elected City Government could not be dissolved by *any* power; the Mayor's person and that of all the members were inviolable; the tyrants, the provocators, the German agents should never be recognized; as for these threats to dissolve us, let them try – only over our dead bodies shall they seize this chamber, where like the Roman senators of old we wait with dignity the coming of the Goths. ...

Resolution, to inform the Dumas and Zemstvos of all Russia by telegraph. Resolution, that it was impossible for the Mayor or the Chairman of the Duma to enter into any relations whatever with representatives of the Military Revolutionary Committee or with the so-called Council of People's Commissars. Resolution, to address another appeal to the population of Petrograd to stand up for the defence of their elected town government. Resolution, to remain in permanent session. ...

In the meanwhile one member arrived with the information that he had telephoned to Smolny, and that the Military Revolutionary Committee said that no orders had been given to surround the Duma, that the troops would be withdrawn. ...

As we went downstairs Riazanov burst in through the front door, very agitated.

'Are you going to dissolve the Duma?' I asked.

'My God, no!' he answered. 'It is all a mistake. I told the Mayor this morning that the Duma would be left alone. ...'

Out on the Nevsky, in the deepening dusk, a long double file of cyclists came riding, guns slung on their shoulders. They halted, and the crowd pressed in and deluged them with questions.

'Who are you? Where do you come from?' asked a fat old man with a cigar in his mouth.

'Twelfth Army. From the Front. We came to support the Soviets against the damn bourgeoisie!'

'Ah!' were furious cries. 'Bolshevik gendarmes! Bolshevik Cossacks!'

A little officer in a leather coat came running down the steps. 'The garrison is turning!' he muttered in my ear. 'It's the beginning of the end of the Bolsheviki. Do you want to see the turn of the tide? Come on!' He started at a half-trot up the Mikhailovsky, and we followed.

'What regiment is it?'

'The Bronneviki. ....' Here was indeed serious trouble. The Bronneviki were the Armoured Car troops, the key to the situation; whoever controlled the Bronneviki controlled the city. 'The Commissars of the Committee for Salvation and the Duma have been talking to them. There's a meeting on to decide. ....'

'Decide what? Which side they'll fight on?'

'Oh, no. That's not the way to do it. They'll never fight against the Bolsheviki. They will vote to remain neutral – and then the *yunkers* and Cossacks –'

The door of the great Mikhailovsky Riding-School yawned blackly. Two sentinels tried to stop us, but we brushed by hurriedly, deaf to their indignant expostulations. Inside only a single arc lamp burned dimly, high up near the roof of the enormous hall, whose forty pilasters and rows of windows vanished in the gloom. Around dimly squatted the monstrous shapes of the armoured cars. One stood alone in the centre of the place, under the light, and round it were gathered some two thousand dun-coloured soldiers, almost lost in the immensity of that imperial building. A dozen men, officers, chairmen of the Soldiers' Committees and speakers, were perched on top of the car, and from the central turret a soldier was speaking. This was Khanjunov, who had been president of last summer's all-Russian Congress of Bronneviki. A lithe, handsome figure in his leather coat with lieutenant's shoulder-straps, he stood, pleading eloquently for neutrality.

'It is an awful thing,' he said, 'for Russians to kill their

Russian brothers. There must not be civil war between soldiers who stood shoulder to shoulder against the Tsar, and conquered the foreign enemy in battles which will go down in history! What have we, soldiers, got to do with these squabbles of political parties? I will not say to you that the Provisional Government was a democratic Government; we want no coalition with the bourgeoisie – no. But we must have a Government of the united democracy, or Russia is lost! With such a Government there will be no need for civil war, and the killing of brother by brother!'

This sounded reasonable – the great hall echoed to the crash of hands and voices.

A soldier climbed up, his face white and strained. 'Comrades!' he cried, 'I come from the Rumanian front, to urgently tell you all: there must be peace! Peace at once! Whoever can give us peace, whether it be the Bolsheviki or this new Government, we will follow. Peace! We at the front cannot fight any longer. We cannot fight either Germans or Russians –' With that he leaped down, and a sort of confused agonized sound rose up from all that surging mass, which burst into something like anger when the next speaker, a Menshevik *oboronets*, tried to say that the war must go on until the Allies were victorious.

'You talk like Kerensky!' shouted a rough voice.

A Duma delegate, pleading for neutrality. Him they listened to, muttering uneasily, feeling him not one of them. Never have I seen men trying so hard to understand, to decide. They never moved, stood staring with a sort of terrible intentness at the speaker, their brows wrinkled with the effort of thought, sweat standing out on their foreheads; great giants of men with the innocent clear eyes of children and the faces of epic warriors. . . .

Now a Bolshevik was speaking, one of their own men, violently, full of hate. They liked him no more than the other. It was not their mood. For the moment they were lifted out of the ordinary run of common thoughts, thinking in terms of Russia, of Socialism, the world, as if it depended on them whether the Revolution were to live or die. . . .

Speaker succeeded speaker, debating amid tense silence, roars of approval, or anger: should we come out or not? Khanjunov returned, persuasive and sympathetic. But wasn't he an officer, and an *oboronets*, however much he talked of peace? Then a workman from Vasili Ostrov, but him they greeted with, 'And are *you* going to give us peace, working-man?' Near us some men, many of them officers, formed a sort of claque to cheer the advocates of neutrality. They kept shouting, 'Khanjunov! Khanjunov!' and whistled insultingly when the Bolsheviki tried to speak.

Suddenly the committee men and officers on top of the automobile began to discuss something with great heat and much gesticulation. The audience shouted to know what was the matter, and all the great mass tossed and stirred. A soldier, held back by one of the officers, wrenched himself loose and held up his hand.

'Comrades!' he cried, 'Comrade Krylenko is here and wants to speak to us.' An outburst of cheers, whistlings, yells of '*Prosim! Prosim! Doloi!* Go ahead! Go ahead! Down with him!' in the midst of which the People's Commissar for Military Affairs clambered up the side of the car, helped by hands before and behind, pushed and pulled from below and above. Rising he stood for a moment, and then walked out on the radiator, put his hands on his hips and looked around smiling, a squat, short-legged figure, bareheaded, without insignia on his uniform.

The claque near me kept up a fearful shouting. 'Khanjunov! We want Khanjunov! Down with him! Shut up! Down with the traitor!' The whole place seethed and roared. Then it began to move like an avalanche bearing down upon us, great black-browed men forcing their way through.

'Who is breaking up our meeting?' they shouted. 'Who is whistling here?' The claque, rudely burst asunder, went flying – nor did they gather again. . . .

'Comrade soldiers!' began Krylenko, in a voice husky with fatigue. 'I cannot speak well to you; I am sorry; but I have not had any sleep for four nights. . . .

'I don't need to tell you that I am a soldier. I don't need to tell you that I want peace. What I must say is that the Bolshevik Party, successful in the Workers' and Soldiers' Revolution, by the help of you and of all the rest of the brave comrades who have hurled down for ever the power of the bloodthirsty bourgeoisie, promised to offer peace to all the peoples, and that has already been done – today!' Tumultuous applause.

'You are asked to remain neutral – to remain neutral while the *yunkers* and the Death Battalions, who are *never* neutral, shoot us down in the streets and bring back to Petrograd Kerensky – or perhaps some other of the gang. Kaledin is marching from the Don. Kerensky is coming from the front. Kornilov is raising the Tekhintsi to repeat his attempt of August. All these Mensheviki and Socialist Revolutionaries who call upon you now to prevent civil war – how have they retained the power except by civil war, that civil war which has endured ever since July, and in which they constantly stood on the side of the bourgeoisie, as they do now?

'How can I persuade you, if you have made up your minds? The question is very plain. On one side are Kerensky, Kaledin, Kornilov, the Mensheviki, Socialist Revolutionaries, Cadets, Dumas, officers. . . . They tell us that their objects are good. On the other side are the workers, the soldiers and sailors, the poorest peasants. The Government is in your hands. You are the masters. Great Russia belongs to you. Will you give it back?'

While he spoke he kept himself up by sheer evident effort of will, and as he went on the deep sincere feeling back of his words broke through the tired voice. At the end he tottered, almost falling; a hundred hands reached up to help him down, and the great dim spaces of the hall gave back the surf of sound that beat upon him.

Khanjunov tried to speak again, but 'Vote! Vote! Vote!' they cried. At length, giving in, he read the resolution: that the Bronneviki withdraw their representative from the Military Revolutionary Committee, and declare their neutrality in the present civil war. All those in favour should go to the right; those opposed, to the left. There was a moment of hesitation, a still expectancy, and then the crowd began to surge faster and faster, stumbling over one another, to the left, hundreds of big soldiers in a solid mass rushing across the dirt floor in the faint light. . . . Near us about fifty men were left stranded, stubbornly in favour, and even as the high roof shook under the shock of victorious roaring, they turned and rapidly walked out of the building – and, some of them, out of the Revolution. . . .

Up at Smolny the new Council of People's Commissars was not idle. Already the first decree was on the presses, to be circulated in thousands through the city streets that night, and shipped in bales by every train southward and east:

In the name of the Government of the Russian Republic, chosen by the All-Russian Congress of Soviets of Workers' and Soldiers' Deputies with participation of peasant deputies, the Council of People's Commissars decrees:

1. That the elections of the Constituent Assembly shall take place at the date determined upon – 12 November.

2. All electoral commissions, organs of self-government, Soviets of Workers', Soldiers', and Peasants' Deputies and soldiers' organizations on the front should make every effort to assure free and regular elections at the date determined upon.

In the name of the Government of the Russian Republic.

President of the Council of People's Commissars,
VLADIMIR ULYANOV – LENIN

In the Municipal building the Duma was in full blast. A member of the Council of the Republic was talking as we came in. The Council, he said, did not consider itself dissolved at all, but merely unable to continue its labours until it secured a new meeting-place. In the meanwhile, its Committee of Elders had determined to enter *en masse* the Committee for Salvation. ... This, I may remark parenthetically, is the last time history mentions the Council of the Russian Republic. ...

Then followed the customary string of delegates from the Ministries, the Vikzhel, the Union of Posts and Telegraphs, for the hundredth time reiterating their determination not to work for the Bolshevik usurpers. A *yunker* who had been in the Winter Palace told a highly coloured tale of the heroism of himself and his comrades, and disgraceful conduct of the Red Guards – all of which was devoutly believed. Somebody read aloud an account in the Socialist Revolutionary paper *Narod*, which stated that five hundred million roubles' worth of damage had been done in the Winter Palace, and describing in great detail the loot and breakage.

From time to time couriers came from the telephone with news. The four Socialist Ministers had been released from prison. Krylenko had gone to Peter-Paul to tell Admiral Verderevsky that the Ministry of Marine was deserted, and to beg him, for the sake of Russia, to take charge under the authority of the Council of People's Commissars; and the old seaman had consented. ... Kerensky was advancing north from Gatchina, the Bolshevik garrisons falling back before him. Smolny had issued another decree, enlarging the powers of the City Duma to deal with food supplies.

This last piece of insolence caused an outburst of fury. He, Lenin, the usurper, the tyrant, whose Commissars had seized the Municipal garage, entered the Municipal warehouses, were interfering with the Supply Committees and the distribution of food – he presumed to define the limits of power of the free, independent, autonomous City Government! One member, shaking his fist, moved to cut off the food of the city if the Bolsheviki dared to interfere with the Supply Committees. ... Another, representative of the Special Supply Committee, reported that the food situation was very grave, and asked that emissaries be sent out to hasten food trains.

Diedonenko announced dramatically that the garrison was wavering. The Semionovsky regiment had already decided to submit to the orders of the Socialist Revolutionary party; the crews of the torpedo-boats on the Neva were shaky. Seven members were at once appointed to continue the propaganda. ...

Then the old mayor stepped into the tribune: 'Comrades and citizens! I have just learned that the prisoners in Peter-Paul are in danger. Fourteen *yunkers* of the Pavlovsk school have been stripped and tortured by the Bolshevik guards. One has gone mad. They are threatening to lynch the Ministers!' There was a whirlwind of indignation and horror, which only grew more violent when a stocky little woman dressed in grey demanded the floor, and lifted up her hard metallic voice. This was Vera Slutskaya, veteran revolutionist and Bolshevik member of the Duma.

'That is a lie and a provocation!' she said, unmoved at the torrent of abuse. 'The Workers' and Peasants' Government, which has abolished the death penalty, cannot permit such deeds. We demand that this story be investigated, at once; if there is any truth in it, the Government will take energetic measures!'

A commission composed of members of all parties was

immediately appointed, and, with the Mayor, sent to Peter-Paul to investigate. As we followed them out, the Duma was appointing another commission to meet Kerensky – to try and avoid bloodshed when he entered the capital. ...

It was midnight when we bluffed our way past the guards at the gates of the fortress, and went forward under the faint glimmer of rare electric lights along the side of the church where lie the tombs of the Tsars, beneath the slender golden spire and chimes, which, for months, continued to play *Bozhe Tsaria Khrani** every day at noon. ... The place was deserted; in most of the windows there were not even lights. Occasionally we bumped into a burly figure stumbling along in the dark, who answered questions with the usual, '*Ya nié znayu*'.

On the left loomed the dark outline of Trubetskoi Bastion, that living grave in which so many martyrs of liberty had lost their lives or their reason in the days of the Tsar, where the Provisional Government had in turn shut up the Ministers of the Tsar, and now the Bolsheviki had shut up the Ministers of the Provisional Government.

A friendly sailor led us to the office of the commandant, in a little house near the Mint. Half a dozen Red Guards, sailors, and soldiers were sitting around a hot room full of smoke, in which a samovar steamed cheerfully. They welcomed us with great cordiality, offering tea. The commandant was not in; he was escorting a commission of '*sabotazhniki*' (sabotageurs) from the City Duma, who insisted that the *yunkers* were all being murdered. This seemed to amuse them very much. At one side of the room sat a bald-headed, dissipated-looking little man in a frock-coat and a rich fur coat, biting his moustache and staring around him like a cornered rat. He had just been arrested. Somebody said, glancing carelessly at him, that he was a Minister or something. ... The little man didn't seem to hear it; he was evidently terrified, although the occupants of the room showed no animosity whatever towards him.

I went across and spoke to him in French. 'Count Tolstoy,' he answered, bowing stiffly. 'I do not understand why I was arrested. I was crossing the Troitsky Bridge on my way home when two of these – of these – persons held me up. I was a

* 'God save the Tsar.'

Commissar of the Provisional Government attached to the General Staff, but in no sense a member of the Government. ...'

'Let him go,' said a sailor. 'He's harmless. ...'

'No,' responded the soldier who had brought the prisoner. 'We must ask the commandant.'

'Oh, the commandant!' sneered the sailor. 'What did you make a revolution for? To go on obeying officers?'

A *praporshchik* of the Pavlovsky regiment was telling us how the insurrection started. 'The *polk* (regiment) was on duty at the General Staff the night of the sixth. Some of my comrades and I were standing guard; Ivan Pavlovich and another man – I don't remember his name – well, they hid behind the window-curtains in the room where the Staff was having a meeting, and they heard a great many things. For example, they heard orders to bring the Gatchina *yunkers* to Petrograd by night, and an order for the Cossacks to be ready to march in the morning. ... The principal points in the city were to be occupied before dawn. Then there was the business of opening the bridges. But when they began to talk about surrounding Smolny, then Ivan Pavlovich couldn't stand it any longer. That minute there was a good deal of coming and going, so he slipped out and came down to the guardroom, leaving the other comrade to pick up what he could.

'I was already suspicious that something was going on. Automobiles full of officers kept coming, and all the Ministers were there. Ivan Pavlovich told me what he had heard. It was half past two in the morning. The secretary of the regimental Committee was there, so we told him and asked what to do.

'"Arrest everybody coming and going!" he says. So we began to do it. In an hour we had some officers and a couple of Ministers, whom we sent up to Smolny right away. But the Military Revolutionary Committee wasn't ready; they didn't know what to do; and pretty soon came back the order to let everybody go and not arrest anybody else. Well, we ran all the way to Smolny, and I guessed we talked for an hour before they finally saw that it was war. It was five o'clock when we got back to the Staff, and by that time most of them were gone. But we got a few, and the garrison was all on the march. ...'

A Red Guard from Vasili Ostrov described in great detail what had happened in his district on the great day of the rising.

'We didn't have any machine-guns over there,' he said, laughing, 'and we couldn't get any from Smolny. Comrade Zalkind, who was a member of the Uprava (Central Bureau) of the Ward Duma, remembered all at once that there was lying in the meeting-room of the Uprava a machine-gun which had been captured from the Germans. So he and I and another comrade went there. The Mensheviki and Socialist Revolutionaries were having a meeting. Well, we opened the door and walked right in on them, as they sat around the table – twelve or fifteen of them, three of us. When they saw us they stopped talking and just stared. We walked right across the room, uncoupled the machine-gun, Comrade Zalkind picked up one part, I the other, we put them on our shoulders and walked out – and not a single man said a word!'

'Do you know how the Winter Palace was captured?' asked a third man, a sailor. 'Along about eleven o'clock we found out there weren't any more *yunkers* on the Neva side. So we broke in the doors and filtered up different stairways one by one or in little bunches. When we got to the top of the stairs the *yunkers* held us up and took away our guns. Still our fellows kept coming up, little by little until we had a majority. Then we turned around and took away the *yunkers*' guns. . . .'

Just then the commandant entered – a merry-looking young non-commissioned officer with his arm in a sling, and deep circles of sleeplessness under his eyes. His eye first fell on the prisoner, who at once began to explain.

'Oh, yes,' interrupted the other. 'You were one of the committee who refused to surrender the Staff Wednesday afternoon. However, we don't want you, citizen. Apologies –' He opened the door and waved his arm for Count Tolstoy to leave. Several of the others, especially the Red Guards, grumbled protests, and the sailor remarked triumphantly, '*Vot!* There! Didn't I say so?'

Two soldiers now engaged his attention. They had been elected a committee of the fortress garrison to protest. The prisoners, they said, were getting the same food as the guards, when there wasn't even enough to keep a man from being hungry. 'Why should the counter-revolutionaries be treated so well?'

'We are revolutionaries, comrades, not bandits,' answered the commandant. He turned to us. We explained that rumours were going about that the *yunkers* were being tortured, and the lives of the Ministers threatened. 'Could we perhaps see the prisoners, so as to be able to tell the world –?'

'No,' said the young soldier irritably. 'I am not going to disturb the prisoners again. I have just been compelled to wake them up – they were sure we were going to massacre them. ... Most of the *yunkers* have been released, anyway, and the rest will go out tomorrow.' He turned abruptly away.

'Could we talk to the Duma commission, then?'

The commandant, who was pouring himself a glass of tea, nodded. 'They are still in the hall,' he said carelessly.

Indeed they stood there just outside the door, in the feeble light of an oil lamp, grouped around the Mayor and talking excitedly.

'Mr Mayor,' I said, 'we are American correspondents. Will you please tell us officially the result of your investigations?'

He turned to us his face of venerable dignity.

'There is no truth in the reports,' he said slowly. 'Except for the incidents which occurred as the Ministers were being brought here, they have been treated with every consideration. As for the *yunkers*, not one has received the slightest injury. ...'

Up the Nevsky, in the empty, after-midnight gloom, an interminable column of soldiers shuffled in silence – to battle Kerensky. In dim back streets automobiles without lights flitted to and fro, and there was a furtive activity in Fontanka 6, headquarters of the Peasants' Soviet, in a certain apartment of a huge building on the Nevsky, and in the Inzhenierny Zamok (School of Engineers); the Duma was illuminated. ...

In Smolny Institute the Military Revolutionary Committee flashed baleful fire, pounding like an overloaded dynamo. ...

7 The Revolutionary Front

Saturday, 10 November. ...

Citizens!

The Military Revolutionary Committee declares that it will not tolerate any violation of revolutionary order.

Theft, brigandage, assault, and attempts at massacre will be severely punished. ...

Following the example of the Paris Commune, the Committee will destroy without mercy any looter or instigator of disorder. ...

Quiet lay the city. Not a hold-up, not a robbery, not even a drunken fight. By night armed patrols went through the silent street, and on the corners, soldiers and Red Guards squatted around little fires, laughing and singing. In the day-time great crowds gathered on the sidewalks listening to interminable hot debates between students and soldiers, businessmen and workmen.

Citizens stopped each other in the street.

'The Cossacks are coming?'

'No. ...'

'What's the latest?'

'I don't know anything. Where's Kerensky?'

'They say only eight versts from Petrograd. ... Is it true that the Bolsheviki have fled to the battleship *Avrora*?'

'They say so. ...'

Only the walls screamed, and the few newspapers; denunciation, appeal, decree. ...

An enormous poster carried the hysterical manifesto of the Executive Committee of the Peasants' Soviets:

... They (the Bolsheviki) dare to say that they are supported by the Soviets of Peasants' Deputies, and that they are speaking on behalf of the peasants' Deputies. ...

Let all the working-class Russia know that this is a LIE AND THAT ALL THE WORKING PEASANTS – in the person of the EXECUTIVE

COMMITTEE OF THE ALL-RUSSIAN SOVIETS OF PEASANTS' DEPU-TIES – refute with indignation all participation of the organized peasantry in this criminal violation of the will of the working class. ...

From the Soldier Section of the Socialist Revolutionary party:

The insane attempt of the Bolsheviki is on the eve of collapse. The garrison is divided. ... The Ministries are on strike and bread is getting scarcer. All factions except the few Bolsheviki have left the Congress. The Bolsheviki are alone. ...

We call upon all sane elements to group themselves around the Committee for Salvation of Country and Revolution, and to prepare themselves to be ready at the first call of the Central Committee. ...

In a handbill the Council of the Republic recited its wrongs:

Ceding to the force of bayonets, the Council of the Republic has been obliged to separate, and temporarily to interrupt its meetings.

The usurpers, with the words 'Liberty and Socialism' on their lips, have set up a rule of arbitrary violence. They have arrested the members of the Provisional Government, closed the newspapers, seized the printing shops. ... This power must be considered the enemy of the people and the Revolution; it is necessary to do battle with it, and to pull it down. ...

The Council of the Republic, until the resumption of its labours, invites the citizens of the Russian Republic to group themselves around the ... local Committees for Salvation of Country and Revolution, which are organizing the overthrow of the Bolsheviki and the creation of a Government capable of leading the country to the Constituent Assembly.

Dielo Naroda said:

A revolution is a rising of all the people. ... But here what have we? Nothing but a handful of poor fools deceived by Lenin and Trotsky. ... Their decrees and their appeals will simply add to the museum of historical curiosities. ...

And *Narodnoye Slovo* (People's Word – Populist Socialist):

'Workers' and Peasants' Government?' That is only a pipe-dream; nobody, either in Russia or in the countries of our Allies, will recognize this 'Government' – or even in the enemy countries. ...

The bourgeois press had temporarily disappeared. ...

Pravda had an account of the first meeting of the new Tsay-ee-kah, now the parliament of the Russian Soviet Republic. Milyutin, Commissar of Agriculture, remarked that the Peasants' Executive Committee had called an All-Russian Peasant Congress for 13 December.

'But we cannot wait,' he said. 'We must have the backing of the peasants. I propose that we call the Congress of Peasants, and do it immediately. ...' The Left Socialist Revolutionaries agreed. An appeal to the Peasants of Russia was hastily drafted, and a committee of five elected to carry out the project.

The question of detailed plans for distributing the land, and the question of the Workers' Control of Industry, were postponed until the experts working on them should submit a report.

Three decrees[36] were read and approved: first, Lenin's 'General Rules for the Press', ordering the suppression of all newspapers inciting to resistance and disobedience to the new Government, inciting to criminal acts, or deliberately perverting the news; the Decree of Moratorium for House-rents; and the Decree Establishing a Workers' Militia. Also orders, one giving the Municipal Duma power to requisition empty apartments and houses, the other directing the unloading of freight-cars in the railroad terminals, to hasten the distribution of necessities and to free the badly needed rolling-stock. ...

Two hours later the Executive Committee of the Peasants' Soviets were sending broadcast over Russia the following telegram:

The arbitrary organization of the Bolsheviki, which is called 'Bureau of Organization for the National Congress of Peasants', is inviting all the Peasants' Soviets to send delegates to the Congress at Petrograd. ...

The Executive Committee of the Soviets of Peasants' Deputies declares that it considers, now as well as before, that it would be dangerous to take away from the provinces at this moment the forces necessary to prepare for elections to the Constituent Assembly, which is the only salvation of the working class and the country. We confirm the date of the Congress of Peasants, *13 December.*

At the Duma all was excitement, officers coming and going, the Mayor in conference with the leaders of the Committee for Salvation. A Councillor ran in with a copy of Kerensky's proclamation, dropped by hundreds from an aeroplane low-flying down the Nevsky, which threatened terrible vengeance on all who did not submit, and ordered soldiers to lay down their arms and assemble immediately in Mars Field.

The Minister-President had taken Tsarskoye Selo, we were told, and was already in the Petrograd campagna, five miles away. He would enter the city tomorrow – in a few hours. The Soviet troops in contact with his Cossacks were said to be going over to the Provisional Government. Chernov was somewhere in between, trying to organize the 'neutral' troops into a force to halt the civil war.

In the city the garrison regiments were leaving the Bolsheviki, they said. Smolny was already abandoned. ... All the Governmental machinery had stopped functioning. The employees of the State Bank had refused to work under Commissars from Smolny, refused to pay out money to them. All the private banks were closed. The Ministries were on strike. Even now a committee from the Duma was making the rounds of the business houses, collecting a fund[37] to pay the salaries of the strikers. ...

Trotsky had gone to the Ministry of Foreign Affairs and ordered the clerks to translate the Decree on Peace into foreign languages, six hundred functionaries had hurled their resignations in his face. ... Shliapnikov, Commissar of Labour, had commanded all the employees of the Ministry to return to their places within twenty-four hours, or lose their places and their pension rights, only the door-servants had responded. ... Some of the branches of the Special Food Supply Committee had suspended work rather than submit to the Bolsheviki. ... In spite of lavish promises of high wages and better conditions, the operators at the Telephone Exchange would not connect Soviet headquarters. ...

The Socialist Revolutionary Party had voted to expel all members who had remained in the Congress of Soviets, and all who were taking part in the insurrection. ...

News from the provinces. Moghilev had declared against the Bolsheviki. At Kiev the Cossacks had overthrown the Soviets and arrested all the insurrectionary leaders. The Soviet and garrison at Luga, thirty thousand strong, affirmed its loyalty to the Provisional Government, and appealed to all Russia to rally around it. Kaledin had dispersed all Soviets and Unions in the Don Basin, and his forces were moving north. ...

Said a representative of the Railway Workers: 'Yesterday we sent a telegram all over Russia demanding that war between the political parties must cease, and insisting on the formation of a coalition Socialist Government. Otherwise we shall call a strike tomorrow night.... In the morning there will be a meeting of all factions to consider the question. The Bolsheviki seem anxious for an agreement....'

'If they last that long!' laughed *he City Engineer, a stout, ruddy man....

As we came up to Smolny – not abandoned, but busier than ever, throngs of workers and soldiers running in and out, and doubled guards everywhere – we met the reporters for the bourgeois and 'moderate' Socialist papers.

'Threw us out!' cried one, from *Volia Naroda*. 'Bonch-Bruevich came down to the Press Bureau and told us to leave! Said we were spies!' They all began to talk at once. 'Insult! Outrage! Freedom of the press!'

In the lobby were great tables heaped with stacks of appeals, proclamations and orders of the Military Revolutionary Committee. Workmen and soldiers staggered past, carrying them to waiting automobiles.

One began:

TO THE PILLORY!

In this tragic moment through which the Russian masses are living, the Mensheviki and their followers and the Right Socialist Revolutionaries have betrayed the working class. They have enlisted on the side of Kornilov, Kerensky, and Savinkov....

They are printing orders of the traitor Kerensky and creating a panic in the city, spreading the most ridiculous rumours of mythical victories by that renegade....

Citizens! Don't believe these false rumours. No power can defeat the People's Revolution.... Premier Kerensky and his followers await speedy and well-deserved punishment....

We are putting them in the Pillory. We are abandoning them to the enmity of the workers, soldiers, sailors, and peasants, on whom they are trying to rivet the ancient chains. They will never be able to wash from their bodies the stain of the people's hatred and contempt....

Shame and curses to the traitors of the People....

The Military Revolutionary Committee had moved into larger quarters, room 17 on the top floor. Red Guards were at the door. Inside, the narrow space in front of the railing was crowded with well-dressed persons, outwardly respectful but inwardly full of murder – bourgeois who want permits for their automobiles, or passports to leave the city, among them many foreigners. . . . Bill Shatov and Peters were on duty. They suspended all other business to read us the latest bulletins.

The One Hundred and Seventy-Ninth Reserve Regiment offers its unanimous support. Five thousand stevedores at the Putilov wharves greet the new Government. Central Committee of the Trade Unions – enthusiastic support. The garrison and squadron at Reval elect Military Committees to cooperate, and dispatch troops. Military Revolutionary Committees control in Pskov and Minsk. Greetings from Soviets of Tsaritzin, Rovno on Don, Chernigovsk, Sevastopol. . . . The Finland Division, the new Committees of the Fifth and Twelfth Armies, offer allegiance. . . .

From Moscow the news is uncertain. Troops of the Military Revolutionary Committee occupy the strategic points of the city; two companies on duty in the Kremlin have gone over to the Soviets, but the Arsenal is in the hands of Colonel Diabtsev and his *yunkers*. The Military Revolutionary Committee demanded arms for the workers, and Diabtsev parleyed with them until this morning, when suddenly he sent an ultimatum to the Committee, ordering Soviet troops to surrender and the Committee to disband. Fighting has begun. . . .

In Petrograd the Staff submitted to Smolny's Commissars at once. The Tsentroflot, refusing, was stormed by Dybenko and a company of Kronstadt sailors, and a new Tsentroflot set up, supported by the Baltic and the Black Sea battleships. . . .

But beneath all the breezy assurances there was a chill premonition, a feeling of uneasiness in the air. Kerensky's Cossacks were coming fast; they had artillery. Skripnik, Secretary of the Factory-Shop Committees, his face drawn and yellow, assured me that there was a whole army corps of them, but he added fiercely, 'They'll never take us alive!' Petrovsky laughed wearily. 'Tomorrow maybe we'll get a sleep – a long one. . . .' Lozovsky, with his emaciated, red-bearded face, said, 'What chance have we? All alone. . . . A mob against trained soldiers!'

South and south-west the Soviets had fled before Kerensky, and the garrisons of Gatchina, Pavlovsk, Tsarskoye Selo were divided – half voting to remain neutral, the rest, without officers, falling back on the capital in the wildest disorder.

In the halls they were posting up bulletins:

FROM KRASNOYE SELO, 10 NOVEMBER, 8 A.M.

To be communicated to all Commanders of Staffs, Commanders-in-Chief, Commanders, everywhere and to all, all, all.

The ex-Minister Kerensky has sent a deliberately false telegram to everyone everywhere to the effect that the troops of revolutionary Petrograd have voluntarily surrendered their arms and joined the armies of the former Government, the Government of Treason, and that the soldiers have been ordered by the Military Revolutionary Committee to retreat. The troops of a free people do not retreat nor do they surrender.

Our troops have left Gatchina in order to avoid bloodshed between ourselves and their mistaken brother-Cossacks, and in order to take a more convenient position, which is at present so strong that if Kerensky and his companions in arms should even increase their forces ten times, still there would be no cause for anxiety. The spirit of our troops is excellent.

In Petrograd all is quiet.

Chief of the Defence of Petrograd and the Petrograd District,
Lieutenant-Colonel MURAVIOV

As we left the Military Revolutionary Committee Antonov entered, a paper in his hand, looking like a corpse.

'Send this,' said he.

TO ALL DISTRICT SOVIETS OF WORKERS' DEPUTIES AND
FACTORY-SHOP COMMITTEES

Order

The Kornilovist bands of Kerensky are threatening the approaches to the capital. All the necessary orders have been given to crush mercilessly the counter-revolutionary attempt against the people and its conquests.

The Army and the Red Guard of the Revolution are in need of the immediate support of the workers.

WE ORDER THE WARD SOVIETS AND FACTORY-SHOP
COMMITTEES:

1. To move out the greatest possible number of workers for the digging of trenches, the erection of barricades and reinforcing of wire entanglements.

2. Wherever it shall be necessary for this purpose to stop work at the factories this shall be done immediately.

3. All common and barbed wire available must be assembled, and also all implements for the digging of trenches and the erection of barricades.

4. All available arms must be taken.

5. THE STRICTEST DISCIPLINE IS TO BE OBSERVED, AND EVERY-ONE MUST BE READY TO SUPPORT THE ARMY OF THE REVOLU-TION BY ALL MEANS.

Chairman of the Petrograd Soviet of Workers' and Soldiers' Deputies,
People's Commissar LEON TROTSKY
Chairman of the Military Revolutionary Committee,
Commander-in-Chief PODVOISKY

As we came out into the dark and gloomy day all around the grey horizon factory whistles were blowing, a hoarse and nervous sound, full of foreboding. By tens of thousands the working-people poured out, men and women; by tens of thousands the humming slums belched out their dun and miserable hordes. Red Petrograd was in danger! Cossacks! South and south-west they poured through the shabby streets towards the Moskovsky Gate, men, women, and children, with rifles, picks, spades, rolls of wire, cartridge-belts over their working clothes. . . . Such an immense, spontaneous outpouring of a city was never seen! They rolled along torrent-like, companies of soldiers borne with them, guns, motor-trucks, wagons – the revolutionary proletariat defending with its breast the capital of the Workers' and Peasants' Republic!

Before the door of Smolny was an automobile. A slight man with thick glasses magnifying his red-rimmed eyes, his speech a painful effort, stood leaning against a mud-guard with his hands in the pockets of a shabby raglan. A great bearded sailor, with the clear eyes of youth, prowled restlessly about, absently toying with an enormous blue-steel revolver, which never left his hand. These were Antonov and Dybenko.

Some soldiers were trying to fasten two military bicycles on the running-board. The chauffeur violently protested; the enamel would get scratched, he said. True, he was a Bolshevik, and the automobile was commandeered from a bourgeois; true, the bicycles were for the use of orderlies. But the chauffeur's professional pride was revolted. . . . So the bicycles were abandoned. . . .

The People's Commissars for War and Marine were going to inspect the revolutionary front – wherever that was. Could we go with them? Certainly not. The automobile only held five – the two Commissars, two orderlies, and the chauffeur. However, a Russian acquaintance of mine, whom I will call Trusishka, calmly got in and sat down, nor could any argument dislodge him. . . .

I see no reason to doubt Trusishka's story of the journey. As they went down the Suvorovsky Prospect someone mentioned food. They might be out for three or four days, in a country indifferently well provisioned. They stopped the car. Money? The Commissar of War looked through his pockets. He hadn't a kopek. The Commissar of Marine was broke. So was the chauffeur. Trusishka bought the provisions. . . .

Just as they turned into the Nevsky a tyre blew out.

'What shall we do?' asked Antonov.

'Commandeer another machine!' suggested Dybenko, waving his revolver. Antonov stood in the middle of the street and signalled a passing machine, driven by a soldier.

'I want that machine,' said Antonov.

'You won't get it,' responded the soldier.

'Do you know who I am?' Antonov produced a paper upon which was written that he had been appointed Commander-in-Chief of all the armies of the Russian Republic, and that everyone should obey him without question.

'I don't care if you're the devil himself,' said the soldier, hotly. 'This machine belongs to the First Machine-Gun Regiment, and we're carrying ammunition in it, and you can't have it. . . .'

The difficulty, however, was solved by the appearance of an old battered taxi-cab, flying the Italian flag. (In time of trouble private cars were registered in the name of foreign consulates, so as to be safe from requisition.) From the interior of this was dislodged a fat citizen in an expensive fur coat, and the party continued on its way.

Arrived at Narvskaya Zastava, about ten miles out, Antonov called for the commandant of the Red Guard. He was led to the edge of the town, where some few hundred workmen had dug trenches and were waiting for the Cossacks.

'Everything all right here, comrade?' asked Antonov.

'Everything perfect, comrade,' answered the commandant. 'The troops are in excellent spirits. . . . Only one thing – we have no ammunition. . . .'

'In Smolny there are two billion rounds,' Antonov told him. 'I will give you an order.' He felt in his pockets. 'Has anyone a piece of paper?'

Dybenko had none – nor the couriers. Trusishka had to offer his note-book. . . .

'Devil! I have no pencil!' cried Antonov. 'Who's got a pencil?' Needless to say, Trusishka had the only pencil in the crowd. . . .

We who were left behind made for the Tsarskoye Selo station. Up the Nevsky, as we passed, Red Guards were marching, all armed, some with bayonets, some without. The early twilight of winter was falling. Heads up they tramped in the chill mud, irregular lines of four, without music, without drums. A red flag crudely lettered in gold, 'Peace! Land!' floated over them. They were very young. The expression on their faces was that of men who know they are going to die. . . . Half-fearful, half-contemptuous, the crowds on the sidewalk watched them pass, in hateful silence. . . .

At the railroad station nobody knew just where Kerensky was, or where the front lay. Trains went no further, however, than Tsarskoye.

Our car was full of commuters and country people going home, laden with bundles and evening papers. The talk was all of the Bolshevik rising. Outside of them, however, one would never have realized that civil war was rending mighty Russia in two, and that the train was headed into the zone of battle. Through the window we could see, in the swiftly deepening darkness, masses of soldiers going along the muddy road towards the city, flinging out their arms in argument. A freight-train, swarming with troops and lit up by huge bonfires, was halted on a siding. That was all. Back along the flat horizon the glow of the city's lights faded down the night. A streetcar crawled distantly along a far-flung suburb. . . .

Tsarskoye Selo station was quiet, but knots of soldiers stood here and there talking in low tones and looking uneasily down the empty track in the direction of Gatchina. I asked some of them which side they were on. 'Well,' said one, 'we don't exactly know the rights of the matter. . . . There is no doubt that Kerensky is a provocator, but we do not consider it right for Russian men to be shooting Russian men.'

In the station commandant's office was a big, jovial, bearded common soldier, wearing the red arm-band of a regimental committee. Our credentials from Smolny commanded immediate respect. He was plainly for the Soviets, but bewildered.

'The Red Guards were here two hours ago, but they went away again. A Commissar came this morning, but he returned to Petrograd when the Cossacks arrived.'

'The Cossacks are here, then?'

He nodded gloomily. 'There has been a battle. The Cossacks came early in the morning. They captured two or three hundred of our men, and killed about twenty-five.'

'Where are the Cossacks?'

'Well, they didn't go this far. I don't know just where they are. Off that way. . . .' He waved his arm vaguely westward.

We had dinner – an excellent dinner, better and cheaper than could be got in Petrograd – in the station restaurant. Near by sat a French officer who had just come on foot from Gatchina. All was quiet there, he said. Kerensky held the town. 'Ah, these Russians,' he went on. 'They are original! What a civil war! Everything except the fighting!'

We sallied out into the town. Just at the door of the station stood two soldiers with rifles and bayonets fixed. They were surrounded by about a hundred business men, Government officials and students, who attacked them with passionate argument and epithet. The soldiers were uncomfortable and hurt, like children unjustly scolded.

A tall young man with a supercilious expression, dressed in the uniform of a student, was leading the attack.

'You realize, I presume,' he said insolently, 'that by taking up arms against your brothers you are making yourselves the tools of murderers and traitors?'

'Now, brother,' answered the soldier earnestly, 'you don't understand. There are two classes, don't you see, the proletariat and the bourgeoisie. We –'

'Oh, I know that silly talk!' broke in the student rudely. 'A bunch of ignorant peasants like you hear somebody bawling a few catch-words. You don't understand what they mean. You just catch them like a lot of parrots.' The crowd laughed. 'I'm a Marxian student. And I tell you that this isn't Socialism you are fighting for. It's just plain pro-German anarchy!'

'Oh, yes, I know,' answered the soldier, with sweat dripping from his brow. 'You are an educated man, that is easy to see, and I am a simple man. But it seems to me –'

'I suppose,' interrupted the other contemptuously, 'that you believe Lenin is a real friend of the proletariat?'

'Yes, I do,' answered the soldier, suffering.

'Well, my friend, do you know that Lenin was sent through Germany in a closed car? Do you know that Lenin took money from the Germans?'

'Well, I don't know much about that,' answered the soldier stubbornly, 'but it seems to me that what he says is what I want to hear, and all the simple men like me. Now there are two classes, the bourgeoisie and the proletariat –'

'You are a fool! Why, my friend, I spent two years in Schlüsselburg for revolutionary activity, when you were still shooting down revolutionists and singing, "God Save the Tsar!" My name is Vasili Georgevich Panyin. Didn't you ever hear of me?'

'I'm sorry to say I never did,' answered the soldier with humility. 'But then, I am not an educated man. You are probably a great hero.'

'I am,' said the student with conviction. 'And I am opposed to the Bolsheviki, who are destroying our Russia, our free Revolution. Now how do you account for that?'

The soldier scratched his head. 'I can't account for it at all,' he said, grimacing with the pain of his intellectual processes. 'To me it seems perfectly simple – but then, I'm not well educated. It seems like there are only two classes, the proletariat and the bourgeoisie –'

'There you go again with your silly formula!' cried the student.

'– only two classes,' went on the soldier, doggedly. 'And whoever isn't on one side is on the other. . . .'

We wandered on up the street, where the lights were few and far between, and where people rarely passed. A threatening silence hung over the place – as of a sort of purgatory between heaven and hell, a political no-man's-land. Only the barber shops were all brilliantly lighted and crowded, and a line formed at the doors of the public bath; for it was Saturday night, when all Russia bathes and perfumes itself. I haven't the slightest doubt that Soviet troops and Cossacks mingled in the places where these ceremonies were performed.

The nearer we came to the Imperial Park, the more deserted were the streets. A frightened priest pointed out the headquarters of the Soviet, and hurried on. It was in the wing of one of the Grand Ducal palaces, fronting the Park. The windows were dark, the door locked. A soldier, lounging about with his hands in the top of his trousers, looked us up and down with gloomy suspicion. 'The Soviet went away two days ago,' said he. 'Where?' A shrug. '*Nié znayu.* I don't know.'

A little further along was a large building, brightly illuminated. From within came a sound of hammering. While we were hesitating, a soldier and a sailor came down the street, hand in hand. I showed them my pass from Smolny. 'Are you for the Soviets?' I asked. They did not answer, but looked at each other in a frightened way.

'What is going on there?' asked the sailor, pointing to the building.

'I don't know.'

Timidly the soldier put out his hand and opened the door a crack. Inside a great hall hung with bunting and evergreens, rows of chairs, a stage being built.

A stout woman with a hammer in her hand and her mouth full of tacks came out. 'What do you want?' she asked.

'Is there a performance tonight?' said the sailor, nervously.

'There will be private theatricals Sunday night,' she answered severely. 'Go away.'

We tried to engage the soldier and sailor in conversation, but they seemed frightened and unhappy, and drew off into the darkness.

We strolled towards the Imperial Palaces, along the edge of the vast, dark gardens, their fantastic pavilions and ornamental bridges looming uncertainly in the night, and soft water splashing from the fountains. At one place, where a ridiculous iron swan spat unceasingly from an artificial grotto, we were suddenly aware of observation, and looked up to encounter the sullen, suspicious gaze of half a dozen gigantic armed soldiers, who stared moodily down from a grassy terrace. I climbed up to them. 'Who are you?' I asked.

'We are the guard,' answered one. They all looked very depressed, as undoubtedly they were, from weeks and weeks of all-day, all-night argument and debate.

'Are you Kerensky's troops or the Soviets'?'

There was a silence for a moment, as they looked uneasily at each other. Then, 'We are neutral,' said he.

We went through the arch of the huge Ekaterina Palace, into the Palace enclosure itself, asking for headquarters. A sentry outside a door in a curving white wing of the Palace said that the commandant was inside.

In a graceful, white Georgian room, divided into unequal parts by a two-sided fire-place, a group of officers stood anxiously talking. They were pale and distracted, and evidently hadn't slept. To one, an oldish man with a white beard, his uniform studded with decorations, who was pointed out as the Colonel, we showed our Bolshevik papers.

He seemed surprised. 'How did you get here without being killed?' he asked politely. 'It is very dangerous in the streets just now. Political passion is running very high in Tsarskoye Selo. There was a battle this morning, and there will be another tomorrow morning. Kerensky is to enter the town at eight o'clock.'

'Where are the Cossacks?'

'About a mile over that way.' He waved his arm.

'And you will defend the city against them?'

'Oh, dear, no!' He smiled. 'We are holding the city for Kerensky.' Our hearts sank, for our passes stated that we were revolutionary to the core. The Colonel cleared his throat. 'About those passes of yours,' he went on. 'Your lives will be in danger if you are captured. Therefore, if you want to see the battle, I will give you an order for rooms in the officers' hotel, and if you will come back here at seven o'clock in the morning, I will give you new passes.'

'So you are for Kerensky?'

'Well, not exactly *for* Kerensky.' The Colonel hesitated. 'You see, most of the soldiers in the garrison are Bolsheviki, and today, after the battle, they all went away in the direction of Petrograd, taking the artillery with them. You might say that none of the *soldiers* are for Kerensky; but some of them just don't want to fight at all. The *officers* have almost all gone over to Kerensky's forces, or simply gone away. We are – ahem – in a most difficult position, as you see. . . .'

He did not believe that there would be any battle. . . .

The Colonel courteously sent his orderly to escort us to the railway station. He was from the south, born of French immigrant parents in Bessarabia. 'Ah,' he kept saying, 'it is not the danger or the hardship that I mind, but being so long, three years, away from my mother. . . .'

Looking out of the window of the train as we sped through the cold dark towards Petrograd, I caught glimpses of clumps of soldiers gesticulating in the light of fires, and of clusters of armoured cars halted together at cross-roads, the chauffeurs hanging out of the turrets and shouting at each other. . . .

All the troubled night over the bleak flats leaderless bands of soldiers and Red Guards wandered, clashing and confused, and the Commissars of the Military Revolutionary Committee hurried from one group to another, trying to organize a defence. . . .

Back in town excited throngs were moving in tides up and down the Nevsky. Something was in the air. From the Warsaw Railway station could be heard far-off cannonade. In the *yunker* schools there was feverish activity. Duma members went from barracks to barracks, arguing and pleading, narrating fearful stories of Bolshevik violence – massacre of the *yunkers* in the Winter Palace, rape of the women soldiers, the shooting of the girl before the Duma, the murder of Prince Tumanov. . . . In the Alexander Hall of the Duma building the Committee for Salvation was in special session; Commissars came and went, running. . . . All the journalists expelled from Smolny were there in high spirits. They did not believe our report of conditions in Tsarskoye. Why, everybody knew that Tsarskoye was in Kerensky's hands, and that the Cossacks were now at Pulkovo. A committee was being elected to meet Kerensky at the railway station in the morning. . . .

One confided to me, in the strictest secrecy, that the counter-revolution would begin at midnight. He showed me two proclamations, one signed by Gotz and Polkovnikov, ordering the *yunker* schools, soldier convalescents in the hospitals, and the Knights of St George to mobilize on a war footing and wait for orders from the Committee for Salvation; the other from the Committee for Salvation itself, which read as follows:

To the Population of Petrograd!
Comrades, workers, soldiers, and citizens of revolutionary Petrograd!
The Bolsheviki, while appealing for peace at the front, are inciting to civil war in the rear.
Do not listen to their provocatory appeals!
Do not dig trenches!
Down with the traitorous barricades!
Lay down your arms!
Soldiers, return to your barracks!
The war begun in Petrograd – is the death of the Revolution!
In the name of liberty, land, and peace, unite all around the Committee for Salvation of Country and Revolution!

As we left the Duma a company of Red Guards, stern-faced and desperate, came marching down the dark, deserted street with a dozen prisoners – members of the local branch of the Council of Cossacks, caught red-handed plotting counter-revolution in their headquarters....

A soldier, accompanied by a small boy with a pail of paste, was sticking up great flaring notices:

By virtue of the present, the city of Petrograd and its suburbs are declared in a state of siege. All assemblies or meetings in the streets, and generally in the open air, are forbidden until further orders.
N. PODVOISKY, President of the Military
Revolutionary Committee

As we went home the air was full of confused sound – automobile horns, shouts, distant shots. The city stirred uneasily, wakeful.

In the small hours of the morning a company of *yunkers*, disguised as soldiers of the Semionovsky Regiment, presented themselves at the Telephone Exchange just before the hour of changing guard. They had the Bolshevik password, and took charge without arousing suspicion. A few minutes later Antonov appeared making a round of inspection. Him they captured and locked in a small room. When the relief came it was met with a blast of rifle-fire, several being killed.

Counter-revolution had begun. . . .

Next morning, Sunday the eleventh, the Cossacks entered Tsarskoye Selo, Kerensky[38] himself riding a white horse and all the church-bells clamouring. From the top of a little hill outside the town could be seen the golden spires and many-coloured cupolas, the sprawling grey immensity of the capital spread along the dreary plain, and beyond, the steely Gulf of Finland.

There was no battle. But Kerensky made a fatal blunder. At seven in the morning he sent word to the Second Tsarskoye Selo Rifles to lay down their arms. The soldiers replied that they would remain neutral, but would not disarm. Kerensky gave them ten minutes in which to obey. This angered the soldiers; for eight months they had been governing themselves by committee, and this smacked of the old régime .... A few minutes later Cossack artillery opened fire on the barracks, killing eight men. From that moment there were no more 'neutral' soldiers in Tsarskoye....

Petrograd woke to bursts of rifle-fire, and the tramping thunder of men marching. Under the high dark sky a cold wind smelt of snow. At dawn the Military Hotel and the Telegraph Agency had been taken by large forces of *yunkers*, and bloodily recaptured. The telephone station was besieged by sailors, who lay behind barricades of barrels, boxes, and tin sheets in the middle of the Morskaya, or sheltered themselves at the corner of the Gorokhovaya, and of St Isaac's Square, shooting at anything that moved. Occasionally an automobile passed in and out, flying the Red Cross flag. The sailors let it pass....

Albert Rhys Williams was in the Telephone Exchange. He went out with the Red Cross automobile which was ostensibly full of wounded. After circulating about the city, the car went by devious ways to the Mikhailovsky *yunker* school, headquarters of the counter-revolution. A French officer, in the courtyard, seemed to be in command.... By this means ammunition and supplies were conveyed to the Telephone Exchange. Scores of these pretended ambulances acted as couriers and ammunition trains for the *yunkers*.

Five or six armoured cars, belonging to the disbanded British Armoured Car Division, were in their hands. As Louise Bryant was going along St Isaac's Square one came rolling up from the Admiralty, on its way to the Telephone Exchange. At the corner of Ulitsa Gogolia, right in front of her, the engine stalled. Some sailors ambushed behind wood-piles began shooting. The machine-gun in the turret of the thing slewed around and spat a hail of bullets indiscriminately into the wood-piles and the crowd. In the archway where Miss Bryant stood seven people were shot dead, among them two little boys. Suddenly, with a shout, the sailors leaped up and rushed into the flaming open, closing around the monster, they thrust their bayonets into the loopholes again and again, yelling.... The chauffeur pretended to be wounded, and they let him go free – to run to the Duma and swell the tale of Bolshevik atrocities.... Among the dead was a British officer....

Later the newspapers told of another French officer, captured in a *yunker* armoured car and sent to Peter-Paul. The French Embassy promptly denied this, but one of the City Councillors told me that he himself had procured the officer's release from prison....

Whatever the official attitude of the Allied Embassies, individual French and British officers were active these days, even to the extent of giving advice at executive sessions of the Committee for Salvation.

All day long in every quarter of the city there were skirmishes between *yunkers* and Red Guards, battles between armoured cars.... Volleys, single shots, and the shrill chatter of machine-guns could be heard, far and near. The iron shutters of the shops were drawn, but business still went on. Even the moving-picture shows, all outside lights dark, played to crowded houses. The streetcars ran. The telephones were all working; when you called Central, shooting could be plainly heard over the wire.... Smolny was cut off, but the Duma and the Committee for Salvation were in constant communication with all the *yunker* schools and with Kerensky at Tsarskoye.

At seven in the morning the Vladimir *yunker* school was visited by a patrol of soldiers, sailors, and Red Guards, who gave the *yunkers* twenty minutes to lay down their arms. The ultimatum was rejected. An hour later the *yunkers* got ready to march, but were driven back by a violent fusillade from the corner of the Grebetskaya and the Bolshoy Prospekt. Soviet troops surrounded the building and opened fire, two armoured cars cruising back and forth with machine-guns raking it. The *yunkers* telephoned for help. The Cossacks replied that they dare not come, because a large body of sailors with two cannon commanded their barracks. The Pavlovsk school was surrounded. Most of the Mikhailov *yunkers* were fighting in the streets....

At half past seven three field-pieces arrived. Another demand to surrender was met by the *yunkers* shooting down two of the Soviet delegates under the white flag. Now began a real bombardment. Great holes were torn in the walls of the school. The *yunkers* defended themselves desperately; shouting waves of Red Guards, assaulting, crumpled under the withering blast.... Kerensky telephoned from Tsarskoye to refuse all parley with the Military Revolutionary Committee.

Frenzied by defeat and their heaps of dead, the Soviet troops opened a tornado of steel and flame against the battered building. Their own officers could not stop the terrible bombardment. A Commissar from Smolny named Kirilov tried to halt it; he was threatened with lynching. The Red Guards' blood was up.

At half past two the *yunkers* hoisted a white flag; they would surrender if they were guaranteed protection. This was promised. With a rush and a shout thousands of soldiers and Red Guards poured through windows, doors, and holes in the wall. Before it could be stopped five *yunkers* were beaten and stabbed to death. The rest, about two hundred, were taken to Peter-Paul under escort, in small groups so as to avoid notice. On the way a mob set upon the party, killing eight more *yunkers*.... More than a hundred Red Guards and soldiers had fallen....

Two hours later the Duma got a telephone message that the victors were marching towards the Inzhenierny Zamok – the Engineers' school. A dozen members immediately set out to distribute among them armfuls of the latest proclamations of the Committee for Salvation. Several did not come back.... All the other schools surrendered without a resistance, and the *yunkers* were sent unharmed to Peter-Paul and Kronstadt....

The Telephone Exchange held out until afternoon, when a Bolshevik armoured car appeared, and the sailors stormed the place. Shrieking, the frightened telephone girls ran to and fro; the *yunkers* tore from their uniforms all distinguishing marks, and one offered Williams *anything* for the loan of his overcoat, as a disguise.... 'They will massacre us! They will massacre us!' they cried, for many of them had given their word at the Winter Palace not to take up arms against the People. Williams offered to mediate if Antonov were released. This was immediately done; Antonov and Williams made speeches to the victorious sailors, inflamed by their many dead – and once more the *yunkers* went free.... All but a few, who in their panic tried to flee over the roofs, or to hide in the attic, and were found and hurled into the street.

Tired, bloody, triumphant, the sailors and workers swarmed into the switchboard room, and finding so many pretty girls, fell back in an embarrassed way and fumbled with awkward feet. Not a girl was injured, not one insulted. Frightened, they huddled in the corners, and then, finding themselves safe, gave vent to their spite. 'Ugh! The dirty, ignorant people! The fools!' ... The sailors and Red Guards were embarrassed. 'Brutes! Pigs!' shrilled the girls indignantly, putting on their coats and hats. Romantic had been their experience passing up cartridges and dressing the wounds of their dashing young defenders, the *yunkers*, many of them members of noble families, fighting to restore their beloved Tsar! These were just common workmen, peasants, 'Dark People'....

The Commissar of the Military Revolutionary Committee, little Vishniak, tried to persuade the girls to remain. He was effusively polite. 'You have been badly treated,' he said. 'The telephone system is controlled by the Municipal Duma. You are paid sixty roubles a month, and have to work ten hours and more.... From now on all that will be changed. The Government intends to put the telephones under control of the Ministry of Posts and Telegraphs. Your wages will be immediately raised to one hundred and fifty roubles, and your working hours reduced. As members of the working class you should be happy –'

Members of the *working class* indeed! Did he mean to infer

that there was anything in common between these – these animals – and *us*? Remain? Not if they offered a thousand roubles!... Haughty and spiteful, the girls left the place. ...

The employees of the building, the line-men and labourers – they stayed. But the switchboards must be operated – the telephone was vital. ... Only half a dozen trained operators were available. Volunteers were called for; a hundred responded, sailors, soldiers, workers. The six girls scurried backwards and forwards, instructing, helping, scolding. ... So, crippled, halting, but *going*, the wires began to hum. The first thing was to connect Smolny with the barracks and the factories; the second, to cut off the Duma and the *yunker* schools. ... Late in the afternoon word of it spread through the city, and hundreds of bourgeois called up to scream, 'Fools! Devils! How long do you think you will last? Wait till the Cossacks come!'

Dusk was already falling. On the almost deserted Nevsky, swept by a bitter wind, a crowd had gathered before the Kazan Cathedral, continuing the endless debate; a few workmen, some soldiers and the rest shopkeepers, clerks, and the like.

'But Lenin won't get Germany to make peace!' cried one.

A violent young soldier replied, 'And whose fault is it? Your damn Kerensky, dirty bourgeois! To hell with Kerensky! We don't want him. We want Lenin. ...'

Outside the Duma an officer with a white arm-band was tearing down posters from the wall, swearing loudly. One read:

To the Population of Petrograd!
At this dangerous hour, when the Municipal Duma ought to use every means to calm the population, to assure it bread and other necessities, the Right Socialist Revolutionaries and the Cadets, forgetting their duty, have turned the Duma into a counter-revolutionary meeting, trying to raise part of the population against the rest, so as to facilitate the victory of Kornilov-Kerensky. Instead of doing their duty, the Right Socialist Revolutionaries and the Cadets have transformed the Duma into an arena of political attack upon the Soviets of Workers', Soldiers', and Peasants' Deputies, against the revolutionary Government of peace, bread, and liberty.
Citizens of Petrograd, we, the Bolshevik Municipal Councillors, elected by you – we want you to know that the Right Socialist Revolutionaries and the Cadets are engaged in a counter-revolutionary action, have forgotten their duty, and are leading the population to famine, to

civil war. We, elected by 183,000 votes, consider it our duty to bring the attention of our constituents to what is going on in the Duma, and declare that we disclaim all responsibility for the terrible but inevitable consequences. ...

Far away still sounded occasional shots, but the city lay quiet, cold, as if exhausted by the violent spasms which had torn it.

In the Nikolai Hall the Duma session was coming to an end. Even the truculent Duma seemed a little stunned. One after another the Commissars reported capture of the Telephone Exchange, street-fighting, the taking of the Vladimir school. ... 'The Duma,' said Trupp, 'is on the side of the democracy in its struggle against arbitrary violence; but in any case, whichever side wins, the Duma will always be against lynchings and torture. ...'

Konovsky, Cadet, a tall old man with a cruel face: 'When the troops of the legal Government arrive in Petrograd, they will shoot down these insurgents, and that will not be lynching!' Protests all over the hall, even from his own party.

Here there was doubt and depression. The counter-revolution was being put down. The Central Committee of the Socialist Revolutionary party had voted lack of confidence in its officers; the left wing was in control; Avksentiev had resigned. A courier reported that the Committee of Welcome sent to meet Kerensky at the railway station had been arrested. In the streets could be heard the dull rumble of distant cannonading, south and southwest. Still Kerensky did not come. ...

Only three newspapers were out – *Pravda*, *Dielo Naroda*, and *Novaya Zhizn*. All of them devoted much space to the new 'coalition' Government. The Socialist Revolutionary paper demanded a Cabinet without either Cadets or Bolsheviki. Gorky was hopeful; Smolny had made concessions. A purely Socialist Government was taking shape – all elements except the bourgeoisie. As for *Pravda*, it sneered:

> We ridicule these coalitions with political parties whose most prominent members are petty journalists of doubtful reputation; our 'coalition' is that of the proletariat and the revolutionary Army with the poor peasants. ...

On the walls a vainglorious announcement of the Vikzhel, threatening to strike if both sides did not compromise:

The conquerors of these riots, the saviours of the wreck of our country, these will be neither the Bolsheviki, nor the Committee for Salvation, nor the troops of Kerensky – but we, the Union of Railwaymen. . . .

Red Guards are incapable of handling a complicated business like the railways; as for the Provisional Government, it has shown itself incapable of holding the power. . . .

We refuse to lend our services to any party which does not act by authority of . . . a Government based on the confidence of all the democracy. . . .

Smolny thrilled with the boundless vitality of inexhaustible humanity in action.

In trade union headquarters Lozovsky introduced me to a delegate of the Railway Workers of the Nikolai line, who said that the men were holding huge mass meetings, condemning the action of their leaders.

'All power to the Soviets!' he cried, pounding on the table. 'The *oborontsi* in the Central Committee are playing Kornilov's game. They tried to send a mission to the Stavka, but we arrested them at Minsk. . . . Our branch has demanded an All-Russian Convention, and they refuse to call it. . . .'

The same situation as in the Soviets, the Army Committees. One after another the various democratic organizations all over Russia were cracking and changing. The Cooperatives were torn by internal struggles; the meetings of the Peasants' Executive broke up in stormy wrangling; even among the Cossacks there was trouble. . . .

On the top floor the Military Revolutionary Committee was in full blast, striking and slacking not. Men went in, fresh and vigorous; night and day and night and day they threw themselves into the terrible machine; and came out limp, blind with fatigue, hoarse and filthy, to fall on the floor and sleep. . . . The Committee for Salvation had been outlawed. Great piles of new proclamations[39] littered the floor:

. . . The conspirators, who have no support among the garrison or the working class above all counted on the suddenness of their attack. Their plan was discovered in time by Sub-Lieutenant Blagonravov, thanks to the revolutionary vigilance of a soldier of the Red Guard, whose name shall be made public. At the centre of the plot was the Committee for Salvation. Colonel Polkovnikov was in command of their forces, and the orders were signed by Gotz, former member of the Provisional Government, allowed at liberty on his word of honour. . . .

Bringing these facts to the attention of the Petrograd population, the Military Revolutionary Committee orders the arrest of all concerned in the conspiracy, who shall be tried before the Revolutionary Tribunal. . . .

From Moscow, word that the *yunkers* and Cossacks had surrounded the Kremlin and ordered the Soviet troops to lay down their arms. The Soviet forces complied, and as they were leaving the Kremlin, were set upon and shot down. Small forces of Bolsheviki had been driven from the Telephone and Telegraph offices; the *yunkers* now held the centre of the city. . . . But all around them the Soviet troops were mustering. Street fighting was slowly gathering way; all attempts at compromise had failed. . . . On the side of the Soviet ten thousand garrison soldiers and a few Red Guards; on the side of the Government, six thousand *yunkers*, twenty-five hundred Cossacks and two thousand White Guards.

The Petrograd Soviet was meeting, and next door the new Tsay-ee-kah, acting on the decrees and orders[40] which came down in a steady stream from the Council of People's Commissars in session upstairs; on the Order in Which Laws Are to be Ratified and Published, Establishing an Eight-hour Day for Workers, and Lunacharsky's 'Basis for a System of Popular Education'. Only a few hundred people were present at the two meetings, most of them armed. Smolny was almost deserted, except for the guards, who were busy at the hall windows, setting up machine-guns to command the flanks of the building.

In the Tsay-ee-kah a delegate of the Vikzhel was speaking:

'We refuse to transport the troops of either party. . . . We have sent a committee to Kerensky to say that if he continues to march on Petrograd we will break his lines of communication. . . .'

He made the usual plea for a conference of all the Socialist parties to form a new Government. . . .

Kameniev answered discreetly. The Bolsheviki would be very glad to attend a conference. The centre of gravity, however, lay not in composition of such a Government, but in its acceptance of the programme of the Congress of Soviets. . . . The Tsay-ee-kah had deliberated on the declaration made by the Left Socialist Revolutionaries and the Social Democrat Internationalists, and had accepted the proposition of proportional representation at the conference, even including delegates from the Army Committees and the Peasants' Soviets. . . .

In the great hall, Trotsky recounted the events of the day.

'We offered the Vladimir *yunkers* a chance to surrender,' he said. 'We wanted to settle matters without bloodshed. But now that blood has been spilled there is only one way – pitiless struggle. It would be childish to think we can win by any other means. . . . The moment is decisive. Everybody must cooperate with the Military Revolutionary Committee, report where there are stores of barbed wire, benzine, guns. . . . We've won the power; now we must keep it!'

The Menshevik Yoffe tried to read his party's declaration, but Trotsky refused to allow 'a debate about principle'.

'Our debates are now in the streets,' he cried. 'The decisive step has been taken. We all, and I in particular, take the responsibility for what is happening. . . .'

Soldiers from the front, from Gatchina, told their stories. One from the Death Battalion, Four Hundred Eighty-First Artillery: 'When the trenches hear of this they will cry, "This is *our* Government!"' A *yunker* from Peterhof said that he and two others had refused to march against the Soviets; and when his comrades had returned from the defence of the Winter Palace they appointed him their Commissar, to go to Smolny and offer their services to the *real* Revolution. . . .

Then Trotsky again, fiery, indefatigable, giving orders, answering questions.

'The petty bourgeoisie, in order to defeat the workers, soldiers, and peasants, would combine with the devil himself!' he said once. Many cases of drunkenness had been remarked the last two days. 'No drinking, comrades! No one must be on the streets after eight in the evening, except the regular guards. All places suspected of having stores of liquor should be searched, and the liquor destroyed.[41] No mercy to the sellers of liquor. . . .'

The Military Revolutionary Committee sent for the delegation from the Viborg section; then for the members from Putilov. They clumped out hurriedly.

'For each revolutionist killed,' said Trotsky, 'we shall kill five counter-revolutionists!'

Down-town again. The Duma brilliantly illuminated and great crowds pouring in. In the lower hall wailing and cries of grief; the throng surged back and forth before the bulletin-board, where was posted a list of *yunkers* killed in the day's fighting – or supposed to be killed, for most of the dead afterwards turned up safe and sound.... Up in the Alexander Hall the Committee for Salvation held forth. The gold-and-red epaulettes of officers were conspicuous, the familiar faces of the Menshevik and Socialist Revolutionary intellectuals, the hard eyes and bulky magnificence of bankers and diplomats, officials of the old régime, and well-dressed women. ...

The telephone girls were testifying. Girl after girl came to the tribune – over-dressed, fashion-aping little girls, with pinched faces and leaky shoes. Girl after girl, flushing with pleasure at the applause of the 'nice' people of Petrograd, of the officers, the rich, the great names of politics – girl after girl, to narrate her sufferings at the hands of the proletariat, and proclaim her loyalty to all that was old-established and powerful. ...

The Duma was again in session in the Nikolai Hall. The Mayor said hopefully that the Petrograd regiments were ashamed of their actions; propaganda was making headway.

... Emissaries came and went, reporting horrible deeds of the Bolsheviki, interceding to save the *yunkers*, busily investigating. ...

'The Bolsheviki,' said Trupp, 'will be conquered by moral force, and not by bayonets. ...'

Meanwhile all was not well on the revolutionary front. The enemy had brought up armoured trains, mounted with cannon. The Soviet forces, mostly raw Red Guards, were without officers and without a definite plan. Only five thousand regular soldiers had joined them; the rest of the garrison was either busy suppressing the *yunker* revolt, guarding the city, or undecided what to do. At ten in the evening, Lenin addressed a meeting of delegates from the city regiments, who voted overwhelmingly to fight. A Committee of five soldiers was elected to serve as General Staff, and in the small hours of the morning the regiments left their barracks in full battle-array. Going home I saw them pass, swinging along with the regular tread of veterans, bayonets in perfect alignment, through the deserted streets of the conquered city....

At the same time, in the headquarters of the Vikzhel down on the Sadovaya, the conference of all the Socialist parties to form a new Government was under way. Abramovich, for the centre Mensheviki, said that there should be neither conquerors nor conquered – that bygones should be bygones.... In this were agreed all the left-wing parties. Dan, speaking in the name of the right Mensheviki, proposed to the Bolsheviki the following conditions of a truce; the Red Guard to be disarmed, and the Petrograd garrison to be placed at the orders of the Duma; the troops of Kerensky not to fire a single shot or arrest a single man; a Ministry of all the Socialist parties *except the Bolsheviki*. For Smolny Riazanov and Kameniev declared that a coalition ministry of all parties was acceptable, but protested at Dan's proposals. The Socialist Revolutionaries were divided; but the Executive Committee of the Peasants' Soviet and the Populist Socialists flatly refused to admit the Bolsheviki.... After bitter quarrelling a commission was elected to draw up a workable plan....

All that night the commission wrangled, and all the next day and the next night. Once before, on the ninth of November, there had been a similar effort at conciliation, led by Martov and Gorky; but at the approach of Kerensky and the activity of the Committee for Salvation, the right wing of the Mensheviki, Socialist Revolutionaries, and Populist Socialists suddenly withdrew. Now they were awed by the crushing of the *yunker* rebellion....

Monday the twelfth was a day of suspense. The eyes of all Russia were fixed on the grey plain beyond the gates of Petrograd, where all the available strength of the old order faced the unorganized power of the new, the unknown. In Moscow a truce had been declared; both sides parleyed, awaiting the result in the capital. Now the delegates to the Congress of Soviets, hurrying on speeding trains to the farthest ends of Asia, were coming to their homes, carrying the fiery cross. In wide-spreading ripples news of the miracle spread over the face of the land, and in its wake towns, cities, and far villages stirred and broke, Soviets and Military Revolutionary Committees against Dumas, Zemstvos, and Government Commissars – Red Guards against White – street fighting and passionate speech.... The result waited on the word from Petrograd....

Smolny was almost empty, but the Duma was thronged and noisy. The old Mayor, in his dignified way, was protesting against the Appeal of the Bolshevik Councillors.

'The Duma is not a centre of counter-revolution,' he said, warmly. 'The Duma takes no part in the present struggle between the parties. But at a time when there is no legal power in the land, the only centre of order is the Municipal Self-Government. The peaceful population recognizes this fact; the foreign Embassies recognize only such documents as are signed by the Mayor of the town. The mind of a European does not admit of any other situation, as the Municipal Self-Government is the only organ which is capable of protecting the interests of the citizens. The City is bound to show hospitality to all organizations which desire to profit by such hospitality, and therefore the Duma cannot prevent the distribution of any newspapers whatever within the Duma building. The sphere of our work is increasing, and we must be given full liberty of action, and our rights must be respected by both parties....

'We are perfectly neutral. When the Telephone Exchange was occupied by the *yunkers* Colonel Polkovnikov ordered the telephones to Smolny disconnected, but I protested, and the telephones were kept going....'

At this there was ironic laughter from the Bolshevik benches and imprecations from the right.

'And yet,' went on Schreider, 'they look upon us as counter-revolutionaries and report us to the population. They deprive us of our means of transport by taking away our last motor-cars. It will not be our fault if there is famine in the town. Protests are of no use....'

Kobozev, Bolshevik member of the Town Board, was doubtful whether the Military Revolutionary Committee had requisitioned the municipal automobiles. Even granting the fact, it was probably done by some unauthorized individual in the emergency.

'The Mayor,' he continued, 'tells us we must not make political meetings out of the Duma. But every Menshevik and Socialist here talks nothing but party propaganda, and at the door they distribute their illegal newspapers, *Iskri* (Sparks), *Soldatski Golos*, and *Rabochaya Gazeta*, inciting to insurrection. What if we Bolsheviki should also begin to distribute our papers here? But this shall not be, for we respect the Duma. We have not attacked the Municipal Self-Government, and we shall not do so. But you have addressed an Appeal to the population, and we are entitled to do so....'

Followed him Shingariov, Cadet, who said that there could be no common language with those who were liable to be brought before the Attorney-General for indictment, and who must be tried on the charge of treason.... He proposed again that all Bolshevik members should be expelled from the Duma. This was tabled, however, for there were no personal charges against the members, and they were active in the Municipal administration.

Then two Mensheviki Internationalists, declaring that the Appeal of the Bolshevik Councillors was a direct incitement to massacre. 'If everything that is against the Bolsheviki is counter-revolutionary,' said Pinkevich, 'then I do not know the difference between revolution and anarchy.... The Bolsheviki are depending upon the passions of the unbridled masses; we have nothing but moral force. We will protest against massacres and violence from both sides, as our task is to find a peaceful issue.'

'The notice posted in the streets under the heading "To the Pillory", which calls upon the people to destroy the Mensheviki and Socialist Revolutionaries,' said Nazariev, 'is a crime which you, Bolsheviki, will not be able to wash away. Yesterday's horrors are but a preface to what you are preparing by such a proclamation.... I have always tried to reconcile you with other parties, but at present I feel for you nothing but contempt!'

The Bolshevik Councillors were on their feet, shouting angrily, assailed by hoarse, hateful voices and waving arms....

Outside the hall I ran into the City Engineer, the Menshevik Gomberg, and three or four reporters. They were all in high spirits.

'See!' they said. 'The cowards are afraid of us. They don't dare arrest the Duma! Their Military Revolutionary Committee doesn't care to send a Commissar into this building. Why, on the corner of the Sadovaya today I saw a Red Guard try to stop a boy selling *Soldatski Golos*.... The boy just laughed at him, and a crowd of people wanted to lynch the bandit. It's only a few hours more now. Even if Kerensky wouldn't come they haven't the men to run a Government. Absurd! I understand they're even fighting among themselves at Smolny!'

A Socialist Revolutionary friend of mine drew me aside. 'I know where the Committee for Salvation is hiding,' he said. 'Do you want to go and talk with them?'

By this time it was dusk. The city had again settled down to normal – shop-shutters up, lights shining, and on the streets great crowds of people slowly moving up and down and arguing....

At Number 86 Nevsky we went through a passage into a courtyard, surrounded by tall apartment buildings. At the door of apartment 229 my friend knocked in a peculiar way. There was a sound of scuffling; an inside door slammed; then the front door opened a crack and a woman's face appeared. After a minute's observation she led us in – a placid-looking, middle-aged lady who at once cried, 'Kyril, it's all right!' In the dining-room, where a samovar steamed on the table and there were plates full of bread and raw fish, a man in uniform emerged from behind the window curtains, and another, dressed like a workman, from a closet. They were delighted to meet an American reporter. With a certain amount of gusto both said that they would certainly be shot if the Bolsheviki caught them. They would not give me their names, but both were Socialist Revolutionaries....

'Why,' I asked, 'do you publish such lies in your newspapers?'

Without taking offence the officer replied, 'Yes, I know; but what can we do?' He shrugged. 'You must admit that it is necessary for us to create a certain frame of mind in the people....'

The other interrupted. 'This is merely an adventure on the part of the Bolsheviki. They have no intellectuals.... The Ministries won't work.... Russia is not a city, but a whole country.... Realizing that they can only last a few days, we have decided to come to the aid of the strongest force opposed to them – Kerensky – and help to restore order.'

'That is all very well,' I said. 'But why do you combine with the Cadets?'

The pseudo-workman smiled frankly. 'To tell you the truth, at this moment the masses of the people are following the Bolsheviki. We have no following – now. We can't mobilize a handful of soldiers. There are no arms available.... The Bolsheviki are right to a certain extent; there are at this moment in Russia only two parties with any force – the Bolsheviki and the reactionaries, who are all hiding under the coat-tails of the Cadets. When we smash the Bolsheviki we shall turn against the Cadets....'

'Will the Bolsheviki be admitted into the new Government?'

He scratched his head. 'That's a problem,' he admitted. 'Of course if they are not admitted, they'll probably do this all over again. At any rate, they will have a chance to hold the balance of power in the Constituent – that is, if there *is* a Constituent.'

'And then, too,' said the officer, 'that brings up the question of admitting the Cadets into the new Government – and for the same reasons. You know the Cadets do not really want the Constituent Assembly – not if the Bolsheviki can be destroyed now.' He shook his head. 'It is not easy for us Russians, politics. You Americans are born politicians; you have had politics all your lives. But for us –'

'What do you think of Kerensky?' I asked.

'Oh, Kerensky is guilty of the sins of the Provisional Government,' answered the other man. 'Kerensky himself forced us to accept coalition with the bourgeoisie. If he had resigned, as he threatened, it would have meant a new Cabinet crisis only sixteen weeks before the Constituent Assembly, and that we wanted to avoid.'

'But didn't it amount to that, anyway?'

'Yes, but how were we to know? They tricked us – the Kerenskys and Avksentievs. Gotz is a little more radical. I stand with Chernov, who is a real revolutionist.... Why, only today Lenin sent word that he would not object to Chernov entering the Government.

'We wanted to get rid of the Kerensky Government too, but we thought it better to wait for the Constituent.... At the beginning of this affair I was with the Bolsheviki, but the Central Committee of my party voted unanimously against it – and what could I do? It was a matter of party discipline....

'In a week the Bolshevik Government will go to pieces; if the

Socialist Revolutionaries could only stand aside and wait, the Government would fall into their hands. But if we wait a week the country will be so disorganized that the German imperialists will be victorious. That is why we began our revolt with only two regiments of soldiers promising to support us – and they turned against us.... That left only the *yunkers*....'

'How about the Cossacks?'

The officer sighed. 'They did not move. At first they said they would come out if they had infantry support. They said, moreover, that they had their men with Kerensky, and that they were doing their part.... Then, too, they said that the Cossacks were always accused of being the hereditary enemies of democracy.... And finally, "The Bolsheviki promise that they will not take away our land. There is no danger to us. We remain neutral."'

During this talk people were constantly entering and leaving – most of them officers, their shoulder-straps torn off. We could see them in the hall, and hear their low, vehement voices. Occasionally, through the half-drawn portières, we caught a glimpse of a door opening into a bathroom, where a heavily built officer in a colonel's uniform sat on the toilet, writing something on a pad held in his lap. I recognized Colonel Polkovnikov, former commandant of Petrograd, for whose arrest the Military Revolutionary Committee would have paid a fortune.

'Our programme?' said the officer. 'That is it. Land to be turned over to the Land Committees. Workmen to have full representation in the control of industry. An energetic peace programme, but not an ultimatum to the world such as the Bolsheviki issued. The Bolsheviki cannot keep their promises to the masses, even in the country itself. We won't let them.... They stole our land programme in order to get the support of the peasants. That is dishonest. If they had waited for the Constituent Assembly –'

'It doesn't matter about the Constituent Assembly!' broke in the other. 'If the Bolsheviki want to establish a Socialist state here, we cannot work with them in any event! Kerensky made the great mistake. He let the Bolsheviki know what he was going to do by announcing in the Council of the Republic that he had ordered their arrest....'

'But what,' I said, 'do you intend to do now?'

The two men looked at one another. 'You will see in a few days. If there are enough troops from the front on our side we shall not compromise with the Bolsheviki. If not, perhaps we shall be forced to....'

Out again on the Nevsky we swung on the step of a streetcar bulging with people, its platform bent down from the weight and scraping along the ground, which crawled with agonizing slowness the long miles to Smolny.

Meshkovsky, a neat, frail little man, was coming down the hall, looking worried. The strikes in the Ministries, he told us, were having their effect. For instance, the Council of People's Commissars had promised to publish the secret treaties; but Neratov, the functionary in charge, had disappeared, taking the documents with him. They were supposed to be hidden in the British Embassy....

Worst of all, however, was the strike in the banks. 'Without money,' said Menzhinsky, 'we are helpless. The wages of the railroad men, and of the telegraph employees, must be paid.... The banks are closed; and the key to the situation, the State Bank, is also shut. All the bank-clerks in Russia have been bribed to stop work....

'But Lenin has issued an order to dynamite the State Bank vaults, and there is a Decree just out, ordering the private banks to open tomorrow, or we will open them ourselves!'

The Petrograd Soviet was in full swing, thronged with armed men, Trotsky reporting:

'The Cossacks are falling back from Krasnoye Selo.' (Sharp, exultant cheering.) 'But the battle is only beginning. At Pulkovo heavy fighting is going on. All available forces must be hurried there....

'From Moscow, bad news. The Kremlin is in the hands of the *yunkers*, and the workers have only a few arms. The result depends upon Petrograd.

'At the front, the decrees on Peace and Land are provoking great enthusiasm. Kerensky is flooding the trenches with tales of Petrograd burning and bloody, of women and children massacred by the Bolsheviki. But no one believes him....

'The cruisers *Oleg*, *Avrora*, and *Respublika* are anchored in the Neva, their guns trained on the approaches to the city....'

'Why aren't you out there with the Red Guards?' shouted a rough voice.

'I'm going now!' answered Trotsky, and left the platform. His face a little paler than usual, he passed down the side of the room, surrounded by eager friends, and hurried out to the waiting automobile.

Kameniev now spoke, describing the proceedings of the re-conciliation conference. The armistice conditions proposed by the Mensheviki, he said, had been contemptuously rejected. Even the branches of the Railwaymen's Union had voted against such a proposition. . . .

'Now that we've won the power and are sweeping all Russia,' he declared, 'all they ask of us are three things: 1. To surrender the power. 2. To make the soldiers continue the war. 3. To make the peasants forget about the land. . . .'

Lenin appeared for a moment to answer the accusations of the Socialist Revolutionaries:

'They charge us with stealing their land programme. . . . If that was so we bow to them. It is good enough for us. . . .'

So the meeting roared on, leader after leader explaining, ex-horting, arguing, soldier after soldier, workman after workman, standing up to speak his mind and his heart. . . . The audience flowed, changing and renewed continually. From time to time men came in, yelling for the members of such and such a detach-ment, to go to the front; others, relieved, wounded, or coming to Smolny for arms and equipment, poured in. . . .

It was almost three o'clock in the morning when, as we left the hall, Holtzman, of the Military Revolutionary Committee, came running down the hall with a transfigured face.

'It's all right!' he shouted, grabbing my hands. 'Telegram from the front. Kerensky is smashed. Look at this!'

He held out the sheet of paper, scribbled hurriedly in pencil, and then, seeing we couldn't read it, he declaimed aloud:

Pulkovo. Staff. 2.10 a.m.

The night of 30 to 31 October* will go down in history. The attempt

* These dates are given according to the Old Calendar, thirteen days behind the Western Calendar, which was only introduced later. The date according to our calendar was 12–13 November. Lower down, as we see, an Order of the Day was dated in the new style.

of Kerensky to move counter-revolutionary troops against the capital of the Revolution has been decisively repulsed. Kerensky is retreating, we are advancing. The soldiers, sailors, and workers of Petrograd have shown that they can and will with arms in their hands enforce the will and authority of the democracy. The bourgeoisie tried to isolate the revolutionary army. Kerensky attempted to break it by the force of the Cossacks. Both plans met a pitiful defeat.

The grand idea of the domination of the worker and peasant democracy closed the ranks of the army and hardened its will. All the country from now on will be convinced that the Power of the Soviets is no ephemeral thing, but an invincible fact. . . . The repulse of Kerensky is the repulse of the landowners, the bourgeoisie, and the Kornilovists in general. The repulse of Kerensky is the confirmation of the right of the people to a peaceful free life, to land, to bread, and power. The Pulkovo detachment by its valorous blow has strengthened the cause of the Workers' and Peasants' Revolution. There is no return to the past. Before us are struggles, obstacles, and sacrifices. But the road is clear and victory is certain.

Revolutionary Russia and the Soviet Power can be proud of their Pulkovo detachment, acting under the command of Colonel Walden. Eternal memory to those who fell! Glory to the warriors of the Revolution, the soldiers and the officers who were faithful to the People!

Long live revolutionary, popular, Socialist Russia!

In the name of the Council,

L. TROTSKY, People's Commissar . . .

Driving home across Znambensky Square, we made out an unusual crowd in front of the Nikolai Railway Station. Several thousand sailors were massed there, bristling with rifles.

Standing on the steps a member of the Vikzhel was pleading with them.

'Comrades, we cannot carry you to Moscow. We are neutral. We do not carry troops for either side. We cannot take you to Moscow, where already there is terrible civil war. . . .'

All the seething square roared at him; the sailors began to surge forward. Suddenly another door was flung wide; in it stood two or three brakemen, a fireman or so.

'This way, comrades!' cried one. 'We will take you to Moscow – or Vladivostok, if you like. Long live the Revolution!'

9 Victory

13 November 1917. 38 minutes past 9 a.m.

After a cruel fight the troops of the Pulkovo detachment completely routed the counter-revolutionary forces, who retreated from their positions in disorder, and under cover of Tsarskoye Selo fell back towards Pavlovsk II and Gatchina.

Our advanced units occupied the north-eastern extremity of Tsarskoye Selo and the station Alexandrovskaya. The Colpinno detachment was on our left, the Krasnoye Selo detachment to our right.

I ordered the Pulkovo forces to occupy Tsarskoye Selo, to fortify its approaches, especially on the side of Gatchina.

Also to pass and occupy Pavlovskoye, fortifying its southern side, and to take up the railroad as far as Dno.

The troops must take all measures to strengthen the positions occupied by them, arranging trenches and other defensive works.

They must enter into close liaison with the detachments of Colpinno and Krasnoye Selo, and also with the Staff of the Commander-in-Chief for the Defence of Petrograd.

Signed,

Commander-in-Chief over all Forces acting against
the Counter-revolutionary Troops of Kerensky,
Lieutenant-Colonel MURAVIOV

Tuesday morning. But how is this? Only two days ago the Petrograd campagna was full of leaderless bands, wandering aimlessly; without food, without artillery, without a plan. What had fused that disorganized mass of undisciplined Red Guards, and soldiers without officers, into an army obedient to its own elected high command, tempered to meet and break the assault of cannon and Cossack cavalry?[42]

People in revolt have a way of defying military precedent. The ragged armies of the French Revolution are not forgotten – Valmy and the Lines of Weissembourg. Massed against the Soviet forces were *yunkers*, Cossacks, landowners, nobility, Black

Hundreds – the Tsar come again, Okhrana and Siberian chains; and the vast and terrible menace of the Germans. ... Victory, in the words of Carlyle, meant 'Apotheosis and Milennium without end!'

Sunday night, the Commissars of the Military Revolutionary Committee returning desperately from the field, the garrison of Petrograd elected its Committee of Five, its Battle Staff, three soldiers and two officers, all certified free from counter-revolutionary taint. Colonel Muraviov, ex-patriot, was in command – an efficient man, but to be carefully watched. At Colpinno, at Obukhovo, at Pulkovo and Krasnoye Selo were formed provisional detachments, increased in size as the stragglers came in from the surrounding country – mixed soldiers, sailors, and Red Guards, parts of regiments, infantry, cavalry, and artillery all together, and a few armoured cars.

Day broke, and the pickets of Kerensky's Cossacks came in touch. Scattered rifle-fire, summons to surrender. Over the bleak plain on the cold quiet air spread the sound of battle, falling upon the ears of roving bands as they gathered about their little fires, waiting. ... So it was beginning! They made towards the battle; and the worker hordes pouring out along the straight roads quickened their pace. ... Thus upon all the points of attack automatically converged angry human swarms, to be met by Commissars and assigned positions, or work to do. This was *their* battle, for *their* world; the officers in command were elected by *them*. For the moment that incoherent multiple will was one will. ...

Those who participated in the fighting described to me how the sailors fought until they ran out of cartridges, and then stormed; how the untrained workmen rushed the charging Cossacks and tore them from their horses; how the anonymous hordes of the people, gathering in the darkness around the battle, rose like a tide and poured over the enemy. ... Before midnight of Monday the Cossacks broke and were fleeing, leaving their artillery behind them, and the army of the proletariat, on a long ragged front, moved forward and rolled into Tsarskoye, before the enemy had a chance to destroy the great Government wireless station, from which now the Commissars of Smolny were hurling out to the world paeans of triumph. ...

TO ALL SOVIETS OF WORKERS' AND SOLDIERS' DEPUTIES

The twelfth of November, in a bloody combat near Tsarskoye Selo, the revolutionary army defeated the counter-revolutionary troops of Kerensky and Kornilov. In the name of the Revolutionary Government I order all regiments to take the offensive against the enemies of the revolutionary democracy, and to take all measures to arrest Kerensky, and also to oppose the adventure which might menace the conquests of the Revolution and the victory of the proletariat.

Long live the Revolutionary Army!

MURAVIOV

News from the provinces. ...

At Sevastopol the local Soviet had assumed the power; a huge meeting of the sailors on the battleships in the harbour had forced their officers to line up and swear allegiance to the new Government. At Nizhni Novgorod the Soviet was in control. From Kazan came reports of a battle in the streets, *yunkers* and a brigade of artillery against the Bolshevik garrison. ...

Desperate fighting had broken out again in Moscow. The *yunkers* and White Guards held the Kremlin and the centre of the town, beaten upon from all sides by the troops of the Military Revolutionary Committee. The Soviet artillery was stationed in Skobeliev Square, bombarding the City Duma building, the Prefecture, and the Hotel Metropole. The cobble-stones of the Tverskaya and Nikitskaya had been torn up for trenches and barricades. A hail of machine-gun fire swept the quarters of the great banks and commercial houses. There were no lights, no telephones; the bourgeois population lived in the cellars. ... The last bulletin said that the Military Revolutionary Committee had delivered an ultimatum to the Committee of Public Safety, demanding the immediate surrender of the Kremlin, or bombardment would follow.

'Bombard the Kremlin?' cried the ordinary citizen. 'They dare not!'

From Vologda to Chita in far Siberia, from Pskov to Sevastopol on the Black Sea, in great cities and little villages, civil war burst into flame. From thousands of factories, peasant communes, regiments, and armies, ships on the wide sea, greetings poured into Petrograd – greetings to the Government of the People.

The Cossack Government of Novocherkask telegraphed to Kerensky, '*The Government of the Cossack troops invites the Provisional Government and the members of the Council of the Republic to come, if possible, to Novocherkask, where we can organize in common the struggle against the Bolsheviki.*'

In Finland, also, things were stirring. The Soviet of Helsingfors and the Tsentrobalt (Central Committee of the Baltic Fleet), jointly proclaimed a state of siege, and declared that all attempts to interfere with the Bolshevik forces, and all armed resistance to its orders, would be severely repressed. At the same time the Finnish Railway Union called a country-wide general strike, to put into operation the laws passed by the Socialist Diet of June 1917, dissolved by Kerensky....

Early in the morning I went out to Smolny. Going up the long wooden sidewalk from the outer gate I saw the first thin, hesi-tating snowflakes fluttering down from the grey, windless sky. 'Snow!' cried the soldier at the door, grinning with delight. 'Good for the health!' Inside, the long, gloomy halls and bleak rooms seemed deserted. No one moved in all the enormous pile. A deep, uneasy sound came to my ears, and looking around, I noticed that everywhere on the floor, along the walls, men were sleeping. Rough, dirty men, workers and soldiers, spattered and caked with mud, sprawled alone or in heaps, in the careless atti-tudes of death. Some wore ragged bandages marked with blood. Guns and cartridge-belts were scattered about.... The victorious proletarian army!

In the upstairs buffet so thick they lay that one could hardly walk. The air was foul. Through the clouded windows a pale light streamed. A battered samovar, cold, stood on the counter, and many glasses holding dregs of tea. Beside them lay a copy of the Military Revolutionary Committee's last bulletin, upside down, scrawled with painful handwriting. It was a memorial written by some soldier to his comrades fallen in the fight against Kerensky, just as he had set it down before falling on the floor to sleep. The writing was blurred with what looked like tears....

Alexei Vinogradov	S. Stolbikov
D. Maskvin	D. Preobrazhensky
A. Voskressensky	V. Laidansky
D. Leonsky	M. Berchikov

These men were drafted into the Army on 15 November 1916. Only three are left of the above.

Mikhail Berchikov.

Alexei Voskressensky.

Dmitri Leonsky.

> *Sleep, warrior eagles, sleep with peaceful soul.*
> *You have deserved, our own ones, happiness and*
> *Eternal peace. Under the earth of the grave*
> *You have straitly closed your ranks. Sleep, Citizens!*

Only the Military Revolutionary Committee still functioned, unsleeping. Skripnik, emerging from the inner room, said that Gotz had been arrested, but had flatly denied signing the proclamation of the Committee of Salvation, as had Avksentiev; and the Committee for Salvation itself had repudiated the Appeal to the garrison. There was still disaffection among the city regiments, Skripnik reported; the Volhynsky Regiment had refused to fight against Kerensky.

Several detachments of 'neutral' troops, with Chernov at their head, were at Gatchina, trying to persuade Kerensky to halt his attack on Petrograd.

Skripnik laughed. 'There can be no "neutrals" now,' he said. 'We've won!' His sharp, bearded face glowed with an almost religious exaltation. 'More than sixty delegates have arrived from the front, with assurances of support by all the armies except the troops on the Roumanian front, who have not been heard from. The Army Committees have suppressed the news from Petrograd, but we now have a regular system of couriers. . . .

Down in the front hall Kameniev was just entering, worn out by the all-night session of the Conference to Form a New Government, but happy. 'Already the Socialist Revolutionaries are inclined to admit us into the new Government,' he told me. 'The right-wing groups are frightened by the Revolutionary Tribunals; they demand, in a sort of panic, that we dissolve them before going any further. . . . We have accepted the proposition of the Vikzhel to form a homogeneous Socialist Ministry, and they're working on that now. You see, it all springs from our victory. When we were down, they wouldn't have us at any price; now everybody's in favour of some agreement with the Soviets. . . .

What we need is a really decisive victory. Kerensky wants an armistice, but he'll have to surrender....'[43]

That was the temper of the Bolshevik leaders. To a foreign journalist who asked Trotsky what statement he had to make to the world, Trotsky replied: 'At this moment the only statement possible is the one we are making through the mouths of our cannon!'

But there was an undercurrent of real anxiety in the tide of victory; the question of finances. Instead of opening the banks, as had been ordered by the Military Revolutionary Committee, the Union of Bank Employees had held a meeting and declared a formal strike. Smolny had demanded some thirty-five million roubles from the State Bank, and the cashier had locked the vaults, only paying out money to the representatives of the Provisional Government. The reactionaries were using the State Bank as a political weapon; for instance, when the Vikzhel demanded money to pay the salaries of the employees of the Government railroads, it was told to apply to Smolny....

I went to the State Bank to see the new Commissar, a red-haired Ukrainian Bolshevik named Petrovich. He was trying to bring order out of the chaos in which affairs had been left by the striking clerks. In all the offices of the huge place perspiring volunteer workers, soldiers and sailors, their tongues sticking out of their mouths in the intensity of their effort, were poring over the great ledgers with a bewildered air....

The Duma building was crowded. There were still isolated cases of defiance towards the new Government, but they were rare. The Central Land Committee had appealed to the Peasants, ordering them not to recognize the Land Decree passed by the Congress of the Soviets, because it would cause confusion and civil war. Mayor Schreider announced that because of the Bolshevik insurrection, the election to the Constituent Assembly would have to be indefinitely postponed.

Two questions seemed to be uppermost in all minds, shocked by the ferocity of the civil war; first, a truce to the bloodshed[44] – second, the creation of a new Government. There was no longer any talk of 'destroying the Bolsheviki' – and very little about excluding them from the Government, except from the Populist Socialists and the Peasants' Soviets. Even the Central Army

Committee at the Stavka, the most determined enemy of Smolny, telephoned from Moghilev: 'If, to constitute the new Ministry, it is necessary to come to an understanding with the Bolsheviki, we agree to admit them *in a minority* to the Cabinet.'

Pravda, ironically calling attention to Kerensky's 'humanitarian sentiments', published his dispatch to the Committee for Salvation:

In accord with the proposals of the Committee for Salvation and all the democratic organizations united around it, I have halted all military action against the rebels. A delegate of the Committee has been sent to enter into negotiations. Take all measures to stop the useless shedding of blood.

The Vikzhel sent a telegram to all Russia:

The Conference of the Union of Railway Workers with the representatives of both the belligerent parties, who admit the necessity of an agreement, protest energetically against the use of political terrorism in the civil war, especially when it is carried on between different factions of the revolutionary democracy, and declare that political terrorism, in whatever form, is in contradiction to the very idea of the negotiations for a new Government. . . .

Delegations from the Conference were sent to the front, to Gatchina. In the Conference itself everything seemed on the point of final settlement. It had even been decided to elect a Provisional People's Council, composed of about four hundred members – seventy-five representing Smolny, seventy-five the old Tsay-ee-kah, and the rest split up among the Town Dumas, the Trade Unions, Land Committees, and political parties. Chernov was mentioned as the new Premier. Lenin and Trotsky, rumour said, were to be excluded. . . .

About noon I was again in front of Smolny, talking with the driver of an ambulance bound for the revolutionary front. Could I go with him? Certainly! He was a volunteer, a University student, and as we rolled down the street shouted over his shoulder to me phrases of execrable German: '*Also, gut! Wir mach die Kasernen zu essen gehen!*' I made out that there would be lunch at some barracks.

On the Kirochnaya we turned into an immense courtyard surrounded by military buildings, and mounted a dark stairway to a low room lit by one window. At a long wooden table were seated some twenty soldiers, eating *shchi* (cabbage soup) from a great tin wash-tub with wooden spoons, and talking loudly with much laughter.

'Welcome to the Battalion Committee of the Sixth Reserve Engineers' Battalion!' cried my friend, and introduced me as an American Socialist. Whereat everyone rose to shake my hand, and one old soldier put his arms around me and gave me a hearty kiss. A wooden spoon was produced and I took my place at the table. Another tub, full of *kasha*, was brought in, a huge loaf of black bread, and of course the inevitable teapots. At once everyone began asking me questions about America: Was it true that people in a free country sold their votes for *money*? If so, how did they get what they wanted? How about this 'Tammany'? Was it true that in a free country a little group of people could control a whole city, and exploited it for their personal benefit? Why did the people stand it? Even under the Tsar such things could not happen in Russia; true, here there was always graft, but to buy and sell a whole city full of people! And in a free country! Had the people no revolutionary feeling? I tried to explain that in my country people tried to change things by law.

'Of course,' nodded a young sergeant, named Baklanov, who spoke French. 'But you have a highly developed capitalist class? Then the capitalist class must control the legislatures and the courts. How then can the people change things? I am open to conviction, for I do not know your country, but to me it is incredible. . . .'

I said that I was going to Tsarskoye Selo. 'I, too,' said Baklanov suddenly. 'And I – and I –' The whole roomful decided on the spot to go to Tsarskoye Selo.

Just then came a knock on the door. It opened, and in it stood the figure of the Colonel. No one rose, but all shouted a greeting. 'May I come in?' asked the Colonel. '*Prosim! Prosim!*' they answered heartily. He entered, smiling, a tall, distinguished figure in a goatskin cape embroidered with gold. 'I think I heard you say that you were going to Tsarskoye Selo, comrades,' he said. 'Could I go with you?'

Baklanov considered. 'I do not think there is anything to be done here today,' he answered. 'Yes, comrade, we shall be very glad to have you.' The Colonel thanked him and sat down, filling a glass of tea.

In a low voice, for fear of wounding the Colonel's pride, Baklanov explained to me. 'You see, I am the chairman of the Committee. We control the Battalion absolutely, except in action, when the Colonel is delegated by us to command. In action his orders must be obeyed, but he is strictly responsible to us. In barracks he must ask our permission before taking any action. . . . You might call him our Executive Officer. . . .'

Arms were distributed to us, revolvers and rifles – 'we might meet some Cossacks, you know' – and we all piled into the ambulance, together with three great bundles of newspapers for the front. Straight down the Liteiny we rattled, and along the Zagorodny Prospect. Next to me sat a youth with the shoulder-straps of a lieutenant, who seemed to speak all European languages with equal fluency. He was a member of the Battalion Committee.

'I am not a Bolshevik,' he assured me emphatically. 'My family is a very ancient and noble one. I, myself, am, you might say, a Cadet. . . .'

'But how –?' I began, bewildered.

'Oh, yes, I am a member of the Committee. I make no secret of my political opinions, but the others do not mind, because they know I do not believe in opposing the will of the majority. . . . I have refused to take any action in the present civil war, however, for I do not believe in taking up arms against my brother Russians. . . .'

'Provocator! Kornilovist!' the others cried at him gaily, slapping him on the shoulder. . . .

Passing under the huge grey stone archway of the Moskovsky Gate, covered with golden hieroglyphics, ponderous Imperial eagles and the names of Tsars, we sped out on the wide, straight highway, grey with the first light fall of snow. It was thronged with Red Guards, stumbling along on foot towards the revolutionary front, shouting and singing; and others, grey-faced and muddy, coming back. Most of them seemed to be mere boys. Women with spades, some with rifles and bandoliers, others wearing the Red Cross on their arm-bands – the bowed, toil-worn women of the slums. Squads of soldiers marching out of step, with an affectionate jeer for the Red Guards; sailors, grim-looking; children with bundles of food for their fathers and mothers; all these, coming and going, trudged through the whitened mud that covered the cobbles of the highway inches deep. We passed cannon, jingling southward with their caissons; trucks bound both ways, bristling with armed men; ambulances full of wounded from the direction of the battle, and once a peasant cart, creaking slowly along, in which sat a white-faced boy bent over his shattered stomach and screaming monotonously. In the fields on either side women and old men were digging trenches and stringing barbed wire entanglements.

Back northward the clouds rolled away dramatically, and the pale sun came out. Across the flat, marshy plain Petrograd glittered. To the right, white and gilded and coloured bulbs and pinnacles; to the left, tall chimneys, some pouring out black smoke; and beyond, a lowering sky over Finland. On each side of us were churches, monasteries.... Occasionally a monk was visible, silently watching the pulse of the proletarian army throbbing on the road.

At Pulkovo the road divided, and there we halted in the midst of a great crowd, where the human streams poured from three directions, friends meeting, excited and congratulatory, describing the battle to one another. A row of houses facing the cross-roads was marked with bullets, and the earth was trampled into mud half a mile around. The fighting had been furious here.... In the near distance riderless Cossack horses circled hungrily, for the grass of the plain had died long ago. Right in front of us an awkward Red Guard was trying to ride one, falling off again and again, to the childlike delight of a thousand rough men.

The left road, along which the remnants of the Cossacks had retreated, led up a little hill to a hamlet, where there was a glorious view of the immense plain, grey as a windless sea, tumultuous clouds towering over, and the imperial city disgorging its thousands along all the roads. Far over to the left lay the little hill of Krasnoye Selo, the parade-ground of the Imperial Guards' summer camp, and the Imperial Dairy. In the middle distance nothing broke the flat monotony but a few walled monasteries and convents, some isolated factories, and several large buildings with unkempt grounds that were asylums and orphanages....

'Here,' said the driver, as we went on over a barren hill, 'here was where Vera Slutskaya died. Yes, the Bolshevik member of the Duma. It happened early this morning. She was in an automobile, with Zalkind and another man. There was a truce, and they started for the front trenches. They were talking and laughing, when all of a sudden, from the armoured train in which Kerensky himself was riding, somebody saw the automobile and fired a cannon. The shell struck Vera Slutskaya and killed her....'

And so we came into Tsarskoye, all bustling with the swaggering heroes of the proletarian horde. Now the palace where the Soviet had met was a busy place. Red Guards and sailors filled the courtyard, sentries stood at the doors, and a stream of couriers and Commissars pushed in and out. In the Soviet room a samovar had been set up, and fifty or more workers, soldiers, sailors, and officers stood around, drinking tea and talking at the top of their voices. In one corner two clumsy-handed working men were trying to make a multigraphing machine go. At the centre table, the huge Dybenko bent over a map, marking out positions for the troops with red and blue pencils. In his free hand he carried, as always, the enormous blue-steel revolver. Anon he sat himself down at a typewriter and pounded away with one finger; every little while he would pause, pick up the revolver, and lovingly spin the chamber.

A couch lay along the wall, and on this was stretched a young workman. Two Red Guards were bending over him, the rest of the company did not pay any attention. In his breast was a hole; through his clothes fresh blood came welling up with every heart-beat. His eyes were closed, and his young, bearded face was greenish-white. Faintly and slowly he still breathed, with every breath sighing, '*Mir boudit! Mir boudit!* (Peace is coming! Peace is coming!).'

Dybenko looked up as we came in. 'Ah,' he said to Baklanov. 'Comrade, will you go up to the Commandant's headquarters and take charge? Wait; I will write you credentials.' He went to the typewriter and slowly picked out the letters.

The new Commandant of Tsarskoye Selo and I went towards the Ekaterina Palace, Baklanov very excited and important. In the same ornate, white room some Red Guards were rummaging curiously around, while my old friend, the Colonel, stood by the

window biting his moustache. He greeted me like a long-lost
brother. At a table near the door sat the French Bessarabian.
The Bolsheviki had ordered him to remain, and continue his
work.

'What could I do?' he muttered. 'People like myself cannot
fight on either side in such a war as this, no matter how much we
may instinctively dislike the dictatorship of the mob. . . . I only
regret that I am so far from my mother in Bessarabia!'

Baklanov was formally taking over office from the Commandant. 'Here,' said the Colonel nervously, 'are the keys to the
desk.'

A Red Guard interrupted. 'Where's the money?' he asked
rudely. The Colonel seemed surprised. 'Money? Money? Ah,
you mean the chest. There it is,' said the Colonel, 'just as I found
it when I took possession three days ago. Keys?' The Colonel
shrugged. 'I have no keys.'

The Red Guard sneered knowingly. 'Very convenient,' he said.

'Let us open the chest,' said Baklanov. 'Bring an axe. Here is an
American comrade. Let him smash the chest open, and write
down what he finds there.'

I swung the axe. The wooden chest was empty.

'Let's arrest him,' said the Red Guard, venomously. 'He is
Kerensky's man. He has stolen the money and given it to
Kerensky.'

Baklanov did not want to. 'Oh, no,' he said. 'It was the
Kornilovist before him. He is not to blame.'

'The devil!' said the Red Guard. 'He is Kerensky's man, I tell
you. If you won't arrest him then we will, and we'll take him to
Petrograd and put him in Peter-Paul, where he belongs!' At this
the other Red Guards growled assent. With a piteous glance at us
the Colonel was led away. . . .

Down in front of the Soviet palace an auto-truck was going to
the front. Half a dozen Red Guards, some sailors, and a soldier or
two, under command of a huge workman, clambered in, and
shouted to me to come along. Red Guards issued from headquarters, each of them staggering under an arm-load of small,
corrugated-iron bombs, filled with *grubit* – which, they say, is ten
times as strong, and five times as sensitive as dynamite; these
they threw into the truck. A three-inch cannon was loaded and

then tied on to the tail of the truck with bits of rope and wire.

We started with a shout, at top speed, of course; the heavy truck swaying from side to side. The cannon leaped from one wheel to the other, and the *grubit* bombs went rolling back and forth over our feet, fetching up against the sides of the car with a crash.

The big Red Guard, whose name was Vladimir Nikolayevich, plied me with questions about America. 'Why did America come into the war? Are the American workers ready to throw over the capitalists? What is the situation in the Mooney case now? Will they extradite Berkman to San Francisco?' and others, very difficult to answer, all delivered in a shout above the roaring of the truck, while we held on to each other and danced amid the caroming bombs.

Occasionally a patrol tried to stop us. Soldiers ran out into the road before us, shouted '*Stoi!*' and threw up their guns.

We paid no attention. 'The devil take you!' cried the Red Guards. 'We don't stop for anybody! We're Red Guards!' And we thundered imperiously on, while Vladimir Nikolayevich bellowed to me about the internationalization of the Panama Canal and such matters....

'Where's the front, brothers?'

The foremost sailor halted and scratched his head. 'This morning,' he said, 'it was about half a kilometre down the road. But the damn thing isn't anywhere now. We walked and walked and walked, but we couldn't find it.'

They climbed into the truck, and we proceeded. It must have been about a mile further that Vladimir Nikolayevich cocked his ear and shouted to the chauffeur to stop.

'Firing!' he said. 'Do you hear it?' For a moment dead silence, and then, a little ahead and to the left, three shots in rapid succession. Along here the side of the road was heavily wooded. Very much excited now, we crept along, speaking in whispers, until the truck was nearly opposite the place where the firing had come from. Descending, we spread out, and every man carrying his rifle, went stealthily into the forest.

Two comrades, meanwhile, detached the cannon and slewed it around until it aimed as nearly as possible at our backs.

It was silent in the woods. The leaves were gone, and the

tree-trunks were a pale wan colour in the low, sickly autumn sun. Not a thing moved, except the ice of little woodland pools shivering under our feet. Was it an ambush?

We went uneventfully forward until the trees began to thin, and paused. Beyond, in a little clearing, three soldiers sat around a small fire, perfectly oblivious.

Vladimir Nikolayevich stepped forward. '*Zra'zvuitye*, comrades!' he greeted, while behind him one cannon, twenty rifles, and a truck-load of *grubit* bombs hung by a hair. The soldiers scrambled to their feet.

'What was the shooting going on around here?'

One of the soldiers answered, looking relieved, 'Why, we were just shooting a rabbit or two, comrade....'

The truck hurtled on towards Romanov, through the bright, empty day. At the first cross-roads two soldiers ran out in front of us, waving their rifles. We slowed down, and stopped.

'Passes, comrades!'

The Red Guards raised a great clamour. 'We are Red Guards. We don't need any passes.... Go on, never mind them!'

But a sailor objected. 'This is wrong, comrades. We must have revolutionary discipline. Suppose some counter-revolutionaries came along in a truck and said: "We don't need any passes"? The comrades don't know you.'

At this there was a debate. One by one, however, the sailors and soldiers joined with the first. Grumbling, each Red Guard produced his dirty *bumaga* (paper). All were alike except mine, which had been issued by the Revolutionary Staff at Smolny. The sentries declared that I must go with them. The Red Guards objected strenuously, but the sailor who had spoken first insisted. 'This comrade we know to be a true comrade,' he said. 'But there are orders of the Committee, and these orders must be obeyed. That is revolutionary discipline....'

In order not to make any trouble, I got down from the truck and watched it disappear careening down the road, all the company waving farewell. The soldiers consulted in low tones for a moment, and then led me to a wall, against which they placed me. It flashed upon me suddenly; they were going to shoot me!

In all three directions not a human being was in sight. The only sign of life was smoke from the chimney of a *dacha*, a rambling wooden house a quarter of a mile up the side road. The two soldiers were walking out in the road. Desperately I ran after them.

'But, comrades! See! Here is the seal of the Military Revolutionary Committee!'

They stared stupidly at my pass, then at each other.

'It is different from the others,' said one, sullenly. 'We cannot read, brother.'

I took him by the arm. 'Come!' I said. 'Let's go to that house. Someone there can surely read.' They hesitated. 'No,' said one. The other looked me over. 'Why not?' he muttered. 'After all, it is a serious crime to kill an innocent man.'

We walked up to the front door of the house and knocked. A short, stout woman opened it, and shrank back in alarm, babbling, 'I don't know anything about them! I don't know anything about them!' One of my guards held out the pass. She screamed. 'Just to read it, comrade.' Hesitatingly she took the paper and read aloud, swiftly:

The bearer of this pass, John Reed, is a representative of the American Social-Democracy, an internationalist. . . .

Out on the road again the two soldiers held another consultation. 'We must take you to the Regimental Committee,' they said. In the fast-developing twilight we trudged along the muddy road. Occasionally we met squads of soldiers, who stopped and surrounded me with looks of menace, handing my pass around and arguing violently as to whether or not I should be killed. . . .

It was dark when we came to the barracks of the Second Tsarskoye Selo Rifles, low, sprawling buildings huddled along the post-road. A number of soldiers slouching at the entrance asked eager questions. A spy? A provocator? We mounted a winding stair and emerged into a great, bare room with a huge stove in the centre, and rows of cots on the floor, where about a thousand soldiers were playing cards, talking, singing, and asleep. In the roof was a jagged hole made by Kerensky's cannon. . . .

I stood in the doorway, and a sudden silence ran among the groups, who turned and stared at me. Of a sudden they began to move, slowly and then with a rush, thundering, with faces full of hate. 'Comrades! Comrades!' yelled one of my guards. 'Committee! Committee!' The throng halted, banked around me, muttering. Out of them shouldered a lean youth, wearing a red arm-band.

'Who is this?' he asked roughly. The guards explained. 'Give me the paper!' He read it carefully, glancing at me with keen eyes. Then he smiled and handed me the pass. 'Comrades, this is an American comrade. I am chairman of the committee, and I welcome you to the regiment....' A sudden general buzz grew into a roar of greeting, and they pressed forward to shake my hand.

'You have not dined? Here we have had our dinner. You shall go the Officers' Club, where there are some who speak your language....'

He led me across the courtyard to the door of another building. An aristocratic-looking youth, with the shoulder-straps of a lieutenant, was entering. The Chairman presented me, and shaking hands, went back.

'I am Stepan Georgevich Morovsky, at your service,' said the lieutenant in perfect French. From the ornate entrance-hall a ceremonial staircase led upward, lighted by glittering lustres. On the second floor billiard-rooms, card-rooms, a library opened from the hall. We entered the dining-room, at a long table in the centre of which sat about twenty officers in full uniform, wearing their gold and silver handled swords, the ribbons and crosses of Imperial decorations. All rose politely as I entered, and made a place for me beside the colonel, a large, impressive man with a grizzled beard. Orderlies were deftly serving dinner. The atmosphere was that of any officers' mess in Europe. Where was the Revolution?

'You are not Bolsheviki?' I asked Morovsky.

A smile went around the table, but I caught one or two glancing furtively at the orderly.

'No,' answered my friend. 'There is only one Bolshevik officer in this regiment. He is in Petrograd tonight. The colonel is a Menshevik. Captain Kherlov there is a Cadet. I myself am a Socialist-Revolutionary of the Right wing.... I should say that most of the officers in the Army are not Bolsheviki, but like me they believe in democracy; they believe that they must follow the soldier-masses....'

Dinner over, maps were brought, and the colonel spread them out on the table. The rest crowded around to see.

'Here,' said the colonel, pointing to pencil marks, 'were our positions this morning. Vladimir Kyrilovich, where is your company?'

Captain Kherlov pointed. 'According to orders, we occupied the position along this road. Karsavin relieved me at five o'clock.'

Just then the door of the room opened, and there stood the chairman of the regimental committee, with another soldier. They joined the group behind the colonel, peering at the map.

'Good,' said the colonel. 'Now the Cossacks have fallen back ten kilometres in our sector. I do not think it is necessary to take up advanced positions. Gentlemen, for tonight you will hold the present line, strengthening the positions by –'

'If you please,' interrupted the chairman of the regimental committee. 'The orders are to advance with all speed, and prepare to engage the Cossacks north of Gatchina in the morning. A crushing defeat is necessary. Kindly make the proper dispositions.'

There was a short silence. The colonel again turned to the map. 'Very well,' he said, in a different voice. 'Stepan Georgevich, you will please –' Rapidly tracing lines with a blue pencil, he gave his orders, while a sergeant made shorthand notes. The sergeant then withdrew, and ten minutes later returned with the orders typewritten, and one carbon copy. The chairman of the committee studied the map with a copy of the orders before him.

'All right,' he said, rising. Folding the carbon copy, he put it in his pocket. Then he signed the other, stamped it with a round seal taken from his pocket, and presented it to the colonel....

Here was the Revolution!

I returned to the Soviet palace in Tsarskoye in the regimental staff automobile. Still the crowds of workers, soldiers, and sailors pouring in and out, still the choking press of trucks, armoured cars, cannon before the door, and the shouting, the laughter of unwonted victory. Half a dozen Red Guards forced their way through, a priest in the middle. This was Father Ivan, they said, who had blessed the Cossacks when they entered the town. I heard afterwards that he was shot....[45]

Dybenko was just coming out, giving rapid orders right and

left. In his hand he carried the big revolver. An automobile stood with racing engine at the kerb. Alone he climbed in the rear seat, and was off – off to Gatchina, to conquer Kerensky.

Towards nightfall he arrived at the outskirts of the town, and went on afoot. What Dybenko told the Cossacks nobody knows, but the fact is that General Krasnov and his staff and several thousand Cossacks surrendered and advised Kerensky to do the same.[46]

As for Kerensky – I reprint here the deposition made by General Krasnov on the morning of 14 November:

'Gatchina, 14 November 1917. Today, about three o'clock (a.m.), I was summoned by the Supreme Commander (Kerensky). He was very agitated, and very nervous.

'"General," he said to me, "you have betrayed me. Your Cossacks declare categorically that they will arrest me and deliver me to the sailors."

'"Yes," I answered, "there is talk of it, and I know that you have no sympathy anywhere."

'"But the officers say the same thing."

'"Yes, most of all it is the officers who are discontented with you."

'"What shall I do? I ought to commit suicide!"

'"If you are an honourable man you will go immediately to Petrograd with a white flag, you will present yourself to the Military Revolutionary Committee, and enter into negotiations as Chief of the Provisional Government."

'"All right. I will do that, general."

'"I will give you a guard and ask that a sailor go with you."

'"No, no, not a sailor. Do you know whether it is true that Dybenko is here?"

'"I don't know who Dybenko is."

'"He is my enemy."

'"There is nothing to do. If you play for high stakes you must know how to take a chance."

'"Yes. I'll leave tonight!"

'"That would be a flight. Leave calmly and openly, so that everyone can see that you are not running away."

'"Very well. But you must give me a guard on which I can count."

'"Good."

'I went out and called the Cossack Russkov, of the Tenth Regiment of the Don, and ordered him to pick out ten Cossacks to accompany the Supreme Commander. Half an hour later the Cossacks came to tell me that Kerensky was not in his quarters, that he had run away.

'I gave the alarm and ordered that he be searched for, supposing that he could not leave Gatchina, but he could not be found. . . .'

And so Kerensky fled alone, 'disguised in the uniform of a sailor', and by that act lost whatever popularity he had retained among the Russian masses. . . .

I went back to Petrograd riding on the front seat of an autotruck, driven by a workman and filled with Red Guards. We had no kerosene, so our lights were not burning. The road was crowded with the proletarian army going home, and new reserves pouring out to take their places. Immense trucks like ours, columns of artillery, wagons, loomed up in the night, without lights, as we were. We hurtled furiously on, wrenched right and left to avoid collisions that seemed inevitable, scraping wheels, followed by the epithets of pedestrians.

Across the horizon spread the glittering lights of the capital, immeasurably more splendid by night than by day, like a dike of jewels on the barren plain.

The old workman who drove held the wheel in one hand, while with the other he swept the far-gleaming capital in an exultant gesture.

'Mine!' he cried, his face all alight. 'All mine now! My Petrograd!'

10 Moscow

The Military Revolutionary Committee, with a fierce intensity, followed up its victory:

14 November.

To all Army corps, divisional and regimental Committees, to all Soviets of Workers', Soldiers', and Peasants' Deputies, to all, all, all.

Conforming to the agreement between the Cossacks, *yunkers*, soldiers, sailors, and workers, it has been decided to arraign Alexander Feodorovich Kerensky before a tribunal of the people. We demand that Kerensky be arrested, and that he be ordered, in the name of the organization hereinafter mentioned, to come immediately to Petrograd and present himself to the tribunal.

Signed,

The Cossacks of the First Division of Ussur Cavalry; the Committee of Yunkers of the Petrograd detachment of Franc-Tireurs; the delegate of the Fifth Army

People's Commissar, DYBENKO

The Committee for Salvation, the Duma, the Central Committee of the Socialist Revolutionary Party – proudly claiming Kerensky as a member – all passionately protested that he could only be held responsible to the Constituent Assembly.

On the evening of 16 November I watched two thousand Red Guards swing down the Zagorodny Prospekt behind a military band playing the *Marseillaise* – and how appropriate it sounded – with blood-red flags over the dark ranks of workmen, to welcome home again their brothers who had defended 'Red Petrograd'. In the bitter dusk they tramped, men and women, their tall bayonets swaying; through streets faintly lighted and slippery with mud, between silent crowds of bourgeois, contemptuous but fearful. . . .

All were against them – business men, speculators, investors, landowners, army officers, politicians, teachers, students, professional men, shopkeepers, clerks, agents. The other Socialist parties hated the Bolsheviki with an implacable hatred. On the side of the Soviets were the rank and file of the workers, the sailors, all the undemoralized soldiers, the landless peasants and a few – a very few – intellectuals.

From the farthest corners of great Russia, whereupon desperate street fighting burst like a wave, news of Kerensky's defeat came echoing back the immense roar of proletarian victory. Kazan, Saratov, Novgorod, Vinnitza – where the streets had run with blood; Moscow, where the Bolsheviki had turned their artillery against the last stronghold of the bourgeoisie – the Kremlin.

'They are bombarding the Kremlin!' The news passed from mouth to mouth in the streets of Petrograd, almost with a sense of terror. Travellers from 'white and shining little mother Moscow' told fearful tales. Thousands killed; the Tverskaya and the Kuznetsky Most in flames; the church of Vasili Blazhenny a smoking ruin; Usspensky Cathedral crumbling down; the Spasskaya Gate of the Kremlin tottering; the Duma burned to the ground.[47]

Nothing that the Bolsheviki had done could compare with this fearful blasphemy in the heart of Holy Russia. To the ears of the devout sounded the shock of guns crashing in the face of the Holy Orthodox Church, and pounding to dust the sanctuary of the Russian nation....

On 15 November Lunacharsky, Commissar of Education, broke into tears at the session of the Council of People's Commissars, and rushed from the room, crying, 'I cannot stand it! I cannot bear the monstrous destruction of beauty and tradition....'

That afternoon his letter of resignation was published in the newspapers:

I have just been informed, by people arriving from Moscow, what has happened there.

The Cathedral of St Basil the Blessed, the Cathedral of the Assumption, are being bombarded. The Kremlin, where are now gathered the most important art treasures of Petrograd and of Moscow, is under artillery fire. There are thousands of victims.

The fearful struggle there has reached a pitch of bestial ferocity.

What is left? What more can happen?

I cannot bear this. My cup is full. I am unable to endure these horrors. It is impossible to work under the pressure of thoughts which drive me mad!

That is why I am leaving the Council of People's Commissars.

I fully realize the gravity of this decision. But I can bear no more. . . .[48]

That same day the White Guards and *yunkers* in the Kremlin surrendered, and were allowed to march out unharmed. The treaty of peace follows:

1. The Committee of Public Safety ceases to exist.

2. The White Guard gives up its arms and dissolves. The officers retain their swords and regulation side-arms. In the Military Schools are retained only the arms necessary for instruction; all others are surrendered by the *yunkers*. The Military Revolutionary Committee guarantees the liberty and inviolability of the person.

3. To settle the question of disarmament, as set forth in section 2, a special commission is appointed, consisting of representatives from all organizations which took part in the peace negotiations.

4. From the moment of the signature of this peace treaty, both parties shall immediately give order to cease firing and halt all military operation, taking measures to ensure punctual obedience to this order.

5. At the signature of the treaty, all prisoners made by the two parties shall be released. . . .

For two days now the Bolsheviki had been in control of the city. The frightened citizens were creeping out of their cellars to see their dead; the barricades in the streets were being removed. Instead of diminishing, however, the stories of destruction in Moscow continued to grow. . . . And it was under the influence of these fearful reports that we decided to go there.

Petrograd, after all, in spite of being for a century the seat of Government, is still an artificial city. Moscow is real Russia, Russia as it was and will be; in Moscow we would get the true feeling of the Russian people about the Revolution. Life was more intense there.

For the past week the Petrograd Military Revolutionary Committee, aided by the rank and file of the Railway Workers, had seized control of the Nikolai Railroad, and hurled trainload after trainload of sailors and Red Guards south-west. . . . We were provided with passes from Smolny, without which no one could leave the capital. . . . When the train backed into the station, a mob of shabby soldiers, all carrying huge sacks of eatables, stormed the doors, smashed the windows and poured into all the compartments, filling up the aisles and even climbing on to the roof. Three of us managed to wedge our way into a compartment, but almost immediately about twenty soldiers entered.... There was room for only four people; we argued, expostulated, and the conductor joined us – but the soldiers merely laughed. Were they to bother about the comfort of a lot of *boorzhui* (bourgeois)? We produced the passes from Smolny; instantly the soldiers changed their attitude.

'Come, comrades,' cried one, 'these are American *tovarishchi*. They have come thirty thousand versts to see our revolution, and they are naturally tired....'

With polite and friendly apologies the soldiers began to leave. Shortly afterwards we heard them breaking into a compartment occupied by two stout, well-dressed Russians, who had bribed the conductor and locked their door....

About seven o'clock in the evening we drew out of the station, an immense long train drawn by a weak little locomotive burning wood, and stumbled along slowly, with many stops. The soldiers on the roof kicked their heels and sang whining peasant songs; and in the corridor, so jammed that it was impossible to pass, violent political debates raged all night long. Occasionally the conductor came through, as a matter of habit, looking for tickets. He found very few except ours, and after a half-hour of futile wrangling, lifted his arms despairingly and withdrew. The atmosphere was stifling, full of smoke and foul odours; if it hadn't been for the broken windows we would doubtless have smothered during the night.

In the morning, hours late, we looked out upon a snowy world. It was bitter cold. About noon a peasant woman got on with a basket full of bread-chunks and a great can of luke-warm coffee-substitute. From then on until dark there was nothing but the packed train, jolting and stopping, and occasional stations where a ravenous mob swooped down on the scantily furnished buffet and swept it clean.... At one of these halts I ran into Nogin and Rykov, the seceding Commissars, who were returning to Moscow to put their grievances before their own Soviet;* and further

* See Chapter 11.

along was Bukharin, a short red-bearded man with the eyes of a fanatic – 'more Left than Lenin', they said of him....

Then the three strokes of the bell and we made a rush for the train, worming our way through the packed and noisy aisle.... A good-natured crowd, bearing the discomfort with humorous patience, interminably arguing about everything from the situation in Petrograd to the British trade-union system, and disputing loudly with the few *boorzhui* who were on board. Before we reached Moscow almost every car had organized a committee to secure and distribute food, and these committees became divided into political factions, who wrangled over fundamental principles....

The station at Moscow was deserted. We went to the office of the Commissar, in order to arrange for our return tickets. He was a sullen youth with the shoulder-straps of a lieutenant; when we showed him our papers from Smolny he lost his temper and declared that he was no Bolshevik, that he represented the Committee of Public Safety.... It was characteristic – in the general turmoil attending the conquest of the city, the chief railway station had been forgotten by the victors....

Not a cab in sight. A few blocks down the street, however, we woke up a grotesquely padded *izvozchik* asleep upright on the box of his little sleigh. 'How much to the centre of the town?'

He scratched his head. 'The *barini* won't be able to find a room in any hotel,' he said. 'But I'll take you around for a hundred roubles....' Before the Revolution it cost *two*! We objected, but he simply shrugged his shoulders. 'It takes a good deal of courage to drive a sleigh nowadays,' he went on. We could not beat him down below fifty.... As we sped along the silent, snowy, half-lighted streets he recounted his adventures during the six days' fighting. 'Driving along, or waiting for a fare on the corner,' he said, 'all of a sudden *pooff!* a cannon ball exploding here, *pooff!* a cannon ball there, *ratt-tatt!* a machine-gun.... I gallop, the devils shooting all around. I get to a nice quiet street and stop, doze a little, *pooff!* another cannon ball, *ratt-tatt....* Devils! Devils! Devils! B-r-r-r!'

In the centre of the town the snow-piled streets were quiet with the stillness of convalescence. Only a few arc-lights were burning, only a few pedestrians hurried along the sidewalks. An icy wind blew from the great plain, cutting to the bone. At the first hotel we entered an office illuminated by two candles.

'Yes, we have some very comfortable rooms, but all the windows are shot out. If the *gospodin* does not mind a little fresh air....'

Down the Tverskaya the shop-windows were broken, and there were shell holes and torn-up paving-stones in the street. Hotel after hotel, all full, or the proprietors still so frightened that all they could say was, 'No, no, there is no room! There is no room!' On the main streets, where the great banking houses and mercantile houses lay, the Bolshevik artillery had been indiscriminately effective. As one Soviet official told me, 'Whenever we didn't know just where the *yunkers* and White Guards were, we bombarded their pocket-books....'

At the big Hotel National they finally took us in; for we were foreigners, and the Military Revolutionary Committee had promised to protect the dwellings of foreigners.... On the top floor the manager showed us where shrapnel had shattered several windows. 'The animals!' said he, shaking his fist at imaginary Bolsheviki. 'But wait! Their time will come; in just a few days now their ridiculous Government will fall, and then we shall make them suffer!'

We dined at a vegetarian restaurant with the enticing name, I Eat Nobody, and Tolstoy's picture prominent on the walls, and then sallied out into the streets.

The headquarters of the Moscow Soviet was in the palace of the former Governor-General, an imposing white building fronting Skobeliev Square. Red Guards stood sentry at the door. At the head of the wide, formal stairway, whose walls were plastered with announcements of committee meetings and addresses of political parties, we passed through a series of lofty ante-rooms, hung with red-shrouded pictures in gold frames, to the splendid state salon, with its magnificent crystal lustres and gilded cornices. A low-voiced hum of talk underlaid with the whirring bass of a score of sewing machines, filled the place. Huge bolts of red and black cotton cloth were unrolled, serpentining across the parqueted floor and over tables, at which sat half a hundred women, cutting and sewing streamers and banners for the Funeral of the Revolutionary Dead. The faces of these women were roughened and scarred with life at its most difficult; they worked now sternly, many of them with eyes red from weeping.... The losses of the Red Army had been heavy.

At a desk in one corner was Rogov, an intelligent, bearded man with glasses, wearing the black blouse of a worker. He invited us to march with the Central Executive Committee in the funeral procession next morning....

'It is impossible to teach the Socialist Revolutionaries and the Mensheviki anything!' he exclaimed. 'They compromise from sheer habit. Imagine! They proposed that we hold a joint funeral with the *yunkers*.'

Across the hall came a man in a ragged soldier-coat and *shapka*, whose face was familiar; I recognized Melnichansky, whom I had known as the watchmaker George Melcher in Bayonne, New Jersey, during the great Standard Oil strike. Now, he told me, he was secretary of the Moscow Metal-Workers' Union, and a Commissar of the Military Revolutionary Committee during the fighting....

'You see me!' he cried, showing his decrepit clothing. 'I was with the boys in the Kremlin when the *yunkers* came the first time. They shut me up in the cellar and swiped my overcoat, my money, watch, and even the ring on my finger. This is all I've got to wear!'

From him I learned many details of the bloody six-day battle which had rent Moscow in two. Unlike Petrograd, in Moscow the City Duma had taken command of the *yunkers* and White Guards. Rudnev, the mayor, and Minor, president of the Duma, had directed the activities of the Committee of Public Safety and the troops. Riabtsev, commandant of the city, a man of democratic instincts, had hesitated about opposing the Military Revolutionary Committee; but the Duma had forced him.... It was the Mayor who had urged the occupation of the Kremlin: 'They will never dare fire on you there,' he said....

One garrison regiment, badly demoralized by long inactivity, had been approached by both sides. The regiment held a meeting to decide what action to take. Resolved, that the regiment remain neutral, and continue its present activities – which consisted in peddling rubbers and sunflower seeds!

'But worst of all,' said Melnichansky, 'we had to organize

while we were fighting. The other side knew just what it wanted; but here the soldiers had their Soviet and the workers theirs.... There was a fearful wrangle over who should be commander-in-chief; some regiments talked for days before they decided what to do; and when the officers suddenly deserted us, we had no battle-staff to give orders....'

Vivid little pictures he gave me. On a cold, grey day he had stood at a corner of the Nikitskaya, which was swept by blasts of machine-gun fire. A throng of little boys were gathered there – street waifs who used to be newsboys. Shrill, excited as if with a new game, they waited until the firing slackened, and then tried to run across the ' street.... Many were killed, but the rest dashed backward and forward, laughing, daring each other....

Late in the evening I went to the Dvorianskoye Sobranie – the Nobles' Club – where the Moscow Bolsheviki were to meet and consider the report of Nogin, Rykov, and the others who had left the Council of People's Commissars.

The meeting-place was a theatre, in which, under the old régime, to audiences of officers and glittering ladies, amateur presentations of the latest French comedy had once taken place.

At first the place filled with the intellectuals – those who lived near the centre of the town. Nogin spoke, and most of his listeners were plainly with him. It was very late before the workers arrived; the working-class quarters were on the outskirts of the town, and no streetcars were running. But about midnight they began to clump up the stairs, in groups of ten or twenty – big, rough men, in coarse clothes, fresh from the battle-line, where they had fought like devils for a week, seeing their comrades fall all about them.

Scarcely had the meeting formally opened before Nogin was assailed with a tempest of jeers and angry shouts. In vain he tried to argue, to explain; they would not listen. He had left the Council of People's Commissars; he had deserted his post while the battle was raging. As for the bourgeois press, here in Moscow there was no more bourgeois press; even the City Duma had been dissolved.[49] Bukharin stood up, savage, logical, with a voice which plunged and struck, plunged and struck.... Him they listened to with shining eyes. Resolution, to support the action of the Council of People's Commissars, passed by overwhelming majority. So spoke Moscow....

Late in the night we went through the empty streets and under the Iberian Gate to the great Red Square in front of the Kremlin. The church of Vasili Blazhenny loomed fantastic, its bright-coloured, convoluted, and blazoned cupolas vague in the darkness. There was no sign of any damage.... Along one side of the square the dark towers and walls of the Kremlin stood up. On the high walls flickered redly the light of hidden flames; voices reached us across the immense place, and the sound of picks and shovels. We crossed over.

Mountains of dirt and rock were piled high near the base of the wall. Climbing these we looked down into two massive pits, ten or fifteen feet deep and fifty yards long, where hundreds of soldiers and workers were digging in the light of huge fires.

A young soldier spoke to us in German. 'The Brotherhood Grave,' he explained. 'Tomorrow we shall bury here five hundred proletarians who died for the Revolution.'

He took us down into the pit. In frantic haste swung the picks and shovels, and the earth-mountains grew. No one spoke. Overhead the night was thick with stars, and the ancient Imperial Kremlin wall towered up immeasurably.

'Here in this holy place,' said the student, 'holiest of all Russia, we shall bury our most holy. Here where are the tombs of the Tsars, our Tsar – the People – shall sleep....' His arm was in a sling, from a bullet wound gained in the fighting. He looked at it. 'You foreigners look down on us Russians because so long we tolerated a medieval monarchy,' said he. 'But we saw that the Tsar was not the only tyrant in the world; capitalism was worse, and in all the countries of the world capitalism was Emperor.... Russian revolutionary tactics are best....'

As we left, the workers in the pit, exhausted and running with sweat in spite of the cold, began to climb wearily out. Across the Red Square a dark knot of men came hurrying. They swarmed into the pits, picked up the tools and began digging, digging, without a word....

So, all the long night volunteers of the People relieved each other, never halting in their driving speed, and the cold light of the dawn laid bare the great square, white with snow, and the yawning brown pits of the Brotherhood Grave, quite finished.

We rose before sunrise, and hurried through the dark streets to Skobeliev Square. In all the great city not a human being could be seen; but there was a faint sound of stirring, far and near, like a deep wind coming. In the pale half-light a little group of men and women were gathered before the Soviet headquarters, with a sheaf of gold-lettered red banners – the Central Executive Committee of the Moscow Soviets. It grew light. From afar the vague stirring sound deepened and became louder, a steady and tremendous bass. The city was rising. We set out down the Tverskaya, the banners flapping overhead. The little street chapels along our way were locked and dark, as was the Chapel of the Iberian Virgin, which each new tsar used to visit before he went to the Kremlin to crown himself, and which, day or night, was always open and crowded, and brilliant with the candles of the devout gleaming on the gold and silver and jewels of the ikons. Now, for the first time since Napoleon was in Moscow, they say, the candles were out.

The Holy Orthodox Church had withdrawn the light of its countenance from Moscow, the nest of irreverent vipers who had bombarded the Kremlin. Dark and silent and cold were the churches; the priests had disappeared. There were no popes to officiate at the Red Burial, there had been no sacrament for the dead, nor were any prayers to be said over the grave of the blasphemers. Tikhon, Metropolitan of Moscow, was soon to excommunicate the Soviets. . . .

Also the shops were closed, and the propertied classes stayed at home – but for other reasons. This was the Day of the People, the rumour of whose coming was thunderous as surf. . . .

Already through the Iberian Gate a human river was flowing, and the vast Red Square was spotted with people, thousands of them. I remarked that as the throng passed the Iberian Chapel, where always before the passer-by had crossed himself, they did not seem to notice it. . . .

We forced our way through the dense mass packed near the Kremlin wall, and stood upon one of the dirt-mountains. Already several men were there, among them Muranov, the soldier who had been elected commandant of Moscow – a tall, simple-looking, bearded man with a gentle face.

Through all the streets to the Red Square, the torrents of people poured, thousands upon thousands of them, all with the look of the poor and the toiling. A military band came marching up playing the *Internationale*, and spontaneously the song caught and spread like wind-ripples on a sea, slow and solemn. From the top of the Kremlin wall gigantic banners unrolled to the ground red, with great letters in gold and in white, saying, 'Martyrs of the Beginning of World Social Revolution', and 'Long Live the Brotherhood of Workers of the World'.

A bitter wind swept the square, lifting the banners. Now from the far quarters of the city the workers of the different factories were arriving, with their dead. They could be seen coming through the Gate, the blare of their banners, and the dull red – like blood – of the coffins they carried. These were rude boxes, made of un-planed wood and daubed with crimson, borne high on the shoulders of rough men who marched with tears streaming down their faces, and followed by women who sobbed and screamed, or walked stiffly, with white, dead faces. Some of the coffins were open, the lid carried behind them; others were covered with gilded or silvered cloth, or had a soldier's hat nailed on the top. There were many wreaths of hideous artificial flowers.

Through an irregular lane that opened and closed again the procession slowly moved towards us. Now through the gate was flowing an endless stream of banners, all shades of red and silver and gold lettering, knots of crepe hanging from the top – and some anarchist flags, black with white letters. The band was play-ing the Revolutionary Funeral March, and against the immense singing of the mass of people, standing uncovered, the paraders sang hoarsely, choked with sobs....

Between the factory workers came companies of soldiers with their coffins, too, and squadrons of cavalry, riding at salute, and artillery batteries, the cannon wound with red and black – for ever, it seemed. Their banners said, 'Long live the Third Inter-national!' or 'We Want an Honest, General, Democratic Peace!'

Slowly the marchers came with their coffins to the entrance of the grave, and the bearers clambered up with their burdens and went down into the pit. Many of them were women – squat, strong proletarian women. Behind the dead came other women –

women young and broken, or old, wrinkled women making noises like hurt animals, who tried to follow their sons and husbands into the Brotherhood Grave, and shrieked when compassionate hands restrained them. The poor love each other so!

All the long day the funeral procession passed, coming in by the Iberian Gate and leaving the square by way of the Nikolskaya, a river of red banners, bearing words of hope and brotherhood and stupendous prophecies, against a background of fifty thousand people – under the eyes of the world's workers and their descendants for ever....

One by one the five hundred coffins were laid in the pits. Dusk fell, and still the banners came drooping and fluttering, the band played the Funeral March, and the huge assemblage chanted. In the leafless branches of the trees above the grave the wreaths were hung, like strange, multi-coloured blossoms. Two hundred men began to shovel in the dirt. It rained dully down upon the coffins with a thudding sound, audible beneath the singing....

The lights came out. The last banners passed, and the last moaning women, looking back with awful intensity as they went. Slowly from the Red Square ebbed the proletarian tide....

I suddenly realized that the devout Russian people no longer needed priests to pray them into heaven. On earth they were building a kingdom more bright than any heaven had to offer, and for which it was a glory to die....

... The first Congress of Soviets, in June of this year, proclaimed the rights of the peoples of Russia to self-determination.

The second Congress of Soviets, in November last, confirmed this inalienable right of the peoples of Russia more decisively and definitely.

Executing the will of these Congresses, the Council of People's Commissars has resolved to establish as a basis for its activity in the question of Nationalities, the following principles:

(1) The equality and sovereignty of the peoples of Russia.

(2) The right of the peoples of Russia to free self-determination, even to the point of separation and the formation of an independent state.

(3) The abolition of any and all national and national-religious privileges and disabilities.

(4) The free development of national minorities and ethnographic groups inhabiting the territory of Russia.

Decrees will be prepared immediately upon the formation of a Commission on Nationalities.

> In the name of the Russian Republic,
> People's Commissar for Nationalities,
> DJUGASHVILI-STALIN
> President of the Council of People's Commissars,
> V. ULYANOV (LENIN)

The Central Rada at Kiev immediately declared Ukraine an independent republic, as did the Government of Finland, through the Senate at Helsingfors. Independent 'Governments' sprang up in Siberia and the Caucasus. The Polish troops in the Russian Army, abolished their committees and established an iron discipline. ...

All these 'Governments' and 'movements' had two characteristics in common; they were controlled by the propertied classes, and they feared and detested Bolshevism. ...

Steadily, amid the chaos of shocking change, the Council of People's Commissars hammered at the scaffolding of the Socialist order. Decree on Social Insurance, on Workers' Control,

Regulations for Volost Land Committees, Abolition of Ranks and Titles, Abolition of Courts and the Creation of People's Tribunals....[52]

Army after army, fleet after fleet, sent deputations, 'joyfully to greet the new Government of the People'.

In front of Smolny, one day, I saw a ragged regiment just come from the trenches. The soldiers were drawn up before the great gates, thin and grey-faced, looking up at the building as if God were in it. Some pointed out the Imperial eagles over the door, laughing.... Red Guards came to mount guard. All the soldiers turned to look, curiously, as if they had heard of them but never seen them. They laughed good-naturedly and pressed out of line to slap the Red Guards on the back, with half-joking, half-admiring remarks....

The Provisional Government was no more. On 15 November, in all the churches of the capital, the priests stopped praying for it. But as Lenin himself told the Tsay-ee-kah, that was 'only the beginning of the conquest of power'. Deprived of arms, the opposition, which still controlled the economic life of the country, settled down to organize disorganization, with all the Russian genius for cooperative action – to obstruct, cripple, and discredit the Soviets.

The strike of Government employees was well organized, financed by the banks and commercial establishments. Every move of the Bolsheviki to take over the Government apparatus was resisted.

Trotsky went to the Ministry of Foreign Affairs; the functionaries refused to recognize him, locked themselves in, and when the doors were forced resigned. He demanded the keys of the archives; only when he brought workmen to force the locks were they given up. Then it was discovered that Neratov, former assistant Foreign Minister, had disappeared with the Secret Treaties....

Shliapnikov tried to take possession of the Ministry of Labour. It was bitterly cold, and there was no one to light the fires. Of all the hundreds of employees, not one would show him where the office of the Minister was....

Alexandra Kollontai, appointed the thirteenth of November Commissar of Public Welfare – the department of charities and public institutions – was welcomed with a strike of all but forty of the functionaries in the Ministry. Immediately the poor of the great cities, the inmates of institutions, were plunged in miserable want; delegations of starving cripples, of orphans, with blue pinched faces, besieged the building. With tears streaming down her face, Kollontai arrested the strikers until they should deliver the keys of the office and the safe; when she got the keys, however, it was discovered that the former Minister, Countess Panina, had gone off with all the funds, which she refused to surrender except on the order of the Constituent Assembly.[53]

In the Ministry of Agriculture, the Ministry of Supplies, the Ministry of Finance, similar incidents occurred. And the employees, summoned to return or forfeit their positions and their pensions, either stayed away or returned to sabotage. . . . Almost all the *intelligentsia* being anti-Bolshevik, there was nowhere for the Soviet Government to recruit new staffs. . . .

The private banks remained stubbornly closed, with a back door open for speculators. When Bolshevik Commissars entered, the clerks left, secreting the books and removing the funds. All the employees of the State Bank struck except the clerks in charge of the vaults and the manufacture of money, who refused all demands from Smolny and privately paid out huge sums to the Committee for Salvation and the City Duma.

Twice a Commissar, with a company of Red Guards, came formally to insist upon the delivery of large sums for Government expenses. The first time, the City Duma members and the Menshevik and Socialist Revolutionary leaders were present in imposing numbers, and spoke so gravely of the consequences that the Commissar was frightened. The second time he arrived with a warrant, which he proceeded to read aloud in due form; but someone called his attention to the fact that it had no date and no seal, and the traditional Russian respect for 'documents' forced him again to withdraw. . . .

The officials of the Credit Chancery destroyed their books, so that all record of the financial relations of Russia with foreign countries was lost.

The Supply Committees, the administrations of the municipal-owned public utilities, either did not work at all, or sabotaged. And when the Bolsheviki, compelled by the desperate needs of the city population, attempted to help or to control the public service, all the employees went on strike immediately, and the Duma flooded Russia with telegrams about Bolshevik 'violation of municipal autonomy'.

At military headquarters, and in the offices of the Ministries of War and Marine, where the old officials had consented to work, the Army Committees and the high command blocked the Soviets in every way possible, even to the extent of neglecting the troops at the front. The Vikzhel was hostile, refusing to transport Soviet troops; every troop train that left Petrograd was taken out by force, and railway officials had to be arrested each time – whereupon the Vikzhel threatened an immediate general strike unless they were released. ...

Smolny was plainly powerless. The newspapers said that all the factories of Petrograd must shut down for lack of fuel in three weeks; the Vikzhel announced that trains must cease running by 1 December, there was food for three days only in Petrograd, and no more coming in; and the Army on the front was starving. ... The Committee for Salvation, the various Central Committees, sent word all over the country, exhorting the population to ignore the Government decrees. And the Allied Embassies were either coldly indifferent or openly hostile. ...

The opposition newspapers, suppressed one day and re-appearing next morning under new names, heaped bitter sarcasm on the new régime.[54] Even *Novaya Zhizn* characterized it as 'a combination of demagoguery and impotence'.

From day to day (it said) the Government of the People's Commissars sinks deeper and deeper into the mire of superficial haste. Having easily conquered the power ... the Bolsheviki cannot make use of it.

Powerless to direct the existing mechanism of Government, they are unable at the same time to create a new one which might work easily and freely according to the theories of social experimenters.

Just a little while ago the Bolsheviki hadn't enough men to run their growing party – a work above all of speakers and writers; where then are they going to find trained men to execute the diverse and complicated functions of government?

The new Government acts and threatens, it sprays the country with decrees, each one more radical and more 'socialist' than the last. But in this exhibition of Socialism on Paper – more likely designed for the stupefaction of our descendants – there appears neither the desire nor the capacity to solve the immediate problems of the day!

Meanwhile the Vikzhel's Conference to Form a New Government continued to meet night and day. Both sides had already agreed in principle to the basis of the Government; the composition of the People's Council was being discussed; the Cabinet was tentatively chosen, with Chernov as Premier; the Bolsheviki were admitted in a large minority, but Lenin and Trotsky were barred. The Central Committees of the Menshevik and Socialist Revolutionary parties, the Executive Committee of the Peasants' Soviets, resolved that, although unalterably opposed to the 'criminal politics' of the Bolsheviki, they would 'in order to halt the fratricidal bloodshed', not oppose their entrance into the People's Council.

The flight of Kerensky, however, and the astounding success of the Soviets everywhere altered the situation. On the sixteenth, in a meeting of the Tsay-ee-kah, the Left Socialist Revolutionaries insisted that the Bolsheviki should form a coalition Government with the other Socialist parties; otherwise they would withdraw from the Military Revolutionary Committee and the Tsay-ee-kah. Malkin said: 'The news from Moscow, where our comrades are dying on both sides of the barricades, determines us to bring up once more the question of organization of power, and it is not only our right to do so but our duty.... We have won the right to sit with the Bolsheviki here within the walls of Smolny Institute, and to speak from this tribune. After the bitter internal party struggle we shall be obliged, if you refuse to compromise, to pass to open battle outside.... We must propose to the democracy terms of an acceptable compromise....'

After a recess to consider this ultimatum the Bolsheviki returned with a resolution, read by Kameniev:

The Tsay-ee-kah considers it necessary that there enter into the Government representatives of *all the Socialist parties comprising the Soviets of Workers', Soldiers', and Peasants' Deputies who recognize the conquests of the Revolution of 7 November – that is to say, the establishment of a Government of Soviets, the decrees on peace, land, workers' control over industry, and the arming of the working-class.* The Tsay-ee-kah therefore resolves to propose negotiations concerning the constitution of the Government to all parties *of the Soviet,* and insists upon the following conditions as a basis:

The Government is responsible to the Tsay-ee-kah. The Tsay-ee-kah shall be enlarged to 150 members. To these 150 delegates of the Soviets of Workers' and Soldiers' Deputies shall be added 75 delegates of the *Provincial* Soviets of Peasants' Deputies, 80 from the front organizations of the Army and Navy, 40 from the Trade Unions (25 from the various All-Russian Unions, in proportion to their importance, 10 from the Vikzhel, and 5 from the Post and Telegraph Workers), and 50 delegates from the Socialist groups in the Petrograd City Duma. In the Ministry itself, at least one half the portfolios must be reserved for the Bolsheviki. The Ministries of Labour, Interior, and Foreign Affairs must be given to the Bolsheviki. The command of the garrisons of Petrograd and Moscow must remain in the hands of delegates of the Moscow and Petrograd Soviets.

The Government undertakes the systematic arming of the workers of all Russia.

It is resolved to insist upon the candidature of comrades Lenin and Trotsky.

Kameniev explained. 'The so-called "People's Council",' he said, 'proposed by the Conference, would consist of about 420 members, of which about 150 would be Bolsheviki. Besides, there would be delegates from the counter-revolutionary old Tsay-ee-kah, 100 members chosen by the Municipal Dumas – Kornilovtsi all; 100 delegates from the Peasants' Soviets – appointed by Avksentiev, and 80 from the old Army Committees, who no longer represent the soldier masses.

'We refuse to admit the old Tsay-ee-kah, and also the representatives of the Municipal Dumas. The delegates from the Peasants' Soviets shall be elected by the Congress of Peasants, which we have called, and which will at the same time elect a new Executive Committee. The proposal to exclude Lenin and Trotsky is a proposal to decapitate our party, and we do not accept it. And finally, we see no necessity for a "People's Council" anyway: the Soviets are open to all Socialist parties, and the Tsay-ee-kah represents them in their real proportions among the masses. . . .'

Karelin, for the Left Socialist Revolutionaries, declared that his party would vote for the Bolshevik resolution, reserving the right to modify certain details, such as the representation of the peasants, and demanding that the Ministry of Agriculture be

reserved for the Left Socialist Revolutionaries. This was agreed
to....

Later, at a meeting of the Petrograd Soviet, Trotsky answered
a question about the formation of the new Government: 'I don't
know anything about that. I am not taking part in the negotiations.... However, I don't think that they are of great importance....'

That night there was great uneasiness in the Conference. The
delegates of the City Duma withdrew....

But at Smolny itself, in the ranks of the Bolshevik party, a
formidable opposition to Lenin's policy was growing. On the
night of 17 November the great hall was packed and ominous for
the meeting of the Tsay-ee-kah.

Larin, Bolshevik, declared that the moment of elections to the
Constituent Assembly approached, and it was time to do away
with 'political terrorism'.

'The measures taken against the freedom of the press should be
modified. They had their reason during the struggle, but now
they have no further excuse. The press should be free, except for
appeals to riot and insurrection.'

In a storm of hisses and hoots from his own party, Larin
offered the following resolution:

The decree of the Council of People's Commissars concerning the
press is herewith repealed.

Measures of political repression can only be employed subject to
decision of a special tribunal, elected by the Tsay-ee-kah proportionately
to the strength of the different parties represented; and this tribunal
shall have the right also to reconsider measures of repression already
taken.

This was met by a thunder of applause, not only from the Left
Socialist Revolutionaries, but also from a part of the Bolsheviki.

Avanessov, for the Leninites, hastily proposed that the question
of the press be postponed until after some compromise between
the Socialist parties had been reached. Overwhelmingly voted
down.

'The revolution which is now being accomplished,' went on
Avanessov, 'has not hesitated to attack private property; and it is

as private property that we must examine the question of the press. . . .'

Thereupon he read the official Bolshevik resolution:

The suppression of the bourgeois press was dictated not only by purely military needs in the course of the insurrection, and for the checking of counter-revolutionary action, but it is also necessary as a measure of transition towards the establishment of a new régime with regard to the press – a régime under which the capitalist owners of printing-presses and of paper cannot be the all-powerful and exclusive manufacturers of public opinion.

We must further proceed to the confiscation of private printing plants and supplies of paper, which should become the property of the Soviets, both in the capital and in the provinces, so that the political parties and groups can make use of the facilities of printing in proportion to the actual strength of the ideas they represent – in other words, proportionally to the number of their constituents.

The re-establishment of the so-called 'freedom of the press', the simple return of printing presses and paper to the capitalists – poisoners of the mind of the people – this would be an inadmissible surrender to the will of capital, a giving up of one of the most important conquests of the Revolution; in other words, it would be a measure of unquestionably counter-revolutionary character.

Proceeding from the above, the Tsay-ee-kah categorically rejects all propositions aiming at the re-establishment of the old régime in the domain of the press, and unequivocally supports the point of view of the Council of People's Commissars on this question against pretensions and ultimatums dictated by petty bourgeois prejudices, or by evident surrender to the interests of the counter-revolutionary bourgeoisie.

The reading of this resolution was interrupted by ironical shouts from the Left Socialist Revolutionaries, and bursts of indignation from the insurgent Bolsheviki. Karelin was on his feet, protesting. 'Three weeks ago the Bolsheviki were the most ardent defenders of the freedom of the press. . . . The arguments in this resolution suggest singularly the point of view of the old Black Hundreds and the censors of the Tsarist régime – for they also talked of "poisoners of the mind of the people".'

Trotsky spoke at length in favour of the resolution. He distinguished between the press during the civil war, and the press after the victory. 'During civil war the right to use violence belongs only to the oppressed....' (Cries of 'Who's the oppressed now? Cannibal!')

'The victory over our adversaries is not yet achieved, and the newspapers are arms in their hands. In these conditions, the closing of the newspapers is a legitimate measure of defence....' Then passing to the question of the press after the victory, Trotsky continued:

'The attitude of Socialists on the question of freedom of the press should be the same as their attitude towards the freedom of business.... The rule of the democracy which is being established in Russia demands that the domination of the press by private property must be abolished, just as the domination of industry by private property.... The power of the Soviets should confiscate all printing plants.' (Cries, 'Confiscate the printing shop of *Pravda*!')

'The monopoly of the press by the bourgeoisie must be abolished. Otherwise it isn't worth while for us to take the power. Each group of citizens should have access to print-shops and paper.... The ownership of print-type and of paper belongs first to the workers and peasants, and only afterwards to the bourgeois parties, which are in a minority.... The passing of the power into the hands of the Soviets will bring about a radical transformation of the essential conditions of existence, and this transformation will necessarily be evident in the press.... If we are going to nationalize the banks, can we then tolerate the financial journals? The old régime must die: that must be understood once and for all....' Applause and angry cries.

Karelin declared that the Tsay-ee-kah had no right to pass upon this important question, which should be left to a special committee. Again, passionately, he demanded that the press be free.

Then Lenin, calm, unemotional, his forehead wrinkled, as he spoke slowly, choosing his words; each sentence falling like a hammer-blow. 'The civil war is not yet finished; the enemy is still with us; consequently it is impossible to abolish the measures of repression against the press.

'We Bolsheviki have always said that when we reached a position of power we would close the bourgeois press. To tolerate the bourgeois newspapers would mean to cease being a Socialist. When one makes a Revolution, one cannot mark time; one must always go forward – or go back. He who now talks about the "freedom of the press" goes backward, and halts our headlong course towards Socialism.

'We have thrown off the yoke of capitalism, just as the first revolution threw off the yoke of Tsarism. *If the first revolution had the right to suppress the monarchist newspapers,* then we have the right to suppress the bourgeois press. It is impossible to separate the question of the freedom of the press from the other questions of the class struggle. We have promised to close these newspapers, and we shall do it. The immense majority of the people is with us!

'Now that the insurrection is over we have absolutely no desire to suppress the papers of the other Socialist parties, except inasmuch as they appeal to armed insurrection, or to disobedience to the Soviet Government. However, we shall not permit them, under the pretence of freedom of the Socialist press, to obtain through the secret support of the bourgeoisie, a monopoly of printing-presses, ink, and paper.... These essentials must become the property of the Soviet Government, and be apportioned, first of all to the Socialist parties in strict proportion to their voting strength....'

Then the vote. The resolution of Larin and the Left Socialist Revolutionaries was defeated by 31 to 22; the Lenin motion was carried by 34 to 24. Among the minority were the Bolsheviki Riazanov and Lozovsky, who declared that it was impossible for them to vote for any restriction on the freedom of the press.

Upon this the Left Socialist Revolutionaries declared they could no longer be responsible for what was being done, and withdrew from the Military Revolutionary Committee and all other positions of executive responsibility.

Five members – Nogin, Rykov, Milyutin, Teodorovich and Shliapnikov – resigned from the Council of People's Commissars, declaring:

We are in favour of a Socialist Government composed of all the parties in the Soviets. We consider that only the creation of such a Government can possibly guarantee the results of the heroic struggle of the working-class and the revolutionary army. Outside of that, there remains only one way: the constitution of a purely Bolshevik Government by means of political terrorism. This last is the road taken by the

Council of People's Commissars. We cannot and will not follow it. We see that this leads directly to the elimination from political life of many proletarian organizations, to the establishment of an irresponsible régime, and to the destruction of the Revolution and the country. We cannot take the responsibility for such a policy, and we renounce before the Tsay-ee-kah our function as People's Commissars.

Other Commissars, without resigning their positions, signed the declaration – Riazanov, Derbychev of the Press Department, Arbuzov of the Government Printing-plant, Yureniev of the Red Guard, Feodorov of the Commissariat of Labour, and Larin, secretary of the Section of Elaboration of Decrees.

At the same time Kameniev, Rykov, Milyutin, Zinoviev, and Nogin resigned from the Central Committee of the Bolshevik Party, making public their reasons:

... The constitution of such a Government (composed of all the parties of the Soviet) is indispensable to prevent a new flow of blood, the coming of famine, the destruction of the Revolution by the Kaledinists, to assure the convocation of the Constituent Assembly at the proper time, and to apply effectively the programme adopted by the Congress of Soviets. ...

We cannot accept the responsibility for the disastrous policy of the Central Committee, carried on against the will of an enormous majority of the proletariat and the soldiers, who are eager to see the rapid end of the bloodshed between the different political parties of the democracy.

... We renounce our title as members of the Central Committee, in order to be able to say openly our opinion to the masses of workers and soldiers. ...

We leave the Central Committee at the moment of victory; we cannot calmly look on while the policy of the chiefs of the Central Committee leads towards the loss of the fruits of victory and the crushing of the proletariat. ...

The masses of the workers, the soldiers of the garrison, stirred restlessly, sending their delegations to Smolny, to the Conference for Formation of the New Government, where the break in the ranks of the Bolsheviki caused the liveliest joy.

But the answer of the Leninites was swift and ruthless. Shliapnikov and Teodorovich submitted to party discipline and returned to their posts. Kameniev was stripped of his powers as president of the Tsay-ee-kah, and Sverdlov elected in his place. Zinoviev was deposed as president of the Petrograd Soviet. On the morning of the fifteenth *Pravda* contained a ferocious proclamation to the people of Russia, written by Lenin, which was printed in hundreds of thousands of copies, posted on the walls everywhere, and distributed over the face of Russia.

The second All-Russian Congress of Soviets gave the majority to the Bolshevik party. Only a Government formed by this party can therefore be a Soviet Government. And it is known to all that the Central Committee of the Bolshevik party, a few hours before the formation of the new Government and before proposing the list of its members to the All-Russian Congress of Soviets, invited to its meeting three of the most eminent members of the Left Socialist Revolutionary group, comrades Kamkov, Spiro, and Karelin, and ASKED THEM to participate in the new Government. We regret infinitely that the invited comrades refused; we consider their refusal inadmissible for revolutionists and champions of the working-class; we are willing at any time to include the Left Socialist Revolutionaries in the Government, but we believe that, as the party of the majority at the second All-Russian Congress of Soviets, we are entitled and BOUND before the people to form a Government. ...

... Comrades! Several members of the Central Committee of our party and the Council of People's Commissars, Kameniev, Zinoviev, Nogin, Rykov, Milyutin, and a few others left yesterday, 17 November, the Central Committee of our party, and the last three the Council of People's Commissars. ...

The comrades who left us acted like deserters, because they not only abandoned the posts entrusted to them, but also disobeyed the direct instructions of the Central Committee of our party, to the effect that they should wait the decisions of the Petrograd and Moscow party organizations before retiring. We blame decisively such desertion. We are firmly convinced that all conscious workers, soldiers, and peasants, belonging to our party or sympathizing with it, will also disapprove of the behaviour of the deserters. ...

Remember, comrades, that two of these deserters, Kameniev and Zinoviev, even before the uprising in Petrograd, appeared as deserters and strike-breakers, by voting at the decisive meeting of the Central Committee, 23 October 1917, against the insurrection; and even AFTER the resolution passed by the Central Committee, they continued their campaign at a meeting of the party workers. ... But the great impulse of the masses, the great heroism of millions of workers, soldiers, and peasants, in Moscow, Petrograd, at the front, in the trenches, in the villages, pushed aside the deserters as a railway train scatters sawdust. ...

Shame upon those who are of little faith, who hesitate, who doubt, who allow themselves to be frightened by the bourgeoisie, or who succumb before the cries of the latter's direct or indirect accomplices. There is NOT A SHADOW of hesitation in the MASSES of Petrograd, Moscow, and the rest of Russia. ...

... We shall not submit to any ultimatums from small groups of intellectuals which are not followed by the masses, which are PRACTICALLY only supported by Kornilovists, Savinkovists, *yunkers*, and so forth. ...

The response from the whole country was like a blast of hot storm. The insurgents never got a chance to 'say openly their opinion to the masses of workers and soldiers'. Upon the Tsay-ee-kah rolled in like breakers the fierce popular condemnation of the 'deserters'. For days Smolny was thronged with angry delegations and committees, from the front, from the Volga, from the Petrograd factories. 'Why did they dare leave the Government? Were they paid by the bourgeoisie to destroy the Revolution? They must return and submit to the decisions of the Central Committee!'

Only in the Petrograd garrison was there still uncertainty.[55] A great soldier meeting was held on 24 November, addressed by representatives of all the political parties. By a vast majority Lenin's policy was sustained, and the Left Socialist Revolutionaries were told that they must enter the government....*

The Mensheviki delivered a final ultimatum, demanding that all Ministers and *yunkers* be released, that all newspapers be allowed full freedom, that the Red Guard be disarmed and the garrison put under command of the Duma. To this Smolny answered that all the Socialist Ministers and also that all but a very few *yunkers* had been already set free, that all newspapers were free except the bourgeois press, and that the Soviet would remain in command of the armed forces.... On the nineteenth the Conference to Form a New Government disbanded, and the opposition one by one slipped away to Moghilev, where, under the wing of the General Staff, they continued to form Government after Government, until the end....

Meanwhile the Bolsheviki had been undermining the power of the Vikzhel. An appeal of the Petrograd Soviet to all railway

* See page 335.

workers called upon them to force the Vikzhel to surrender its power. On the fifteenth the Tsay-ee-kah, following its procedure towards the peasants, called an All-Russian Congress of Railway Workers for 1 December; the Vikzhel immediately called its own Congress for two weeks later. On 16 November, the Vikzhel members took their seats in the Tsay-ee-kah. On the night of 2 December, at the opening session of the All-Russian Congress of Railway Workers, the Tsay-ee-kah formally offered the post of Commissar of Ways and Communications to the Vikzhel – which accepted. . . .

Having settled the question of power, the Bolsheviki turned their attention to problems of practical administration. First of all the city, the country, the Army must be fed. Bands of sailors and Red Guards scoured the warehouses, the railway terminals, even the barges in the canals, unearthing and confiscating thousands of *poods*** of food held by private speculators. Emissaries were sent to the provinces, where with the assistance of the Land Committees they seized the storehouses of the great grain dealers. Expeditions of sailors, heavily armed, were sent out in groups of five thousand to the South, to Siberia, with roving commissions to capture cities still held by the White Guards, establish order and *get food*. Passenger traffic on the Trans-Siberian Railroad was suspended for two weeks, while thirteen trains, loaded with bolts of cloth and bars of iron assembled by the Factory-Shop Committees, were sent out eastward, each in charge of a Commissar, to barter with the Siberian peasants for grain and potatoes. . . .

Kaledin being in possession of the coal mines of the Don, the fuel question became urgent. Smolny shut off all electric lights in theatres, shops, and restaurants, cut down the number of street-cars, and confiscated the private stores of firewood held by the fuel dealers. . . . And when the factories of Petrograd were about to close down for lack of coal, the sailors of the Baltic Fleet turned over to the workers two hundred thousand *poods* from the bunkers of battleships. . . .

Towards the end of November occurred the 'wine-pogrom'[56] – looting of the wine cellars – beginning with the plundering of the Winter Palace vaults. For days there were drunken soldiers on the

* A *pood* is thirty-six pounds.

streets.... In all this was evident the hand of the counter-revolutionists, who distributed among the regiments plans showing the location of the stores of liquor. The Commissars of Smolny began by pleading and arguing, which did not stop the growing disorder, followed by pitched battles between soldiers and Red Guards.... Finally the Military Revolutionary Committee sent out companies of sailors with machine-guns, who fired mercilessly upon the rioters, killing many; and by executive order the wine-cellars were invaded by Committees with hatchets, who smashed the bottles – or blew them up with dynamite....[57]

Companies of Red Guards, disciplined and well-paid, were on duty at the headquarters of the Ward Soviets day and night, replacing the old Militia. In all quarters of the city small elective Revolutionary Tribunals were set up by the workers and soldiers to deal with petty crime....

The great hotels, where the speculators still did a thriving business, were surrounded by Red Guards, and the speculators thrown into jail....[58]

Alert and suspicious, the working class of the city constituted itself a vast spy system, through the servants prying into bourgeois households, and reporting all information to the Military Revolutionary Committee, which struck with an iron hand, unceasing. In this way was discovered the Monarchist plot led by a former Duma-member Purishkevich and a group of nobles and officers, who had planned an officers' uprising, and had written a letter inviting Kaledin to Petrograd....[59] In this way was unearthed the conspiracy of the Petrograd Cadets, who were sending money and recruits to Kaledin....

Neratov, frightened at the outburst of popular fury provoked by his flight, returned and surrendered the Secret Treaties to Trotsky, who began their publication in *Pravda*, scandalizing the world....

The restrictions on the press were increased by a decree[60] making advertisements a monopoly of the official Government newspaper. At this all the other papers suspended publication as a protest, or disobeyed the law and were closed.... Only three weeks later did they finally submit.

Still the strike of the Ministries went on, still the sabotage of the old officials, the stoppage of normal economic life. Behind

Smolny was only the will of the vast, unorganized popular masses; and with them the Council of People's Commissars dealt, directing revolutionary mass action against its enemies. In eloquent proclamations,[61] couched in simple words and spread over Russia, Lenin explained the Revolution, urged the people to take the power into their own hands, by force to break down the resistance of the propertied classes, by force to take over the institutions of Government. Revolutionary order. Revolutionary discipline! Strict accounting and control! No strikes! No loafing![62]

On the twentieth of November the Military Revolutionary Committee issued a warning:

> The rich classes oppose the power of the Soviets – the Government of workers, soldiers, and peasants. Their sympathizers halt the work of the employees of the Government and the Duma, incite strikes in the banks, try to interrupt communication by the railways, the post, and the telegraph. ...
>
> We warn them that they are playing with fire. The country and the Army are threatened with famine. To fight against it the regular functioning of all services is indispensable. The Workers' and Peasants' Government is taking every measure to assure the country and the Army all that is necessary. Opposition to these measures is a crime too against the People. We warn the rich classes and their sympathizers that if they do not cease their sabotage and their provocation in halting the transportation of food they will be the first to suffer. They will be deprived of the right of receiving food. All reserves which they possess will be requisitioned. The property of the principal criminals will be confiscated.
>
> We have done our duty in warning those who play with fire.
>
> We are convinced that in case decisive measures become necessary we shall be solidly supported by all workers, soldiers, and peasants.

On the twenty-second of November the walls of the city were placarded with a sheet headed 'EXTRAORDINARY COMMUNICATION':

> The Council of People's Commissars has received an urgent telegram from the Staff of the Northern Front. ...
>
> 'There must be no further delay; do not let the Army die of hunger; the armies of the Northern Front have not received a crust of bread for several days now, and in two or three days they will not have any more biscuits – which are being doled out to them from reserve supplies until

now never touched. . . . Already delegates from all parts of the front are talking of a necessary removal of part of the Army to the rear, foreseeing that in a few days there will be headlong flight of the soldiers, dying from hunger, ravaged by the three years' war in the trenches, sick, insufficiently clothed, bare-footed, driven mad by superhuman misery.'

The Military Revolutionary Committee brings this to the notice of the Petrograd garrison and the workers of Petrograd. The situation at the front demands the most urgent and decisive measures. . . . Meanwhile the higher functionaries of the Government institutions, banks, railroads, post, and telegraph are on strike and impeding the work of the Government in supplying the front with provisions. . . . Each hour of delay may cost the life of thousands of soldiers. The counter-revolutionary functionaries are most dishonest criminals towards their hungry and dying brethren on the front. . . .

THE MILITARY REVOLUTIONARY COMMITTEE GIVES THESE CRIMINALS A LAST WARNING. In the event of the least resistance or opposition on their part the harshness of the measures which will be adopted against them will correspond to the seriousness of their crime. . . .

The masses of workers and soldiers responded by a savage tremor of rage, which swept all Russia. In the capital the Government and bank employees got out hundreds of proclamations and appeals,[63] protesting, defending themselves, such as this one:

TO THE ATTENTION OF ALL CITIZENS
THE STATE BANK IS CLOSED!
WHY?

Because the violence exercised by the Bolsheviki against the State Bank has made it impossible for us to work. The first act of the People's Commissars was to DEMAND TEN MILLION ROUBLES, and on 27 November THEY DEMANDED TWENTY-FIVE MILLIONS, without any indication as to where the money was to go.

. . . We functionaries cannot take part in plundering the people's property. We stopped work.

CITIZENS! The money in the State Bank is yours, the people's money acquired by your labour, your sweat, your blood. CITIZENS! Save the people's property from robbery, and us from violence, and we shall immediately resume work.

EMPLOYEES OF THE STATE BANK

From the Ministry of Supplies, the Ministry of Finance, from the Special Supply Committee, declarations that the Military Revolutionary Committee made it impossible for the employees to work, appeals to the population to support them against Smolny.... But the dominant worker and soldier did not believe them; it was firmly fixed in the popular mind that the employees were sabotaging, starving the Army, starving the people.... In the long bread lines, which as formerly stood in the iron winter streets, it was not the *Government* which was blamed, as it had been under Kerensky, but the *chinovniki*, the sabotageurs; for the Government was *their* Government, *their* Soviets – and the functionaries of the Ministries were against it....

At the centre of all this opposition was the Duma, and its militant organ, the Committee for Salvation, protesting against all the decrees of the Council of People's Commissars, voting again and again not to recognize the Soviet Government, openly cooperating with the new counter-revolutionary 'Governments' set up at Moghilev.... On the seventeenth of November, for example, the Committee for Salvation addressed 'all Municipal Governments, Zemstvos, and all democratic and revolutionary organizations of peasants, workers, soldiers, and other citizens', in these words:

Do not recognize the Government of the Bolsheviki, and struggle against it.

Form local Committees for Salvation of Country and Revolution, who will unite all democratic forces, so as to aid the All-Russian Committee for Salvation in the tasks it has set itself....

Meanwhile the elections for the Constituent Assembly in Petrograd[64] gave an enormous plurality to the Bolsheviki; so that even the Mensheviki Internationalists pointed out that the Duma ought to be re-elected, as it no longer represented the political composition of the Petrograd population.... At the same time floods of resolutions from workers' organizations, from military units, even from the peasants in the surrounding country, poured in upon the Duma, calling it 'counter-revolutionary, Kornilovist', and demanding that it resign. The last days of the Duma were stormy with the bitter demands of the Municipal workers for decent living wages, and the threat of strikes....

On the twenty-third a formal decree of the Military Revolutionary Committee dissolved the Committee for Salvation. On the twenty-ninth, the Council of People's Commissars ordered the dissolution and re-election of the Petrograd City Duma:

In view of the fact that the Central Duma of Petrograd, elected 2 September ... has definitely lost the right to represent the population of Petrograd, being in complete disaccord with its state of mind and its aspirations ... and in view of the fact that the personnel of the Duma majority, although having lost all political following, continues to make use of its prerogatives to resist in a counter-revolutionary manner the will of the workers, soldiers, and peasants, to sabotage and obstruct the normal work of the Government – the Council of People's Commissars considers it its duty to invite the population of the capital to pronounce judgement on the policy of the organ of Municipal autonomy.

To this end the Council of People's Commissars resolves:

(1) To dissolve the Municipal Duma: the dissolution to take effect 30 November 1917.

(2) All functionaries elected or appointed by the present Duma shall remain at their posts and fulfil the duties confided to them, until their places shall be filled by representatives of the new Duma.

(3) All Municipal employees shall continue to fulfil their duties; those who leave the service of their own accord shall be considered discharged.

(4) The new elections for the Municipal Duma of Petrograd are fixed for 9 December 1917. ...

(5) The Municipal Duma of Petrograd shall meet 11 December, at two o'clock.

(6) Those who disobey this decree, as well as those who intentionally harm or destroy the property of the Municipality, shall be immediately arrested and brought before the Revolutionary Tribunals. ...

The Duma met defiantly, passing resolutions to the effect that it would 'defend its position to the last drop of its blood', and appealing desperately to the population to save their 'own elected City Government'. But the population remained indifferent or hostile. On the thirty-first, Mayor Schreider and several members were arrested, interrogated and released. That day and the next the Duma continued to meet, interrupted frequently by Red Guards and sailors, who politely requested the assembly to disperse. At the meeting of 2 December, an officer and some sailors entered the Nikolai Hall while a member was speaking, and ordered the members to leave or force would be used. They did so, protesting to the last, but finally 'ceding to violence'.

The new Duma, which was elected ten days later, and for which the 'Moderate' Socialists refused to vote, was almost entirely Bolshevik....[65]

There remained several centres of dangerous opposition, such as the 'republics' of Ukraine and Finland, which were showing definitely anti-Soviet tendencies. Both at Helsingfors and at Kiev the Governments were gathering troops which could be depended upon, and entering upon campaigns of crushing Bolshevism, and of disarming and expelling Russian troops. The Ukrainian Rada had taken command of all southern Russia, and was furnishing Kaledin reinforcements and supplies. Both Finland and Ukraine were beginning secret negotiations with the Germans, and were promptly recognized by the Allied Governments, which loaned them huge sums of money, joining with the propertied classes to create counter-revolutionary centres of attack upon Soviet Russia. In the end, when Bolshevism had conquered in both these countries, the defeated bourgeoisie called in the Germans to restore them to power....

But the most formidable menace to the Soviet Government was internal and two-headed – the Kaledin movement, and the Staff at Moghilev, where General Dukhonin had assumed command.

The ubiquitous Muraviov was appointed commander of the war against the Cossacks, and a Red Army was recruited from among the factory workers. Hundreds of propagandists were sent to the Don. The Council of People's Commissars issued a proclamation to the Cossacks,[66] explaining what the Soviet Government was, how the propertied classes, the *chinovniki*, landlords, bankers, and their allies, the Cossack princes, landowners, and generals, were trying to destroy the Revolution, and prevent the confiscation of their wealth by the people.

On 27 November a committee of Cossacks came to Smolny to see Trotsky and Lenin. They demanded if it were true that the Soviet Government did not intend to divide the Cossack lands among the peasants of Great Russia? 'No,' answered Trotsky. The Cossacks deliberated for a while. 'Well,' they asked, 'does the Soviet Government intend to confiscate the estates of our great Cossack landowners and divide them among the Cossacks?' To this Lenin replied. 'That,' he said, 'is for you to do. We shall support the working Cossacks in all their actions. ... The best way to begin is to form Cossack Soviets; you will be given representation in the Tsay-ee-kah, and then it will be *your* Government, too. . . .'

The Cossacks departed, thinking hard. Two weeks later General Kaledin received a deputation from his troops. 'Will you,' they asked, 'promise to divide the great estates of the Cossack landlords among the working Cossacks?'

'Only over my dead body,' responded Kaledin. A month later, seeing his army melt away before his eyes, Kaledin blew out his brains. And the Cossack movement was no more. . . .

Meanwhile at Moghilev were gathered the old Tsay-ee-kah, the 'moderate' Socialist leaders – from Avksentiev to Chernov – the active chiefs of the old Army Committees, and the reactionary officers. The Staff steadily refused to recognize the Council of People's Commissars. It had united about it the Death Battalions, the Knights of St George, and the Cossacks of the front, and was in close and secret touch with the Allied military attachés, and with the Kaledin movement and the Ukrainian Rada. . . .

The Allied Governments had made no reply to the Peace decree of 8 November, in which the Congress of Soviets had asked for a general armistice.

On 20 November Trotsky addressed a note to the Allied Ambassadors:[67]

I have the honour to inform you, Mr Ambassador, that the All-Russian Congress of Soviets . . . on 8 November constituted a new Government of the Russian Republic, in the form of the Council of People's Commissars. The President of the Government is Vladimir Ilyich Lenin. The direction of foreign affairs has been entrusted to me, as People's Commissar for Foreign Affairs. . . .

In drawing your attention to the text approved by the All-Russian Congress, of the proposition of an armistice and a democratic peace without annexations or indemnities, based on the right of self-determination of peoples, I have the honour to request you to consider that document as a formal proposal of an immediate armistice on all fronts, and the opening of immediate peace negotiations; a proposal which the authorized Government of the Russian Republic addresses at the same time to all the belligerent peoples and their Governments.

Please accept, Mr Ambassador, the profound assurance of the esteem of the Soviet Government towards your people, who cannot but wish for peace, like all the other peoples exhausted and drained by this unexampled butchery. . . .

The same night the Council of People's Commissars telegraphed to General Dukhonin:

> ... The Council of People's Commissars considers it indispensable without delay to make a formal proposal of armistice to all the powers both enemy and Allied. A declaration conforming to this decision has been sent by the Commissar for Foreign Affairs to the representatives of the Allied powers in Petrograd.
>
> The Council of People's Commissars orders you, Citizen Commander, ... to propose to the enemy military authorities immediately to cease hostilities, and enter into negotiations for peace. In charging you with the conduct of these preliminary pourparlers, the Council of People's Commissars orders you:
>
> 1. To inform the Council by direct wire immediately of any and all steps in the pourparlers with the representatives of the enemy armies.
>
> 2. Not to sign the act of armistice until it has been passed upon by the Council of People's Commissars.

The Allied Ambassadors received Trotsky's note with contemptuous silence, accompanied by anonymous interviews in the newspapers, full of spite and ridicule. The order to Dukhonin was characterized openly as an act of treason....

As for Dukhonin, he gave no sign. On the night of 22 November he was communicated with by telephone, and asked if he intended to obey the order. Dukhonin answered that he could not, unless it emanated from 'a Government sustained by the Army and the country'.

By telegraph he was immediately dismissed from the post of Supreme Commander, and Krylenko appointed in his place. Following his tactics of appealing to the masses, Lenin sent a radio to all regimental, divisional, and corps Committees, to all soldiers and sailors of the Army and the Fleet, acquainting them with Dukhonin's refusal, and ordering that 'the regiments on the front shall elect delegates to begin negotiations with the enemy detachments opposite their positions...'.

On the twenty-third the military attachés of the Allied nations, acting on instructions from their Governments, presented a note to Dukhonin, in which he was solemnly warned not to 'violate the conditions of the treaties concluded between the Powers of the Entente'. The note went on to say that if a separate armistice with Germany were concluded, that act 'would result in the most serious consequences' to Russia. This communication Dukhonin at once sent out to all the soldiers' Committees....

Next morning Trotsky made another appeal to the troops, characterizing the note of the Allied representatives as a flagrant interference in the internal affairs of Russia, and a bald attempt 'to force by threats the Russian Army and the Russian people to continue the war in execution of the treaties concluded by the Tsar...'.

From Smolny poured out proclamation after proclamation,[68] denouncing Dukhonin and the counter-revolutionary officers about him, denouncing the reactionary politicians gathered at Moghilev, rousing, from one end of the thousand-mile front to the other, millions of angry, suspicious soldiers. And at the same time Krylenko, accompanied by three detachments of fanatical sailors, set out for the Stavka, breathing threats of vengeance,[69] and received by the soldiers everywhere with tremendous ovations – a triumphal progress. The Central Army Committee issued a declaration in favour of Dukhonin; and at once ten thousand troops moved upon Moghilev....

On 2 December the garrison of Moghilev rose and seized the city, arresting Dukhonin and the Army Committee, and going out with victorious red banners to meet the new Supreme Commander. Krylenko entered Moghilev next morning, to find a howling mob gathered about the railway-car in which Dukhonin had been imprisoned. Krylenko made a speech in which he implored the soldiers not to harm Dukhonin, as he was to be taken to Petrograd and judged by the Revolutionary Tribunal. When he had finished, suddenly Dukhonin himself appeared at the window, as if to address the throng. But with a savage roar the people rushed the car, and falling upon the old general, dragged him out and beat him to death on the platform....

So ended the revolt of the Stavka....

Immensely strengthened by the collapse of the last important stronghold of hostile military power in Russia the Soviet Government began with confidence the organization of the State. Many of the old functionaries flocked to its banner, and many members of other parties entered the Government service. The financially ambitious, however, were checked by the decree on Salaries of Government Employees, fixing the salaries of the People's

Commissars – the highest – at five hundred roubles (about fifty dollars) a month.... The strike of Government employees, led by the Union of Unions, collapsed, deserted by the financial and commercial interests which had been backing it. The bank clerks returned to their jobs....

With the decree on the Nationalization of Banks, the formation of the Supreme Council of People's Economy, the putting into practical operation of the Land Decree in the villages, the democratic reorganization of the Army, and the sweeping changes in all branches of the Government and of life – with all these, effective only by the will of the masses of workers, soldiers, and peasants, slowly began, with many mistakes and hitches, the moulding of proletarian Russia.

Not by compromise with the propertied classes, or with the other political leaders; not by conciliating the old Government mechanism, did the Bolsheviki conquer the power. Nor by the organized violence of a small clique. If the masses all over Russia had not been ready for insurrection it must have failed. The only reason for Bolshevik success lay in their accomplishing the vast and simple desires of the most profound strata of the people, calling them to the work of tearing down and destroying the old, and afterwards, in the smoke of falling ruins, cooperating with them to erect the framework of the new....

12 The Peasants' Congress

It was on 18 November that the snow came. In the morning we woke to window-ledges heaped white, and snowflakes falling so whirling thick that it was impossible to see ten feet ahead. The mud was gone; in a twinkling the gloomy city became white, dazzling. The *droshki* with their padded coachmen turned into sleighs, bounding along the uneven street at headlong speed, their drivers' beards stiff and frozen. . . . In spite of Revolution, all Russia plunging dizzily into the unknown and terrible future, joy swept the city with the coming of the snow. Everybody was smiling; people ran into the streets, holding out their arms to the soft, falling flakes, laughing. Hidden was all the greyness; only the gold and coloured spires and cupolas, with heightened barbaric splendour, gleamed through the white snow.

Even the sun came out, pale and watery, at noon. The colds and rheumatism of the rainy months vanished. The life of the city grew gay, and the very Revolution ran swifter. . . .

I sat one evening in a *traktir* – a kind of lower-class inn – across the street from the gates of Smolny; a low-ceilinged, loud place called 'Uncle Tom's Cabin', much frequented by Red Guards. They crowded it now, packed close around the little tables with their dirty table-cloths and enormous china teapots, filling the place with foul cigarette smoke, while the harassed waiters ran about crying '*Seichass! Seichass!* In a minute! Right away!'

In one corner sat a man in the uniform of a captain, addressing the assembly, which interrupted him at every few words.

'You are no better than murderers!' he cried. 'Shooting down your Russian brothers on the streets!'

'When did we do that?' asked a worker.

'Last Sunday you did it, when the *yunkers* –'

'Well, didn't they shoot us?' One man exhibited his arm in a sling. 'Haven't I got something to remember them by, the devils?'

The captain shouted at the top of his voice. 'You should remain neutral! You should remain neutral! Who are you to destroy the legal Government? Who is Lenin? A German –'

'Who are you? A counter-revolutionist! A provocator!' they bellowed at him.

When he could make himself heard the captain stood up. 'All right!' said he. 'You call yourselves the people of Russia. But you're not the people of Russia. The peasants are the people of Russia. Wait until the peasants –'

'Yes,' they cried, 'wait until the peasants speak. We know what the peasants will say.... Aren't they working-men like ourselves?'

In the long run everything depended upon the peasants. While the peasants had been politically backward, still they had their own peculiar idea, and they constituted more than eighty per cent of the people of Russia. The Bolsheviki had a comparatively small following among the peasants; and a permanent dictatorship of Russia by the industrial workers was impossible.... The traditional peasant party was the Socialist Revolutionary Party; of all the parties now supporting the Soviet Government, the Left Socialist Revolutionaries were the logical inheritors of peasant leadership – and the Left Socialist Revolutionaries, who were at the mercy of the organized city proletariat, desperately needed the backing of the peasants....

Meanwhile Smolny had not neglected the peasants. After the Land Decree, one of the first actions of the Tsay-ee-kah had been to call a Congress of Peasants, over the head of the Executive Committee of the Peasants' Soviets. A few days later was issued detailed Regulations for the Volost (Township) Land Committees, followed by Lenin's *Instruction to Peasants*,[70] which explained the Bolshevik revolution and the new Government in simple terms; and on 16 November Lenin and Milyutin published the *Instructions to Provisional Emissaries*, of whom thousands were sent by the Soviet Government into the villages.

1. Upon his arrival in the province to which he is accredited the emissary should call a joint meeting of the Central Executive Committees of the Soviets of Workers', Soldiers', and Peasants' Deputies, to whom he should make a report on the agrarian laws, and then demand that a joint plenary session of the Soviets be summoned. ...

2. He must study the aspects of the agrarian problem in the province.
   (a) Has the landowners' property been taken over, and if so, in what districts?
   (b) Who administers the confiscated land – the former proprietors or the Land Committees?
   (c) What has been done with the agricultural machinery and with the farm animals?

3. Has the ground cultivated by the pea sants been augmented?

4. How much and in what respect do es the amount of land now under cultivation differ from the amount fixed by the Government as an average minimum?

5. The emissary must insist that, after the peasants have received the land, it is imperative that they increase the amount of cultivated land as quickly as possible, and that they hasten the sending of grain to the cities, as the only means of avoiding famine.

6. What are the measures projected or put into effect for the transfer of land from the landowners to the Land Committees and similar bodies appointed by the Soviets?

7. It is desirable that agricultural p roperties well appointed and well organized should be administered by Soviets composed of the regular employees of those properties, unde r the direction of competent agricultural scientists.

All through the villages a ferment of change was going on, caused not only by the electrifying action of the Land Decree, but also by thousands of revolutionary-minded peasant-soldiers returning from the front. . . . These men, especially, welcomed the call to a Congress of Peasants.

Like the old Tsay-ee-kah in the matter of the second Congress of Workers' and Soldiers' Soviets, the Executive Committee tried to prevent the Peasant Congress summoned by Smolny. And like the old Tsay-ee-kah, finding its resistance futile, the Executive Committee sent frantic telegrams ordering the election of Conservative delegates. Word was even spread among the peasants that the Congress would meet at Moghilev, and some delegates went there; but by 23 November about four hundred had gathered in Petrograd, and the party caucuses had begun.

The first session took place in the Alexander Hall of the Duma building, and the first vote showed that more than half of all the delegates were Left Socialist Revolutionaries, while the Bolsheviki controlled a bare fifth, the conservative Socialist

Revolutionaries a quarter, and all the rest were united only in their opposition to the old Executive Committee, dominated by Avksentiev, Chaikovsky, and Peshekhonov. . . .

The great hall was jammed with people and shaken with continual clamour; deep, stubborn bitterness divided the delegates into angry groups. To the right was a sprinkling of officers' epaulettes and the patriarchal, bearded faces of the older, more substantial peasants; in the centre were a few peasants, non-commissioned officers, and some soldiers; and on the left almost all the delegates wore the uniforms of common soldiers. These last were the young generation, who had been serving in the army. . . The galleries were thronged with workers – who, in Russia, still remember their peasant origin. . . .

Unlike the old Tsay-ee-kah, the Executive Committee, in opening the session, did not recognize the Congress as official; the official Congress was called for 13 December; amid a hurricane of applause and angry cries, the speaker declared that this gathering was merely 'Extraordinary Conference. . .'. But the 'Extraordinary Conference' soon showed its attitude towards the Executive Committee by electing as presiding officer Maria Spiridonova, leader of the Left Socialist Revolutionaries.

Most of the first day was taken up by a violent debate as to whether the representatives of Volost Soviets should be seated, or only delegates from the provincial bodies; and just as in the Workers' and Soldiers' Congress, an overwhelming majority declared in favour of the widest possible representation. Whereupon the old Executive Committee left the hall. . . .

Almost immediately it was evident that most of the delegates were hostile to the Government of the People's Commissars. Zinoviev, attempting to speak for the Bolsheviki, was hooted down, and as he left the platform, amid laughter, there were cries 'There's how a People's Commissar sits in a mud-puddle!'

'We Left Socialist Revolutionaries refuse,' cried Nazariev, a delegate from the Provinces, 'to recognize this so-called Workers' and Peasants' Government until the peasants are represented in it. At present it is nothing but a dictatorship of the workers. . . . We insist upon the formation of a new Government which will represent the entire democracy!'

The reactionary delegates shrewdly fostered this feeling,

declaring, in the face of protests from the Bolshevik benches, that the Council of People's Commissars intended either to control the Congress or dissolve it by force of arms – an announcement which was received by the peasants with bursts of fury. . . .

On the third day Lenin suddenly mounted the tribune; for ten minutes the room went mad. 'Down with him!' they shrieked. 'We will not listen to any of your People's Commissars! We don't recognize your Government!'

Lenin stood there quite calmly, gripping the desk with both hands, his little eyes thoughtfully surveying the tumult beneath. Finally, except for the right side of the hall, the demonstration wore itself out somewhat.

'I do not come here as a member of the Council of People's Commissars,' said Lenin, and waited again for the noise to subside, 'but as a member of the Bolshevik faction, duly elected to this Congress.' And he held his credentials up so that all might see them.

'However,' he went on in an unmoved voice, 'nobody will deny that the present Government of Russia has been formed by the Bolshevik Party' – he had to wait a moment – 'so that for all purposes it is the same thing. . . .' Here the right benches broke into deafening clamour, but the centre and left were curious, and compelled silence.

Lenin's argument was simple. 'Tell me frankly, you peasants, to whom we have given the lands of the *pomieshchiki*; do you want to prevent the workers from getting control of industry? This is class war. The *pomieshchiki* of course oppose the peasants, and the manufacturers oppose the workers. Are you going to allow the ranks of the proletariat to be divided? Which side will you be on?

'We, the Bolsheviki, are the party of the proletariat – of the peasant proletariat as well as the industrial proletariat. We, the Bolsheviki, are the protectors of the Soviets – of the Peasants' Soviets as well as those of the Workers' and Soldiers'. The present Government is a Government of Soviets; we have not only invited the Peasants' Soviets to join that Government, but we have also invited representatives of the Left Socialist Revolutionaries to enter the Council of People's Commissars. . . .

'The Soviets are the most perfect representatives of the people –

of the workers in the factories and mines, of the workers in the fields. Anybody who attempts to destroy the Soviets is guilty of an anti-democratic and counter-revolutionary act. And I serve notice here on you, comrades Right Socialist Revolutionaries – and on you, Messrs Cadets – that if the Constituent Assembly attempts to destroy the Soviets we shall not permit the Constituent Assembly to do this thing!'

On the afternoon of 25 November Chernov arrived in hot haste from Moghilev, summoned by the Executive Committee. Only two months before considered an extreme revolutionist, and very popular with the peasants, he was now called to check the dangerous drift of the Congress towards the Left. Upon his arrival Chernov was arrested and taken to Smolny, where, after a short conversation, he was released.

His first act was bitterly to rebuke the Executive Committee for leaving the Congress. They agreed to return, and Chernov entered the hall, welcomed with great applause by the majority, and the hoots and jeers of the Bolsheviki.

'Comrades! I have been away. I participated in the Conference of the Twelfth Army on the question of calling a Congress of all the Peasant delegates of the armies of the Western Front, and I know very little about the insurrection which occurred here –'

Zinoviev rose in his seat, and shouted, 'Yes, you were away – for a few minutes!' Fearful tumult. Cries, 'Down with the Bolsheviki!'

Chernov continued. 'The accusation that I helped lead an army on Petrograd has no foundation, and is entirely false. Where does such an accusation come from? Show me the source!'

Zinoviev: '*Izvestia* and *Dielo Naroda* – your own paper – that's where it comes from!'

Chernov's wide face, with the small eyes, waving hair and greyish beard, became red with wrath, but he controlled himself and went on. 'I repeat, I know practically nothing about what has happened here, and I did not lead any army except this army (he pointed to the peasant delegates), which I am largely responsible for bringing here!' Laughter and shouts of 'Bravo!'

'Upon my return I visited Smolny. No such accusation was made against me there. . . . After a brief conversation I left – and that's all! Let anyone present make such an accusation!'

An uproar followed, in which the Bolsheviki and some of the Left Socialist Revolutionaries were on their feet all at once, shaking their fists and yelling, and the rest of the assembly tried to yell them down.

'This is an outrage, not a session!' cried Chernov, and he left the hall; the meeting was adjourned because of the noise and disorder. . . .

Meanwhile the question of the status of the Executive Committee was agitating all minds. By declaring the assembly 'Extraordinary Conference' it had been planned to block the re-election of the Executive Committee. But this worked both ways: the Left Socialist Revolutionists decided that if the Congress had no power over the Executive Committee, then the Executive Committee had no power over the Congress. On 25 November the assembly resolved that the powers of the Executive Committee be assumed by the Extraordinary Conference, in which only members of the Executive who had been elected as delegates might vote. . . .

The next day, in spite of the bitter opposition of the Bolsheviki, the resolution was amended to give all the members of the Executive Committee, whether elected as delegates or not, voice and vote in the assembly.

On the twenty-seventh occurred the debate on the land question, which revealed the differences between the agrarian programme of the Bolsheviki, and the Left Socialist Revolutionaries.

Kolchinsky, for the Left Socialist Revolutionaries, outlined the history of the land question during the Revolution. The first Congress of Peasants' Soviets, he said, had voted a precise and formal resolution in favour of putting the landed estates immediately into the hands of the Land Committees. But the directors of the Revolution, and the bourgeois in the Government, had insisted that the question could not be solved until the Constituent Assembly met. . . . The second period of the Revolution, the period of 'compromise', was signalled by the entrance of Chernov into the Cabinet. The peasants were convinced that now the practical solution of the land question would begin; but in spite of the imperative decision of the first Peasant Congress the reactionaries and conciliators in the Executive Committee had prevented any action. This policy provoked a series of agrarian disorders, which appeared as the natural expression of impatience and thwarted energy on the part of the peasants. The peasants understood the exact meaning of the Revolution – they tried to turn words into action....

'The recent events,' said the orator, 'do not indicate a simple riot, or a "Bolshevik adventure", but, on the contrary, a real popular rising, which has been greeted with sympathy by the whole country....

'The Bolsheviki in general took the correct attitude towards the land question; but in recommending that the peasants seize the land by force they committed a profound error.... From the first days the Bolsheviki declared that the peasants should take over the land "by revolutionary mass action". This is nothing but anarchy; the land can be taken over in an organized manner.... For the Bolsheviki it was important that the problems of the Revolution should be solved in the quickest possible manner – but the Bolsheviki were not interested in how these questions were to be solved....

'The land decree of the Congress of Soviets is identical in its fundamentals with the decisions of the first Peasants' Congress. Why then did not the new Government follow the tactics outlined by that Congress? Because the Council of People's Commissars wanted to hasten the settlement of the land question, so that the Constituent Assembly would have nothing to do....

'But also the Government saw that it was necessary to adopt practical measures, so without further reflection it adopted the Regulations for Land Committees, thus creating a strange situation; for the Council of People's Commissars abolished private property in land, but the Regulations drawn up by the Land Committees are based on private property.... However, no harm has been done by that; for the Land Committees are paying no attention to the Soviet decrees, but are putting into operation their own practical decisions – decisions based on the will of the vast majority of the peasants....

'These Land Committees are not attempting the legislative solution of the land question, which belongs to the Constituent Assembly alone.... But will the Constituent Assembly desire to do the will of the Russian peasants? Of that we cannot be sure. . . . All we can be sure of is that the revolutionary determination of the peasants is now aroused, and that the Constituent will be forced to settle the land question the way the peasants want it settled. . . . The Constituent Assembly will not dare to break with the will of the people. . . .'

Followed him Lenin, listened to now with absorbing intensity. 'At this moment we are not only trying to solve the land question, but the question of Social Revolution – not only here in Russia, but all over the world. The land question cannot be solved independently of the other problems of the Social Revolution. . . . For example, the confiscation of the landed estates will provoke the resistance not only of Russian landowners, but also of foreign capital – with whom the great landed properties are connected through the intermediary of the banks. . . .

'The ownership of the land in Russia is the basis for immense oppression, and the confiscation of the land by the peasants is the most important step of our Revolution. But it cannot be separated from the other steps, as is clearly manifested by the stages through which the Revolution has had to pass. The first stage was the crushing of autocracy and the crushing of the power of the industrial capitalists and landowners, whose interests are closely related. The second stage was the strengthening of the Soviets and the political compromise with the bourgeoisie. The mistake of the Left Socialist Revolutionaries lies in the fact that at that time they did not oppose the policy of compromise, because they held the theory that the consciousness of the masses was not yet fully developed. . . .

'*If Socialism can only be realized when the intellectual development of all the people permits it, then we shall not see Socialism for at least five hundred years*. . . . The Socialist political party – this is the vanguard of the working class; it must not allow itself to be halted by the lack of education of the mass average, but it must lead the masses, using the Soviets as organs of revolutionary initiative. . . . But in order to lead the wavering, the comrades Left Socialist Revolutionaries themselves must stop hesitating. . . .

'In July last a series of open breaks began between the popular masses and the "compromisers"; but now, in November, the Left Socialist Revolutionaries are still holding out their hand to Avksentiev, who is pulling the people with his little finger. . . .

If compromise continues the Revolution disappears. No compromise with the bourgeoisie is possible; its power must be absolutely crushed. . . .

'We Bolsheviki have not changed our land programme; we have not given up the abolition of private property in the land, and we do not intend to do so. We adopted the Regulations for Land Committees – which are *not* based on private property at all – because we want to accomplish the popular will in the way the people have themselves decided to do it, so as to draw closer the coalition of all the elements who are fighting for the Social Revolution.

'We invite the Left Socialist Revolutionaries to enter that coalition, insisting, however, that they cease looking backward, and that they break with the "conciliators" of their party. . . .

'As far as the Constituent Assembly is concerned, it is true, as the preceding speaker has said, that the work of the Constituent Assembly will depend on the revolutionary determination of the masses. I say: Count on the revolutionary determination, but don't forget your gun!'

Lenin then read the Bolshevik resolution:

The Peasants' Congress, fully supporting the Land decree of 8 November . . . approves of the Provisional Workers' and Peasants' Government of the Russian Republic, established by the second All-Russian Congress of Soviets of Workers' and Soldiers' Deputies.

The Peasants' Congress . . . invites all peasants unanimously to sustain that law, and to apply it immediately to themselves; and at the same time invites the peasants to appoint to posts and positions of responsibility only persons who have proved, not by words but by acts, their entire devotion to the interests of the exploited peasant-workers, their desire and their ability to defend these interests against all resistance on the part of the great landowners, the capitalists, their partisans and accomplices.

The Peasants' Congress, at the same time, expresses its conviction that the complete realization of all the measures which make up the Land decree can only be successful through the triumph of the Workers' Social Revolution, which began 7 November 1917; for only the Social Revolution can accomplish the definite transfer, without possibility of return, of the land to the peasant-workers, the confiscation of model farms, and their surrender to the peasant communes, the confiscation of agricultural machinery belonging to the great landowners, the safeguarding of the interests of the agricultural workers by the complete abolition of wage-slavery, the regular and methodical distribution among all regions of Russia of the products of agriculture and industry, and the seizure of the banks (without which the possession of land by the whole people would be impossible, after the abolition of private property), and all sorts of assistance by the State to the workers. ...

For these reasons the Peasants' Congress sustains entirely the Revolution of 7 November ... as a social revolution, and expresses its unalterable will to put into operation, with whatever modifications are necessary, but without hesitation, the social transformation of the Russian Republic.

The indispensable conditions of the victory of the Socialist Revolution, which alone will secure the lasting success and the complete realization of the land decree, is the close union of the peasant-workers with the industrial working-class, with the proletariat of all advanced countries. From now on, in the Russian Republic, all the organization and administration of the State, from top to bottom, must rest on that union. That union, crushing all attempts, direct or indirect, open or dissimulated, to return to the policy of conciliation with the bourgeoisie – conciliation, damned by experience, with the chiefs of bourgeois politics – can alone ensure the victory of Socialism throughout the world.

The reactionaries of the Executive Committee no longer dared openly to appear. Chernov, however, spoke several times, with a modest and winning impartiality. He was invited to sit on the platform.... On the second night of the Congress an anonymous note was handed up to the chairman, requesting that Chernov be made honorary President. Ustinov read the note aloud, and immediately Zinoviev was on his feet, screaming that this was a trick of the old Executive Committee to capture the convention; in a moment the hall was one bellowing mass of waving arms and angry faces, on both sides.... Nevertheless, Chernov remained very popular.

In the stormy debates on the land question and the Lenin resolution, the Bolsheviki were twice on the point of quitting the assembly, both times restrained by their leaders.... It seemed to me as if the Congress were hopelessly deadlocked.

But none of us knew that a series of secret conferences was already going on between the Left Socialist Revolutionaries and the Bolsheviki at Smolny. At first the Left Socialist Revolutionaries had demanded that there be a Government composed of all the Socialist parties in and out of the Soviets, to be responsible to a People's Council, composed of an equal number of delegates from the Workers' and Soldiers' organization, and that of the Peasants, and completed by representatives of the City Dumas and the Zemstvos; Lenin and Trotsky were to be eliminated, and the Military Revolutionary Committee and other repressive organs dissolved.

Wednesday morning, 28 November, after a terrible all-night struggle, an agreement was reached. The Tsay-ee-kah composed of 108 members, was to be augmented by 108 members elected proportionately from the Peasants' Congress; by 100 delegates elected directly from the Army and the Fleet; and by 50 representatives of the Trade Unions (35 from the general unions, 10 Railway Workers, and 5 from the Post and Telegraph Workers). The Dumas and Zemstvos were dropped. Lenin and Trotsky remained in the Government, and the Military Revolutionary Committee continued to function.

The sessions of the Congress had now been removed to the Imperial Law School building, Fontanka 6, headquarters of the Peasants' Soviets. There in the great meeting-hall the delegates gathered on Wednesday afternoon. The old Executive Committee had withdrawn, and was holding a rump convention of its own in another room of the same building, made up of bolting delegates and representatives of the Army Committees.

Chernov went from one meeting to the other, keeping a watchful eye on the proceedings. He knew that an agreement with the Bolsheviki was being discussed, but he did not know that it had been concluded.

He spoke to the rump convention. 'At present, when everybody is in favour of forming an all-Socialist Government, many people forget the first Ministry, which was not a coalition Government, and in which there was only one Socialist – Kerensky; a Government which, in its time, was very popular. Now people accuse Kerensky; they forget that he was raised to power, not only by the Soviets, but also by the popular masses. . . .

'Why did public opinion change towards Kerensky? The savages set up gods to which they pray, and which they punish if one of their prayers is not answered. . . . That is what is happening at this moment.... Yesterday Kerensky; today Lenin and Trotsky; another tomorrow....

'We have proposed to both Kerensky and the Bolsheviki to retire from the power. Kerensky has accepted – today he announced from his hiding-place that he has resigned as Premier; but the Bolsheviki wish to retain the power, and they do not know how to use it....

'If the Bolsheviki succeed, or if they fail, the fate of Russia will not be changed. The Russian villages understand perfectly what they want, and they are now carrying out their own measures.... The villages will save us in the end....'

In the meanwhile, in the great hall Ustinov had announced the agreement between the Peasants' Congress and Smolny, received by the delegates with the wildest joy. Suddenly Chernov appeared and demanded the floor.

'I understand,' he began, 'that an agreement is being concluded between the Peasants' Congress and Smolny. Such an agreement would be illegal, seeing that the true Congress of Peasants' Soviets does not meet until next week....

'Moreover, I want to warn you now that the Bolsheviki will never accept your demands....'

He was interrupted by a great burst of laughter; and realizing the situation, he left the platform and the room, taking his popularity with him....

Late in the afternoon of Thursday, 29 November, the Congress met in extraordinary session. There was a holiday feeling in the air; on every face was a smile.... The remainder of the business before the assembly was hurried through, and then old Nathanson, the white-bearded dean of the left wing of the Socialist Revolutionaries, his voice trembling and tears in his eyes, read the report of the 'wedding' of the Peasants' Soviets with the Workers' and Soldiers' Soviets. At every mention of the word 'union' there was ecstatic applause.... At the end Ustinov announced the arrival of a delegation from Smolny, accompanied by representatives of the Red Army, greeted with a rising ovation. One after another a workman, a soldier, and a sailor took the floor, hailing them.

Then Boris Reinstein, delegate of the American Socialist Labour Party: 'The day of the union of the Congress of Peasants and the Soviets of Workers' and Soldiers' Deputies is one of the great days of the Revolution. The sound of it will ring with resounding echoes throughout the whole world – in Paris, in London, and across the ocean – in New York. This union will fill with happiness the hearts of all toilers.

'A great idea has triumphed. The West and America expected from Russia, from the Russian proletariat, something tremendous. . . . The proletariat of the world is waiting for the Russian Revolution, waiting for the great things that it is accomplishing. . . .'

Sverdlov, president of the Tsay-ee-kah, greeted them. And with the shout, 'Long live the end of civil war! Long live the United Democracy!' the peasants poured out of the building.

It was already dark, and on the ice-covered snow glittered the pale light of moon and star. Along the bank of the canal were drawn up in full marching order the soldiers of the Pavlovsky Regiment, with their band, which broke into the *Marseillaise*. Amid the crashing full-throated shouts of the soldiers, the peasants formed in line, unfurling the great red banner of the Executive Committee of the All-Russian Peasants' Soviets, embroidered newly in gold, 'Long live the union of the revolutionary and toiling masses!' Following were other banners; of the District Soviets – of Putilov Factory, which read, 'We bow to this flag in order to create the brotherhood of all peoples!'

From somewhere torches appeared, blazing orange in the night, a thousand times reflected in the facets of the ice, streaming smokily over the throng as it moved down the bank of the Fontanka singing, between crowds that stood in astonished silence.

'Long live the Revolutionary Army! Long live the Red Guard! Long live the Peasants!'

So the great procession wound through the city, growing and unfurling ever new red banners lettered in gold. Two old peasants, bowed with toil, were walking hand in hand, their faces illumined with child-like bliss.

'Well,' said one, 'I'd like to see them take away our land again, *now!*'

Near Smolny the Red Guard was lined up on both sides of the street, wild with delight. The other old peasant spoke to his comrade, 'I am not tired,' he said. 'I walked on air all the way!'

On the steps of Smolny about a hundred Workers' and Soldiers' Deputies were massed, with their banner, dark against the blaze of light streaming out between the arches. Like a wave they rushed down, clasping the peasants in their arms and kissing them; and the procession poured in through the great door and up the stairs, with a noise like thunder. . . .

In the immense white meeting-room the Tsay-ee-kah was waiting, with the whole Petrograd Soviet and a thousand spectators beside, with that solemnity which attends great conscious moments in history.

Zinoviev announced the agreement with the Peasants' Congress, to a shaking roar which rose and burst into storm as the sound of music blared down the corridor, and the head of the procession came in. On the platform the presidium rose and made place for the Peasants' presidium, the two embracing; behind them the two banners were intertwined against the white wall, over the empty frame from which the Tsar's picture had been torn. . . .

Then opened the 'triumphal session'. After a few words of welcome from Sverdlov, Maria Spiridonova, slight, pale, with spectacles, and hair drawn flatly down, and the air of a New England school-teacher, took the tribune – the most loved and the most powerful woman in all Russia.

'. . . Before the workers of Russia open new horizons which history has never known. . . . All workers' movements in the past have been defeated. But the present movement is international, and that is why it is invincible. There is no force in the world which can put out the fire of the Revolution! The old world crumbles down, the new world begins. . . .'

Then Trotsky, full of fire: 'I wish you welcome, comrades peasants! You come here not as guests, but as masters of this house, which holds the heart of the Russian Revolution. The will of millions of workers is now concentrated in this hall. . . . There is now only one master of the Russian land: the union of the workers, soldiers, and peasants. . . .'

With biting sarcasm he went on to speak of the Allied diplomats, till then contemptuous of Russia's invitation to an armistice, which had been accepted by the Central Powers.

'A new humanity will be born of this war.... In this hall we swear to workers of all lands to remain at our revolutionary post. If we are broken, then it will be in defending our flag....'

Krylenko followed him, explained the situation at the front, where Dukhonin was preparing to resist the Council of People's Commissars. 'Let Dukhonin and those with him understand well that we shall not deal gently with those who bar the road to peace!'

Dybenko saluted the assembly in the name of the Fleet, and Krushinsky, member of the Vikzhel, said, 'From this moment, when the union of all true Socialists is raised, the whole army of railway workers places itself absolutely at the disposition of the revolutionary democracy!' And Lunacharsky, almost weeping, and Proshian, for the Left Socialist Revolutionaries, and finally Saharashvili, for the United Social Democrats Internationalists, composed of members of Martov's and of Gorky's groups, who declared:

'We left the Tsay-ee-kah because of the uncompromising policy of the Bolsheviki, and to force them to make concessions in order to realize the union of all the revolutionary democracy. Now that that union is brought about, we consider it a sacred duty to take our places once more in the Tsay-ee-kah.... We declare that all those who have withdrawn from the Tsay-ee-kah should now return.'

Stachkov, a dignified old peasant of the presidium of the Peasants' Congress, bowed to the four corners of the room. 'I greet you with the christening of a new Russian life and freedom!'

Gronsky, in the name of the Polish Social Democracy; Skripnik, for the Factory-Shop Committees; Tifonov, for the Russian soldiers at Salonika; and others, interminably, speaking out of full hearts, with the happy eloquence of hopes fulfilled....

It was late in the night when the following resolution was put and passed unanimously:

'The Tsay-ee-kah, united in extraordinary session with the Petrograd Soviet and the Peasants' Congress, confirms the Land and Peace decrees adopted by the Second Congress of Soviets of Workers' and Soldiers' Deputies, and also the decree on Workers' Control adopted by the Tsay-ee-kah.

'The joint session of the Tsay-ee-kah and the Peasants' Congress expresses its firm conviction that the union of workers, soldiers, and peasants, this fraternal union of all the workers and all the exploited, will consolidate the power conquered by them, that it will take all revolutionary measures to hasten the passing of the power into the hands of the working class in other countries, and that it will assure in this manner the lasting accomplishment of a just peace and the victory of Socialism.'[71]

Appendix

Chapter 1

1 (p. 29).

Oborontsi – 'Defenders'. All the 'moderate' Socialist groups adopted or were given this name, because they consented to the continuation of the war under Allied leadership, on the ground that it was a war of National Defence. The Bolsheviki, the Left Socialist Revolutionaries, the Mensheviki Internationalists (Martov's faction), and the Social Democrats Internationalists (Gorky's group) were in favour of forcing the Allies to declare democratic war-aims, and to offer peace to Germany on those terms.

2 (p. 30). WAGES AND COST OF LIVING BEFORE AND DURING THE REVOLUTION

The following table of wages and costs were compiled, in October 1917, by a joint Committee from the Moscow Chamber of Commerce and the Moscow section of the Ministry of Labour, and published in *Novaya Zhizn*, 26 October 1917:

Wages per Day (roubles and kopeks)

Trade	July 1914	July 1916	August 1917
Carpenter, Cabinet-maker	1·60–2·0	4·0 –6·0	8·50
Terrassier	1·30–1·50	3·0 –3·50	—
Mason, plasterer	1·70–2·35	4·0 –6·0	8·0
Painter, upholsterer	1·80–2·20	3·0 –5·50	8·0
Blacksmith	1·0 –2·25	4·0 –5·0	8·50
Chimney-sweep	1·50–2·0	4·0 –5·50	7·50
Locksmith	0·90–2·0	3·50–6·0	9·0
Helper	1·0 –1·50	2·50–4·50	8·0

In spite of numerous stories of gigantic advances in wages, immediately following the Revolution of March 1917, these figures, which were published by the Ministry of Labour as characteristic of conditions all over Russia, show that wages did not rise immediately after the Revolution, but little by little. On an average wages increased slightly more than 500 per cent. . . .

But at the same time, the value of the rouble fell to less than one third its former purchasing power, and the cost of necessities of life increased enormously.

The following table was compiled by the Municipal Duma of Moscow, where food was cheaper and more plentiful than in Petrograd:

Cost of Food (roubles and kopeks)

		August 1914	August 1917	Per cent increase
Black bread	(*Funt*)	0·02	0·12	330
White bread	(*Funt*)	0·05	0·20	300
Beef	(*Funt*)	0·22	1·10	400
Veal	(*Funt*)	0·26	2·15	727
Pork	(*Funt*)	0·23	2·0	770
Herring	(*Funt*)	0·06	0·52	767
Cheese	(*Funt*)	0·40	3·50	754
Butter	(*Funt*)	0·48	3·20	557
Eggs	(*Doz.*)	0·30	1·60	443
Milk	(*Krushka*)	0·07	0·40	471

On an average, food increased in price 556 per cent, or 51 per cent more than wages.

As for the other necessities, the price of these increased tremendously.

The following table was compiled by the Economic section of the Moscow Soviet of Workers' Deputies, and accepted as correct by the Ministry of Supplies of the Provisional Government.

Cost of Other Necessities (roubles and kopecks)

		August 1914	August 1917	Per cent increase
Calico	(*Arshin*)	0·11	1·40	1,173
Cotton cloth	(*Arshin*)	0·15	2·0	1,233
Dress goods	(*Arshin*)	2·0	40·0	1,900
Castor cloth	(*Arshin*)	6·0	80·0	1,233
Men's shoes	(*Pair*)	12·0	144·0	1,097

		August 1914	August 1917	Per cent increase
Rubbers	(*Pair*)	2·50	15·0	500
Men's clothing	(*Suit*)	40·0	400–55	900–1,109
Tea	(*Funt*)	4·50	18·0	300
Sole leather		20·0	400·0	1,900
Matches	(*Cartons*)	0·10	0·50	400
Soap	(*Pood*)	4·50	40·0	780
Gasoline	(*Vedro*)	1·70	11·0	547
Candles	(*Pood*)	8·50	100·0	1,076
Caramel	(*Funt*)	0·30	4·50	1,406
Firewood	(*Load*)	10·0	120·0	1,100
Charcoal		0·80	13·0	1,523
Sundry metal ware		1·0	20·0	1.900

On an average the above categories of necessities increased about 1,109 per cent in price, more than twice the increase of salaries. The difference, of course, went into the pockets of speculators and merchants.

In September 1917, when I arrived in Petrograd, the average daily wage of a skilled industrial worker – for example, a steelworker, in the Putilov Factory – was about 8 roubles. At the same time, profits were enormous. . . . I was told by one of the owners of the Thornton Woollen Mills, an English concern on the outskirts of Petrograd, that while wages had increased about 300 per cent in his factory, his profits had gone up 900 per cent.

3 (p. 31). THE SOCIALIST MINISTERS

The history of the efforts of the Socialists in the Provisional Government of July to realize their programme in coalition with the bourgeois Ministers is an illuminating example of class struggle in politics. Says Lenin, in explanation of this phenomenon:

The capitalists . . . seeing that the position of the Government was untenable, resorted to a method which since 1848 has been for decades practised by the capitalists in order to befog, divide, and finally overpower the working-class. This method is the so-called 'Coalition Ministry', composed of bourgeois and of renegades from the Socialist camp.

In those countries where political freedom and democracy have existed side by side with the revolutionary movement of the workers – for example, in England and France – the capitalists make use of this subterfuge, and very successfully too. The 'Socialist' leaders, upon entering the Ministries, invariably prove mere figure-heads, puppets, simply a shield for the capitalists, a tool with which to defraud the workers. The 'democratic' and 'republican' capitalists in Russia set in motion this very same scheme. The Socialist Revolutionaries and Mensheviki fell victim to it, and on 1 June a 'Coalition' Ministry, with the participation of Chernov, Tseretelly, Skobeliev, Avksentiev, Savinkov, Zarudny, and Nikitin became an accomplished fact. ...' – *Problems of the Revolution*

4 (p. 33). SEPTEMBER MUNICIPAL ELECTIONS IN MOSCOW

In the first week of October 1917, *Novaya Zhizn* published the following comparative table of election results, pointing out that this meant the bankruptcy of the policy of Coalition with the propertied classes. 'If civil war can yet be avoided, it can only be done by a united front of all the revolutionary democracy. ...'

Elections for the Moscow Central and Ward Dumas (numbers of Members)

	June 1917	September 1917
Socialist Revolutionaries	58	14
Cadets	17	30
Mensheviki	12	4
Bolsheviki	11	47

5 (p. 33). GROWING ARROGANCE OF THE REACTIONARIES

18 September. The Cadet Shulgin, writing in a Kiev newspaper, said that the Provisional Government's declaration that Russia was a Republic constituted a gross abuse of its powers. 'We cannot admit either a Republic or the present Republican Government.... And we are not sure that we want a Republic in Russia....'

23 October. At a meeting of the Cadet party held at Riazan, M. Dukhonin declared, 'On 1 March we established a Constitutional Monarchy. We must not reject the legitimate heir to the throne, Mikhail Alexandrovich....'

27 October. Resolution passed by the Conference of Business Men at Moscow:

The Conference ... insists that the Provisional Government take the following immediate measures in the Army:

1. Forbidding of all political propaganda; the Army must be out of politics.

2. Propaganda of anti-national and international ideas and theories deny the necessity for armies, and hurt discipline; it should be forbidden, and all propagandists punished. ...

3. The function of the Army Committees must be limited to economic questions exclusively. All their decisions should be confirmed by their superior officers, who have the right to dissolve the Committees at any time. ...

4. The salute to be re-established and made obligatory. Full establishment of disciplinary power in the hands of officers, with right of review of sentence. ...

5. Expulsion from the Corps of Officers of those who dishonour it by participating in the movement of the soldier-masses, which teaches them disobedience. ... Re-establishment for this purpose of the Courts of Honour. ...

6. The Provisional Government should take the necessary measures to make possible the return to the army of generals and other officers unjustly discharged under the influence of Committees, and other irresponsible organizations. ...

Chapter 2

6 (p. 42).

The Kornilov revolt is treated in detail in my forthcoming volume, *Kornilov to Brest-Litovsk*. The responsibility of Kerensky for the situation which gave rise to Kornilov's attempt is now pretty clearly established. Many apologists for Kerensky say that he knew of Kornilov's plans, and by a trick drew him out prematurely, and then crushed him. Even Mr A. J. Sack, in his book, *The Birth of the Russian Democracy*, says:

> Several things ... are almost certain. The first is that Kerensky knew about the movement of several detachments from the front towards Petrograd, and it is possible that as Prime Minister and Minister of War, realizing the growing Bolshevist danger, he called for them. ...

The only flaw in that argument is that there was no 'Bolshevist danger' at the time, the Bolsheviki still being a powerless minority in the Soviets, and their leaders in jail or hiding.

7 (p. 43). DEMOCRATIC CONFERENCE

When the Democratic Conference was first proposed to Kerensky he suggested an assembly of all the elements of the nation – 'the live forces', as he called them – including bankers, manufacturers, landowners, and representatives of the Cadet party. The Soviet refused, and drew up the following table of representation (numbers of delegates), which Kerensky agreed to:

100 All-Russian Soviets Workers' and Soldiers' Deputies
100 All-Russian Soviets Peasants' Deputies
 50 Provincial Soviets Workers' and Soldiers' Deputies
 50 Peasants' District Land Committees
100 Trade Unions
 84 Army Committees at the Front
150 Workers' and Peasants' Cooperative Societies
 20 Railway Workers' Union
 10 Post and Telegraph Workers' Union
 20 Commercial Clerks
 15 Liberal Professions – Doctors, Lawyers, Journalists, etc.
 50 Provincial Zemstvos
 50 Nationalist Organizations – Poles, Ukrainians, etc.

This proportion was altered twice or three times. The final disposition of delegates was:

300 All-Russian Workers', Soldiers', and Peasants' Deputies	150 Provincial Zemstvos
	200 Trade Unions
300 Cooperative Societies	100 Nationalist organizations
300 Municipalities	200 Several small groups
150 Army Committees at the Front	

8, (p. 43). THE FUNCTION OF THE SOVIETS IS ENDED

On 28 September 1917, *Izvestia*, organ of the Tsay-ee-kah, published an article which said, speaking of the last Provisional Ministry:

At last a truly democratic government born of the will of all classes of the Russian people, the first rough form of the future liberal parliamentary régime has been formed. Ahead of us is the Constituent Assembly, which will solve all questions of fundamental law and whose composition will be essentially democratic. The function of the Soviets is at an end, and the time is approaching when they must retire, with the rest of the revolutionary machinery, from the stage of a free and victorious people, whose weapons shall hereafter be the peaceful ones of political action.

The leading article of *Izvestia* for 23 October was called 'The Crisis in the Soviet Organizations'. It began by saying that travellers reported a lessening activity of local Soviets everywhere.

This is natural [said the writer]. For the people are becoming interested in the more permanent legislative organs – the Municipal Dumas and the Zemstvos.

In the important centres of Petrograd and Moscow, where the Soviets were best organized, they did not take in all the democratic elements. . . . The majority of the intellectuals did not participate, and many workers also; some of the workers because they were politically backward, others because the centre of gravity for them was in their unions. . . . We cannot deny that these organizations are firmly united with the masses, whose everyday needs are better served by them. . . .

That the local democratic administrations are being energetically organized is highly important. The City Dumas are elected by universal suffrage, and in purely local matters have more authority than the Soviets. Not a single democrat will see anything wrong in this. . . .

. . . Elections to the Municipalities are being conducted in a better and more democratic way than the elections of the Soviets. . . . All classes are represented in the Municipalities. . . . And as soon as the local Self-Governments begin to organize life in the Municipalities, the role of the local Soviets naturally ends. . . .

. . . There are two factors in the falling off of interest in the Soviets. The first we may attribute to the lowering of political interest in the masses; the second, to the growing effort of provincial and local governing bodies to organize the building of new Russia. . . . The more the tendency lies in this latter direction, the sooner disappears the significance of the Soviets. . . .

We ourselves are being called the 'undertakers' of our organization. In reality we ourselves are the hardest workers in constructing the new Russia. . . .

When autocracy and the whole bureaucratic régime fell we set up the Soviets as a barracks in which all the democracy could find temporary shelter. Now, instead of barracks, we are building the permanent edifice of a new system, and naturally the people will gradually leave the barracks for more comfortable quarters.

9 (p. 43). TROTSKY'S SPEECH AT THE COUNCIL OF THE RUSSIAN REPUBLIC

The purpose of the Democratic Conference, which was called by the Tsay-ee-kah, was to do away with the irresponsible personal government which produced Kornilov, and to establish a responsible government which would be capable of finishing the war, and ensure the calling of the Constituent Assembly at the given time. In the meanwhile, behind the back of the Democratic Conference, by trickery, by deals between Citizen Kerensky, the Cadets, and the leaders of the Menshevik and Socialist Revolutionary parties, we received the opposite result from the officially announced purpose. A power was created around which and in which we have open and secret Kornilovs playing leading parts. The irresponsibility of the Government is officially proclaimed, when it is announced that the Council of the Russian Republic is to be a *consultative* and not a *legislative* body. In the eighth month of the Revolution, the irresponsible Government creates a cover for itself in this new edition of Bulygin's Duma.

The propertied classes have entered this Provisional Council in a proportion which clearly shows, from elections all over the country, that many of them have no right here whatever. In spite of that the Cadet party which until yesterday wanted the Provisional Government to be responsible to the State Duma – this same Cadet party secured the independence of the Government from the Council of the Republic. In the Constituent Assembly the propertied classes will no doubt have a less favourable position than they have in this Council, and they will not be able to be irresponsible to the Constituent Assembly.

If the propertied classes were really getting ready for the Constituent Assembly six weeks from now, there could be no reason for establishing the irresponsibility of the Government at this time. The whole truth is that the bourgeoisie, which directs the politics of the Provisional Government, has for its aim to break the Constituent Assembly. At present this is the main purpose of the propertied classes, which control our entire national policy – external and internal. In the industrial, agrarian, and supply departments the politics of the propertied classes, acting with the Government, increases the natural disorganization caused by the war. The classes which are provoking civil war, and openly hold their course on the bony hand of hunger, with which they intend to overthrow the Revolution and finish with the Constituent Assembly!

No less criminal also is the international policy of the bourgeoisie and its Government. After forty months of war the capital is threatened with mortal danger. In reply to this arises a plan to move the Government to Moscow. The idea of abandoning the capital does not stir the indignation of the bourgeoisie. Just the opposite. It is accepted as a natural part of the general policy designed to promote counter-revolutionary conspiracy. .... Instead of recognizing that the salvation of the country lies in concluding peace, instead of throwing openly the idea of immediate peace to all the war-worn peoples, over the heads of diplomats and imperialists, and making the continuation of the war impossible –

the Provisional Government, by order of the Cadets, the Counter-Revolutionists, and the Allied Imperialists, without sense, without purpose and without a plan, continues to drag on the murderous war, sentencing to useless death new hundreds of thousands of soldiers and sailors, and preparing to give up Petrograd, and to wreck the Revolution. At a time when Bolshevik soldiers and sailors are dying with other soldiers and sailors as a result of the mistakes and crimes of others, the so-called Supreme Commander (Kerensky) continues to suppress the Bolshevik press. The leading parties of the Council are acting as a voluntary cover for these policies.

We, the faction of Social Democrats Bolsheviki, announce that with this Government of Treason to the People we have nothing in common. We have nothing in common with the work of these Murderers of the People which goes on behind official curtains. We refuse either directly or indirectly to cover up one day of this work. While Wilhelm's troops are threatening Petrograd, the Government of Kerensky and Kornilov is preparing to run away from Petrograd and turn Moscow into a base of counter-revolution!

We warn the Moscow workers and soldiers to be on their guard. Leaving this Council, we appeal to the manhood and wisdom of the workers, peasants, and soldiers of all Russia. Petrograd is in danger! The Revolution is in danger! The Government has increased the danger – the ruling classes intensify it. Only the people themselves can save themselves and the country.

We appeal to the people. Long live immediate, honest, democratic peace! All power to the Soviets! All land to the people! Long live the Constituent Assembly!

10 (p. 45). THE 'NAKAZ' TO SKOBELIEV (*Resumé*)

Passed by the Tsay-ee-kah and given to Skobeliev as an instruction for the representative of the Russian Revolutionary democracy at the Paris Conference.

The peace treaty must be based on the principle, 'No annexations, no indemnities, the right of self-determination of peoples'.

Territorial Problems

(1) Evacuation of German troops from invaded Russia. Full right of self-determination to Poland, Lithuania, and Livonia.

(2) For Turkish Armenia autonomy, and later complete self-determination, as soon as local Governments are established.

(3) The question of Alsace-Lorraine to be solved by a plebiscite, after the withdrawal of all foreign troops.

(4) Belgium to be restored. Compensation for damages from an international fund.

(5) Serbia and Montenegro to be restored, and aided by an international relief fund. Serbia to have an outlet on the Adriatic. Bosnia and Herzegovina to be autonomous.

(6) The disputed provinces in the Balkans to have provisional autonomy, followed by a plebiscite.

(7) Rumania is to be restored, but forced to give complete self-determination to the Dobrudja.... Rumania must be forced to execute the clauses of the Berlin Treaty concerning the Jews, and recognize them as Rumanian citizens.

(8) In Italia Irridenta a provisional autonomy, followed by a plebiscite to determine state dependence.

(9) The German colonies to be returned.

(10) Greece and Persia to be restored.

Freedom of the Seas

All straits opening into inland seas, as well as the Suez and Panama Canals, are to be neutralized. Commercial shipping to be free. The right of privateering to be abolished. The torpedoing of commercial ships to be forbidden.

Indemnities

All combatants to renounce demands for any indemnities, either direct or indirect – as, for instance, charges for the maintenance of prisoners. Indemnities and contributions collected during the war must be refunded.

Economic Terms

Commercial treaties are not to be part of the peace terms. Every country must be independent in its commercial relations, and must not be obliged to, or prevented from, concluding an economic treaty, by the Treaty of Peace. Nevertheless, all nations should bind themselves, by the Peace Treaty, not to practise an economic blockade after the war, nor to form separate tariff agreements. The right of most favoured nation must be given to all countries without distinction.

Guarantees of Peace

Peace is to be concluded at the Peace Conference by delegates elected by the national representative institution of each country. The peace terms are to be confirmed by these parliaments.

Secret diplomacy is to be abolished; all parties are to bind themselves not to conclude any secret treaties. Such treaties are declared in contradiction of international law, and void. All treaties, until confirmed by the parliaments of the different nations, are to be considered void.

Gradual disarmament both on land and sea, and the establishment of a militia system. The 'League of Nations' advanced by President Wilson may become a valuable aid to international law, provided that (a) all nations are to be obliged to participate in it with equal rights, and (b) international politics are to be democratized.

Ways to Peace

The Allies are to announce immediately that they are willing to open peace negotiations as soon as the enemy powers declare their consent to the renunciation of all forcible annexations.

The Allies must bind themselves not to begin any peace negotiations, nor to conclude peace, except in a general Peace Conference with the participation of delegates from all the neutral countries.

All obstacles to the Stockholm Conference are to be removed, and passports are to be given immediately to all delegates of parties and organizations who wish to participate.

The Executive Committee of the Peasants' Soviets also issued a *nakaz*, which differs little from the above.

11 (p. 46). PEACE AT RUSSIA'S EXPENSE

The Ribot revelations of Austria's peace-offer to France; the so-called 'Peace Conference' at Berne, Switzerland, during the summer of 1917, in which delegates participated from all the belligerent countries, representing large financial interests in all these countries; and the attempted negotiations of an English agent with a Bulgarian church dignitary; all pointed to the fact that there were strong currents, on both sides, favourable to patching up a peace at the expense of Russia. In my next book, *Kornilov to Brest-Litovsk,* I intend to treat this matter at some length, publishing several secret documents discovered in the Ministry of Foreign Affairs at Petrograd.

12 (p. 46). RUSSIAN SOLDIERS IN FRANCE

Official Report of the Provisional Government

From the time the news of the Russian Revolution reached Paris, Russian newspapers of extreme tendencies immediately began to appear; and these newspapers, as well as individuals, freely circulated among the soldier masses and began a Bolshevik propaganda, often spreading false news which appeared in the French journals. In the

absence of all official news, and of precise details, this campaign provoked discontent among the soldiers. The result was a desire to return
to Russia, and a hatred towards the officers.

Finally it all turned into rebellion. In one of their meetings the
soldiers issued an appeal to refuse to drill, since they had decided to
fight no more. It was decided to isolate the rebels, and General
Zankievich ordered all soldiers loyal to the Provisional Government to
leave the camp of Courtine, and to carry with them all ammunition.
On 25 June the order was executed; there remained at the camp only the
soldiers who said they would submit 'conditionally' to the Provisional
Government. The soldiers at the camp of Courtine received several
times the visit of the Commander-in-Chief of the Russian Armies
abroad, of Rapp, the Commissar of the Ministry of War, and of several
distinguished former exiles who wished to influence them, but these
attempts were unsuccessful, and finally Commissar Rapp insisted that
the rebels lay down their arms, and, in sign of submission, march in
good order to a place called Clairvaux. The order was only partially
obeyed; first 500 men went out, of whom 22 were arrested; 24 hours
later about 6,000 followed. ... About 2,000 remained. ...

It was decided to increase the pressure; their rations were diminished,
their pay was cut off, and the roads towards the village of Courtine
were guarded by French soldiers. General Zankievich, having discovered that a Russian artillery brigade was passing through France,
decided to form a mixed detachment of infantry and artillery to reduce
the rebels. A deputation was sent to the rebels; the deputation returned
several hours later, convinced of the futility of the negotiations. On 1
September General Zankievich sent an ultimatum to the rebels demanding that they lay down their arms, and menacing in case of refusal
to open fire with artillery if the order was not obeyed by 3 September at
10 o'clock.

The order not being executed, a light fire of artillery was opened on
the place at the hour agreed upon. Eighteen shells were fired, and the
rebels were warned that the bombardment would become more intense.
In the night of 3 September 160 men surrendered. On 4 September the
artillery bombardment recommenced and at 11 o'clock, after 36 shells
had been fired, the rebels raised two white flags and began to leave the
camp without arms. By evening 8,300 men had surrendered; 150 men
who remained in the camp opened fire with machine-guns that night.
The fifth of September, to make an end of the affair, a heavy barrage
was laid on the camp, and our soldiers occupied it little by little. The
rebels kept up a heavy fire with their machine-guns. On 6 September, at
9 o'clock, the camp was entirely occupied. ... After the disarmament of
the rebels, 81 arrests were made. ...

Thus the report. From secret documents discovered in the Ministry of Foreign Affairs, however, we knew that the account is not strictly accurate. The first trouble arose when the soldiers tried to form a Committee, as their comrades in Russia were doing. They demanded to be sent back to Russia, which was refused; and then, being considered a dangerous influence in France, they were ordered to Salonika. They refused to go, and the battle followed.... It was discovered that they had been left in camp without officers for about two months, and badly treated, before they became rebellious. All attempts to find out the name of the 'Russian artillery brigade' which had fired on them were futile; the telegrams discovered in the Ministry left it to be inferred that French artillery was used. ...

After their surrender more than two hundred of the mutineers were shot in cold blood.

13 (p. 46). TERESHCHENKO'S SPEECH (*Resumé*)

... The questions of foreign policy are closely related to those of national defence. ... And so, if in questions of national defence you think it is necessary to hold session in secret, also in our foreign policy we are sometimes forced to observe the same secrecy. ...

German diplomacy attempts to influence public opinion. ... Therefore the declarations of directors of great democratic organizations who talk loudly of a revolutionary Congress, and the impossibility of another winter campaign, are dangerous. ... All these declarations cost human lives. ...

I wish to speak merely of governmental logic, without touching the questions of the honour and dignity of the State. From the point of view of logic, the foreign policy of Russia ought to be based on a real comprehension of the *interests* of Russia. ... These interests mean that it is impossible that our country remain alone, and that the present alignment of forces with us (the Allies) is satisfactory. ... All humanity longs for peace, but in Russia no one will permit a humiliating peace which would violate the State interests of our fatherland!

The orator pointed out that such a peace would for long years, if not for centuries, retard the triumph of democratic principles in the world, and would inevitably cause new wars.

All remember the days of May, when the fraternization on our Front threatened to end the war by a simple cessation of military operations, and lead the country to a shameful separate peace ... and what efforts it was necessary to use to make the soldier masses at the front understand that it was not by this method that the Russian State must end the war and guarantee its interest.

He spoke of the miraculous effect of the July offensive, what strength it gave to the words of the Russian ambassadors abroad, and the despair in Germany caused by the Russian victories. And also, the disillusionment in Allied countries which followed the Russian defeat. . . .

As to the Russian Government, it adhered strictly to the formula of May, 'No annexations and no punitive indemnities'. We consider it essential not only to proclaim the self-determination of peoples, but also to renounce imperialistic aims. . . .

Germany is continually trying to make peace. The only talk in Germany is of peace; she knows she cannot win.

I reject the reproaches aimed at the Government which allege that Russian foreign policy does not speak clearly enough about the aims of the war. . . .

If the question arises as to what ends the Allies are pursuing, it is indispensable first to demand what aims the Central Powers have agreed upon. . . .

The desire is often heard that we publish the details of the treaties which bind the Allies, but people forget that, up to now, we do not know the treaties which bind the Central Powers. . . .

Germany, he said, evidently wants to separate Russia from the West by a series of weak buffer-states.

This tendency to strike at the vital interests of Russia must be checked. . . .

And will the Russian democracy, which has inscribed on its banner the rights of nations to dispose of themselves, allow calmly the continuation of oppression upon the most civilized peoples (in Austria-Hungary)?

Those who fear that the Allies will try to profit by our difficult situation, to make us support more than our share of the burden of war, and to solve the questions of peace at our expense, are entirely mistaken. . . .

Our enemy looks upon Russia as a market for its products. The end of the war will leave us in a feeble condition, and with our frontier open the flood of German products can easily hold back for years our industrial development. Measures must be taken to guard against this. . . .

I say frankly and openly: the combination of forces which unites us to the Allies is *favourable to the interests of Russia*. . . . It is therefore important that our views on the question of war and peace shall be in accord with the views of the Allies as clearly and precisely as possible. . . . To avoid all misunderstanding, I must say frankly that Russia must present to the Paris Conference *one point of view*. . . .

He did not want to comment on the *nakaz* to Skobeliev, but he referred to the Manifesto of the Dutch-Scandinavian Committee, just published in Stockholm. This Manifesto declared for the autonomy of Lithuania and Livonia; 'but it is clearly impossible,' said Tereshchenko, 'for Russia must have free ports on the Baltic all the year round. . .'.

In this question the problems of foreign policy are also closely related to interior politics, for if there existed a strong sentiment of unity of all great Russia, one would not witness the repeated manifestations, everywhere, of a desire of people to separate from the Central Government. . . . Such separations are contrary to the interests of Russia, and the Russian delegates cannot raise the issue. . . .

14 (p. 47). THE BRITISH FLEET (*etc.*)

At the time of the naval battle of the Gulf of Riga, not only the Bolsheviki, but also the Ministers of the Provisional Government, considered that the British Fleet had deliberately abandoned the Baltic, as one indication of the attitude so often expressed publicly by the British press, and semi-publicly by British representatives in Russia, 'Russia's finished! No use bothering about Russia!'

See interview with Kerensky (Appendix 18).

GENERAL GURKO was a former Chief of Staff of the Russian armies under the Tsar. He was a prominent figure in the corrupt Imperial court. After the Revolution he was one of the very few persons exiled for his political and personal record. The Russian naval defeat in the Gulf of Riga coincided with the public reception, by King George in London, of General Gurko, a man whom the Russian Provisional Government considered dangerously pro-German as well as reactionary!

15 (p. 57). APPEALS AGAINST INSURRECTION

To the Workers and Soldiers

'Comrades! The Dark Forces are increasingly trying to call forth in Petrograd and other towns DISORDERS AND *Pogroms*. Disorder is necessary to the Dark Forces, for disorder will give them an opportunity for crushing the revolutionary movement in blood. Under the pretext of establishing order, and of protecting the inhabitants, they hope to establish the domination of Kornilov, which the revolutionary people succeeded in suppressing not long ago. Woe to the people if these hopes are realized! The triumphant counter-revolution will destroy the Soviets and the Army Committees, will disperse the Constituent Assembly, will stop the transfer of the land to the Land Committees, will put an end to all the hopes of the people for a speedy peace, and will fill all the prisons with revolutionary soldiers and workers.

In their calculations, the counter-revolutionists and Black Hundred leaders are counting on the serious discontent of the unenlightened part of the people with the disorganization of the food supply, the continuation of the war, and the general difficulties of life. They hope to transform every demonstration of soldiers and workers into a *pogrom*, which will frighten the peaceful population and throw it into the arms of the Restorers of Law and Order.

Under such conditions every attempt to organize a demonstration in these days, although for the most laudable object, would be a crime. All conscious workers and soldiers who are displeased with the policy of the Government will only bring injury to themselves and to the Revolution if they indulge in demonstrations.

THEREFORE THE TSAY-EE-KAH ASKS ALL WORKERS NOT TO OBEY ANY CALLS TO DEMONSTRATE.

WORKERS AND SOLDIERS! DO NOT YIELD TO PROVOCATION! REMEMBER YOUR DUTY TO YOUR COUNTRY AND THE REVOLUTION! DO NOT BREAK THE UNITY OF THE REVOLUTIONARY FRONT BY DEMONSTRATIONS WHICH ARE BOUND TO BE UNSUCCESSFUL!

The Central Committee of the Soviets of Workers' and Soldiers'
Deputies (Tsay-ee-kah)

Russian Social Democratic Labour Party

THE DANGER IS NEAR!

To All Workers and Soldiers
(Read and Hand to Others)

Comrades Workers and Soldiers!
Our country is in danger. On account of this danger our freedom

and our Revolution are passing through difficult days. The enemy is at the gates of Petrograd. The disorganization is growing with every hour. It becomes more and more difficult to obtain bread for Petrograd. All, all from the smallest to the greatest, must redouble their efforts, must endeavour to arrange things properly. . . . We must save our country, save freedom. . . . More arms and provisions for the Army! Bread – for the great cities. Order and organization in the country.

And in these terrible critical days rumours creep about that SOMEWHERE a demonstration is being prepared, that SOMEONE is calling on the soldiers and workers to destroy revolutionary peace and order. . . . *Rabochi Put*, the newspaper of the Bolsheviki, is pouring oil on the flames: it is flattering, trying to please the unenlightened people, tempting the workers and soldiers, urging them against the Government, promising them mountains of good things. . . . The confiding, ignorant men believe, they do not reason. . . . And from the other side come also rumours – rumours that the Dark Forces, the friends of the Tsar, the German spies, are rubbing their hands with glee. They are ready to join the Bolsheviki, and with them fan the disorders into civil war.

The Bolsheviki and the ignorant soldiers and workers seduced by them cry senselessly: 'Down with the Government! All power to the Soviets!' And the Dark servants of the Tsar and the spies of Wilhelm will egg them on: 'Beat the Jews, beat the shopkeepers, rob the markets, devastate the shops, pillage the wine stores! Slay, burn, rob!'

And then will come a terrible confusion, a war between one part of the people and the other. All will become still more disorganized, and perhaps once more blood will be shed on the streets of the capital. And then – what then?

Then the road to Petrograd will be open to Wilhelm. Then, no bread will come to Petrograd, the children will die of hunger. Then, the Army at the front will remain without support, our brothers in the trenches will be delivered to the fire of the enemy. Then, Russia will lose all prestige in other countries, our money will lose its value; everything will be so dear as to make life impossible. Then the long awaited Constituent Assembly will be postponed – it will be impossible to convene it in time. And then – Death to the Revolution, Death to our Liberty. . . .

Is it this that you want, workers and soldiers? No! If you do not, then go, go to the ignorant people seduced by the betrayers, and tell them the whole truth, which we have told you!

Let all know that EVERY MAN WHO IN THESE TERRIBLE DAYS CALLS ON YOU TO COME OUT IN THE STREETS AGAINST THE GOVERNMENT, IS EITHER A SECRET SERVANT OF THE TSAR, A

PROVOCATOR, OR AN UNWISE ASSISTANT OF THE ENEMIES OF
THE PEOPLE, OR A PAID SPY OF WILHELM!

Every conscious worker revolutionist, every conscious peasant, every
revolutionary soldier, all who understand what harm a demonstration
or a revolt against the Government might cause to the people, must
join together and not allow the enemies of the people to destroy our
freedom.

The Petrograd Electoral Committee of the Mensheviki-oborontsi

16 (p. 59). LENIN'S 'LETTER TO THE COMRADES'

This series of articles appeared in *Rabochi Put* several days
running, at the end of October and beginning of November 1917.
I give here only extracts from two instalments:

1. Kameniev and Riazanov say that we have not a majority
among the people, and that without a majority insurrection is
hopeless.

Answer: People capable of speaking such things are falsifiers,
pedants, or simply don't want to look the real situation in the face. In
the last elections we received in all the country more than fifty per cent
of all the votes. . . .

The most important thing in Russia today is the peasants' revolution.
In Tambov Government there has been a real agrarian uprising with
wonderful political results. . . . Even *Dielo Naroda* has been scared into
yelling that the land must be turned over to the peasants, and not only
the Socialist Revolutionaries in the Council of the Republic, but also
the Government itself, have been similarly affected. Another valuable
result was the bringing of bread which had been hoarded by the
pomieshchiki to the railroad stations in that province. The *Russkaya
Volia* had to admit that the stations were filled with bread after the
peasants' uprising. . . .

2. We are not sufficiently strong to take over the Government, and
the bourgeoisie is not sufficiently strong to prevent the Constituent
Assembly.

Answer: This is nothing but timidity, expressed by pessimism as
regards workers and soldiers, and optimism as regards the failure of the
bourgeoisie. If *yunkers* and Cossacks say they will fight, you believe
them; if workmen and soldiers say so, you doubt it. What is the distinction between such doubts and siding politically with the bourgeoisie?

Kornilov proved that the Soviets were really a power. To believe
Kerensky and the Council of the Republic, if the bourgeoisie is not
strong enough to break the Soviets, it is not strong enough to break the

Constituent. But that is wrong. The bourgeoisie will break the Constituent by sabotage, by lock-outs, by giving up Petrograd, by opening the front to the Germans. This has already been done in the case of Riga. ...

3. The Soviets must remain a revolver at the head of the Government to force the calling of the Constituent Assembly, and to suppress any further Kornilov attempts.

Answer: Refusal of insurrection is refusal of 'All Power to the Soviets'. Since September the Bolshevik party has been discussing the question of insurrection. Refusing to rise means to trust our hopes in the faith of the good bourgeoisie, who have 'promised' to call the Constituent Assembly. When the Soviets have all the power, the calling of the Constituent is guaranteed, and its success assured.

Refusal of insurrection means surrender to the 'Lieber-Dans'. Either we must drop 'All Power to the Soviets' or make an insurrection; there is no middle course.

4. The bourgeoisie cannot give up Petrograd, although the Rodziankos want it, because it is not the bourgeoisie who are fighting, but our heroic soldiers and sailors.

Answer: This did not prevent two admirals from running away at the Moonsund battle. The Staff has not changed; it is composed of Kornilovtsi. If the Staff, with Kerensky at its head, wants to give up Petrograd, it can do it doubly or trebly. It can make arrangements with the Germans or the British; open the fronts. It can sabotage the Army's food supply. At all these doors has it knocked.

We have no right to wait until the bourgeoisie chokes the Revolution. Rodzianko is a man of action, who has faithfully and truthfully served the bourgeoisie for years. ... Half the Lieber-Dans are cowardly compromisers; half of them simple fatalists. ...

5. We are getting stronger every day. We shall be able to enter the Constituent Assembly as a stronger opposition. Then why should we play everything on one card?

Answer: This is the argument of a sophomore with no practical experience, who reads that the Constituent Assembly is being called and trustfully accepts the legal and constitutional way. Even the voting of the Constituent Assembly will not do away with hunger or beat Wilhelm. ... The issue of hunger and of surrendering Petrograd cannot be decided by waiting for the Constituent Assembly. Hunger is not waiting. The peasants' Revolution is not waiting. The Admirals who ran away did not wait.

Blind people are surprised that hungry people, betrayed by admirals and generals, do not take an interest in voting.

6. If the Kornilovtsi make an attempt, we will show them our

strength. But why should we risk everything by making an attempt ourselves?.

Answer: History doesn't repeat. 'Perhaps Kornilov will some day
make an attempt!' What a serious base for proletarian action! But
suppose Kornilov waits for starvation, for the opening of the fronts,
what then? This attitude means to build the tactics of a revolutionary
party on one of the bourgeoisie's former mistakes.

Let us forget everything except that there is no way out but by the
dictatorship of the proletariat – either that or the dictatorship of
Kornilov.

Let us wait, comrades, for – a miracle!

17 (p. 59). MILYUKOV'S SPEECH (*Resumé*)

Everyone admits, it seems, that the defence of the country is our principal task, and that, to assure it, we must have discipline in the Army
and order in the rear. To achieve this there must be a power capable of
daring, not only by persuasion but also by force. . . . The germ of all
our evils comes from the point of view, original, truly Russian, concerning foreign policy, which passes for the International point of view.

The noble Lenin only imitates the noble Keroyevsky when he holds
that from Russia will come the New World which shall resuscitate the
aged West, and which will replace the old banner of doctrinary Socialism by the new direct action of starving masses – and that will push
humanity forward and force it to break in the doors of the social para-
dise. . . .

These men sincerely believed that the decomposition of Russia
would bring about the decomposition of the whole capitalist régime.
Starting from that point of view, they were able to commit the unconscious treason, in wartime, of calmly telling the soldiers to abandon
the trenches, and instead of fighting the external enemy, creating internal
civil war and attacking the proprietors and capitalists. . . .

Here Milyukov was interrupted by furious cries from the Left,
demanding what Socialist had ever advised such action. . . .

Martov says that only the revolutionary pressure of the proletariat
can condemn and conquer the evil will of imperialist cliques and break
down the dictatorship of these cliques. . . . Not by an accord between
Governments for a limitation of armaments, but by the disarming of
these Governments and the radical democratization of the military
system. . . .

He attacked Martov viciously, and then turned on the Mensheviki and Socialist Revolutionaries, whom he accused of enter-

ing the Government as Ministers with the avowed purpose of carrying on the class struggle!

The Socialists of Germany and of the Allied countries contemplated these gentlemen with ill-concealed contempt, but they decided that it was for Russia, and sent us some apostles of the Universal Conflagration. . . .

The formula of our democracy is very simple; no foreign policy, no art of diplomacy, an immediate democratic peace, a declaration to the Allies, 'We want nothing, we haven't anything to fight with!' And then our adversaries will make the same declaration, and the brotherhood of peoples will be accomplished!

Milyukov took a fling at the Zimmerwald Manifesto, and declared that even Kerensky has not been able to escape the influence of 'that unhappy document which will for ever be your indictment'. He then attacked Skobeliev, whose position in foreign assemblies, where he would appear as a Russian delegate, yet opposed to the foreign policy of his Government, would be so strange that people would say, 'What's that gentleman carrying, and what shall we talk to him about?' As for the *nakaz*, Milyukov said that he himself was a pacifist; that he believed in the creation of an International Arbitration Board, and the necessity for a limitation of armaments, and parliamentary control over secret diplomacy, which did not mean the abolition of secret diplomacy.

As for the Socialist ideas in the *nakaz*, which he called 'Stockholm ideas' – peace without victory, the right of self-determination of peoples, and renunciation of the economic war –

The German successes are directly proportionate to the successes of those who call themselves the revolutionary democracy. I do not wish to say, 'to the successes of the Revolution', because I believe that the defeats of the revolutionary democracy are victories for the Revolution. . . .

The influence of the Soviet leaders abroad is not unimportant. One had only to listen to the speech of the Minister of Foreign Affairs to be convinced that, in this hall, the influence of the revolutionary democracy on foreign policy is so strong that the Minister does not dare to speak face to face with it about the honour and dignity of Russia!

We can see, in the *nakaz* of the Soviets, that the ideas of the Stockholm Manifesto have been elaborated in two directions – that of Utopianism and that of German interests. ...

Interrupted by the angry cries of the Left, and rebuked by the President, Milyukov insisted that the proposition of peace concluded by popular assemblies, not by diplomats, and the proposal to undertake peace negotiations as soon as the enemy had renounced annexations, were pro-German. Recently Kuhlman said that a personal declaration bound only him who made it. ... 'Anyway, we will imitate the Germans before we will imitate the Soviet of Workers' and Soldiers' Deputies. ...'

The sections treating of the independence of Lithuania and Livonia were symptoms of nationalist agitation in different parts of Russia, supported, said Milyukov, by German money. ... Amid bedlam from the Left, he contrasted the clauses of the *nakaz* concerning Alsace-Lorraine, Rumania, and Serbia with those treating of the nationalities in Germany and Austria. The *nakaz* embraced the German and Austrian point of view, said Milyukov, being afraid to speak the thought in his mind, and even afraid to think in terms of the greatness of Russia. The Dardanelles must belong to Russia. ...

You are continually saying that the soldier does not know why he is fighting, and that when he does know he'll fight. ... It is true that the soldier doesn't know why he is fighting, but now you have told him that there is no reason for him to fight, that we have no national interests, and that we are fighting for alien ends. ...

Paying tribute to the Allies, who, he said, with the assistance of America, 'will yet save the cause of humanity', he ended:

Long live the light of humanity, the advanced democracies of the West, who for a long time have been travelling the way we now only begin to enter, with ill-assured and hesitating steps! Long live our brave Allies!

18 (p. 59). INTERVIEW WITH KERENSKY

The Associated Press man tried his hand. 'Mr Kerensky,' he began, 'in England and France people are disappointed with the Revolution –'

'Yes, I know,' interrupted Kerensky, quizzically. 'Abroad the Revolution is no longer fashionable!'

'What is your explanation of why the Russians have stopped fighting?'

'That is a foolish question to ask.' Kerensky was annoyed. 'Russia of all the Allies entered the war first and for a long time she bore the whole brunt of it. Her losses have been inconceivably greater than those of all the other nations put together. Russia has now the right to demand of the Allies that they bring greater force of arms to bear.' He stopped for a moment and stared at his interlocutor. 'You are asking why the Russians have stopped fighting, and the Russians are asking where is the British fleet – with German battleships in the Gulf of Riga?' Again he ceased suddenly, and as suddenly burst out. 'The Russian Revolution hasn't failed and the revolutionary Army hasn't failed. It is not the Revolution which caused disorganization in the army – that disorganization was accomplished years ago by the old régime. Why aren't the Russians fighting? I will tell you. Because the masses of the people are economically exhausted – and because they are disillusioned with the Allies!'

The interview of which this is an excerpt was cabled to the United States, and in a few days sent back by the American State Department, with a demand that it be 'altered'. This Kerensky refused to do; but it was done by his secretary, Dr David Soskice – and, thus purged of all offensive references to the Allies, was given to the press of the world....

Chapter 3

19 (p. 64). RESOLUTION OF THE FACTORY-SHOP COMMITTEES

Workers' Control

1. (See page 64.)

2. The organization of Workers' Control is a manifestation of the same healthy activity in the sphere of industrial production as are party organizations in the sphere of politics, trade unions in employment, cooperatives in the domain of consumption, and literary clubs in the sphere of culture.

3. The working-class has much more interest in the proper and un-interrupted operation of factories ... than the capitalist class. Workers' Control is a better security in this respect for the interests of modern society, of the whole people, than the arbitrary will of the owners, who are guided only by their selfish desire for material profits or political

privileges. Therefore Workers' Control is demanded by the proletariat not only in their own interest, but in the interests of the whole country, and should be supported by the revolutionary peasantry as well as the revolutionary army.

4. Considering the hostile attitude of the majority of the capitalist class towards the Revolution, experience shows that proper distribution of raw materials and fuel, as well as the most efficient management of factories, is impossible without Workers' Control.

5. Only Workers' Control over capitalist enterprises, cultivating the workers' conscious attitude towards work, and making clear its social meaning, can create conditions favourable to the development of a firm self-discipline in labour, and the development of all labour's possible productivity.

6. The impending transformation of industry from a war to a peace basis, and the redistribution of labour all over the country, as well as among the different factories, can be accomplished without great disturbances only by means of the democratic self-government of the workers themselves.... Therefore the realization of Workers' Control is an indispensable preliminary to the demobilization of industry.

7. In accordance with the slogan proclaimed by the Russian Social Democratic Labour Party (Bolsheviki), Workers' Control on a national scale, in order to bring results, must extend to all capitalist concerns, and not be organized accidentally, without system; it must be well planned, and not separated from the industrial life of the country as a whole.

8. The economic life of the country – agriculture, industry, commerce, and transport – must be subjected to one unified plan, constructed so as to satisfy the individual and social requirements of the wide masses of the people; it must be approved by their elected representatives, and carried out under the direction of these representatives by means of national and local organizations.

9. That part of the plan which deals with land-labour must be carried out under supervision of the peasants' and land-workers' organizations; that relating to industry, trade, and transport operated by wage-earners, by means of Workers' Control; the natural organs of Workers' Control inside the industrial plant will be the Factory-Shop and similar Committees; and in the labour market, the Trade Unions.

10. The collective wage agreements arranged by the Trade Unions for the majority of workers in any branch of labour, must be binding on all the owners of plants employing this kind of labour in the given district.

11. Employment bureaux must be placed under the control and management of the Trade Unions, as class organizations acting within

the limits of the whole industrial plan, and in accordance with it.

12. Trade Unions must have the right, upon their own initiative, to begin legal action against all employers who violate labour contracts or labour legislation, and also on behalf of any individual worker in any branch of labour.

13. On all questions relating to Workers' Control over production, distribution, and employment the Trade Unions must confer with the workers of individual establishments through their Factory-Shop Committees.

14. Matters of employment and discharge, vacations, wage scales, refusal of work, degree of productivity and skill, reasons for abrogating agreements, disputes with the administration, and similar problems of the internal life of the factory, must be settled exclusively according to the findings of the Factory-Shop Committee, which has the right to exclude from participation in the discussion any members of the factory administration.

15. The Factory-Shop Committee forms a commission to control the supplying of the factory with raw materials, fuel, orders, labour power, and technical staff (including equipment), and all other supplies and arrangements, and also to assure the factory's adherence to the general industrial plan. The factory administration is obliged to surrender to the organs of Workers' Control, for their aid and information, all data concerning the business; to make it possible to verify this data, and to produce the books of the company upon demand of the Factory-Shop Committee.

16. Any illegal acts on the part of the administration discovered by the Factory-Shop Committees, or any suspicion of any such illegal acts, which cannot be investigated or remedied by the workers alone, shall be referred to the district central organization of Factory-Shop Committees charged with the particular branch of labour involved, which shall discuss the matter with the institutions charged with the execution of the general industrial plan, and find means to deal with the matter, even to the extent of confiscating the factory.

17. The union of the Factory-Shop Committees of different concerns must be accomplished on the basis of the different trades, in order to facilitate control over the whole branch of industry, so as to come within the general industrial plan; and so as to create an effective plan of distribution among the different factories, of orders, raw materials, fuel, technical and labour power, and also to facilitate cooperation with the Trade Unions, which are organized by trades.

18. The central councils of Trade Unions and Factory-Shop Committees represent the proletariat in the corresponding provincial and local institutions formed to elaborate and carry out the general in-

dustrial plan, and to organize economic relations between the towns and the villages (workers and peasants). They also possess final authority for the management of Factory-Shop Committees and Trade Unions, so far as Workers' Control in their district is concerned, and they shall issue obligatory regulations concerning workers' discipline in the routine of production – which regulations, however, must be approved by vote of the workers themselves.

20 (p. 65). THE BOURGEOIS PRESS ON THE BOLSHEVIKI

Russkaya Volia, 28 October:

The decisive moment approaches. . . . It is decisive for the Bolsheviki. Either they will give us . . . a second edition of the events of 16–18 July or they will have to admit that with their plans and intentions, with their impertinent policy of wishing to separate themselves from everything consciously national, they have been definitely defeated. . . .

What are the chances of Bolshevik success?

It is difficult to answer that question, for their principal support is the . . . ignorance of the popular masses. They speculate on it, they work upon it by a demagogy which nothing can stop. . . .

The Government must play its part in this affair. Supporting itself morally by the Council of the Republic, the Government must take a clearly defined attitude towards the Bolsheviki. . . .

And if the Bolsheviki provoke an insurrection against the legal power, and thus facilitate the German invasion, they must be treated as mutineers and traitors. . . .

Birzhevya Viedomosti, 28 October:

Now that the Bolsheviki have separated themselves from the rest of the democracy, the struggle against them is very much simpler – and it is not reasonable, in order to fight against Bolshevism, to wait until they make a manifestation. The Government should not even allow the manifestation. . . .

The appeals of the Bolsheviki to insurrection and anarchy are acts punishable by the criminal courts, and in the freest countries their authors would receive severe sentences. For what the Bolsheviki are carrying on is not a political struggle against the Government, or even for the power; it is propaganda for anarchy, massacres, and civil war. This propaganda must be extirpated at its roots; it would be strange to wait, in order to begin an action against an agitation for *pogroms*, until the *pogroms* actually occurred. . . .

Novoye Vremya, 1 November:

. . . Why is the Government excited only about 2 November (date of calling of the Congress of Soviets), and not about 12 September, or 3 October?

This is not the first time that Russia burns and falls in ruins, and that the smoke of the terrible conflagration makes the eyes of our Allies smart. . . .

Since it came to power has there been a single order issued by the Government for the purpose of halting anarchy, or has anyone attempted to put out the Russian conflagration?

There were other things to do. . . .

The Government turned its attention to a more immediate problem. It crushed an insurrection (the Kornilov attempt) concerning which everyone is now asking, 'Did it ever exist?'

21 (p. 66). MODERATE SOCIALIST PRESS ON THE BOLSHEVIKI

Dielo Naroda, 28 October (Socialist Revolutionary):

The most frightful crime of the Bolsheviki against the Revolution is that they impute exclusively to the bad intentions of the revolutionary Government all the calamities which the masses are so cruelly suffering; when as a matter of fact these calamities spring from objective causes.

They make golden promises to the masses, knowing in advance that they can fulfil none of them; they lead the masses on a false trail, deceiving them as to the source of all their troubles. . . .

The Bolsheviki are the most dangerous enemies of the Revolution. . . .

Dien, 30 October (Menshevik):

Is this really 'the freedom of the press'? Every day *Novaya Rus* and *Rabochi Put* openly incite to insurrection. Every day these papers commit in their columns actual crimes. Every day they urge *pogroms*. . . . Is that 'the freedom of the press'? . . .

The Government ought to defend itself and defend us. We have the right to insist that the Government machinery does not remain passive while the threat of bloody riots endangers the lives of its citizens. . . .

22 (p. 66). 'YEDINSTVO'

Plekhanov's paper, *Yedinstvo*, suspended publication a few weeks after the Bolsheviki seized the power. Contrary to popular report, *Yedinstvo* was not suppressed by the Bolshevik Government; an announcement in the last number admitted that it was unable to continue *because there were too few subscribers.* . . .

23 (p. 67). WERE THE BOLSHEVIKI CONSPIRATORS?

The French newspaper *Entente* of Petrograd, on 15 November, published an article of which the following is a part:

The Government of Kerensky discusses and hesitates. The Government of Lenin and Trotsky attacks and acts.

This last is called a Government of Conspirators, but that is wrong. Government of usurpers, yes, like all revolutionary Governments which triumph over their adversaries. Conspirators – no!

No! They did not conspire. On the contrary, openly, audaciously, without mincing words, without dissimulating their intentions, they multiplied their agitation, intensified their propaganda in the factories, the barracks, at the front, in the country, everywhere, even fixing in advance the date of their taking up arms, the date of their seizure of the power. . . .

They – conspirators? Never. . . .

24 (p. 75). APPEAL AGAINST INSURRECTION
From the Central Army Committee

. . . Above everything we insist upon the inflexible execution of the organized will of the majority of the people, expressed by the Provisional Government in accord with the Council of the Republic and the Tsay-ee-kah as organ of the popular power. . . .

Any demonstration to dispose this power by violence, at a moment when a Government crisis will infallibly create disorganization, the ruin of the country, and civil war, will be considered by the Army as a counter-revolutionary act, and repressed by force of arms. . . .

The interests of private groups and classes should be submitted to a single interest – that of augmenting industrial production, and distributing the necessities of life with fairness. . . .

All who are capable of sabotage, disorganization, or disorder, all deserters, all slackers, all looters, should be forced to do auxiliary service in the rear of the Army. . . .

We invite the Provisional Government to form, out of these violators of the people's will, these enemies of the Revolution, labour detachments to work in the rear, on the front, in the trenches under enemy fire. . . .

25 (p. 87). EVENTS OF THE NIGHT, 6 NOVEMBER

Towards evening bands of Red Guards began to occupy the printing-shops of the bourgeois press, where they printed *Rabochi Put*, *Soldat*, and various proclamations by the hundred thousand.

The City Militia was ordered to clear these places, but found the offices barricaded, and armed men defending them. Soldiers who were ordered to attack the print-shops refused.

About midnight a colonel with a company of *yunkers* arrived at the club 'Free Mind', with a warrant to arrest the editor of *Rabochi Put*. Immediately an enormous mob gathered in the street outside and threatened to lynch the *yunkers*. The Colonel thereupon begged that he and the *yunkers* be arrested and taken to Peter-Paul prison for safety. This request was granted.

At 1 a.m. a detachment of soldiers and sailors from Smolny occupied the Telegraph Agency. At 1.35 the Post Office was occupied. Towards morning the Military Hotel was taken, and at 5 o'clock the Telephone Exchange. At dawn the State Bank was surrounded. And at 10 a.m. a cordon of troops was drawn about the Winter Palace.

Chapter 4

26 (p. 89). EVENTS OF 7 NOVEMBER

From 4 a.m. until dawn Kerensky remained at the Petrograd Staff Headquarters, sending orders to the Cossacks and to the *yunkers* in the Officers' Schools in and around Petrograd – all of whom answered that they were unable to move.

Colonel Polkovnikov, Commandant of the City, hurried between the Staff and the Winter Palace, evidently without any plan. Kerensky gave an order to open the bridges; three hours passed without any action, and then an officer and five men went out on their own initiative, and putting to flight a picket of Red Guards, opened the Nikolai Bridge. Immediately after they left, however, some sailors closed it again.

Kerensky ordered the print-shops of *Rabochi Put* to be occupied. The officer detailed to the work was promised a squad of soldiers; two hours later he was promised some *yunkers*; then the order was forgotten.

An attempt was made to recapture the Post Office and the Telegraph Agency; a few shots were fired, and the Government troops announced that they would no longer oppose the Soviets.

To a delegation of *yunkers* Kerensky said, 'As chief of the

Provisional Government and as Supreme Commander, I know nothing. I cannot advise you; but as a veteran revolutionist I appeal to you, young revolutionists, to remain at your post and defend the conquests of the Revolution.'

*

Orders of Kishkin, 7 November:

By decree of the Provisional Government. ... I am invested with extraordinary powers for the re-establishment of order in Petrograd, in complete command of all civil and military authorities. ...

In accordance with the powers conferred upon me by the Provisional Government, I herewith relieve from his functions as Commandant of the Petrograd Military District Colonel George Polkovnikov. ...

*

Appeal to the Population signed by Vice-Premier Konovalov, 7 November:

Citizens! Save the fatherland, the republic, and your freedom. Maniacs have raised a revolt against the only government power chosen by the people, the Provisional Government. ...

The members of the Provisional Government fulfil their duty, remain at their post, and continue to work for the good of the fatherland, the re-establishment of order, and the convocation of the Constituent Assembly, future sovereign of Russia and of all the Russian peoples. ...

Citizens, you must support the Provisional Government. You must strengthen its authority. You must oppose these maniacs, with whom are joined all the enemies of liberty and order, and the followers of the Tsarist régime, in order to wreck the Constituent Assembly, destroy the conquests of the Revolution, and the future of our dear fatherland. ...

Citizens! Organize around the Provisional Government for the defence of its temporary authority, in the name of order and the happiness of all peoples. ...

*

Proclamation of the Provisional Government

The Petrograd Soviet ... has declared the Provisional Government overthrown and has demanded that the Governmental power be turned over to it, under threat of bombarding the Winter Palace with the cannon of Peter-Paul Fortress, and of the cruiser *Avrora*, anchored in the Neva.

The Government can surrender its authority only to the Constituent Assembly; for that reason it has decided not to submit, and to demand aid from the population and the Army. A telegram has been sent to the Stavka; and an answer received says that a strong detachment of troops is being sent. ....

Let the Army and the People reject the irresponsible attempts of the Bolsheviki to create a revolt in the rear. ....

About 9 a.m. Kerensky left for the front.

Towards evening two soldiers on bicycles presented themselves at the Staff Headquarters, as delegates of the garrison of Peter-Paul Fortress. Entering the meeting-room of the Staff, where Kishkin, Rutenburg, Palchinsky, General Bagratouni, Colonel Paradielov and Count Tolstoy were gathered, they demanded the immediate surrender of the Staff; threatening, in case of refusal, to bombard headquarters. .... After two panicky conferences the Staff retreated to the Winter Palace, and the headquarters were occupied by Red Guards. ....

Late in the afternoon several Bolshevik armoured cars cruised around the Palace Square, and Soviet soldiers tried unsuccessfully to parley with the *yunkers*. ....

Firing on the Palace began about 7 o'clock in the evening. ....

At 10 p.m. began an artillery bombardment from three sides, in which most of the shells were blanks, only three small shrapnels striking the façade of the Palace. ....

27 (p. 92). KERENSKY IN FLIGHT

Leaving Petrograd in the morning of 7 November, Kerensky arrived by automobile at Gatchina, where he demanded a special train. Towards evening he was in Ostrov, Province of Pskov. The next morning, extraordinary session of the local Soviet of Workers' and Soldiers' Deputies, with participation of Cossack delegates – there being 6,000 Cossacks at Ostrov.

Kerensky spoke to the assembly, appealing for aid against the Bolsheviki, and addressed himself almost exclusively to the Cossacks. The soldier delegates protested.

'Why did you come here?' shouted voices. Kerensky answered, 'To ask the Cossacks' assistance in crushing the Bolshevik insurrection!' At this there were violent protestations, which increased when he continued, 'I broke the Kornilov attempt, and

I will break the Bolsheviki!' The noise became so great that he had
to leave the platform....

The soldier deputies and the Ussuri Cossacks decided to arrest
Kerensky, but the Don Cossacks prevented them, and got him
away by train.... A Military Revolutionary Committee, set up
during the day, tried to inform the garrison of Pskov, but the
telephone and telegraph wires were cut....

Kerensky did not arrive at Pskov. Revolutionary soldiers had
cut the railway line, to prevent troops being sent against the
capital. On the night of 8 November he arrived by automobile at
Luga, where he was well received by the Death Battalions
stationed there.

Next day he took train for the South-West Front, and visited
the Army Committee at headquarters. The Fifth Army, however,
was wild with enthusiasm over the news of the Bolshevik success,
and the Army Committee was unable to promise Kerensky any
support.

From there he went to the Stavka, at Moghilev, where he
ordered ten regiments from different parts of the front to move
against Petrograd. The soldiers almost unanimously refused; and
those regiments which did start halted on the way. About five
thousand Cossacks finally followed him....

28 (p. 109). LOOTING OF THE WINTER PALACE

I do not mean to maintain that there was no looting in the Winter
Palace. Both after and *before* the Winter Palace fell there was
considerable pilfering. The statement of the Socialist Revolutionary paper *Narod*, and of members of the City Duma, to the effect
that precious objects to the value of 500,000,000 roubles had been
stolen, was, however, a gross exaggeration.

The most important art treasures of the Palace – paintings,
statues, tapestries, rare porcelains, and armouries – had been
transferred to Moscow during the month of September; and they
were still in good order in the basement of the Imperial Palace
there, ten days after the capture of the Kremlin by Bolshevik
troops. I can personally testify to this....

Individuals, however, especially the general public, which was
allowed to circulate freely through the Winter Palace for several
days after its capture, made away with table silver, clocks,

bedding, mirrors, and some odd vases of valuable porcelain and semi-precious stones, to the value of about 50,000 dollars.

The Soviet Government immediately created a special commission, composed of artists and archaeologists, to recover the stolen objects. On 1 November two proclamations were issued:

CITIZENS OF PETROGRAD!

We urgently ask all citizens to exert every effort to find whatever possible of the objects stolen from the Winter Palace on the night of 7–8 November, and to forward them to the Commandant of the Winter Palace.

Receivers of stolen goods, antiquarians, and all who are proved to be hiding such objects will be held legally responsible and punished with all severity.

Commissars for the Protection of Museums and Artistic Collections,
G. YATMANOV, B. MANDELBAUM

*

To REGIMENTAL AND FLEET COMMITTEES

In the night of 7–8 November, in the Winter Palace, which is the inalienable property of the Russian people, valuable objects of art were stolen.

We urgently appeal to all to exert every effort, so that the stolen objects are returned to the Winter Palace.

Commissars,
G. YATMANOV, B. MANDELBAUM

About half the loot was recovered, some of it in the baggage of foreigners leaving Russia.

A conference of artists and archaeologists, held at the suggestion of Smolny, appointed a commission to make an inventory of the Winter Palace treasures, which was given complete charge of the Palace and of all artistic collections and State museums in Petrograd. On 16 November the Winter Palace was closed to the public while the inventory was being made. . . .

During the last week of November a decree was issued by the Council of People's Commissars, changing the name of the Winter Palace to 'People's Museum', entrusting it to the complete charge of the artistic-archaeological commissions, and declaring that henceforth all Government activities within its walls were prohibited....

29 (p. 112). RAPE OF THE WOMEN'S BATTALION

Immediately following the taking of the Winter Palace all sorts of sensational stories were published in the anti-Bolshevik press, and told in the City Duma, about the fate of the Women's Battalion defending the Palace. It was said that some of the girl-soldiers had been thrown from the windows into the street, most of the rest had been violated, and many had committed suicide as a result of the horrors they had gone through.

The City Duma appointed a commission to investigate the matter. On 16 November the commission returned from Leva-shovo, headquarters of the Women's Battalion. Madame Tyrkova reported that the girls had been at first taken to the barracks of the Pavlovsky Regiment, and that there some of them had been badly treated; but that at present most of them were at Levashovo, and the rest scattered about the city in private houses. Dr Mandel-baum, another of the commission, testified dryly that *none* of the women had been thrown out of the windows of the Winter Palace, that *none* were wounded, that three had been violated, and that one had committed suicide, leaving a note which said that she had been 'disappointed in her ideals'.

On 21 November the Military Revolutionary Committee officially dissolved the Women's Battalion, at the request of the girls themselves, who returned to civilian clothes.

In Louise Bryant's book, *Six Red Months in Russia*, there is an interesting description of the girl-soldiers during this time.

Chapter 5

30 (p. 118). APPEALS AND PROCLAMATIONS
From the Military Revolutionary Committee, 8 November

To All Army Committees and All Soviets of Soldiers' Deputies

The Petrograd garrison has overturned the Government of Kerensky, which had risen against the Revolution and the People.... In sending this news to the front and the country, the Military Revolutionary Committee requests all soldiers to keep vigilant watch on the conduct of officers. Officers who do not frankly and openly declare for the Revolution should be immediately arrested as enemies.

The Petrograd Soviet interprets the programme of the new Government as: immediate proposals of a general democratic peace, the immediate transfer of the Constituent Assembly. The people's revolutionary Army must not permit troops of doubtful morale to be sent to Petrograd. Act by means of arguments, by means of moral suasion – but if that fails halt the movement of troops by implacable force.

The present order must be immediately read to all military units of every branch of the service. Whoever keeps the knowledge of this order from the soldier-masses . . . commits a serious crime against the Revolution, and will be punished with all the rigour of revolutionary law.

Soldiers! For peace, bread, land, and popular government!

*

To All Front and Rear Army, Corps, Divisional, Regimental, and Company Committees, and All Soviets of Workers', Soldiers', and Peasants' Deputies.

Soldiers and Revolutionary officers!

The Military Revolutionary Committee, by agreement with the majority of the workers, soldiers, and peasants, has decreed that General Kornilov and all the accomplices of his conspiracy shall be brought immediately to Petrograd for incarceration in Peter-Paul Fortress and arraignment before a military revolutionary court-martial. . . .

All who resist the execution of this decree are declared by the Committee to be traitors to the Revolution, and their orders are herewith declared null and void.

The Military Revolutionary Committee Attached to the Petrograd Soviet of Workers' and Soldiers' Deputies

*

To all Provincial and District Soviets of Workers', Soldiers', and Peasants' Deputies.

By resolution of the All-Russian Congress of Soviets, all arrested members of Land Committees are immediately set free. The Commissars who arrested them are to be arrested.

From this moment all power belongs to the Soviets. The Commissars of the Provisional Government are removed. The presidents of the various local Soviets are invited to enter into direct relations with the revolutionary Government.

Military Revolutionary Committee

31 (p. 125). PROTEST OF THE MUNICIPAL DUMA

The Central City Duma, elected on the most democratic principles, has undertaken the burden of managing Municipal affairs and food supplies at the time of the greatest disorganization. At the present moment the Bolshevik party, three weeks before the elections to the Constituent Assembly, and in spite of the menace of the external enemy, having removed by armed force the only legal revolutionary authority, is making an attempt against the rights and independence of the Municipal Self-Government, demanding submission to its Commissars and its illegal authority.

In this terrible and tragic moment the Petrograd City Duma, in the face of its constituents, and of all Russia, declares loudly that it will not submit to any encroachments on its rights and its independence, and will remain at the post of responsibility to which it has been called by the will of the population of the capital.

The Central City Duma of Petrograd appeals to all Dumas and Zemstvos of the Russian Republic to rally to the defence of one of the greatest conquests of the Russian Revolution – the independence and inviolability of popular self-government.

32 (p. 134). LAND DECREE – PEASANTS' 'NAKAZ'

The land question can only be permanently settled by the general Constituent Assembly.

The most equitable solution of the land question should be as follows:

1. The right of private ownership of land abolished for ever; land cannot be sold, nor leased, nor mortgaged, nor alienated in any way. All dominical lands, lands attached to titles, lands belonging to the Emperor's cabinet, to monasteries, churches, possession lands, entailed lands, private estates, communal lands, peasant freeholds, and others, are confiscated without compensation, and become national property, and are placed at the disposition of the workers who cultivate them.

Those who are damaged because of this social transformation of the rights of property are entitled to public aid during the time necessary for them to adapt themselves to the new conditions of existence.

2. All the riches beneath the earth – ores, oil, coal, salt, etc. – as well as forest and waters having a national importance, become the exclusive property of the State. All minor streams, lakes, and forests are placed in the hands of the communities, on condition of being managed by the local organs of government.

3. All plots of land scientifically cultivated – gardens, plantations, nurseries, seed-plots, green-houses, and others – shall not be divided,

but transformed into model farms, and pass into the hands of the State or of the community, according to their size and importance.

Buildings, communal lands, and villages with their private gardens and their orchards remain in the hands of their present owners; the dimensions of these plots and the rates of taxes for their use shall be fixed by law.

4. All studs, governmental and private cattle-breeding and bird-breeding establishments, and others, are confiscated and become national property, and are transferred either to the State or to the community, according to their size and importance.

All questions of compensation for the above are within the competence of the Constituent Assembly.

5. All inventoried agricultural property of the confiscated lands, machinery, and livestock are transferred without compensation to the State or the community, according to their quality and importance.

The confiscation of such machinery or livestock shall not apply to the small properties of peasants.

6. The right to use the land is granted to all citizens, without distinction of sex, who wish to work the land themselves, with the help of their families, or in partnership, and only so long as they are able to work. No hired labour is permitted.

In the event of the incapacity for work of a member of the commune for a period of two years, the commune shall be bound to render him assistance during this time by working the land in common.

Farmers who through old age or sickness have permanently lost the capacity to work the land themselves, shall surrender their land and receive instead a Government pension.

7. The use of the land shall be equalized – that is to say, the land shall be divided among the workers according to local conditions, the unit of labour, and the needs of the individual.

The way in which land is to be used may be individually determined upon: as homesteads, as farms, by communes, by partnerships, as will be decided by the villages and settlements.

8. All land upon its confiscation is pooled in the general People's Land Fund. Its distribution among the workers is carried out by the local and central organs of administration, beginning with the village democratic organizations and ending with the central provincial institutions – with the exception of urban and rural societies.

The Land Fund is subject to periodical redistribution according to the increase of population and the development of productivity and rural economy.

In case of modification of the boundaries of allotments, the original centre of the allotment remains intact.

The lands of persons retiring from the community return to the Land Fund; providing that near relations of the persons retiring, or friends designated by them, shall have preference in the redistribution of those lands.

When lands are returned to the Land Fund the money expended for manuring or improving the land, which has not been exhausted, shall be reimbursed.

If in some localities the Land Fund is insufficient to satisfy the local population, the surplus population should emigrate.

The organization of the emigration, also the costs thereof, and the providing of emigrants with the necessary machinery and livestock, shall be the business of the State.

The emigration shall be carried out in the following order: first, the peasants without land who express their wish to emigrate, then the undesirable members of the community, deserters, etc., and finally by drawing lots on agreement.

All which is contained in this *nakaz*, being the expression of the indisputable will of the great majority of conscious peasants of Russia, is declared to be a temporary law, and until the convocation of the Constituent Assembly, becomes effective immediately so far as is possible, and in some parts of it gradually, as will be determined by the District Soviets of Peasants' Deputies.

33 (p. 138). THE LAND AND THE DESERTERS

The Government was not forced to make any decision concerning the rights of deserters to the land. The end of the war and the demobilization of the army automatically removed the deserter problem. . . .

34 (p. 138). THE COUNCIL OF PEOPLE'S COMMISSARS

The Council of People's Commissars was at first composed entirely of Bolsheviki. This was not entirely the fault of the Bolsheviki, however. On 8 November they offered portfolios to members of the Left Socialist Revolutionaries, who declined.

Chapter 6

35 (p. 147). APPEALS AND DENUNCIATIONS

Appeal to all Citizens and to the Military Organizations of the Socialist Revolutionary Party.

The senseless attempt of the Bolsheviki is on the eve of complete failure. The garrison is disaffected. ... The Ministries are idle, bread is lacking. All factions, except a handful of Bolsheviki have left the Congress of Soviets. The Bolsheviki are alone! Abuses of all sorts, acts of vandalism and pillage, the bombardment of the Winter Palace, arbitrary arrests – all these crimes committed by the Bolsheviki have aroused against them the resentment of the majority of the sailors and soldiers. The Tsentroflot refuses to submit to the orders of the Bolsheviki. ...

We call upon all sane elements to gather around the Committee for Salvation of Country and Revolution; to take serious measures to be ready, at the first call of the Central Committee of the Party, to act against the counter-revolutionists, who will doubtless attempt to profit by these troubles provoked by the Bolshevik adventure, and to watch closely the external enemy, who also would like to take advantage of this opportune moment when the front is weakened. ...

> *The Military Section of the Central Committee*
> *of the Socialist Revolutionary Party*

*

From *Pravda*:

What is Kerensky?

A usurper, whose place is in Peter-Paul prison, with Kornilov and Kishkin.

A criminal and a traitor to the workers, soldiers, and peasants, who believed in him.

Kerensky? A murderer of soldiers!

Kerensky? A public executioner of peasants!

Kerensky? A strangler of workers!

Such is the second Kornilov who now wants to butcher liberty!

Chapter 7

36 (p. 166). TWO DECREES

On the Press

In the serious decisive hour of the Revolution and the days immediately following it, the Provisional Revolutionary Committee is compelled to adopt a series of measures against the counter-revolutionary press of all shades.

Immediately on all sides are cries that the new Socialist authority is in this violating the essential principles of its own programme by an attempt against the freedom of the press.

The Workers' and Peasants' Government calls the attention of the population to the fact that in our country, behind this liberal shield, is hidden the opportunity of the wealthier classes to seize the lion's share of the whole press, and by this means to poison the popular mind and bring confusion into the consciousness of the masses.

Everyone knows that the bourgeois press is one of the most powerful weapons of the bourgeoisie. Especially in this critical moment, when the new authority of the workers and peasants is in process of consolidation, it is impossible to leave it in the hands of the enemy, at a time when it is not less dangerous than bombs and machine-guns. This is why temporary and extraordinary measures have been adopted for the purpose of stopping the flow of filth and calumny in which the yellow and green press would be glad to drown the young victory of the people.

As soon as the new order is consolidated, all administrative measures against the press will be suspended; full liberty will be given it within the limits of responsibility before the law, in accordance with the broadest and most progressive regulations. . . .

Bearing in mind, however, the fact that any restrictions of the freedom of the press, even in critical moments, are admissible only within the bounds of necessity, the Council of People's Commissars decrees as follows:

1. The following classes of newspaper shall be subject to closure: (a) Those inciting to open resistance or disobedience to the Workers' and Peasants' Government; (b) those creating confusion by obviously and deliberately perverting the news; (c) those inciting to acts of a criminal character punishable by the laws.

2. The temporary or permanent closing of any organ of the press shall be carried out by virtue of a resolution of the Council of People's Commissars.

3. The present decree is of a temporary nature and will be revoked by a special *ukaz* when normal conditions of public life are re-established.

President of the Council of People's Commissars

VLADIMIR ULYANOV (LENIN)

◆

On Workers' Militia

1. All Soviets of Workers' and Soldiers' Deputies shall form a Workers' Militia.

2. This Workers' Militia shall be entirely at the orders of the Soviets of Workers' and Soldiers' Deputies.

3. Military and Civil authorities must render every assistance in arming the workers and in supplying them with technical equipment,

even to the extent of requisitioning arms belonging to the War Department of the Government.

4. This decree shall be promulgated by telegraph.

Petrograd, 10 November 1917.

People's Commissar of the Interior,

A. I. RYKOV

*

This decree encouraged the formation of companies of Red Guards all over Russia, which became the most valuable arm of the Soviet Government in the ensuing civil war.

37 (p. 167). THE STRIKE FUND

The fund for the striking Government employees and bank clerks was subscribed by banks and business houses of Petrograd and other cities, and also by foreign corporations doing business in Russia. All who consented to strike against the Bolsheviki were paid full wages, and in some cases their pay was increased. It was the realization of the strike fund contributors that the Bolsheviki were firmly in power, followed by their refusal to pay strike benefits, which finally broke the strike.

Chapter 8

38 (p. 181). KERENSKY'S ADVANCE

On 9 November Kerensky and his Cossacks arrived at Gatchina, where the garrison, hopelessly split into two factions, immediately surrendered. The members of the Gatchina Soviet were arrested, and at first threatened with death; later they were released on good behaviour.

The Cossack advance-guards, practically unopposed, occupied Pavlovsk, Alexandrovsk, and other stations, and reached the outskirts of Tsarskoye Selo next morning – 10 November. At once the garrison divided into three groups – the officers, loyal to Kerensky; part of the soldiers and non-commissioned officers, who declared themselves 'neutral'; and most of the rank and file, who were for the Bolsheviki. The Bolshevik soldiers, who were without leaders or organization, fell back towards the capital. The local Soviet also withdrew to the village of Pulkovo.

From Pulkovo six members of the Tsarskoye Selo Soviet went

with an automobile load of proclamations to Gatchina, to propagandize the Cossacks. They spent most of the day going around Gatchina from one Cossack barracks to another, pleading, arguing, and explaining. Towards evening some officers discovered their presence and they were arrested and brought before General Krasnov, who said, 'You fought against Kornilov, now you are opposing Kerensky. I'll have you all shot!'

After reading aloud to them the order appointing him commander-in-chief of the Petrograd District, Krasnov asked if they were Bolsheviki. They replied in the affirmative, upon which Krasnov went away; a short time later an officer came and set them free, saying it was by order of General Krasnov....

In the meantime delegations continued to arrive from Petrograd; from the Duma, the Committee for Salvation, and, last of all, from the Vikzhel. The Union of Railway Workers insisted that some agreement be reached to halt the civil war, and demanded that Kerensky treat with the Bolsheviki, and that he stop the advance on Petrograd. In case of refusal the Vikzhel threatened a general strike at midnight of 11 November.

Kerensky asked to be allowed to discuss the matter with the Socialist Ministers and with the Committee for Salvation. He was plainly undecided.

On the eleventh Cossack outposts reached Krasnoye Selo, from which the local Soviet and the heterogeneous forces of the Military Revolutionary Committee precipitately retired, some of them surrendering.... That night they also touched Pulkovo, where the first real resistance was encountered....

Cossack deserters began to dribble into Petrograd, declaring that Kerensky had lied to them, that he had spread broadcast over the front proclamations which said that Petrograd was burning, that the Bolsheviki had invited the Germans to come in, and that they were murdering women and children and looting indiscriminately....

39 (p. 187). PROCLAMATIONS OF THE MILITARY REVOLUTIONARY COMMITTEE

To All Soviets of Workers', Soldiers', and Peasants' Deputies.

The All-Russian Congress of Soviets of Workers', Soldiers', and Peasants' Deputies charges the local Soviets immediately to take the most energetic measures to oppose all counter-revolutionary anti-

Semitic disturbances, and all *pogroms* of whatever nature. The honour of the workers', peasants', and soldiers' Revolution cannot tolerate any disorders. ...

The Red Guard of Petrograd, the revolutionary garrison, and the sailors have maintained complete order in the capital.

Workers, soldiers, and Cossacks, on us falls the duty of keeping real revolutionary order.

All revolutionary Russia and the whole world have their eyes on you. ...

*

The All-Russian Congress of Soviets decrees:

To abolish capital punishment at the front, which was reintroduced by Kerensky.

Complete freedom of propaganda is to be re-established in the country. All soldiers and revolutionary officers now under arrest for so-called political 'crimes' are at once to be set free.

*

The ex-Premier Kerensky, overthrown by the people, refuses to submit to the Congress of Soviets and attempts to struggle against the legal Government elected by the All-Russian Congress – the Council of People's Commissars. The front has refused to aid Kerensky. Moscow has rallied to the new Government. In many cities (Minsk, Moghilev, Kharkov) the power is in the hands of the Soviets. No infantry detachment consents to march against the Workers' and Peasants' Government, which, in accord with the firm will of the Army and the people, has begun peace negotiations and has given the land to the peasants. ...

We give public warning that if the Cossacks do not halt Kerensky, who has deceived them and is leading them against Petrograd, the revolutionary forces will rise with all their might for the defence of the precious conquests of the Revolution – Peace and Land.

Citizens of Petrograd! Kerensky fled from the city, abandoning the authority to Kishkin, who wanted to surrender the capital to the Germans; Rutenburg, of the Black Band, who sabotaged the Municipal Food Supply; and Palchinsky, hated by the whole democracy. Kerensky has fled, abandoning you to the Germans, to famine, to bloody massacres. The revolting people have arrested Kerensky's Ministers, and you have seen how the order and supplying of Petrograd at once improved. Kerensky, at the demand of the aristocrat proprietors, the capitalists, speculators, marches against you for the purpose of giving back the land to the landowners, and continuing the hated and ruinous war.

Citizens of Petrograd! We know that the great majority of you are in favour of the peoples' revolutionary authority, against the Kornilovtsi led by Kerensky. Do not be deceived by the lying declarations of the impotent bourgeois conspirators, who will be pitilessly crushed.

Workers, soldiers, peasants! We call upon you for revolutionary devotion and discipline.

Millions of peasants and soldiers are with us.

The victory of the people's Revolution is assured!

40 (p. 188). ACTS OF THE COUNCIL OF PEOPLE'S COMMISSARS

In this book I am giving only such decrees as are in my opinion pertinent to the Bolshevik conquest of power. The rest belong to a detailed account of the structure of the Soviet State, for which I have no place in this work. This will be dealt with very fully in the second volume, now in preparation, *Kornilov to Brest-Litovsk*.

Concerning Dwelling-Places

1. The independent Municipal Self-Governments have the right to sequestrate all unoccupied or uninhabited dwelling-places.

2. The Municipalities may, according to laws and arrangements established by them, install in all available lodgings citizens who have no place to live, or who live in congested or unhealthy lodgings.

3. The Municipalities may establish a service of inspection of dwelling-places, organize it, and define its powers.

4. The Municipalities may issue orders on the institution of House Committees, define their organization, their powers, and give them juridical authority.

5. The Municipalities may create Housing Tribunals, define their powers and their authority.

6. This decree is promulgated by telegraph.

People's Commissar of the Interior,

A. I. RYKOV

∗

On Social Insurance

The Russian proletariat has inscribed on its banners the promise of complete Social Insurance of wage-workers, as well as of the town and village poor. The Government of the Tsar, the proprietors and the capitalists, as well as the Government of coalition and conciliation, failed to realize the desires of the workers with regard to Social Insurance.

The Workers' and Peasants' Government, relying upon the support of the Soviets of Workers', Soldiers', and Peasants' Deputies, announces to the working class of Russia and to the town and village poor, that it will immediately prepare laws on Social Insurance based on the formulas proposed by the Labour organizations:

1. Insurances for all wage-earners without exception, as well as for all urban and rural poor.

2. Insurance to cover all categories of loss of working capacity, such as illness, infirmities, old age, child-birth, widowhood, orphanage, and unemployment.

3. All the costs of insurance to be charged to employers.

4. Compensation of at least full wages in all loss of working capacity and unemployment.

5. Complete workers' self-government of all Insurance institutions.

In the name of the Government of the Russian Republic.

The People's Commissar of Labour,

ALEXANDER SHLIAPNIKOV

•

On Popular Education

Citizens of Russia!

With the insurrection of 7 November the working masses have won for the first time the real power.

The All-Russian Congress of Soviets has temporarily transferred this power both to its Executive Committee and the Council of People's Commissars.

By the will of the revolutionary people, I have been appointed People's Commissar of Education.

The work of guiding in general the people's education, inasmuch as it remains with the central government, is, until the Constituent Assembly meets, entrusted to a Commission on the People's Education, whose chairman and executive is the People's Commissar.

Upon what fundamental proposition will rest this State Commission? How is its sphere of competence determined?

The General Line of Educational Activity: Every genuinely democratic power must, in the domain of education, in a country where illiteracy and ignorance reign supreme, make its first aim in the struggle against this darkness. It must acquire in the shortest time *universal literacy*, by organizing a network of schools answering to the demands of modern pedagogics; it must introduce universal, obligatory, and free tuition for all, and establish at the same time a series of such teachers' institutes and seminaries as will in the shortest time furnish a powerful army of people's teachers so necessary for the universal instruction of the population of our boundless Russia.

Decentralization: The State Commission on People's Education is by no means a central power governing the institutions of instruction and education. On the contrary, the entire school work ought to be transferred to the organs of local self-government. The independent work of the workers, soldiers, and peasants, establishing on their own initiative cultural educational organizations, must be given full autonomy, both by the State centre and the Municipal centres.

The work of the State Commission serves as a link and helpmate to organize resources of material and moral support to the Municipal and private institutions, particularly to those with a class-character established by the workers.

The State Committee on People's Education: A whole series of invaluable law projects was elaborated from the beginning of the Revolution by the State Committee for People's Education, a tolerably democratic body as to its composition, and rich in experts. The State Commission sincerely desires the collaboration of this Committee.

It has addressed itself to the bureau of the Committee, with the request at once to convoke an extraordinary session of the Committee for the fulfilment of the following programme.

1. The revision of rules of representation in the Committee, in the sense of greater democratization.

2. The revision of the Committee's rights in the sense of widening them, and of converting the Committee into a fundamental State institute for the elaboration of law projects calculated to recognize public instruction and education in Russia upon democratic principles.

3. The revision, jointly with the new State Commission, of the laws already created by the Committee, a revision required by the fact that in editing them the Committee had to take into account the bourgeois spirit of previous Ministries, which obstructed it even in this its narrowed form.

After this revision these laws will be put into effect without any bureaucratic red tape, in the revolutionary order.

The Pedagogues and the Societists: The State Commission welcomes the pedagogues to the bright and honourable work of educating the people – the masters of the country.

No one measure in the domain of the people's education ought to be adopted by any power without the attentive deliberation of those who represent the pedagogues.

On the other hand, a decision cannot by any means be reached exclusively through the cooperation of specialists. This refers as well to reforms of the institutes of general education.

The cooperation of the pedagogues with the social forces: this is how the Commission will work both in its own constitution, in the State Committee, and in all its activities.

As its first task the Commission considers the improvement of the teachers' status, and first of all of those very poor though almost most important contributors to the work of culture – the elementary school-teachers. Their just demands ought to be satisfied at once and at any cost. The proletariat of the schools has in vain demanded an increase of salary to one hundred roubles per month. It would be a disgrace any longer to keep in poverty the teachers of the overwhelming majority of the Russian people.

But a real democracy cannot stop at mere literacy, at universal elementary instruction. It must endeavour to organize a uniform secular school of several grades. The ideal is, equal and if possible higher education for all citizens. So long as this idea has not been realized for all, the natural transition through all the schooling grades up to the university – a transition to a higher stage – must depend entirely upon the pupil's aptitude, and not upon the resources of his family.

The problem of a genuinely democratic organization of instruction is particularly difficult in a country impoverished by a long, criminal, imperialistic war; but the workers who have taken the power must remember that education will serve them as the greatest instrument in their struggle for a better lot and for a spiritual growth. However needful it may be to curtail other articles of the people's budget, the expenses on education must stand high. A large educational budget is the pride and glory of a nation. The free and enfranchised peoples of Russia will not forget this.

The fight against illiteracy and ignorance cannot be confined to a thorough establishment of school education for children and youths. Adults, too, will be anxious to save themselves from the debasing position of a man who cannot read and write. The school for adults must occupy a conspicuous place in the general plan of popular instruction.

Instruction and Education: One must emphasize the difference between instruction and education.

Instruction is the transmission of ready knowledge by the teacher to his pupil. Education is a creative process. The personality of the individual is being 'educated' throughout life, is being formed, grows richer in content, stronger and more perfect.

The toiling masses of the people – workmen, the peasants, the soldiers – are thirsting for elementary and advanced instruction. But they are also thirsting for education. Neither the government nor the intellectuals nor any other power outside of themselves can give it to them. The school, the book, the theatre, the museum, etc., may here be only aids. They have their own ideas, formed by their social position, so different from the position of those ruling classes and intellectuals who have hitherto created culture. They have their own ideas, their own emotions, their own ways of approaching the problems of personality and society. The city labourer, according to his own fashion, the rural toiler according to his, will each build his clear world-conception permeated with the class-idea of the workers. There is no more superb or beautiful phenomenon than the one of which our nearest descendants will be both witnesses and participants: the building by collective Labour of its own general, rich, and free soul.

Instruction will surely be an important but not a decisive element. What is more important here is the criticism, the creativeness of the masses themselves; for science and art have only in some of their parts a general human importance. They suffer radical changes with every far-reaching class upheaval.

Throughout Russia, particularly among the city labourers, but also among the peasants, a powerful wave of cultural educational movement has arisen; workers' and soldiers' organizations of this kind are multiplying rapidly. To meet them, to lend them support, to clear the road before them, is the first task of a revolutionary and popular government in the domain of democratic education.

The Constituent Assembly will doubtless soon begin its work. It alone can permanently establish the order of national and social life in our country, and at the same time the general character of the organization of popular education.

Now, however, with the passage of power to the Soviets, the really democratic character of the Constituent Assembly is assured. The line which the State Commission, relying upon the State Committee, will follow, will hardly suffer any modification under the influence of the Constituent Assembly. Without predetermining it, the new People's Government considers itself within its rights in enacting in this domain a series of measures which aim at encircling and enlightening as soon as possible the spiritual life of the country.

The Ministry: The present work must in the interim proceed through the Ministry of the People's Education. Of all the necessary alterations in its composition and construction the State Commission will have charge, elected by the Executive Committee of the Soviets and the State Committee. Of course the order of State authority in the domain of the people's education will be established by the Constituent Assembly. Until then the Ministry must play the part of the executive apparatus for both the State Committee and the State Commission for People's Education.

The pledge of the country's effort of the working people and of the honest enlightened intellectuals will lead the country out of its painful crisis, and through complete democracy to the reign of Socialism and the brotherhood of nations.

People's Commissar on Education,

A. V. LUNACHARSKY

*

On the Order in Which the Laws are to be Ratified and Published

1. Until the convocation of the Constituent Assembly, the enacting and publishing of laws shall be carried out in the order decreed by the present Provisional Workmen's and Peasants' Government, elected by the All-Russian Congress of Workers', Peasants', and Soldiers' Deputies.

2. Every Bill is presented for consideration of the Government by the respective Ministry, signed by the duly authorized People's Commissar; or it is presented by the legislative section attached to the Government, signed by the chief of the section.

3. After its ratification by the Government the decree in its final edition, in the name of the Russian Republic, is signed by the president of the Council of People's Commissars, or for him by the People's Commissar who presented it for the consideration of the Government, and is then published.

4. The date of publishing it in the official *Gazette of the Provisional Workmen's and Peasants' Government* is the date of its becoming law.

5. In the decree there may be appointed a date, other than the date of publication, on which it shall become law, or it may be promulgated by telegraph; in which case it is to be regarded in every locality as becoming law upon the publication of the telegram.

6. The promulgation of legislative Acts of the Government of the State Senate is abolished. The Legislative Section attached to the Council of People's Commissars issues periodically a collection of regulations and orders of the Governments which possess the force of law.

7. The Central Executive Committee of the Soviets of Workers', Peasants', and Soldiers' Deputies (Tsay-ee-kah) has at all times the right to cancel, alter, or annul any of the Government decrees.

In the name of the Russian Republic, the President of the Council of People's Commissars,

V. ULYANOV-LENIN

41 (p. 189). THE LIQUOR PROBLEM

Order Issued by the Military Revolutionary Committee

1. Until further order the production of alcohol and alcoholic drinks is prohibited.

2. It is ordered to all producers of alcohol and alcoholic drinks to inform not later than on the twenty-seventh inst. of the exact site of their stores.

3. All culprits against this order will be tried by a Military Revolutionary Court.

THE MILITARY REVOLUTIONARY COMMITTEE

*

ORDER NO. 2

From the Committee of the Finland Guard Reserve Regiment to all House Committees and to the citizens of Vasili Ostrov.

The bourgeoisie has chosen a very sinister method of fighting against the proletariat; it has established in various parts of the city huge wine depots, and distributes liquor among the soldiers, in this manner attempting to sow dissatisfaction in the ranks of the Revolutionary army.

It is herewith ordered to all house committees that at 3 o'clock, the time set for posting this order, they shall in person and secretly notify the President of the Committee of the Finland Guard Regiment, concerning the amount of wine in their premises.

Those who violate this order will be arrested and given trial before a merciless court, and their property will be confiscated, and the stock of wine discovered will be

BLOWN UP WITH DYNAMITE
two hours after this warning

because more lenient measures, as experience has shown, do not bring the desired results.

REMEMBER, THERE WILL BE NO OTHER WARNING BEFORE THE EXPLOSIONS

Regimental Committee of the Finland Guard Regiment

Chapter 9

42 (p. 200). MILITARY REVOLUTIONARY COMMITTEE.
BULLETIN NO. 2

November the twelfth, in the evening, Kerensky sent a proposition to the revolutionary troops · 'to lay down their arms'. Kerensky's men opened artillery fire. Our artillery answered and compelled the enemy to be silent. The Cossacks assumed the offensive. The deadly fire of the sailors, the Red Guards, and the soldiers forced the Cossacks to retreat. Our armoured cars rushed in among the ranks of the enemy. The enemy is fleeing. Our troops are in pursuit. The order has been given to arrest Kerensky. Tsarskoye Selo has been taken by the revolutionary troops.

The Lettish Riflemen: The Military Revolutionary Committee has received precise information that the valiant Lettish Riflemen have arrived from the front and taken up a position in the rear of Kerensky's bands.

From the Staff of the Military Revolutionary Committee

The seizure of Gatchina and Tsarskoye Selo by Kerensky's detachments is to be explained by the complete absence of artillery and machine-guns in these places, whereas Kerensky's cavalry was provided with artillery from the beginning. The last two days were days of enforced work for our Staff, to provide the necessary quantity of guns, machine-guns, field telephones, etc., for the revolutionary troops. When this work - with the energetic assistance of the District Soviets and the factories (the Putilov Works, Obukhov and others) - was accomplished, the issue of the expected encounter left no place for doubt; on the side of the revolutionary troops there was not only a surplus in quantity and such a powerful material base as Petrograd, but also an enormous moral advantage. All the Petrograd regiments moved out to the positions with tremendous enthusiasm. The Garrison Conference elected a Control Commission of five soldiers, thus securing a complete unity between the commander-in-chief and the garrison. At the Garrison Conference it was unanimously decided to begin decisive action.

The artillery fire on the twelfth of November developed with extra-ordinary force by 3 p.m. The Cossacks were completely demoralized. A parlementaire came from them to the staff of the detachment at Krasnoye Selo, and proposed to stop the firing, threatening otherwise to take 'decisive' measures. He was answered that the firing would cease when Kerensky laid down his arms.

In the developing encounter all sections of the troops - the sailors, soldiers, and the Red Guard - showed unlimited courage. The sailors continued to advance until they had fired their last cartridges. The number of casualties has not been established yet, but it is larger on the part of the counter-revolutionary troops, who experienced great losses through one of our armoured cars.

Kerensky's staff, fearing that they would be surrounded, gave the order to retreat, which retreat speedily assumed a disorderly character. By 11-12 p.m. Tsarskoye Selo, including the wireless station, was entirely occupied by the troops of the Soviets. The Cossacks retreated towards Gatchina and Colpinno.

The morale of the troops is beyond all praise. The order has been given to pursue the retreating Cossacks. From the Tsarskoye Selo station a radio-telegram was sent immediately to the front and to all local Soviets throughout Russia. Further details will be communicated. ...

43 (p. 205). EVENTS OF THE THIRTEENTH IN PETROGRAD

Three regiments of the Petrograd garrison refused to take any part in the battle against Kerensky. On the morning of the thirteenth they summoned to a joint conference sixty delegates from the front, in order to find some way to stop the civil war. This conference appointed a committee to go and persuade Kerensky's troops to lay down their arms. They proposed to ask the Government soldiers the following questions: Will the soldiers and Cossacks of Kerensky recognize the Tsay-ee-kah as the repository of Government power, responsible to the Congress of Soviets? Will the soldiers and Cossacks accept the Land and Peace decrees? Will they agree to cease hostilities and return to their units? Will they consent to the arrest of Kerensky, Krasnov, and Savinkov?

At the meeting of the Petrograd Soviet, Zinoviev said,

It would be foolish to think that this committee could finish the affair. The enemy can only be broken by force. However, it would be a crime for us not to try every peaceful means to bring the Cossacks over to us. ... What we need is a military victory. ... The news of an armistice is premature. Our Staff will be ready to conclude an armistice when the enemy can no longer do any harm. ...

At present the influence of our victory is creating new political conditions. ... Today the Socialist Revolutionaries are inclined to admit the Bolsheviki into the new Government. ... A decisive victory is indispensable, so that those who hesitate will have no further hesitation. ...

At the City Duma all attention was concentrated on the formation of the new Government. In many factories and barracks already Revolutionary Tribunals were operating, and the Bolsheviki were threatening to set up more of these, and try Gotz and Avksentiev before them. Dan proposed that an ultimatum be sent demanding the abolition of these Revolutionary Tribunals, or the other members of the Conference would immediately break off all negotiations with the Bolsheviki.

Shingariov, Cadet, declared that the Municipality ought not to take part in any agreement with the Bolsheviki. ...

Any agreement with the maniacs is impossible until they lay down their arms and recognize the authority of independent courts of law. . . .

Yartsev, for the Yedinstvo group, declared that any agreement with the Bolsheviki would be equivalent to a Bolshevik victory. . . .

Mayor Schreider, for the Socialist Revolutionaries, stated that he was opposed to all agreement with the Bolsheviki. . . .

As for a Government, that ought to spring from the popular will; and since the popular will has been expressed in the municipal elections, the popular will which can create a Government is actually concentrated in the Duma. . . .

After other speakers, of which only the representative of the Mensheviki Internationalists was in favour of considering the admission of the Bolsheviki in the new Government, the Duma voted to continue its representatives in the Vikzhel's conference, but to insist upon the restoration of the Provisional Government before everything, and to exclude the Bolsheviki from the new power. . . .

44 (p. 205). TRUCE. KRASNOV'S ANSWER TO THE COMMITTEE FOR SALVATION

In answer to your telegram proposing an immediate armistice, the Supreme Commander, not wishing further futile bloodshed, consents to enter into negotiations and to establish relations between the armies of the Government and the insurrectionists. He proposes to the General Staff of the insurrectionists to recall its regiments to Petrograd, to declare the line Ligovno-Pulkovo-Colpinno neutral, and to allow the advance-guards of the Government cavalry to enter Tsarskoye Selo, for the purpose of establishing order. The answer to this proposal must be placed in the hands of our envoys before eight o'clock tomorrow morning.

KRASNOV

45 (p. 216). EVENTS AT TSARSKOYE SELO

On the evening that Kerensky's troops retreated from Tsarskoye Selo, some priests organized a religious procession through the streets of the town, making speeches to the citizens, in which they asked the people to support the rightful authority, the Provisional Government. When the Cossacks had retreated, and the first Red Guards entered the town, witnesses reported that the priests had incited the people against the Soviets, and had said prayers at the grave of Rasputin, which lies behind the Imperial Palace. One of the priests, Father Ivan Kuchurov, was arrested and shot by the infuriated Red Guards. . . .

Just as the Red Guards entered the town the electric lights were shut off, plunging the streets in complete darkness. The director of the electric light plant, Lubovich, was arrested by the Soviet troops and asked why he had shut off the lights. He was found some time later in the room where he had been imprisoned with a revolver in his hand and a bullet hole in his temple.

The Petrograd anti-Bolshevik papers came out next day with headlines, 'Plekhanov's temperature 39 degrees!' Plekhanov lived at Tsarskoye Selo, where he was lying ill in bed. Red Guards arrived at the house and searched it for arms, questioning the old man.

'What class of society do you belong to?' they asked him.

'I am a revolutionist,' answered Plekhanov, 'who for forty years has devoted his life to the struggle for liberty!'

'Anyway,' said a workman, 'you have now sold yourself to the bourgeoisie!'

The workers no longer knew Plekhanov, pioneer of the Russian Social Democracy!

46 (p. 217). APPEAL OF THE SOVIET GOVERNMENT

The detachments at Gatchina, deceived by Kerensky, have laid down their arms and decided to arrest Kerensky. The chief of the counter-revolutionary campaign has fled. The Army, by an enormous majority, has pronounced in favour of the second All-Russian Congress of Soviets, and of the Government which it has created. Scores of delegates from the front have hastened to Petrograd to assure the Soviet Government of the Army's fidelity. No twisting of the facts, no calumny against the revolutionary workers, soldiers, and peasants have been able to defeat the People. The Workers' and Soldiers' Revolution is victorious. . . .

The Tsay-ee-kah appeals to the troops which march under the flag of the counter-revolution, and invites them immediately to lay down their arms – to shed no longer the blood of their brothers in the interests of a handful of landowners and capitalists. The Workers', Soldiers', and Peasants' Revolution curses those who remain even for a moment under the flag of the People's enemies. . . .

Cossacks! Come over to the rank of the victorious People! Railway-men, postmen, telegraphers – all, all support the new Government of the People!

Chapter 10

47 (p. 220). DAMAGE TO THE KREMLIN

I myself verified the damage to the Kremlin, which I visited imme-diately after the bombardment. The Little Nikolai Palace, a building of no particular importance, which was occupied occasionally by receptions of one of the Grand Duchesses, had served as barracks for the *yunkers*. It was not only bombarded, but pretty well sacked; fortunately there was nothing in it of particular historical value.

Usspensky Cathedral had a shell-hole in one of the cupolas, but except for a few feet of mosaic in the ceiling was undamaged. The frescoes on the porch of Blagoveshchensky Cathedral were badly damaged by a shell. Another shell hit the corner of Ivan Veliki. Chudovsky Monastery was hit about thirty times, but only one shell went through a window into the interior, the others breaking the brick window-moulding and the roof-cornices.

The clock over the Spasskaya Gate was smashed. Troitsky Gate was battered, but easily reparable. One of the lower towers had lost its brick spire.

The church of St Basil was untouched, as was the great Im-perial Palace, with all the treasures of Moscow and Petrograd in its cellar, and the crown jewels in the Treasury. These places were not even entered.

48 (p. 221). LUNACHARSKY'S DECLARATION

Comrades! You are the young masters of the country, and although now you have much to do and think about, you must know how to defend your artistic and scientific treasures.

Comrades! That which is happening in Moscow is a horrible, irre-parable misfortune. .... The People in its struggle for the power has mutilated our glorious capital.

It is particularly terrible in these days of violent struggle, of destruc-tive warfare, to be Commissar of Public Education. Only the hope of the victory of Socialism, the source of a new and superior culture, brings me comfort. On me weighs the responsibility of protecting the artistic wealth of the people. . . . Not being able to remain at my post, where I had no influence, I resigned. My comrades, the other Commissars considered this resignation inadmissible. I shall therefore remain at my post. . . . And, moreover, I understand that the damage done to the Kremlin is not as serious as has been reported. . . .

But I beg you, comrades, to give me your support. . . . Preserve for yourselves and your descendants the beauty of our land; be the guardians of the property of the People.

Soon, very soon, even the most ignorant, who have been held in ignorance so long, will awake and understand what a source of joy, strength, and wisdom is art. . . .

49 (p. 226). REVOLUTIONARY FINANCIAL MEASURE

Order

In virtue of the powers vested in me by the Military Revolutionary Committee attached to the Moscow Soviet of Workers' and Soldiers' Deputies, I decree:

1. All banks with branches, the Central State Savings Bank with branches, and the savings banks at the Post and Telegraph offices are to be opened beginning 22 November, from 11 a.m. to 1 p.m., until further order.

2. On current accounts and on the books of the savings banks, payments will be made by the above-mentioned institutions of not more than 150 roubles during the course of the next week.

3. Payments of amounts exceeding 150 roubles a week on current accounts and savings bank books, also payments on other accounts of all kinds will be allowed during the next three days, 22, 23, and 24 November, only in the following cases:

(a) On the accounts of military organizations for the satisfaction of their needs;

(b) For the payment of salaries of employees and the earnings of workers according to the tables and lists certified by the Factory Committees or Soviets of Employees, and attested by the signatures of the Commissars, or the representatives of the Military Revolutionary Committee, and the district Military Revolutionary Committee.

4. Not more than 150 roubles are to be paid against drafts; the remaining sums are to be entered on current account, payments on which are to be made in the order established by the present decree.

5. All other banking operations are prohibited during these three days.

6. The receipt of money on all accounts is allowed for any amount.

7. The representatives of the Finance Council for the certification of the authorization indicated in Clause 3 will hold their office in the building of the Stock Exchange, Ilyinka Street, from 10 a.m. to 2 p.m.

8. The Banks and Savings Banks shall send the totals of daily cash operations by 5 p.m. to the headquarters of the Soviet, Skobeliev Square, to the Military Revolutionary Committee, for the Finance Council.

9. All employees and managers of credit institutions of all kinds who refuse to comply with this decree shall be responsible as enemies of the Revolution, and of the mass of the population, before the Revolutionary Tribunals. Their names shall be published for general information.

10. For the control of the operations of Branches of the Savings Banks and Banks within the limits of this decree, the district Military Revolutionary Committees shall elect three representatives and appoint their place of business.

Fully Authorized Commissar of the Military Revolutionary Committee,
S. SHEVERDIN-MAKSIMENKO

Chapter 11

50 (p. 231). LIMITATIONS TO THIS CHAPTER

This chapter extends over a period of two months, more or less. It covers the time of negotiations with the Allies, the negotiations and armistice with the Germans, and the beginning of the Peace negotiations at Brest-Litovsk, as well as the period in which were laid the foundations of the Soviet State.

However, it is no part of my purpose in this book to describe and interpret these very important historical events, which require more space. They are therefore reserved for another volume, *Kornilov to Brest-Litovsk*.

In this chapter, then, I have confined myself to the Soviet Government's attempts to consolidate its political power at home, and sketched its successive conquests of hostile domestic elements – which process was temporarily interrupted by the disastrous Peace of Brest-Litovsk.

51 (p. 231). PREAMBLE – DECLARATION OF THE RIGHTS OF THE PEOPLES OF RUSSIA

The October Revolution of the workers and peasants began under the common banner of Emancipation.

The peasants are being emancipated from the power of the landowners, for there is no longer the landowners' property right in the land – it has been abolished. The soldiers and sailors are being emancipated from the power of autocratic generals, for generals will henceforth be elective and subject to recall. The working men are being emancipated from the whims and arbitrary will of the capitalists, for henceforth there will be established the control of the workers over mills and factories. Everything living and capable of life is being emancipated from the hateful shackles.

There remain only the peoples of Russia, who have suffered and are suffering oppression and arbitrariness, and whose emancipation must immediately begin, whose liberation must be effected resolutely and definitely.

During the period of Tsarism the peoples of Russia were systematically incited one against another. The results of such a policy are known; massacres and *pogroms* on the one hand, slavery of peoples on the other.

There can be and there must be no return to this disgraceful policy. Henceforth the policy of a voluntary and honest union of the peoples of Russia must be substituted.

In the period of imperialism, after the March revolution, when the power was transferred into the hands of the Cadet bourgeoisie, the naked policy of provocation gave way to one of cowardly distrust of the peoples of Russia, to a policy of fault-finding, of meaningless 'freedom', and 'equality' of peoples. The results of such a policy are known; the growth of national enmity, the impairment of mutual confidence.

An end must be put to this unworthy policy of falsehood and distrust, of fault-finding and provocation. Henceforth it must be replaced by an open and honest policy leading to the complete mutual confidence of the peoples of Russia. Only as the result of such a trust can there be found an honest and lasting union of the peoples of Russia. Only as the result of such a union can the workers and peasants of the peoples of Russia be cemented into one revolutionary force able to resist all attempts on the part of the imperialist-annexationist bourgeoisie.

52 (p. 232). DECREES

On the Nationalization of the Banks

In the interest of the regular organization of the national economy, of the thorough eradication of bank speculation and the complete emancipation of the workers, peasants, and the whole labouring population from the exploitation of banking capital, and with a view to the establishment of a single national bank of the Russian Republic which shall serve the real interests of the people and the poorer classes, the Central Executive Committee (Tsay-ee-kah) resolves:

1. The banking business is declared a State monopoly.

2. All existing private joint-stock banks and banking offices are merged in the State Bank.

3. The assets and liabilities of the liquidated establishments are taken over by the State Bank.

4. The order of the merger of private banks in the State Bank is to be determined by a special decree.

5. The temporary administration of the affairs of the private banks is entrusted to the board of the State Bank.

6. The interests of the small depositors will be safeguarded.

*

On the Equality of Rank of All Military Men

In realization of the will of the revolutionary people regarding the prompt and decisive abolition of all remnants of former inequality in the Army, the Council of People's Commissars decrees:

1. All ranks and grades in the Army, beginning with the rank of Corporal and ending with the rank of General, are abolished. The Army of the Russian Republic consists now of free and equal citizens, bearing the honourable title of Soldiers of the Revolutionary Army.

2. All privileges connected with the former ranks and grades, also all outward marks of distinction, are abolished.

3. All addressing by titles is abolished.

4. All decorations, orders, and other marks of distinction are abolished.

5. With the abolition of the rank of officer all separate officers' organizations are abolished.

Note. – Orderlies are left only for headquarters, chanceries, Committees, and other Army organizations.

President of the Council of People's Commissars,
VL. ULYANOV (LENIN)
People's Commissar for Military and Naval Affairs,
N. KRYLENKO
People's Commissar for Military Affairs,
N. PODVOISKY
Secretary of the Council, N. GORBUNOV

*

On the Elective Principle and the Organization of Authority in the Army

1. The army serving the will of the toiling people is subject to its supreme representative – the Council of People's Commissars.

2. Full authority within the limits of military units and combinations is vested in the respective Soldiers' Committees of Soviets.

3. Those phases of life and activity of the troops which are already under the jurisdiction of the Committees are now formally placed in their direct control. Over such branches of activity which the Committees cannot assume, the control of the Soldiers' Soviets is established.

4. The election of commanding Staff and officers is introduced. All commanders up to the commanders of regiments, inclusive, are elected by general suffrage of squads, platoons, companies, squadrons, batteries, divisions (artillery, 2–3 batteries), and regiments. All commanders higher than the commander of a regiment, and up to the Supreme Commander, inclusive, are elected by congresses or conferences of Committees.

Note. – By the term 'conference' must be understood a meeting of the respective Committees together with delegates of committees one degree lower in rank. [Such as a 'conference' of Regimental Committees with delegates from Company Committees. – Author.]

5. The elected commanders above the rank of commander of regiment must be confirmed by the nearest Supreme Committee.

Note. – In the event of a refusal by a Supreme Committee to confirm an elected commander, with a statement of reasons for such refusal, a commander elected by the lower Committee a second time must be confirmed.

6. The commanders of Armies are elected by Army congresses. Commanders of Fronts are elected by congresses of the respective Fronts.

7. To posts of a technical character, demanding special knowledge or other practical preparation, namely: doctors, engineers, technicians, telegraph and wireless operators, aviators, automobilists, etc., only such persons as possess the required special knowledge may be elected, by the Committees of the units of the respective services.

8. Chiefs of Staff must be chosen from among persons with special military training for that post.

9. All other members of the Staff are appointed by the Chief of Staff, and confirmed by the respective congresses.

Note. – All persons with special training must be listed in a special list.

10. The right is reserved to retire from the service all commanders on active service who are not elected by the soldiers to any post, and who consequently are ranked as privates.

11. All other functions besides these pertaining to the command, with the exception of posts in the economic departments, are filled by the appointment of the respective elected commanders.

12. Detailed instructions regarding the election of the commanding
Staff will be published separately.

President of the Council of People's Commissars,

VL. ULYANOV (LENIN)

People's Commissar for Military and Naval Affairs,

N. KRYLENKO

People's Commissar for Military Affairs,

N. PODVOISKY

Secretary of the Council,   N. GORBUNOV

∗

On the Abolition of Classes and Titles

1. All classes and class divisions, all class privileges and delimita-
tions, all class organizations and institutions and all civil ranks are
abolished.

2. All classes of society (nobles, merchants, petty bourgeois, etc.),
and all titles (Prince, Count, and others), and all denominations of
civil rank (Privy State Councillors and others), are abolished, and there
is established the general denomination of Citizen of the Russian
Republic.

3. The property and institutions of the classes of nobility are transferred to the corresponding autonomous Zemstvos.

4. The property of merchant and bourgeois organizations is transferred immediately to the Municipal Self-Government.

5. All class institutions of any sort, with their property, their rules of
procedure, and their archives, are transferred to the administration of
the Municipalities and Zemstvos.

6. All articles of existing laws applying to these matters are herewith
repealed.

7. The present decree becomes effective on the day it is published and
applied by the Soviets of Workers', Soldiers', and Peasants' Deputies.

The present decree has been confirmed by the Tsay-ee-kah at the
meeting of 23 November 1917, and signed by:

President of the Tsay-ee-kah,

SVERDLOV

President of the Council of People's Commissars,

VL. ULYANOV (LENIN)

Executive of the Council of People's Commissars,

V. BONCH-BRUEVICH

Secretary of the Council,   N. GORBUNOV

On 3 December the Council of People's Commissars resolved
'to reduce the salaries of functionaries and employees in all

Governmental institutions and establishments, general or special, without exception'.

To begin with, the Council fixed the salary of a People's Commissar at 500 roubles per month, with 100 roubles additional for each grown member of the family incapable of work....

This was the highest salary paid to any Government official....

53 (p. 233).

Countess Panina was arrested and brought to trial before the first Supreme Revolutionary Tribunal. The trial is described in the chapter on 'Revolutionary Justice' in my forthcoming volume, *Kornilov to Brest-Litovsk*. The prisoner was sentenced to 'return the money, and then be liberated to the public contempt'. In other words, she was set free!

54 (p. 234). RIDICULE OF THE NEW RÉGIME

From *Drug Naroda* (Mensheviki), 18 November:

The story of the 'immediate peace' of the Bolsheviki reminds us of a joyous moving-picture film.... Neratov runs – Trotsky pursues; Neratov climbs a wall, Trotsky too; Neratov dives into the water – Trotsky follows; Neratov climbs on to the roof – Trotsky right behind him; Neratov hides under the bed – and Trotsky has him! He has him! Naturally peace is immediately signed. ...

All is empty and silent at the Ministry of Foreign Affairs. The couriers are respectful, but their faces wear a caustic expression....

How about arresting an ambassador and signing an armistice or a Peace Treaty with him? But they are strange folk, these ambassadors. They keep silent as if they had heard nothing. Hola, hola, England, France, Germany! We have signed an armistice with you! Is it possible that you know nothing about it? Nevertheless, it has been published in all the papers and posted on the walls. On a Bolshevik's word of honour, Peace has been signed. We're not asking much of you; you just have to write two words. ...

The ambassadors remain silent. The Powers remain silent. All is empty and silent in the office of the Minister of Foreign Affairs.

'Listen,' says Robespierre-Trotsky to his assistant Marat-Uritsky, 'run over to the British Ambassador's, tell him we're proposing peace.'

'Go yourself,' says Marat-Uritsky. 'He's not receiving.'

'Telephone him, then.'

'I've tried. The receiver's off the hook.

'Send him a telegram.'

'I did.'

'Well. with what result?'

Marat-Uritsky sighs and does not answer. Robespierre-Trotsky spits furiously into the corner. . . .

'Listen, Marat,' recommences Trotsky, after a moment. 'We must absolutely show that we're conducting an active foreign policy. How can we do that ?'

'Launch another decree about arresting Neratov,' answers Uritsky, with a profound air.

'Marat, you're a blockhead!' cries Trotsky. All of a sudden he arises, terrible and majestic, looking at this moment like Robespierre.

'Write, Uritsky!' he says with severity. 'Write a letter to the British ambassador, a registered letter with receipt demanded. Write! I also will write! The peoples of the world await an immediate peace!'

In the enormous and empty Ministry of Foreign Affairs are to be heard only the sound of two typewriters. With his own hands Trotsky is conducting an active foreign policy. . . .

55 (p. 243). ON THE QUESTION OF AN AGREEMENT

[Announcement, posted on the walls of Petrograd, of the result of a meeting of representatives of the garrison regiments, called to consider the question of forming a new Government.]

To the attention of All Workers and All Soldiers.

November eleventh, in the club of the Preobrazhensky Regiment, was held an extraordinary meeting of representatives of all the units of the Petrograd garrison.

The meeting was called upon the initiative of the Preobrazhensky and Semionovsky Regiments, for the discussion of the question as to which Socialist parties are for the power of the Soviets, which are against, which are for the people, which against, and if an agreement between them is possible.

The representatives of the Tsay-ee-kah, of the Municipal Duma, of the Avksentiev Peasants' Soviets, and of all the political parties from the Bolsheviki to the Populist Socialists, were invited to the meeting.

After long deliberation, having heard the declarations of all parties and organizations, the meeting by a tremendous majority of votes agreed that only the Bolsheviki and the Left Socialist Revolutionaries are for the people, and that all the other parties are only attempting under cover of seeking an agreement, to deprive the people of the conquests won in the days of the great Workers' and Peasants' Revolution of November.

Here is the text of the resolution carried at this meeting of the Petro-grad garrison, by 61 votes against 11, and 12 not voting:

'The garrison conference, summoned at the initiative of the Semion-ovsky and Preobrazhensky Regiments, on hearing the representatives of all the Socialists parties and popular organizations on the question of an agreement between the different political parties finds that:

'1. The representatives of the Tsay-ee-kah, the representatives of the Bolshevik party and the Left Socialist Revolutionaries, declared definitely that they stand for a Government of the Soviets, for the decrees on Land, Peace, and Workers' Control of Industry, and that upon this platform they are willing to agree with all the Socialist parties.

'2. At the same time the representatives of the other parties (Men-sheviki, Socialist Revolutionaries) either gave no answer at all, or declared simply that they were opposed to the power of the Soviets and against the decrees on Land, Peace, and Workers' Control.

'In view of this the meeting resolves:

'"1. To express censure of all parties which, under cover of an agree-ment, wish practically to annul the popular conquests of the Revolution of November.

'"2. To express full confidence in the Tsay-ee-kah and the Council of People's Commissars, and to promise them complete support."

'At the same time the meeting deems it necessary that the comrades Left Socialist Revolutionaries should enter the People's Government.'

56 (p. 244). WINE 'POGROMS'

It was afterwards discovered that there was a regular organiza-tion, maintained by the Cadets, for provoking rioting among the soldiers. There would be telephone messages to the different barracks, announcing that wine was being given away at such and such an address, and when the soldiers arrived at the spot an individual would point out the location of the cellar. . . .

The Council of People's Commissars appointed a Commissar for the Fight Against Drunkenness, who, besides mercilessly putting down the wine riots, destroyed hundreds of thousands of bottles of liquor. The Winter Palace cellars, containing rare vintages valued at more than five million dollars, were at first flooded, and then the liquor was removed to Kronstadt and destroyed.

In this work the Kronstadt sailors, 'flower and pride of the

revolutionary forces', as Trotsky called them, acquitted themselves with iron self-discipline....

57 (p. 245). OBLIGATORY ORDINANCE

1. The city of Petrograd is declared to be in a state of siege.
2. All assemblies, meetings, and congregations on the streets and
squares are prohibited.
3. Attempts to loot wine-cellars, warehouses, factories, stores,
business premises, private dwellings, etc., etc., *will be stopped by
machine-gun fire without warning*.
4. House Committees, doormen, janitors, and Militiamen are
charged with the duty of keeping strict order in all houses, courtyards,
and in the streets, and house-doors and carriage entrances must be
locked at 9 o'clock in the evening, and opened at 7 o'clock in the
morning. After 9 o'clock in the evening only tenants may leave the
house, under strict control of the House Committees.
5. Those guilty of the distribution, sale, or purchase of any kind of
alcoholic liquor, and also those guilty of the violation of sections 2 and
4 will be immediately arrested and subjected to the most severe punishment.

Petrograd, 6 December, 3 o'clock in the night.

> *Committee to Fight Against Pogroms, attached to the Executive
> Committee of the Soviet of Workers' and Soldiers' Deputies*

58 (p. 245). SPECULATORS

Two orders concerning them:

*Council of People's Commissars
To the Military Revolutionary Committee*

The disorganization of the food supply created by the war, and the
lack of system, is becoming to the last degree acute, thanks to
the speculators, marauders, and their followers on the railways, in
the steamship offices, forwarding offices, etc.

Taking advantage of the nation's greatest misfortune, these criminal
spoliators are playing with the health and life of millions of soldiers and
workers, for their own benefit.

Such a situation cannot be borne a single day longer.

The Council of People's Commissars proposes to the Military Revolutionary Committee to take the most decisive measures towards the
uprooting of speculation, sabotage, hiding of supplies, fraudulent
detention of cargoes, etc.

All persons guilty of such actions shall be subject, by special orders of the Military Revolutionary Committee, to immediate arrest, and Confinement in the prisons of Kronstadt, pending their arraignment before the Revolutionary Tribunal.

All the popular organizations are invited to cooperate in the struggle against the spoliators of food supplies.

> *President of the Council of People's Commissar,*
>
> Accepted for execution,   V. ULYANOV (LENIN)
>
> *Military Revolutionary Committee attached to the*
>
> *C.E.C. of the Soviets of W. and S. Deputies*

Petrograd, 23 November 1917

*

To All Honest Citizens
The Military Revolutionary Committee Decrees:

Spoliators, marauders, speculators, are declared to be enemies of the People. . . .

The Military Revolutionary Committee proposes to all public organizations, to all honest citizens: to inform the Military Revolutionary Committee immediately of all cases of spoliation, marauding, speculation, which become known to them.

The struggle against this evil is the business of all honest people. The Military Revolutionary Committee expects the support of all to whom the interests of the People are dear.

The Military Revolutionary Committee will be merciless in pursuit of speculators and marauders.

> THE MILITARY REVOLUTIONARY COMMITTEE

Petrograd, 2 December 1917

59 (p. 245). PURISHKEVICH'S LETTER TO KALEDIN

The situation at Petrograd is desperate. The City is cut off from the outside world and is entirely in the power of the Bolsheviki. . . . People are arrested in the streets, thrown into the Neva, drowned and imprisoned without any charge. Even Burtzev is shut up in Peter-Paul fortress, under strict guard.

The organization, at whose head I am, is working without rest to unite all the officers and what is left of the *yunker* schools, and to arm them. The situation cannot be saved except by creating regiments of officers and *yunkers*. Attacking with these regiments, and having gained a first success, we could later gain the aid of the garrison troops but without that first success it is impossible to count on a single soldier, because thousands of them are divided and terrorized by the scum which exists in every regiment. Most of the Cossacks are tainted by Bolshevik propaganda, thanks to the strange policy of General Dutov, who allowed to pass the moment when by decisive action something could have been obtained. The policy of negotiations and concessions has borne its fruits; all that is respectable is persecuted, and it is the *plebs* and the criminals who dominate – and nothing can be done except by shooting and hanging them.

We are awaiting you here, General, and at the moment of your arrival we shall advance with all the forces at our disposal. But for that we must establish some communication with you, and before all, clear up the following points:

(1) Do you know that in your name officers who could take part in the fight are being invited to leave Petrograd on the pretext of joining you?

(2) About when can we count on your arrival at Petrograd? We should like to know in order to coordinate our actions.

In spite of the criminal inaction of the conscious people here, which allowed the yoke of Bolshevism to be laid upon us – in spite of the extraordinary pig-headedness of the majority of officers, so difficult to organize – we believe in spite of all that Truth is on our side, and that we shall conquer the vicious and criminal forces who say that they are acting for motives of love of country and in order to save it. Whatever comes, we shall not permit ourselves to be struck down, and shall remain firm until the end.

Purishkevich, being brought to trial before the Revolutionary Tribunal, was given a short term of prison. . . .

60 (p. 245). THE DECREE ON THE MONOPOLY OF ADVERTISEMENTS

1. The printing of advertisements, in newspapers, books, bill-boards, kiosks, in offices and other establishments is declared to be a State monopoly.

2. Advertisements may only be published in the organs of the Provisional Workers' and Peasants' Government at Petrograd, and in the organs of local Soviets.

3. The proprietors of newspapers and advertising offices, as well as all employees of such establishments, should remain at their posts until the transfer of their advertisement business to the Government . . . superintending the uninterrupted continuation of their houses, and turning over to the Soviets all private advertising and the sums received therefor, as well as all accounts and copy.

4. All managers of publications and businesses dealing with paid advertising, as well as their employees and workers, shall agree to hold a

City Congress, and to join, first the City Trade Unions and then the All-Russian Unions, to organize more thoroughly and justly the advertising business in the Soviet publications, as well as to prepare better rules for the public utility of advertising.

5. All persons found guilty of having concealed documents or money, or having sabotaged the regulations indicated in paragraphs 3 and 4, will be punished by a sentence of not more than three years' imprisonment, and all their property will be confiscated.

6. The paid insertion of advertisements ... in private publications, or under a masqued form, will also be severely penalized.

7. Advertising offices are confiscated by the Government, the owners being entitled to compensation in cases of necessity. Small proprietors, depositors and stockholders of the confiscated establishments will be reimbursed for all moneys held by them in the concern.

8. All buildings, offices, counters, and in general every establishment doing a business in advertising, should immediately inform the Soviet of Workers' and Soldiers' Deputies of its address, and proceed to the transfer of its business, under penalty of the punishment indicated in paragraph 5.

President of the Council of People's Commissars,

V. ULYANOV (LENIN)

People's Commissar for Public Instruction,

A. V. LUNACHARSKY

Secretary of the Council, N. GORBUNOV

61 (p. 246). TWO PROCLAMATIONS

Lenin, *To the People of Russia*:

Comrades, workers. Soldiers, peasants – all toilers!

The Workers' and Peasants' Revolution has won at Petrograd, at Moscow. ... From the front and the village arrive every day, every hour, greetings to the new Government. ... The victory of the Revolution ... is assured, seeing that it is sustained by the majority of the people.

It is entirely understandable that the proprietors and the capitalists, the employees and functionaries closely allied with the bourgeoisie – in a word, all the rich and all those who join hands with them – regard the new Revolution with hostility, oppose its success, threaten to halt the activity of the banks, and sabotage or obstruct the work of other establishments.... Every conscious worker understands perfectly well that we cannot avoid this hostility, because the high officials have set themselves against the People and do not wish to abandon their posts without resistance. The majority of the people is for us. For us is the majority of the workers and the oppressed of the whole world. We have justice on our side. Our ultimate victory is certain.

The resistance of the capitalists and high officials will be broken. No one will be deprived of his property without a special law on the nationalization of banks and financial syndicates. This law is in preparation. Not a worker will lose a single kopek; on the contrary, he will be assisted. Without at this moment establishing the new taxes, the new Government considers one of its primary duties to make a severe accounting and control on the reception of taxes decreed by the former régime. ...

Comrades, workers! Remember that you yourselves direct the Government. No one will help you unless you organize yourselves and take into your own hands the affairs of the State. Your Soviets are now the organs of governmental power. ... Strengthen them, establish a severe revolutionary control, pitilessly crush the attempts at anarchy on the part of drunkards, brigands, counter-revolutionary *yunkers*, and Kornilovists.

Establish a strict control over production and the accounting for products. Arrest and turn over to the Revolutionary Tribunal of the People everyone who injures the property of the People, by sabotage in production, by concealment of grain reserves, reserves of other products, by retarding the shipments of grain, by bringing confusion into the railroads, the posts, and the telegraphs, or in general opposing the great work of bringing Peace and transferring the Land to the peasants. ...

Comrades, workers, soldiers, peasants – all toilers!

Take immediately all local power into your hands. ... Little by little, with the consent of the majority of peasants, we shall march firmly and unhesitatingly towards the victory of Socialism, which will fortify the advance-guards of the working class of the most civilized countries, and give to the peoples an enduring peace, and free them from every slavery and every exploitation.

62 (p. 246).

To All Workers of Petrograd!

Comrades! The Revolution is winning – the revolution has won. All the power has passed to our Soviets. The first weeks are the most difficult ones. The broken reaction must be finally crushed, a full triumph must be secured to our endeavours. The working class ought to – must – show in these days THE GREATEST FIRMNESS AND ENDURANCE, in order to facilitate the execution of all the aims of the new People's Government of Soviets. In the next few days decrees on the Labour question will be issued, and among the very first will be the decree on

Workers' Control over the production and regulation of industry.
STRIKES AND DEMONSTRATIONS OF THE WORKER MASSES IN PETROGRAD NOW CAN ONLY DO HARM.

We ask you to cease immediately all economic and political strikes, to take up your work, and do it in perfect order. The work in the factories and all the industries is necessary for the new Government of Soviets, because any interruption of this work will only create new difficulties for us, and we have enough as it is. All to your places.

The best way to support the new Government of Soviets in these days – is by doing your job.

LONG LIVE THE IRON FIRMNESS OF THE PROLETARIAT! LONG LIVE THE REVOLUTION!

> Petrograd Soviet of W. and S.D.
> Petrograd Council of Trade Unions
> Petrograd Council of Factory-Shop Committees

63 (p. 247). APPEALS AND COUNTER-APPEALS

From the Employees of the State and Private Banks
To the Population of Petrograd

Comrades, workers, soldiers, and citizens!

The Military Revolutionary Committee in an 'extraordinary notice' is accusing the workers of the State and private banking and other institutions of 'impeding the work of the Government, directed towards the ensuring of the front with provisions'.

Comrades and citizens, do not believe this calumny, brought against us, who are part of the general army of labour.

However difficult it is for us to work under the constant threat of interference by acts of violence in our hard-working life, however depressing it be to know that our Country and the Revolution are on the verge of ruin, we, nevertheless, all of us, from the highest to the lowest, employees, *artelshchiki*, counters, labourers, couriers, etc., are continuing to fulfil our duties which are connected with the ensuring of provisions and munitions to the front and country.

Counting upon your lack of information, comrades, workers, and soldiers, in questions of finance and banking, you are being incited against workers like yourselves, because it is desirable to divert the responsibility for the starving and dying brother-soldiers at the front from the guilty persons to the innocent workers who are accomplishing their duty under the burden of general poverty and disorganization.

REMEMBER, WORKERS AND SOLDIERS! THE EMPLOYEES HAVE ALWAYS STOOD UP FOR ALL AND WILL ALWAYS STAND UP FOR

THE INTERESTS OF THE TOILING PEOPLE, PART OF WHICH THEY
ARE THEMSELVES, AND NOT A SINGLE KOPEK NECESSARY FOR
THE FRONT AND THE WORKERS HAS EVER BEEN DETAINED AND
WILL NOT BE DETAINED BY THE EMPLOYEES.

From 6 November to 23 November, i.e., during seventeen days,
500,000,000 roubles were dispatched to the front, and 120,000,000
roubles to Moscow, besides the sums sent to other towns.

Keeping guards over the wealth of the people, the master of which
can be only the Constituent Assembly, representing the whole nation,
the employees refuse to give out money for purposes which are unknown to them.

DO NOT BELIEVE THE CALUMNIATORS CALLING YOU TO TAKE
THE LAW INTO YOUR OWN HANDS.

> *Central Board of the All-Russian Union of Employees*
> *of the State Bank*
> *Central Board of the All-Russian Trade Union of*
> *Employees of Credit Institutions*

*

To the Population of Petrograd

CITIZENS: Do not believe the falsehood which irresponsible people
are trying to suggest to you by spreading terrible calumnies against the
employees of the Ministry of Supplies and the workers in other Supply
organizations who are labouring in these dark days for the salvation of
Russia. Citizens! In posted placards you are called upon to lynch us, we
are accused falsely of sabotage and strikes, we are blamed for all the
woes and misfortunes that the people are suffering, although we have
been striving indefatigably and uninterruptedly, and are still striving,
to save the Russian people from the horrors of starvation. Notwith-
standing all that we are bearing as citizens of unhappy Russia, we have
not for one hour abandoned our heavy and responsible work of supplying the Army and population with provisions.

The image of the Army, cold and hungry, saving our very existence
by its blood and its tortures, does not leave us for a single moment.

Citizens! If we have survived the blackest days in the life and history
of our people, if we have succeeded in preventing famine in Petrograd,
if we have managed to procure to the suffering army bread and forage
by means of enormous, almost superhuman, efforts, it is because we
have honestly continued and are still continuing to do our work. ...

To the 'last warning' of the usurpers of the power we reply: It is not
for you who are leading the country to ruin to threaten us who are
doing all we can not to allow the country to perish. We are not afraid of
threats: before us stands the sacred image of tortured Russia. We will

continue our work of supplying the Army and the people with bread to our last efforts, so long as you will not prevent us from accomplishing our duty to our country. In the contrary case the Army and the people will stand before the horrors of famine, but the responsibility therefor belongs to the perpetrators of violence.

Executive Committee of the Employees of the
Ministry of Supplies

*

To the Chinovniki (Government Officials)

It is notified hereby that all officials and persons who have quitted the service in Government and public institutions or have been dismissed for sabotage or for having failed to report for work on the day fixed, and who have, nevertheless, received their salary paid in advance for the time they have not served, are bound to return such salary not later than on 27 November 1917 to those institutions where they were in service.

In the event of this not being done, these persons will be rendered answerable for stealing the Treasury's property and tried by the Military Revolutionary Court.

The Military Revolutionary Committee

7 December 1917

From the Special Board for Supplies

CITIZENS!

The conditions of our work for the supplying of Petrograd are getting more and more difficult every day.

The interference with our work – which is so ruinous to our business – of the Commissars of the Military Revolutionary Committee is still continuing.

THEIR ARBITRARY ACTS, their annulling of our orders, MAY LEAD TO A CATASTROPHE.

Seals have been affixed to one of the cold storages where the meat and butter destined for the population are kept, and we cannot regulate the temperature SO THAT THE PRODUCTS WOULD NOT BE SPOILT.

One carload of potatoes and one carload of cabbages have been seized and carried away no one knows where to.

Cargoes which are not liable to requisition (*khalva*) are requisitioned by the Commissars and, as was the case one day, five boxes of *khalva* were seized by the Commissar for his own use.

WE ARE NOT IN A POSITION TO DISPOSE OF OUR STORAGE, where the self-appointed Commissars do not allow the cargoes to be taken out, and terrorize our employees, threatening them with arrest.

ALL THAT IS GOING ON IN PETROGRAD IS KNOWN IN THE
PROVINCES, AND FROM THE DON, FROM SIBERIA, FROM VORO-
NEZH AND OTHER PLACES PEOPLE ARE REFUSING TO SEND FLOUR
AND BREAD.

THIS CANNOT GO ON MUCH LONGER.

The work is simply falling out of our hands.

OUR DUTY is to let the population know of this.

To the last possibility we will remain on guard of the interests of the
population.

WE WILL DO EVERYTHING TO AVOID THE ONCOMING FAMINE,
BUT IF UNDER THESE DIFFICULT CONDITIONS OUR WORK IS
COMPELLED TO STOP LET THE PEOPLE KNOW THAT IT IS NOT
OUR FAULT....

64 (p. 248). ELECTIONS TO THE CONSTITUENT ASSEMBLY IN PETROGRAD

There were nineteen tickets in Petrograd. The results are as
follows, published 30 November:

Party	Vote
Christian Democrats	3,707
Cadets	245,006
Populist Socialists	19,109
Bolsheviki	424,027
Socialist Universalists	158
S.D. and S.R. Ukrainian and Jewish Workers	4,219
League of Women's Rights	5,310
Left Socialist Revolutionaries	152,230
Socialist Revolutionaries (*oborontsi*)	4,696
League of People's Development	385
Radical Democrats	413
Orthodox Parishes	24,139
Feminine League for Salvation of Country	318
Independent League of Workers, Soldiers, Peasants	4,942
Christian Democrats (Catholics)	14,382
Unified Social Democrats	11,740
Mensheviki	17,427
Yedinstvo group	1,823
League of Cossack Troops	6,712

65 (p. 250). FROM THE COMMISSION ON PUBLIC EDUCATION ATTACHED TO THE CENTRAL CITY DUMA

Comrades, Working Men and Working Women!
A few days before the holidays, a strike has been declared by the

teachers of the public schools. The teachers side with the bourgeoisie against the Workers' and Peasants' Government.

Comrades, organize parents' committees and pass resolutions against the strike of the teachers. Propose to the Ward Soviets of Workers' and Soldiers' Deputies, the Trade Unions, the Factory-Shop and Party Committees, to organize protest meetings. Arrange with your own resources Christmas trees and entertainments for the children, and demand the opening of the schools, after the holidays, at the date which will be set by the Duma.

Comrades, strengthen your position in matters of public education, insist on the control of the proletarian organizations over the schools.

Commission on Public Education attached to the Central City Duma

66 (p. 250). FROM THE COUNCIL OF PEOPLE'S COMMISSARS TO THE TOILING COSSACKS

Brother Cossacks.

You are being deceived. You are being incited against the People. You are told that the Soviets of Workers', Soldiers', and Peasants' Deputies are your enemies, that they want to take away your Cossack land, your Cossack liberty. Don't believe it, Cossacks. ... Your own Generals and landowners are deceving you, in order to keep you in darkness and slavery. We, the Council of People's Commissars, address ourselves to you, Cossacks, with these words. Read them attentively and judge yourselves which is the truth and which is cruel deceit. The life and service of a Cossack were always bondage and penal servitude. At the first call of the authorities a Cossack always had to saddle his horse and ride out on campaign. All his military equipment a Cossack had to provide with his own hardly earned means. A Cossack is on service, his farm is going to rack and ruin. Is such a condition fair? No, it must be altered for ever. THE COSSACKS MUST BE FREED FROM BONDAGE. The new People's Soviet power is willing to come to the assistance of the toiling Cossacks. It is only necessary that the Cossacks themselves should resolve to abolish the old order, that they should refuse submission to their slave-driver officers, landowners, rich men, that they should throw off the cursed yoke from their necks. Arise, Cossacks! Unite! The Council of People's Commissars calls upon you to enter a new, fresh, more happy life.

In November and December in Petrograd there were All-Russian Congresses of Soviets of Soldiers', Workers', and Peasants' Deputies. Congresses conferred all the authority in the different localities into the hands of the Soviets, i.e., into the hands of men elected by the People. From now on there must be in Russia no rulers or functionaries who

command the People from above and drive them. The People create the
authority themselves. A General has no more rights than a soldier. All
are equal. Consider, Cossacks, is this wrong or right? We are calling
upon you, Cossacks, to join this new order and to create your own
Soviets of Cossacks' Deputies. To such Soviets all the power must
belong in the different localities. Not to *hetmans* with the rank of
General, but to the elected representatives of the toiling Cossacks, to
your own trustworthy reliable men.

The All-Russian Congress of Soldiers', Workers', and Peasants'
Deputies have passed a resolution to transfer all landowners' land into
the possession of the toiling people. Is not that fair, Cossacks? The
Kornilovs, Kaledins, Dutovs, Karaulovs, Bardizhes, all defend with
their whole souls the interests of the rich men, and they are ready to
drown Russia in blood if only the lands remain in the hands of the
landowners. But you, the toiling Cossacks, do not you suffer yourselves
from poverty, oppression, and lack of land? How many Cossacks are
there who have more than 4–5 *dessiatins* per head? But the landowners,
who have thousands of *dessiatins* of their own land wish besides to get
into their hands the lands of the Cossack Army. According to the new
Soviet laws, the lands of Cossack landowners must pass without compensation into the hands of the Cossack workers, the poorer Cossacks.
You are being told that the Soviets wish to take away your lands from
you. Who is frightening you? The rich Cossacks, who know that the
Soviet AUTHORITY WISHES to transfer the landowners' land to you.
Choose then, Cossacks, for whom you will stand: for the Kornilovs and
Kaledins, for the Generals and rich men or for the Soviets of Peasants',
Soldiers', Workers', and Cossacks' Deputies.

THE COUNCIL OF PEOPLE'S COMMISSARS elected by the All-Russian Congress HAS PROPOSED TO ALL NATIONS AN IMMEDIATE
ARMISTICE AND AN HONOURABLE DEMOCRATIC PEACE WITH-
OUT LOSS OR DETRIMENT TO ANY NATION. All the capitalists, landowners, Generals-Kornilovists have risen against the peaceful policy of
the Soviets. The war was bringing them profits, power, distinctions.
And you, Cossacks, privates? You were perishing without reason,
without purpose, like your brother-soldiers and sailors. It will soon be
three years and a half that this accursed war has gone on, a war devised
by the capitalists and landowners of all countries for their own profit,
their world robberies. To the toiling Cossacks the war has only brought
ruin and death. The war has drained all the resources of the Cossack
farm life. The only salvation for the whole of our country and for the
Cossacks in particular, is a prompt and honest peace. The Council of
People's Commissars has declared to all Governments and peoples: We
do not want other people's property, and we do not wish to give away

our own. Peace without annexations and without indemnities. Every nation must decide its own fate. There must be no oppressing of one nation by another. Such is the honest, democratic, People's peace which the Council of People's Commissars is proposing to all Governments, to all peoples, allies, and enemies. And the results are visible: ON THE RUSSIAN FRONT AN ARMISTICE HAS BEEN CONCLUDED.

The soldiers' and the Cossacks' blood is not flowing there any more. Now, Cossacks, decide: do you wish to continue this ruinous, senseless, criminal slaughter? Then support the Cadets, the enemies of the people, support Chernov, Tseretelly, Skobeliev, who drove you into the offensive of 1 July; support Kornilov, who introduced capital punishment for soldiers and Cossacks at the front. BUT IF YOU WISH A PROMPT AND HONEST PEACE, THEN ENTER THE RANKS OF THE SOVIETS AND SUPPORT THE COUNCIL OF PEOPLE'S COMMISSARS.

Your fate, Cossacks, lies in your own hands. Our common foes, the landowners, capitalists, officers-Kornilovists, bourgeois newspapers are deceiving you and driving you along the road to ruin. In Orenburg, Dutov has arrested the Soviet and disarmed the garrison. Kaledin is threatening the Soviets in the province of the Don. He has declared the province to be in a state of war and is assembling his troops. Karaulov is shooting the local tribes in the Caucasus. The Cadet bourgeoisie is supplying them with its millions. Their common aim is to suppress the People's Soviets, to crush the workers and peasants, to introduce again the discipline of the whip in the army, and to eternalize the bondage of the toiling Cossacks.

Our revolutionary troops are moving to the Don and the Ural in order to put an end to this criminal revolt against the people. The commanders of the revolutionary troops have received orders not to enter into any negotiations with the mutinous generals, to act decisively and mercilessly.

Cossacks! On you depends now whether your brothers' blood is to flow still. We are holding out our hands to you. Join the whole people against its enemies. Declare Kaledin, Kornilov, Dutov, Karaulov, and all their aiders and abettors to be the enemies of the people, traitors and betrayers. Arrest them with your own forces and turn them over into the hands of the Soviet authority, which will judge them in open and public Revolutionary Tribunal. Cossacks! Form Soviets of Cossacks' Deputies. Take into your toil-worn hands the management of all the affairs of the Cossacks. Take away the lands of your own wealthy landowners. Take over their grain, their inventoried property and livestock for the cultivation of the lands of the toiling Cossacks, who are ruined by the war.

Forward, Cossacks, to the fight for the common cause of the people!

Long live the toiling Cossacks!

Long live the union of the Cossacks, the soldiers, peasants, and workers!

Long live the power of the Soviets of Cossacks', Soldiers', Workers', and Peasants' Deputies.

Down with the war! Down with the landowners and the Kornilovist-Generals!

Long live Peace and the Brotherhood of Peoples!

Council of People's Commissars

67 (p. 251). DIPLOMATIC CORRESPONDENCE OF THE SOVIET GOVERNMENT

The notes issued by Trotsky to the Allies and to the neutral Powers, as well as the note of the Allied military attachés to General Dukhonin, are too voluminous to give here. Moreover, they belong to another phase of the history of the Soviet Republic, with which this book has nothing to do – the foreign relations of the Soviet Government. This I treat at length in the next volume, *Kornilov to Brest-Litovsk.*

68 (p. 253). APPEALS TO THE FRONT AGAINST DUKHONIN

... The struggle for peace has met with the resistance of the bourgeoisie and the counter-revolutionary generals. ... From the accounts in the newspapers, at the Stavka of former Supreme Commander Dukhonin are gathering the agents and allies of the bourgeoisie, Verkhovsky, Avksentiev, Chernov, Gotz, Tseretelly, etc. It seems even that they want to form a new power against the Soviets.

Comrades, soldiers! All the persons we have mentioned have been Ministers already. They have acted in accord with Kerensky and the bourgeoisie. They are responsible for the offensive of 1 July and for the prolongation of the war. They promised the land to the peasants and then arrested the Land Committees. They re-established capital punishment for soldiers. They obey the orders of the French, English, and American financiers. ...

General Dukhonin, for having refused to obey orders of the Council of People's Commissars, has been dismissed from his position as Supreme Commander. ... For answer he is circulating among the troops the note from the Military Attachés of the Allied imperialist Powers, and attempting to provoke counter-revolution. ...

Do not obey Dukhonin! Pay no attention to his provocation! Watch him and his group of counter-revolutionary generals carefully. ...

69 (p. 253). FROM KRYLENKO

Order Number Two

The ex-Supreme Commander, General Dukhonin, for having opposed resistance to the execution of orders, for criminal action susceptible of provoking a new civil war, is declared the enemy of People. All persons who support Dukhonin will be arrested, without respect to their social or political position or their past. Persons equipped with special authority will operate these arrests. I charge General Manikhovsky with the execution of the above-mentioned dispositions. ...

Chapter 12

70 (p. 256). INSTRUCTIONS TO PEASANTS

In answer to the numerous inquiries coming from peasants, it is hereby explained that the whole power in the country is from now on held by the Soviets of the Workers', Soldiers', and Peasants' Deputies. The Workers' Revolution, after having conquered in Petrograd and in Moscow, is now conquering in all other centres of Russia. The Workers' and Peasants' Government safeguards the interests of the masses and workers against the landowners and against the capitalists.

Hence the Soviets of Peasants' Deputies, and before all the District Soviets, and subsequently those of the Provinces, are from now on and until the Constituent Assembly meets, full-powered bodies of State authority in their localities. All landlords' titles to the land are cancelled by the second All-Russian Congress of Soviets. A decree regarding the land has already been issued by the present Provisional Workers' and Peasants' Government. On the basis of the above decree all lands hitherto belonging to landlords now pass entirely and wholly into the hands of the Soviets of Peasants' Deputies. The Volost (a group of several villages forms a Volost) Land Committees are immediately to take over all land from the landlords, and to keep a strict account over it, watching that order be maintained, and that the whole estate be well guarded, seeing that from now on all private estates become public property and must therefore be protected by the people themselves.

All orders given by the Volost Land Committees, adopted with the assent of the District Soviets of Peasants' Deputies, in fulfilment of the decrees issued by the revolutionary power, are absolutely legal and are to be forthwith and irrefutably brought into execution.

The Workers' and Peasants' Government appointed by the second All-Russian Congress of Soviets has received the name of the Council of People's Commissars.

The Council of People's Commissars summons the Peasants to take the whole power into their hands in every locality.

The workers will in every way absolutely and entirely support the peasants, arrange for them all that is required in connexion with machines and tools, and in return they request the peasants to help with the transport of grain.

President of the Council of People's Commissars,
Petrograd, 18 November 1917   V. ULYANOV (LENIN)

71 (p. 271).

The full-powered Congress of Peasants' Soviets met about a week later, and continued for several weeks. Its history is merely an expanded version of the history of the 'Extraordinary Conference'. At first the great majority of the delegates were hostile to the Soviet Government, and supported the hostile wing. Several days later the assembly was supporting the moderates with Chernov. And several days after that the vast majority of the Congress was voting for the faction of Maria Spiridonova, and sending their representatives into the Tsay-ee-kah at Smolny.... The Right Wing then walked out of the Congress and called a Congress of its own, which went on, dwindling from day to day, until it finally dissolved....

THE STORY OF PENGUIN CLASSICS

Before 1946 ...'Classics' are mainly the domain of academics and students, without readable editions for everyone else. This all changes when a little-known classicist, E. V. Rieu, presents Penguin founder Allen Lane with the translation of Homer's *Odyssey* that he has been working on and reading to his wife Nelly in his spare time.

1946 *The Odyssey* becomes the first Penguin Classic published, and promptly sells three million copies. Suddenly, classic books are no longer for the privileged few.

1950s Rieu, now series editor, turns to professional writers for the best modern, readable translations, including Dorothy L. Sayers's *Inferno* and Robert Graves's *The Twelve Caesars*, which revives the salacious original.

1960s The Classics are given the distinctive black jackets that have remained a constant throughout the series's various looks. Rieu retires in 1964, hailing the Penguin Classics list as 'the greatest educative force of the 20th century'.

1970s A new generation of translators arrives to swell the Penguin Classics ranks, and the list grows to encompass more philosophy, religion, science, history and politics.

1980s The Penguin American Library joins the Classics stable, with titles such as *The Last of the Mohicans* safeguarded. Penguin Classics now offers the most comprehensive library of world literature available.

1990s The launch of Penguin Audiobooks brings the classics to a listening audience for the first time, and in 1999 the launch of the Penguin Classics website takes them online to a larger global readership than ever before.

The 21st Century Penguin Classics are rejacketed for the first time in nearly twenty years. This world famous series now consists of more than 1300 titles, making the widest range of the best books ever written available to millions – and constantly redefining the meaning of what makes a 'classic'.

The Odyssey continues ...

The best books ever written

PENGUIN CLASSICS

SINCE 1946